ARMY PRO

A Memoir of a Soldier's Life

LTC. Floyd R. Mulvany, US Army
Military Assistance Command Việt Nam (MACV/HQ)
Studies and Observations Group (SOG)
Deputy Director – (OPS-35)
August 1969

ARMY PRO

A Memoir of a Soldier's Life

LTC. FLOYD RUSSELL MULVANY, JR.,
US Army (Retired)
with CHRISTOPHER J. O'SHEA V

Army Pro

A Memoir of a Soldier's Life

By

Lieutenant Colonel Floyd Russell Mulvany, Jr., US Army (Retired)

With

Christopher J. O'Shea V

ISBN 978-1-7368062-0-3   [print]

ISBN 978-1-7368062-1-0   [mobi]

ISBN 978-1-7368062-2-7   [ePub]

Interior design by Booknook.biz.

Cover design by Shelley Savoy

CONTENTS

"Personal Meditations"

"No man is an island entire of itself; every man
Is a piece of the continent, a part of the main;
If a clod be washed away by the sea, Europe
Is the less, as well as if a promontory were, as
Well as any manner of thy friends or of thine
Own were; any man's death diminishes me,
Because I am involved in mankind.
And therefore never send to know for whom
The bell tolls; it tolls for thee."

MEDITATION XVII

Devotions upon Emergent Occasions

John Donne
(1572 – 1631)

INTRODUCTION

Floyd Russell ("Russ") Mulvany, Jr. (August 22, 1922 – June 18, 2019) joined the United States Army Air Corps, on January 23, 1941. Lieutenant Colonel (LTC) Mulvany retired from active duty with the United States Army on August 1, 1972.

This work is an historical narrative based on a memoir begun in 1989 and completed in 1994. It is a chronicle in which the strengths and limitations of the author are on full display. At the same time, it is also the story of an idealist and visionary who aspired from early youth to pursue a career as a professional soldier in service to the nation.

LTC. Mulvany served in three wars: World War II, the Korean Conflict, and the Vietnam War. In addition to his enlisted service in the US Army Air Corps during the Second World War, he later served in the Officers Corps as a proud member of US Army Infantry, Airborne, and Special Forces units. His honors included, among others, the Army Meritorious Service Medal, Distinguished Flying Cross, Bronze Star Medal w/Oak Leaf Cluster, Army Commendation Medal, Purple Heart Medal, World War II Victory Medal w/2 service stars, World War II American Campaign Medal, Korean Service Medal, United Nations Service Medal, and Vietnam Service Medal w/5 Campaign Stars.

This book is not a work of scholarly history, but it is a very personal military memoir. Its contents were derived initially from the Mulvany's often vivid personal recollections of disparate events which took place over a span of nearly 50 years. His recollections were supplemented at the time of writing by limited and itinerant access to official historical resources, government records, and occasional spates of correspondence with former comrades-in-arms. In addition to Xerox copies of the initial typewritten transcription manuscript, regrettably only scattered bits of Mulvany's original hand-written notes, snippets of personal correspondence, and a few hundred well weathered photographs are known to exist. Mulvany's stated purpose in creating his memoir was to *"relate [his] life as a professional soldier, an 'Army Pro', to the loved ones [he would leave] behind."*

In April 2018, he rededicated himself to revising his memoir in close collaboration with the co-author of the present work. As presented here, this work is organized in three parts, comprising twenty-two chapters, and totaling more than 490 pages. Readers are encouraged to approach this narrative with curiosity, an open mind, and a critical but sympathetic eye towards the main protagonist vis-à-vis the context of his circumstances and his times. LTC. Mulvany was passionate in his devotion to the United States Army, the profession-of-arms, and as demanding of others as he was with himself. He was not one to suffer fools gladly and, for better or worse, seldom shied away from calling things the way he saw them.

LTC. Mulvany was a purist committed to the highest standards of his profession, the welfare of his troops, and the advancement of the common good. He led a full and rich life before, during, and after his return to civilian life. Although not without his faults, he is remembered by many as a loyal friend, fearless competitor, inveterate contrarian, and above all else, a leader-of-men in peace and war, an officer and a gentleman.

Christopher J. O'Shea V

Editor and Co-Author

Boryspil, Kyivs'ka Oblast

Ukraine 08301

March 8, 2021

Endnotes

(1) The original "ARMY PRO" manuscript was a single-spaced document which totaled 253 typewritten pages. It was generally well organized on a macro level, but lacked sufficient detail in almost every respect in terms of its actual structure and content. Its contents were unedited transcriptions of hand-

written narratives largely derived from memories accrued over a life span of then more than 67 years. His first-cut at the memoir, begun in 1989 and completed in 1994, was devoid of any illustrations, footnotes, and corroborating documentation which might provide evidence to support various aspects of the author's recollections concerning his military service, experiences and professional milestones.

When Mulvany began the process of recording his story for posterity, he had been retired from the US Army for about 17 years. At the time, he had in his possession relatively few artifacts derived from his time in service, viz., a dress uniform, a complete rack of service devices, a collection of covers from different stages of his career, a foot locker, a few bits of 'official' government correspondence from the period 1944–1947, several framed photographs, a few photo albums, and a single portrait of himself rendered from a color photograph taken in the Spring of 1972. What he lacked most notably were certifiable copies of his official service records – most of which were destroyed in a disastrous fire at the National Personnel Records Center, Military Personnel Records Center, in Overland, Missouri, on July 12, 1973.

In order to bring the author's story to life, there were many challenges which had to be identified, met, and overcome. First and foremost, there was a pressing need to reconstruct in detail and as accurately as possible the arc of the author's actual service career. Accomplishing this task alone took more than 30 months of conscientious historical research, fact checking, line editing, copy editing, and proof-reading by a small and dedicated band of brothers.

PART I

FORMATIVE YEARS
1922 – 1941

"The truth is rarely pure and never simple."

The Importance of Being Earnest (1898)

Oscar Wilde
(1854 – 1900)

CHAPTER 1

THE ROAD FROM EL DORADO, KS TO LOS ANGELES, CA (AUGUST 22, 1922 – JANUARY 23, 1941)

"So long, it's been good to know yuh …
And I got to be driftin' along."

"Dusty Old Dust"
Words and Music by Woody Guthrie (1940)

Woodie Guthrie
(1912 – 1967)

El Dorado, KS
1922 - 1928

I, Floyd Russell Mulvany Jr., was born at around 5:00 AM on Tuesday, August 22, 1922, in the oil fields outside El Dorado, Kansas. My paternal father worked in the fields. He was 22 years old and my mother, Hazel Velma (nee Robertson), had just turned 18. In filling out my birth certificate, my father spelled our name M-U-L-V-A-N-E-Y. I did not learn of this until 1982 when I obtained a copy of his birth certificate. Even to the present day, the name is spelled both ways by certain of my relatives from my dad's side. I have not been able to find out why this is so. I do know that in Ireland the spelling is M-U-L-V-A-N-Y and pronounced MUL VAH NY.

The family of my paternal father's mother, Dora, has been traced back in America to 1692. As far as we could tell, the first Mulvany turned up in Tennessee around 1847. So, by the time I entered the picture my family was pretty far removed from the old sod. My mother and father separated when I was two or three years old. I remember seeing my father only once in my entire life. At the time, I was about seven and visiting his mother and father (my grandparents) in Kansas City, Missouri. This was the only time I remember seeing them as well. Grandpa Mulvany, Marion, died in 1930, just a year or so after I had seen him. Grandmother Dora remarried and lived until 1940.

Early in 1926, I saw my stepfather for the first time. I remember that first encounter clearly. He came up the stairs to where I was in bed, wearing a coat and cap having come to take my mother out for the evening. His name was Felix Fay Ferguson. Felix and my mother were married in May 1926, shortly before my fourth birthday. He became the only father I knew and the best dad any kid could have ever had. I was an only child as it turned out, so all efforts at child rearing by both my parents were directed at me alone.

I got their undivided attention.

Master Floyd Russell Mulvany, Jr.
"Birthday Boy"
August 22, 1926

Details of my early life are skimpy, but I do remember some things about those times. For example, when I was three or four years old, I was in the hospital with Scarlet Fever. I clearly recall the nurses taking care of me because I was in isolation. My mother could not even enter the room because Scarlet Fever was so dangerous and contagious. She did come to the window with a pint of ice cream quite frequently. I was lucky, I guess, since I had no lasting ill effects from the fever. I also remember that Pop drove a bus between Denver, where we lived, and Kansas City, Missouri. Mom often went with him, while I stayed with my Grandmother Robertson. She was born Nina Bell (Winnie) Spradlin in Paintsville, Kentucky, on January 24, 1868.

Winnie's family moved to Kansas while she was still a young girl. Her father had been a Captain in the Union Army during the Civil War. While living in Coffeeville, she said she saw the infamous Dalton Gang rob a bank across the street from the restaurant where she was waiting tables. She claimed to have witnessed the robbery on October 5, 1892 from start to finish. Later that same day, it was said the whole gang was wiped out nearby during the course of a second bank robbery.

She married my grandfather, Phillip Robertson, later and in the years to come gave birth to my Aunt Madge (Magdalena) in 1899, my uncle Howard Nathaniel Blossom, in 1901, and my mother Hazel Velma, in June 1904. Winnie's family, on her mother's side, had been traced directly back to the parents of the American Revolutionary War Patriot Ethan Allen (January 21, 1738 – February 12, 1789). He was the leader of the *"Green Mountain Boys"* from Vermont. It was Allen's militia troops which captured Fort Ticonderoga *"in the name of Jehovah and the Continental Congress."*

My grandmother was a bona fide member of the Daughters of the American Revolution. Alas, she died in January 1929. All I know about her and her family was learned many years after her death. I have pleasant memories of lying in her arms in bed while she told me ghost stories before we went to sleep. I came to know Grandfather Robertson only after I reached maturity because he and Nina divorced before I was born. For a variety of reasons, I grew up not having the pleasure of being with my maternal grandparents.

My mother, her husband Felix, and I were a close-knit group. My parents seldom went anywhere without me, even to dances where they held me between them as they danced. It was said that I could do the *"Charleston"* by the age of five years old. As a kid,

I learned how to play all the popular card games such as Poker, Canasta, and Pinochle, and even sat in with the grownups at seven years old.

All their good friends became my *"aunts and uncles."* I was treated like one of their Gang. One such uncle, Red Grant, told me about his experiences in World War I. He was a hero to me. Two other best friends, Al and Emma Agee, were older and both were born in the 1880s. My first visit to a farm was their birthplace in Trenton, Missouri. Later, we lived in the same apartment house as the Agee family in Denver, Colorado.

Denver, CO
1928 - 1934

Family Life

It was just one big happy family house with an upstairs, a large dining room, and a large bathroom on the second floor. The house was located right next door to what was to be (and is now) the Denver Mint. I played in the big construction site for the Mint and still have a scar on my leg from tearing it on a large nail.

I distinctly remember Emma telling me she was going to vote for Herbert Hoover for President of the United States in 1928. I also remember that I fell over the railing on the second floor of the apartment and landed flat on my face. The fall spilt my chin wide open. I can still feel the doctor pulling the cat gut through my chin, taking 10 to 15 stitches to sew me back together. I still have the scar to prove it. I guess I was pretty lucky, because I just missed hitting the piano, which sat almost directly under the spot from which I fell.

It seemed as though we were constantly moving from place to place in Denver. I don't remember all the places, just snatches of some. In one place I had a toy steam shovel that I played with in the snow. In another, I had a cast-iron tractor and a tin bread box which I used as the tractor's garage. I also made cars from kitchen match boxes by cutting the lid in half, folding the lid upward to make the windshield, and gluing buttons on the sides of the box for wheels. At another place, while walking down the street one day, I looked up and saw a pair of enormous wings flapping. Something very large was flying by at a great distance from me. I have always believed it was my *"Guardian Angel."*

Being an only child, I have always picked one special friend to be my *"brother."* I became very attached to these boys and it hurt whenever I had to move away and leave them behind. Moving so frequently and meeting new people really benefitted me in later life, however. It has always been easy for me to adjust to new places and new people.

My Dad was a great automobile mechanic and always had a job, even in the deepest part of the Depression Era. We had a place to live, clothes to wear, and food to eat. He was an excellent provider and, with my mother's help, I never knew what it meant to be poor or hungry. This doesn't mean that we had a high life by any means. My parents just never allowed me to know what it was to be poor or hungry.

Consequently, I had a very happy childhood without any emotional hang-ups. Both Mom and Dad were very hard workers. Even though their combined salaries seldom exceeded $25.00 a week, they seemed to have managed our household really well. We could go to a movie once a week and come home for a cup of hot chocolate. We had a radio and went to friends' homes for cards and eats. Everyone made home brew, too.

I know my Dad always had a crock of yeast and malt brewing somewhere in the house. Homemade beer brewing was very popular during the days of prohibition. Never once, however, was I ever offered a drink of beer by my parents or their friends. It just wasn't done in those days.

Childhood Pastimes

All of us kids made our own fun from what we had available to us. It was not a time of having everything given to you because there wasn't enough money to buy such things. We did for ourselves.

An old inner tube could be cut into strips to make ammunition for our rubber gun pistols or rifles. These guns were cut from a single piece of wood. A clothes pin was tightly bound around the end of the butt so that when we pressed down on the outer side of the pin, the rubber strip which we had stretched over the end of the barrel would be released and fly through the air 10 to 15 feet. The tighter the stretch, the farther the rubber would fly. We couldn't really be hurt by getting hit with it. We all had several pistols and rifles of this type with plenty of ammunition that would allow for several hours of *"combat."* The ultimate type of rubber gun was one from which several strips of tube could be fired without reloading each time. Eventually, we graduated from rubber guns to BB guns. We played war with them and it is a wonder none of us had our eyes shot out. We never aimed for the head, but there are always accidents. I shot a sparrow once and never got over it. I never again killed a bird.

Another favorite of all of us was our skateboard. Not at all like the modern-day type, our skateboards were built from either apple or orange crates nailed upright on a 2" x 4" board that was two to three feet long. A single skate, taken apart so two wheels were nailed to the front and rear underside of the 2" x 4" board, provided the means for mobility. A handle on top of the crate, either straight across the top or in a *"V"* from the top of the center, permitted us to hold on with both hands, put one foot on the 2" x 4" board, and push with the other foot, just like on a scooter. We usually embellished the front of the crate with two tin cans for headlights, black tape around the handles for hand grips, and some paint here and there for the sake of beauty and style. Talk about having fun. Those skateboards were really great.

We also made our own games. For example, an old piece of plywood about two- or three-feet square would be hung on a nail diamond-wise, not square-wise. On the board, we would pound in nails so they would stick out about two inches. Under each nail, we would put a number. The nails nearest the center of the board got the highest numbers. We then got rubber rings from canning jars that our mothers always had on hand. Standing back from the board 10 to 15 feet, we would throw the rubber rings, hoping they would catch on the nail nearest the center. After so many throws, we would add up our scores. A great many hours were passed playing this game, which cost nothing to make.

Another popular activity was playing marbles. Our stock of marbles was our pride and joy. We had *clearies*, *soapies*, *glassies*, *peewees*, *steelies*, and at least one *agate shooter*[1], if we had

---

[1] Agate is a colored variety of quartz that was hand-ground into marbles. They were a favorite of many marble players, especially as shooters, throughout the 20th century. A quality shooter marble made it easier to knock an opponent's marble out of the ring. A player needs only one shooter to play the game. Although shooters varied in diameter from one marble to the next, they tended to be about .75 in, or about 19 mm, in diameter. See: https://www.marblecollecting.com/marble-reference/online-marble-id-guide/agate-and-other-mineral/.

25 cents to buy one that is. We had marbles that we could lose in a game, if it came to that, and other ones that we would buy or could trade. Usually, we had a knuckle pad to lay on the ground so we could shoot better. The best knuckle pads were small pieces of fur that we picked out of the taxidermist's trash bin. There were quite a few neighborhood taxidermists in those days. I had a real keen piece of deerskin I used as a pad. It smelled pretty earthy, but I used it all the time. We also had a canvas or leather bag in which to carry our marbles. I still have my boyhood marbles in the same old pocketbook given to me by Mom.

Of course, all red-blooded American boys played baseball. Every day in school, after school, and on weekends during baseball season at least one boy would have a bat. Maybe we had a real baseball at times, but mostly we made our own baseballs by wrapping electrician tape layer upon layer around a golf ball. Talk about something that would travel far if you hit it far. Mom paid 50 cents for a catcher's mitt for me. I used it no matter what position I played -- it was all I had.

Another popular pastime was playing war. It must be remembered that when I was a kid, we were only a few years removed from the end of World War I. Armistice Day was a national holiday. Now known as Veterans Day, it's still celebrated on November 11th. Somewhere I acquired a World War I steel helmet. It had no liner, but it did have the original chin strap. I stuffed paper in it to keep it from bouncing around. It made me a bona fide American soldier. We had trenches and built command posts from scraps of old lumber and cardboard boxes. On homemade message pads, we sent messages from the command post to the front-line trenches. Of course, the enemy Germans were always simulated because no one ever wanted to be a German soldier. The World War I propaganda against Germany still largely prevailed for years after the end of the war. We would play for hours at war. I guess it came naturally for me. For rations, we usually had a potato or two, which we baked in a fire in a hole in the ground. They always tasted good.

We also played Cowboys and Indians. It was a great game, because almost all of the movies we saw were about the Old West. One of my greatest possessions besides the steel helmet was an imitation cowhide holster with a six-shooter cap gun. No one else had one like it. Of course, I was always a cowboy and our horses were old broom handles with a piece of rope or string for a bridle. We'd put them between our legs, hold on to the bridle with one hand, and slap our thighs with the other as we ran around and chased each other.

Grade School Years

I started school in Denver in the autumn of 1928. I was six years old and went directly into first grade. I don't know why I didn't go into kindergarten first. The very first day I went to school, Mom dressed me in a velvet Lord Fauntleroy suit. I was really embarrassed wearing such an outfit. For the record, it was the first and only time I ever wore that suit. I learned quickly and got good report cards each time. I skipped from grade 3B to grade 4B – a whole semester. My first six years of school were all in Denver.

Shortly after our arrival, I was baptized in Saint Andrew's High Episcopal Church where my Godmother was a nun and my Godfather was a Priest. It was a small parish as I remember, but there were several resident nuns and a few priests. In about the 4th grade, I became an Altar Boy, wore a red skull cap, red gown and white hassock whenever serving Mass. One of the most embarrassing moments of my young life occurred when I dropped the incense jar in front of the altar, spilling lots of ash on the floor, then I tried to scoop it up with the very small incense spoon.

Denver was a great town to live in, at least for me. We lived all over the place during my childhood. I had good friends to play with, appeared in all the school plays and participated in many other programs. I reached the sixth grade without too many incidents of note, save for one in particular which became the source of some considerable anxiety years later.

I never did have my own bicycle. Bicycles were expensive and besides my parents thought I was too small for one and they were right. Nevertheless, after school one day, I borrowed a racing bike and rode around the block several times. As I was getting off of it, my left foot got caught in the pedal strap. The bike fell over and I crash landed with my left arm extended reflexively to break the fall. Unfortunately, I broke my left elbow in the process. The best the doctor could do was to get it back within two degrees or so of normal. I was in a cast for several weeks, during which period my left arm withered away to almost nothing before the cast was removed. I was unable to bend my arm for a period of several months, but eventually I recovered full use of it though it's always been slightly out of alignment.

At 11 years old, I got my first pair of real undershorts and did away with the one-piece BVD under suits that all young boys wore at the time. School was easy for me and I had lots of friends. I even found my first true love, a 10-year-old girl named Helen Rice. Her dad owned the apartment house we lived in. We went to the movies each weekend. It cost 10 cents to see three cowboy features, a cartoon, and a serial. For another five cents, you could get a whole bag of candy or large bag of popcorn. Life was good.

Kansas City, MO
1934 – 1935

Grammar School

At the end of my 6th grade school year, during the late spring of 1934, we moved from Denver to Kansas City. I had to leave my friends again. As usual, however, I soon settled into a new home, a new school, and new friends. We first lived in a duplex which was close to my new school, Longfellow Grammar School, which was located at 2830 Holmes Street. Then we moved to an apartment at 25th and Brooklyn which was quite near Muehlbock Field, home of the Kansas City Blues baseball team.

There was a very high billboard sign across the street from Muehlbock Park. One could see the whole inside ballpark from the top of it. My mom's brother, Uncle Howard, and I would climb on top and watch the games. At the end of every seventh inning, they would open the gates to the ballpark and let everyone waiting outside in for free. Eventually I joined the so-called Knot Hole Gang. As a member, I could go to a game each Friday for 10 cents and sit directly behind home plate for the whole game.

I did really well in 7th grade. In addition to earning good marks, I won Silver Medal by placing second in an oral essay contest sponsored by the American Legion. I spoke about Benjamin Franklin. The boy who won first place also spoke about Benjamin Franklin just before I did – only better. I was also elected president of my 7th grade class and gave the commencement speech that year. In addition, I caught the measles three times, played touch football for the school every Saturday, and played baseball pretty much every day. I made a bevy friends, most of whom I've always remembered by name. Usually, I cannot generally remember names, for some reason I do remember those of my Kansas City boyhood friends. By the time I finished 7th grade, I was adept at reading, writing, and speaking in public.

It was also a memorable year in my young life for other reasons. I met a beautiful girl who I fell madly in (puppy) love with. When I was introduced to her mother and she heard my last name, she asked if my father had been called *"Bud."* I replied in the affirmative and subsequently learned she had gone with my paternal father after he and my mom were divorced.

Los Angeles, CA
1935 – 1941

In early of August 1935, Dad was offered a very good job as a mechanic at the Hillcrest Cadillac Agency in Beverly Hills. He accepted the job, so we departed for California in a 1930 two-door Ford that Dad and Uncle Howard had rebuilt after it had been crushed by a street car. We arrived in Los Angeles on my 13th birthday.

Visiting California was not an entirely new thing to me. In 1929, Uncle Howard and his wife, Ella, Grandpa Robertson, and I traveled there in a canvas-top touring car. Just before we reached Albuquerque, New Mexico, a car sideswiped us and kept on going. The roof support brace was broken in the mishap, so the top was flailing in the wind. We arrived in Albuquerque flat broke, but holed up in a motel [2] in the old part of town. To make myself useful, I went door to door telling everyone how hungry I was and asking for help.

By the Grace of God, complete strangers gave me enough money to buy us some food. Since my uncle and aunt had run out of money and the car needed repair, there was no way we could go on to California without further assistance. As best I can recall, my Mom sent enough money by Western Union to pay for the necessary car repairs, gas, and food to enable us to continue the trek westward. Well, we *eventually* made it to California.

---

[2] When I passed through Albuquerque in 1962, that old motel was still there!

The first thing we all noticed about California was all the orange groves. Folks could buy 12 dozen oranges for about one dollar. Our first home was in Hollywood on Lexington Avenue, just two doors off Vine Street. We lived in a typical California-style bungalow – part of a courtyard arrangement. Six to eight one story affairs were lined up opposite each other with a small side yard for each and a single common walkway down the center. Ours was the second or third one down from the front and right outside the kitchen window grew a fig tree. I had never seen one before and I didn't like figs at all.

I noticed that everyone my age was taller than me. This, coupled with the fact that my name was Floyd, always seemed to invite trouble and occasionally got me into some serious fights. All through school I was most often getting into fights with guys bigger than I was. I learned to be quicker and beat their heads against the ground as my best means of defense. I didn't always win, but I didn't always lose either.

There was a boy who lived next door to us who was about my age, only much taller. This fellow was really mean. He didn't know how to be nice and never had anything good to say about anybody. He was always bad mouthing everyone. As is usually the case with big mouth types, he was also a coward. He was 14 and I was 13. It was here that I first learned to deal with these types of individuals, ignore what they say and act completely indifferent towards them. Without any response, they soon have nothing left to say and, not infrequently, they are reluctant to act out their tough guy impulses.

Soon after our arrival, we moved across the street into a fine old house with a front porch, a big front and back yard, Eucalyptus trees all around, and a fireplace in the living room. Mom and Uncle Howard, who came out to Hollywood on his own, worked in a café directly across the street from Warner Brothers Studios in Burbank. My parents had to be at work every morning at 6:00 AM. Dad got up and took both of them to work each morning. Mom always sent me a chocolate-covered doughnut back with Dad.

There were many big movie stars at Warner Brothers in those days. Quite a few of them ate in the café. Mom had many stories to tell about some of them. A few stories were good and entertaining ones. Other stories didn't reflect too well on some of the stars and would be stars.

Joseph Le Conte Junior High School
1935 – 1936

I entered Le Conte Junior High School in the autumn of 1935. It's still located at 1316 North Bronson Avenue in Hollywood. School administrators allowed me to skip the entire 8th grade because Missouri schools were so far advanced scholastically over the California system. So, there I was, 13 years old and in the 9th grade.

I was not only the smallest one in the 9th grade, but I was also among the youngest in my class. Most of the girls were at least a head or more taller than me. My diminutive stature was something I simply had to learn to live with at the time. I had no problems with the school work, despite the fact that I had skipped 8th grade. Spelling, English, Algebra, and History were all easy for me. Being reasonably bright was a big help. Having a flawless, healthy complexion free of pimples and blemishes endeared me to many of the girls. Most thought I was cute and treated me well, but my physical size did seem to have prevented any serious relationships.

Despite my physical stature and age, it happened by chance that I was appointed 'Commissioner of Halls'. This was a job supervising all the 'Hall Monitors' in the school. At recess, during the noon hour, and auditorium hours, no student was permitted to traverse the halls without a written pass. Monitors were stationed in all hallways to enforce this rule. And, imagine that, I was in charge of all those individuals. As a practical matter, this assignment taught me responsibility at an important stage in my life.

The girls at Le Conte, for the most part, were real lookers – healthy, well-endowed, typical California females. At age 12, Bonita Granville was already a child star having appeared in at least one popular movie by the time of my arrival. She later gained significant acclaim for her starring role in the 'Nancy Drew' film series of the late 1930s. Alexis Smith was there too, standing by, just waiting for her first big break at 14 years of age. Alexis went on to have a notable career in films commencing in the 1940s. In 1972, she won a Tony Award as Best Actress in a Musical for her role as an aging showgirl in Stephen Sondheim's Broadway musical *"Follies"*.

There were so many things to do at that age, such as roller skating at the old Warner Brothers Studios on Sunset Boulevard. A converted sound stage was made into one of the biggest skating rinks in the world. We also played a lot of touch football. There were both male and female professional baseball teams. Many movie stars attended games on a regular basis. They liked being seen in the public's eye and the public liked mingling with them.

Hollywood was a great town to live in during that period. Hollywood Boulevard was world famous as was the Hollywood Hotel, Vine Street, Sunset Boulevard, the Sunset Strip, the Palladium Ballroom, and Earl Carroll's Theatre Restaurant where you could have dinner with the floor show for $5.00 a head. There was no smog, the skies were blue, and the beaches were free of trash and debris.

The star's homes were scattered all over the Hollywood Hills and along various beaches, such as Santa Monica and Malibu. The population was not too large, probably because California was still a long way away from most other population centers to the east and the Great Depression was not yet over. Plainly speaking, most ordinary people could not afford to travel too far away from where ever they called home.

A drive from Hollywood to Long Beach along the future route of the Pacific Coast Highway, California State Route 1, was a favorite Sunday afternoon's diversion. The horse races at Santa Anita and midget or large-size car racing were a nightly affair. There was no winter, only some rain now and then. Southern California really was a great place to grow up. In late 1935, we moved from Lexington near Vine to North Mariposa Street, east of Vine and just north of Sunset Boulevard. At the time, Sunset Boulevard was the longest single street in the world. It ran all the way from First and Main in Los Angeles to the beach above Santa Monica, a distance of about 16 miles. Both Sunset Boulevard and Wilshire Boulevard were also world famous.

I graduated from the 9th grade in June of 1936. That summer we went back to Kansas City for a visit. We saw my Aunt Madge, Grandpa Robertson, Uncle Jack, and Dad's brothers and sisters. Dad regaled family members with stories about the many benefits of living in California. He told his story so passionately that eventually three of his sisters soon moved out to the West Coast. While visiting Kansas City, I saw also some old school chums from my Longfellow days. In addition, Dad had my hair cut to about one-half inch long so it would last for our whole time in Kansas City.

It did.

Hollywood High School [3]
1936 – 1939

I entered Hollywood High in September of 1936. It's still located at 1521 N. Highland Avenue, close to the intersection of North Highland Avenue and West Sunset Boulevard in Hollywood. Even in those days, the school was well-known for the eclectic make up of its student body and the neighborhood itself was already the stuff of legend.

I was 14 years old and hadn't grown an inch taller during my time at Le Conte. From the moment of my matriculation at Hollywood High, I was intrigued by the uniforms that the Reserve Officer Training Corps (ROTC) cadets wore. My fascination led me to sign up for ROTC, rather than gymnasium classes. I got my uniform *and* a regulation U.S. Army Model 1903 Springfield rifle. The top of the barrel came up to my armpit which, of course, made it easier for me to hold the rifle up straight. The Hollywood High ROTC Battalion had three rifle companies, a 40-piece band, and a full Battalion staff. The unit was advised by a Regular Army Lieutenant Colonel and a Sergeant. We had a small-bore rifle range and various classrooms where we were taught military subjects.

I ate it up. I pressed my uniform every night. We wore the olive drab shirt and pants four days a week. On Friday's, we put on a white shirt and blouse and had a parade in the afternoon. To get promoted to any rank in the ROTC, we had to successfully pass a written test. I never had any problems with any military subject. In three years of my ROTC training, I went from Private to Cadet Major and won the *"Best Officer"* medal in my final year. In those days, officers wore Sam Brown belts and carried sabers. We looked sharp and, of course, some of the girls always preferred a man in uniform.

Other than ROTC, my high school days were quite normal except that I never owned a car. I had worked all the summer of 1937 in a drug store for $5.00 a week. Dad told me that if I saved the entire amount I earned, he would match it and buy me a car. I saved the money but I was not yet 16 years old, so I had to wait a year to learn to drive and get a license.

---

[3] Over the decades, Hollywood High School has educated a long list of noteworthy public figures. Not surprisingly, many graduates have gone on enjoy successful careers in stage and film. Others have had distinguished careers in other walks of life such as public service, journalism, and the performing arts. See: https://en.wikipedia.org/wiki/Hollywood_High_School#Notable_alumni.

Quite suddenly, when I was still in the 11th grade, I grew to my present height of 5 feet, 10 inches. Now, I could look down on my former head taller girlfriends. I felt great about the physical changes that had so suddenly come over me. Lacking either a driver's license or my own car didn't pose too much of a problem, since there was usually someone to ride with if I needed one so everything generally worked out okay. There were football games, drive-in movies, dances at the Palladium and the Pasadena Civic Auditorium, and my falling in and out of love several times a month.

Cadet Major Floyd R. Mulvany, Jr.
ROTC | Hollywood High School
(1939)

Hollywood High, like Le Conte, was noted for its beautiful girls. As my height increased my self-confidence improved, I started spending more and more time hanging around with girls. Of course, almost all of them were two years older than me and I was still very naïve about them. With some girls this didn't seem to matter, because I still had my peaches and crème complexion and was an officer in the ROTC.

I went through three years of high school without ever being absent or tardy. It wasn't difficult for me to be on time because Dad drove me to school every morning on his way to work in Beverly Hills. He had to be at work at 8:00 AM. As a result, I was at school by 7:15 or 7:30 every day. Never having missed any classes can be attributed to the fact that I was healthy, highly motivated, and really enjoyed learning about the world.

Los Angeles City College
1939 – 1940

There were drawbacks to being the youngest kid in my high school graduating class. For example, I could not join the Army until I was 18 years of age and couldn't obtain a commission until I turned 21. In other words, I had to wait 2-4 years to do what I really wanted to do – join the US Army and become an officer. Since I had already completed three years of Junior ROTC in high school, I would be eligible for Senior ROTC when I started college. In those days, the best Senior ROTC program was at Pasadena Junior College. The next best program was at the University of California at Los Angeles (UCLA). I could not go to Pasadena since we did not live in the proper school district. I had hoped to attend UCLA, but my parents couldn't afford the tuition. So, there was to be no Senior ROTC for me.

While biding my time, I decided to matriculate at Los Angeles City College (LACC) because we lived in the district and it had minimal tuition costs. I opted to take subjects which would prepare me for a degree in Archaeology. I had always been an avid student of history and the social sciences. I was more interested in the past than the present or the future. I began to dabble in Egyptian hieroglyphics when I was about twelve years old. If I couldn't be a soldier, then I reckoned I would become an Archaeologist.

The year at LACC (1939-1940) was probably the worst year of my young life. Except for dating Donna Reed [4], who was in my French class, and being friends with Alexis Smith, whom I had known since Le Conte days, the whole thing was a real drag. On top of everything else, my academic load required a maximum amount of homework – French, College Algebra, Literature, and Anthropology. I had no car (yet), I had no money to speak of, and I was far from mature. I finished the year, but in June of 1940, I told my parents I would not go back to LACC – no matter what.

---

[4] Donna Reed (born Donna Belle Mullenger, January 27, 1921 – January 14, 1986) was an American film, television actress, and producer. Her career spanned more than 40 years, with performances in more than 40 films. She is well known for her role as Mary Hatch Bailey in Frank Capra's 1946 film *It's a Wonderful Life*. In 1953, she received the Academy Award for Best Supporting Actress for her performance as Lorene Burke in the war drama *From Here to Eternity*. Her hit television series, "*The Donna Reed Show*" ran from 1958-1966. See: https://www.en.wikipedia.org/wiki/Donna_Reed.

Following my freshman year in college, I got a job in Hollywood with the Red Arrow Messenger Service (a subsidiary of United Parcel Service) at the grand salary of $17.00 a week, plus tips. I rode a one-speed, balloon tire bike all over Hollywood. There wasn't a hill in the whole town that I couldn't climb on my bike. My uniform was a pass into all the studios, offices, and other inner sanctums of Hollywood.

Around the time I turned 18, I bought my first car which was a used 1932 Chevrolet Roadster. It was jet black and sported a brand-new beige top. I could supplement my $17.00 salary by taking a few automobile deliveries, which also paid mileage. The only problem with the Chevy was that it was always blowing spark plugs – at least two or three of the four. Incidentally, this also happened one night as I was taking Donna Reed home down Hollywood Boulevard. When three cylinders blew, it sounded like a drum. Donna didn't mind, though, she was a really sweet gal. We shared a big laugh over my misfortune.

I soon figured out that although the studios had many beautiful girls working for them, there were even more beautiful women working in the various offices around town. It was tough on my young body gazing at and being proximate to them. I enjoyed my work and getting to know more about people and life, but I knew that I would not and could not be a messenger all of my life. Each delivery I made was only 25 cents anywhere within the confines of Hollywood. Almost all of the studios, offices, actors, lawyers, airlines, and so on used our services. It was a great lesson in sociology for me. I met all kinds of people from all walks of life.

My professional ambitions lay in another direction. World War II had started in Europe in September of 1939. I knew for sure that the United States would get totally involved sooner or later, despite all the talk by Roosevelt and the other peaceniks about isolationism. I also knew that my chances of going back to finish college were probably nil. I had turned 18 in August of 1940. I did not want to get drafted into the service, because I would have had no choice whatsoever about where I would be assigned. I knew I would be much better off if I enlisted and had my choice of a job and duty station.

I could get into the Army if one of my parents would sign the consent papers. I started talking about enlisting and being one of the thirty men selected each year to attend West Point Preparatory School who would then go on to West Point to get a commission. The more I talked about enlistment, the more adamant my parents became in opposing my proposed course of action. I was determined, however, to pursue my dreams and persisted in making my case. I had a good I.Q. and a full year of college credits under my belt. In those days, less than 10 percent of all high school graduates went on to attend a college or university.

In the end, I wore my parents down. They finally understood what I wanted to do and gave their permission. It was coming time for me to leave the nest.

PART II

US ARMY AIR CORPS | US ARMY AIR FORCES
JANUARY 25, 1941 – OCTOBER 30, 1946

"We aren't no thin red 'eroes, nor we aren't no blackguards too,
But single men in barricks, most remarkable like you;
An' if sometimes our conduck isn't all your fancy paints,
Why, single men in barricks don't grow into plaster saints"

The Barrack-Room Ballads (1892)
Rudyard Kipling
(1865 – 1936)

CHAPTER 2

US ARMY AIR CORPS [1]
(JANUARY – JUNE, 1941)

Recruit Training, Fort MacArthur, San Pedro, CA
(January – March 1941) | Advance Training, 17th
Bombardment Group, 89th Reconnaissance Squadron,
McChord Air Base, WA/Pendleton Airfield, OR
(April – December 1941)

For it's Tommy this, an' Tommy that, an' "Chuck him out, the brute."
But it's "Saviour of 'is country" when the guns begin to shoot"

The Barrack-Room Ballads (1892)
Rudyard Kipling
(1865 – 1936)

The prospect of a career in the United States military was widely regarded as right-minded career choice in 1941. The profession-of-arms was well-respected and held in high esteem by practically everyone who knew anything about military service. An officer could always be trusted to be honorable and his word was accepted as fact. The

---

[1] The United States Army Air Corps (USAAC) was established by an act of Congress on July 2, 1926. See: https://en.wikipedia.org/wiki/United_States_Army_Air_Corps.

Army was small organization in those days and competition for advancement was intense. It would be a challenging career path, but I thought I could make a go of it over time. After thirty years' service, I could expect to retire with honor, respect, and good retirement pay.

In the 1940s, an individual was considered a minor until turning 21. At the time, I was only 18 years of age and had to start my Army career as an enlisted man. Later, I could try to become an officer by working my way up through the ranks. It was my belief at the time that the best way to obtain a commission would be through graduation from the US Military Academy at West Point. Naturally, my parents were reluctant to let me go off on my own and leave the nest unprepared for the responsibility of living on my own.

It is sobering to reflect upon how incredibly naïve I was about the ways of the world in my youth. I was raised, after all, in relatively sheltered environment where parental guidance, stalwart support, and steadfast encouragement were relied upon to resolve almost any and all problems. As such, I had been completely dependent on my parents for almost everything in life. They took great care to provide for all of my material wants and needs. Nevertheless, my desire to leave home was really strong. It ultimately proved irresistible.

I was determined to join the Army. A few months before heading off to the service, I packed my bags in anticipation of my departure. Once my parents decided to allow me to join up, they never deviated from doing all they could to help me make my new life successful and happy.

Enlistment, Army Recruiting Office, Los Angeles County Courthouse

January 11, 1941

Mom and I visited the Army Recruiting Office on the 12th floor of the Los Angeles County Courthouse on Saturday, January 11, 1941. I had decided that I was going to join the *"Horse Cavalry."* I guess this idea came from having read so many great stories about the horse soldiers in the Old West – particularly those written by James Warner Bellah (1899–1976).

As one might expect, the listings of position openings for the entire Army were posted in the recruiting office. As I recall there were openings in all branches -- *except* for the Horse Calvary! I was really disappointed, but oddly it never once entered my mind to simply join the Infantry. To this day, I can't say why this was the case. Naturally, all my ROTC training had been Infantry. Moreover, all of my high school friends in the California National Guard were in the Infantry.

There were openings in all the Infantry units in the United States and overseas. For the life of me, I can't tell you why I didn't join one of those Infantry outfits. With the benefit of hindsight, of course, I know now that I should have gone in that direction from the get-go. In any event, I filled out the necessary papers for enlistment that day without making a decision about what branch I'd actually join. Instead, Mom and I agreed to return to the recruitment office in a couple of weeks to make a selection and finalize my enlistment.

When Mom and I returned to the recruitment office on January 23rd, I again looked over the lists of occupational specialties within the various branches of the Army. *What is the mission of the Air Corps*, I asked? Well, I got an answer nine yards long all about the *"wild blue yonder"*, the big birds flying and diving and shooting and bombing in the fastest way, the 'special pay', and the special treatment flyers received because they were the cream of the crop and the most highly trained.

> *"Will I be able to fly right away?" I asked. "Sure, as soon as you're trained", replied the Major. "Can I go anywhere I want in the whole world?' I asked. "Sure, we have openings all over the world," said the Major. "The Air Corps is really expanding fast, he declared."*

Now that was it. My ignorance went into overdrive. I was sold!

I decided that I would join the 89th Reconnaissance Squadron at McChord Field in Tacoma, Washington. Situated on the West Coast, it was not too far from home which meant I could get home pretty fast when I got my first leave. Maybe, I could even fly home in a big airplane to see my folks.

Mom and I had signed my enlistment papers on January 11th, but I didn't take my induction oath until the 23rd. Not until 1978 did I realize that those enlistment papers had my first name as Lloyd rather than Floyd. Although only a technicality, this error could have gotten me released from my service obligation had I been looking for an out as the country drifted towards war.

As a further aside, while completing the necessary paperwork to join the Army Air Corps, I very nearly selected a squadron that was soon thereafter transferred to the Philippines in mid-1941. It was an element of the 24th Pursuit Group [2], I believe, whose survivors were later decimated while fighting as an Infantry unit on Bataan. I didn't know it at the time, of course, but this decision *almost* made was just the first of many which were to be made largely by chance over the course of my career, any one of which might well have led to an early grave, but for the *"Luck of the Irish."*

Fort Arthur MacArthur [3]
Recruit Training

January 25 – April 12, 1941

Following my swearing in ceremony on January 23rd, I was told to report for basic training at Fort MacArthur in San Pedro within the ensuing 48 hours. Fort Mac was located in San Pedro about 20 miles south of Los Angeles. It was a gathering place for one-year draftees and Regular Army enlistees, prior to being shipped out to their designated units.

Fort Mac was not new to me. As a member of my high school ROTC unit, we had visited there during my senior year in the autumn of 1938. It was originally one of the coastal artillery forts which guarded the entrance to Los Angeles harbor and featured gigantic, rail mounted, 14-inch coastal guns. On top of these huge tubes, which were as long as railroad flatbed cars (~53'), were mounted a single Browning M2 .50 caliber machine gun. During our field trip to Fort Mac, gun crews fired the Browning M2 .50 caliber machine guns instead of the Big Guns. At the time, this demonstration was a real disappointment to everyone in our unit. In retrospect, however, I'm sure it was just as well because later during the war Fort Mac's gunners actually fired the big guns. The

---

[2] See: https://en.wikipedia.org/wiki/24th_Pursuit_Group.

[3] See: https://en.wikipedia.org/wiki/Fort_MacArthur.

collective blast effects blew out windows inland for a radius of about twelve miles. As far as I know, their gunners never fired any of those big guns again – ever.

Rendezvous with Destiny
Introduction to Army Life

Saturday - January 25, 1941

In 1941, the US Army's Recruit Training Course was carried out over a six-week period. Its curriculum focused on indoctrination relating to basic military general orders, military conduct, close order and open order drill. After successful completion of basic training, individual recruits were shipped out to their respective prospective service units.

Mom and Pop drove me down to Fort Mac. They urged me to be careful and to come back home to visit as soon as circumstances might permit. Of course, I thought it would be a long time before I would see them again. I turned away and 1 walked through the Main Gate carrying a little bag with my toilet articles and some goodies from home. It was an ominous feeling to know that from that moment on I was on my own.

When I reported to Fort Mac, it quickly dawned upon me that I was like a child amongst men -- all 139 pounds of me. I knew about drilling and wearing a uniform from the ROTC, but I could only guess what it would be like to be a *"yardbird"* [4] Buck Private in the Regular Army. As a former Junior ROTC Officer, I had been accustomed to giving orders. Now it would be the other way around, since *everyone* outranked a Private.

Upon my arrival, I discovered there were quite a few recruits either reporting in or already there, most of whom were older than me. To my amazement, some recruits were as old as 30 years of age. There were others who had been in the service before,

---

[4] In the United States Army and some other branches of the US's military, a "yardbird" is defined as an inexperienced, untrained, or clumsy soldier, especially one employed on menial duties, customarily either a recent recruit or Private/Specialist (Grade 7/no insignia).

but had been out for more than three years, and had to go through recruit training all over again.

Everyone was assigned to specific barracks. Each barracks had two floors, each floor held 20 double bunks, one on top of the other. This meant 40 men on each floor, 80 men to a barracks, plus two or three Privates First Class (PFCs) and Corporals. Reveille was at 4:30 AM. A bell rang over a loudspeaker system that likely could have been heard as far away as San Diego. We raw recruits had five minutes maximum to get up, get dressed, fold our sheets and blankets, place them on top of our folded mattress, and fall in outside for roll call.

Our barracks of 80 men was in the charge of an old and grizzled Sergeant (Grade 4/three stripes), who had earned about seven or eight hash marks. Each hash mark was a diagonal piece of cloth sewn on the left sleeve of the uniform blouse, just above the cuff, and represented three years of service. He had seen service in World War I and acted as if he was the Almighty One. As far as we recruits were concerned, he was certainly *that* and then some.

In the *'Old Army'*, as a practical matter, the Non-Commissioned Officers ("*NCOs*", i.e., Corporals and Sergeants) *actually* ran the Army. Officers were very seldom seen around enlisted men. The NCOs took care of everything and the officers knew it. We recruits were divided into platoons of about 40 men with a Corporal or a PFC assigned to lead us around. It was made very clear to us that we would not move or do anything unless we were told to do so by one of these leaders. We were not to think. We were always to do as told. This was, after all, the initial period of basic training used to instill the discipline which is essential to every military unit.

All formations and calls were sounded by bugle. By the time we had had our roll call, the Bugler blew reveille at 5:30 AM for the rest of the troops on the post. The Bugler blew each call at the same time every day, so we always knew what time it was. A soldier did not need to own a watch, because the bugle calls always let us know what time of the day it was and what we were supposed to do: reveille; mess call; work call; mail call; and so forth.

Our hair was cut very short. All recruits were practically skinned – no sideburns, high in back, and no more than one-half inch on top. My hair stuck straight up and out and nothing I tried could make it lay down flat.

The barracks at Fort Mac were located right at the edge of Los Angeles Harbor. There was scant pavement anywhere, only dirt. A very large drill area was located just behind the barracks. It was on this very plot of ground we were drilled in the rudiments of close-order drill several hours a day. It was dusty and quickly dissolved into a muddy quagmire in the rain.

The Morning After: Physicals, Aptitude Tests, Paperwork, and Drills

Sunday – January 26, 1941

On our second day, we were taken to the post hospital for a physical exam. Because I hoped to attend the US Military Academy at West Point someday, I really took this exam seriously. I did not want anything to hurt my chances of getting accepted into the Academy. We were given pretty thorough physicals. I passed the exam with flying colors except for one thing – I was classified as having flat feet.

Such a classification wasn't considered serious, of course, given that 80-90 percent of the men with me were also classified that way. However, it really shook me up to think that I was not 100 percent physically perfect. At the time, this classification seemed pretty absurd since I had always been told I actually had high arches. As an aside, this diagnosis seems even more silly in retrospect since I went on to serve more than twenty-six years in Infantry, Airborne, and Special Forces units without ever once having experienced any sort of foot trouble whatsoever.

Following our physical examinations, the Army General Classification Test (AGCT) was administered to serve as a measure of *"general learning ability"* that could be used to assign new recruits to jobs. I got a score of 133 out of a possible 150, which put me in the 'genius' class. In 1941, a score of 70 was considered outstanding. Next, we were then fingerprinted and questioned: *"what had we done before joining the service"*; *"what were our hobbies"*; *"what was our language of fluency"*; *"how much schooling we had"*, and so on, and so on and so on. As far as schooling went, at 18, I was again way above the norm because I had completed one year of college by that time. In 1941, by contrast with the population-at-large, the average educational level was only 4th or 5th grade.

Finally, we signed a bunch of papers and were told that as soon as we were certified as healthy by the doctors and non-criminal by the Federal Bureau of Investigation (FBI), we would be fully welcomed into the Army. This was usually a matter of only a few days at the most. In the meantime, we were given close-order drill several hours a day – *"right face," "left face," "about face," "step off with the left foot", "always the left foot."*

Since I had three years of ROTC training under my belt, I knew the drill and quite a few things more. The Sergeant in charge soon noticed that I knew the drill and asked me where I learned it. I told him and later that day I was detailed as Barracks Leader for the downstairs floor of my barracks. Being only 18 years old and the youngest member of my platoon, the other men, particularly the prior-service men, took an immediate dislike for the situation and complained. It didn't help matters at all when I was given my own private room in the barracks. I didn't have much to do other than turn on the lights at reveille and turn them off at taps. I was still just another yardbird doing everything everyone else had to do, except repetitious close-order drill. I spent a large proportion of my time, in fact, assisting the NCOs in teaching the other recruits how to get the hang of close order drills.

Most of the recruits stayed at Fort Mac about one week or so before being shipped out to their assigned units. This was the case for both draftees and Regular Army types. I did not leave when my week was up. Officials at the base told me that the FBI field office had lost my fingerprint record, though I knew it was far more likely that the folks at Fort Mac had lost them. In any event, I was fingerprinted again and told I could spend the weekend at home.

Completion of Week #1 and
An Unexpected Weekend Pass

Saturday – February 1, 1941

A 48-hour pass was unheard of especially for fellows like me, a raw recruit. I hadn't even been issued a uniform yet. If I had wanted to go *"Absent Without Official Leave"* (AWOL), I could have done so and not gotten into any trouble because technically I had not yet been welcomed into the fold and thus was not officially subject to Army regulations. Of course, the officers and NCOs knew this, but we poor yardbirds didn't know what we didn't know. Anyway, I wanted to be a soldier, so it didn't even enter my mind not to return to Fort MacArthur.

When the word got out in the old neighborhood that I was home for the weekend, naturally everyone came to visit. All my aunts and uncles and friends stopped by the house. Each one of them, including my Mom and Dad, were quick to ask without fail, *"What have they done to you?"* Everyone was referring, of course, to my short hair. All the females had tears in their eyes when they asked me the question. At this early stage of my life, I had a very large wave in the front of my hair which was my pride and joy. After the Army trim, I looked like a porcupine in the defensive position – all the quills were sticking straight out.

I had to explain that it was customary for every recruit to have a short haircut. This practice was born of necessity in the early Army days, when living conditions at most Army posts were not conducive to modern sanitary methods. Head lice were commonplace and infections from such lice could only be prevented and easily detected by mandating short hair.

The practice of short haircuts for all recruits persists, but not for the same reasons. Short hair is a form of initiation, a rite of passage if you will, into the highly structured and disciplined military lifestyle. Except for the same question from everyone and female tears shed for me, I enjoyed my pass and was sad to leave again as it expired. Mom and Dad drove me back to Fort Mac. It was a cold and windy night in early February.

Return to Fort Mac and a Sudden Wake-Up Call

Sunday – February 2, 1941

The Fort appeared to be deserted and I again experienced some pangs of regret for leaving the good life, to which I was so well-accustomed. I entered the main gate and walked slowly down the hill past the 14-inch coastal gun emplacements. Suddenly, I was challenged by a loud voice shouting, *"Halt!"* *"Who goes there?"* It was a sentry on duty at one of the emplacements. He undoubtedly knew that I would not have been in the area unless there was good reason, but it helped to break the monotony of sentry duty on the lonely post. I learned this many times over during all the later guard duty I pulled. I relate this incident so the reader will know that it was in that moment, I realized abruptly that I had reentered the military world of regulations and orders.

Resumption of Recruit Training
A Visit to the Outfitters

Monday – February 3, 1941

Early on Monday morning, a large group of us was taken to the warehouse to fetch our uniform issue. Here's what I received: three pairs of white cotton drawers, three pairs of white cotton undershirts, three pairs of khaki cotton socks, one pair of Garrison shoes (ankle-high shoes), one khaki web belt with buckle, two pairs of blue (yes, blue.) fatigue jackets and pants, one blue fatigue hat (a round, saucer – shaped hat with a narrow brim all the way around), and a 1918 World War I olive drab wool uniform complete with choke collar, flared-out breeches, wrap-around puttees (two strips of wool cloth, two inches wide, six feet long), two olive drab (OD) wool shirts, one wool 1918-type overseas cap, and one wool 1918-type overcoat.

I was utterly flabbergasted at the thought of wearing a vintage uniform and blue fatigues. I just couldn't believe it. Maybe that stuff was acceptable for one-year draftees who had no intention of staying in the Army, but it was definitely not okay in my book for an aspiring professional soldier in the Regular Army. So, I told the Supply Sergeant that I was Regular Army, not a draftee, and asked about the uniform. His response was, *"Shut your mouth and move on."* I didn't like it, but what recourse was there for a yardbird? That was that.

While cheap and available in large quantities, this explanation is in no way a justification for the issue of blue fatigues to the Army. I could never understand why no one in the Army ever told our big-brothers in civilian government that the color blue made a man stand out like a sore thumb in the field. After all, Mother Nature doesn't create the sort of blue foliage that would camouflage a man in a blue suit and prevent him from becoming an easy battlefield target.

Very few men who were issued these uniforms found that they were properly tailored for the average man. They were either too large or too small and separate articles of clothing often did not match. In the military of that time, it was customary for the small men to be issued large sizes and the large men to receive the small sizes. There could be no trading of pieces since the last four digits of each man's serial number were stamped on each item of issue. More than once, I was issued trousers and jackets that would have suited a man twice my size. When I held out my arms to the sides, my fatigue jacket looked like bat wings. The side seams appeared to fall straight down from my wrists. I had to fold the trousers halfway around my side to buckle my belt. The fatigue hat was held up only by my ears. At the time, it was my opinion that everything that could be done was done to make us look and feel ridiculous.

Thank goodness we did not have to get into the *"Blues"* very often. On the other hand, I did not do too badly with my 1918 blouse and breeches. The blouse was snug and the choke collar made me hold my head up high. It was either that or have my chin rubbed raw. The trousers were too big around the waist by an inch or two and I couldn't lace the breeches around my legs. Fortunately, the six-feet long, two-inch wide wool wraparound puttees covered the gaps nicely. My overseas cap was about a size 12 and my overcoat was tailored for a man at least six-feet, six-inches tall. When I donned my cap and overcoat, nothing showed except the lower half of my face and the tips of my shoes. I had no need to wear gloves since the sleeves of the coat extended beyond my fingertips. That worked out nicely because I didn't have any. On reflection, I supposed, something good could come out of the situation no matter how fouled the circumstances.

Speaking of *"puttees"*, I would be remiss if I failed to mention there was a right and a wrong way to put on the wraparound puttees. The right way was to start wrapping them at the ankle so that each succeeding wrap would cover the preceding one. In this way, rain would run down from the top without getting inside and the final top fold would fit nicely beneath the small hangover of cloth resulting from the flare in the breeches. The other way (*the wrong one!*) was to wrap from the top of the calf to the ankle, which was how 99 percent of the recruits did it. I had learned from an ex-service type how to correctly wrap them the first time I put them on. Tucking in the roll at the top helped stop the puttee from coming unwrapped until you took them off – or, so the Army Regulations stated. On many occasions during our close-order drills at

Fort Mac, in fact, a man's puttee would come unwrapped and trail out behind him. Invariably, it would be stepped on by the first or second man behind him. This abruptly stopped the man dead in his tracks and, of course, brought the drill to an abrupt halt. [5]

Selective Training and Service Act of 1940 [6]
Reintroduction of Universal Conscription

US Army Volunteers and Draftees

The United States instituted the Selective Training and Service Act of 1940, September 16, 1940, which required all men between the ages of 21 and 45 to register for the military draft. It was the fourth incarnation of nominally universal military conscription in our nation's history. It was implemented so as to ensure that the United States of America would not be caught short in the event of war, as we had been in previous wars, viz. World War I.

Historically, in peacetime, Regular military forces were typically cut to the bone owing to the inherently American political notion that large standing armies are a *"no-no."* At least in 1940, someone in the government had the foresight to see that it was inevitable and the United States would be drawn into the conflict that had been raging in Europe, Asia and parts of Africa since the 1930s. For this reason, it was necessary to have trained personnel available before we were inevitably drawn into the whole affair.

An Army cannot be assembled, outfitted, and trained overnight. It takes quite a while to make units combat ready. The drafting of men for one year of training was thought to be sufficient preparation for war. Of course, so-called 'draftees' were invariably looked down upon by military professionals. It was always this way and probably will remain so because draftees do not ask to be soldiers and usually have no

---

[5] Further explanation is also needed about the World War I era uniforms and blue fatigues. With the draft in 1940 and 1941, the Army grew so rapidly that standard uniforms and equipment items were not produced rapidly enough to keep up with the increases. By late 1941, just before the Japanese attacked Pearl Harbor, this situation was pretty well rectified. But this development wasn't of much consolation to us early joiners. By my reckoning, sometime in 1938, someone sold the government a real bill of goods about the excellent durability of the WWI-era fatigues.

[6] See: https://en.wikipedia.org/wiki/Conscription_in_the_United_States.

intention of making a full-time profession of the military. A professional full-timer in any organization (military or civilian) resents part-timers to some degree. In 1940 and 1941, draftees in camps such as Fort MacArthur were kept separate from regulars in barracks and drill formations.

Draftees usually outnumbered the Regulars, so it was not easy to entirely avoid them. This created a rivalry that was kept going by both factions. For their part, the Draftees kept reminding the Regulars that they would be home in a year. The Regulars kept reminding the Draftees that no one had to drag them out to serve their country. As it turned out, most Draftees served until the end of the war in 1945 (five years rather than one) and a great many of them made a career of the service.

Graduation from Recruit Training
Saturday – April 12, 1941

In the waning days of basic training, our original platoon got smaller and smaller as the men were sworn in and shipped out. Soon I was the only one left and for a time thought that something was wrong that the Army hadn't told me about. Not so.

Orders to Report for Duty [7]
McChord Army Air Base

Tacoma, WA

On April 13th, less than 24 hours after graduation from the basic training course, I finally received orders to report for duty. I was assigned to the 17th Bombardment Group (M), 89th Reconnaissance Squadron, at McChord Army Air Base, Tacoma, Washington. In that moment, I felt that I had *really* become Private Floyd Russell Mulvany, Jr., Serial Number RA 19051508.

---

[7] At the time of my enlistment, the 17th Bombardment Group (M) was under the command of Lieutenant Colonel Walter R. Peck (USMA 1916 - 1917). Peck retired from the US Air Force with the rank of Brigadier General in 1948. The 89th Reconnaissance Squadron was under the command of Major John A. Hilger (Texas A&M - Class of 1932), who would later become famous as second-in-command to Lieutenant Colonel James H. ("Jimmy") Doolittle in connection with the daring 'Raid on Tokyo' which took place on April 18, 1942. Hilger retired from the US Air Force with the rank of Brigadier General in 1966.

The 89th Reconnaissance Squadron had a complement of about 30 individuals, all Regular Army. As a Private, I was on my way, and there was only *one way* I could go and that was up. It was taken as a given that my career would go the distance. Anything less than a full 30-year career was unimaginable.

My US Army Serial Number contained a lot of information. It was RA 19051508. The "1" signified Regular Army, as opposed to a "2" for National Guard, or a "3", "4", or "5" for draftees. The "9" signified the 9th Corps area, which was comprised of the nine western states of the continental United States. The country was divided into a total of nine corps areas, numbered consecutively from East to West. The digits "051508" meant that I was the 51,508th Regular Army soldier to enlist since the new serial number designation system was started in 1939. Prior to 1939, all Regular Army serial numbers began with a "6" and had only seven digits. Irrespective of his component (Regular Army, National Guard, or draftee), a man's serial number was always his alone. If he left the service and never returned, the number was never used again. If he was killed or died in the service, the number was never used again. If a soldier left the service and later returned, he assumed his same number again.

This system for assigning serial numbers was in effect until July 1, 1969, at which time all serial numbers were replaced by social security numbers. From then on, no longer did a man have an individual serial number that would identify him as a professional regular, a National Guardsman, or a draftee, or which would identify the part of the country where he enlisted. From my point-of-view, this change was just another step in the direction of diminishing the organizational integrity of the United States military.

17th Bombardment Group (M)
89th Reconnaissance Squadron
McChord Army Air Base, Tacoma, WA

April – June 1941

The area around Fort Lewis and McChord Field was known to all of us as *"Consumption Gulch."* At night there was always coughing and hacking throughout the camp. It couldn't be helped. Most of us, even those from the Northwest, were not used to the climate and it would take newcomers at least six months to get acclimated.

Shipments of personnel from Fort Mac were mostly by train with the cheapest accommodations available. For a trip requiring one or more nights, this meant that two men slept head-to-toe in a single Pullman berth. I shared a berth to Tacoma with a young recruit going to Fort Lewis and the Infantry. We were both in our 1918 uniforms and it was embarrassing. His fit the same as mine, so we both vowed we would not leave the train and would stay out of sight as much as possible.

Veterans of World War I could probably have had fond memories if they had seen us, but anyone else could only have wondered what we were. I remember that our woolen puttees started to itch, so we removed them. We also took our blouses off and were down to our undershirts. Around 9:00 PM, we took a chance that the lounge car would be empty and went to sit in the soft, comfortable chairs. No sooner had we stretched out when four or five Army officers came in and immediately went bug-eyed upon seeing us. Since we wore no insignia of any kind, they apparently didn't recognize us as soldiers. They did not say anything, they just stared at us. We took about one minute of this and left in a hurry. We did not want them to start asking questions. It was certainly no place for a couple of yardbirds. We were on the train for two more days and nights and we stayed in our seat with our puttees on.

Plenty of snow covered the countryside. Being from Southern California, it was quite a change of scenery for me. It was cold and dreary when we rolled into Tacoma. We were met at the train by some PFCs from McChord and Fort Lewis. They pulled duty at the train station and herded recruits like us into a truck for the ride to our duty stations. I bid goodbye to my train buddy and never saw or heard from him again. As I was soon to learn, meeting, leaving, and never seeing people again was an ordinary thing in the military. Also ordinary for military life was meeting the same people again and again at various stations throughout the world. Sometimes at ten, fifteen, or even twenty-year intervals.

Small Unit Training

Small unit training was conducted over a 12-week period. During this time, new recruits were not permitted to leave the base. Throughout this period, we were herded around in platoon-sized groups under the supervision of a Staff Sergeant (Grade 3/3 stripes up, 1 down), a Corporal (Grade 5/2 stripes up), and a couple of PFC's (Grade 6/1 stripe up) who were on detached duty (TDY) from the 89th.

Our Staff Sergeant will always be remembered for repeatedly saying "*As you was*" instead of the proper phrase "*As you were.*" This command was usually given when we were standing "*at ease*" in ranks and someone in authority started to speak. Talking was not permitted while at ease. You could move one foot at a time or scratch or stretch. It was a sort of an "*in-ranks*" rest period. Many times, we drilled close to the draftees and during rest periods the banter back and forth got really hot. Of course, we wouldn't break ranks, so it was all just talk. The Drill Sergeants kept us in our proper places.

At this stage in my Army career, the most important thing I learned was how to live in a man's world. Remember, this was before any women, other than nurses, were in the military services. There weren't any females around and there weren't any pin-ups either. It was an all-male environment. To paraphrase Rudyard Kipling, from his "*Barrack-Room Ballads*" (1892), there's a reason "… *Why, single men in barracks don't grow into plaster saints.*" I found that the same maxim applied to tent life. Being a very naïve and inexperienced youngster, I didn't find it very easy to learn all I needed to know, even though I had a lot of help. Instead, I learned most of what I had to know the hard way. Any experience learned the hard way is not soon forgotten and I had plenty of them. I was the butt of many jokes in those days.

Camp Life

The recruit training area at McChord was a genuine tent city. It was situated about three miles across the reservation from the main post. It was full of draftees and enlistees being trained for duty under less-than-ideal circumstances. All recruits lived together in the same general area – six men to a tent. Other men, assigned to different squadrons in the 17th Bombardment Group, were bivouacked in close proximity. The tents were "*Sibleys*", the same type first introduced and put into use during the American Civil War (1861-1865). Round and conical in shape, they could sleep six men without too much crowding. We had wooden floors, which was a good break for us because Washington State was so damp in the winter.

In the center of each tent was a Sibley stove. The fuel for the stove was a product called "*Prestologs*." It was made from sawdust that had been compressed into a cylindrical shape, hard as concrete, and difficult to ignite. Once started, a single Prestolog would keep the tent warm for about two hours. There was a trick to getting them to burn, a trick I never quite mastered. Never once could start one burning on my own. Invariably, someone always had to get up and assist me with lighting the fire. In short order, I became a very unpopular bunkmate at least temporarily.

There weren't any recreational facilities in camp. We had no movies, no canteens, and no post exchange - no nothing. We had to make our own amusement during non-duty hours, so most of our free time was spent letter writing, sleeping, and often reading. In basic training, our pay was the magnificent sum of $21.00 a month. Out of that came $3.00 for laundry and $.10 for the Old Soldiers Home. These were mandatory deductions, so we never saw the money. This left $16.90 to do with as we wished. In addition, I took out $1,000.00 in life insurance at $5.00 per month. [8] I saved $5.00 of the $11.90 that remained, which left me $6.90 to fool around with. I did not smoke or drink. So, as it happened, this amount of money was sufficient to meet my ordinary wants and needs.

At the end of our twelve weeks of boot camp, we all thought that we would be freed from the Sibleys. At that point, we were sure we'd soon be moving into the big, new, modern barracks where the rest of the squadron lived. Contrary to our expectations, we moved back into another row of Sibleys, just outside the big, new, modern barracks. As matters played out, the tents were good enough for what little time we would spend in them. There was no way we yardbirds were going to be spoiled. Besides, there weren't any other Privates in the squadron and there hadn't been for some time. In high clover, the squadron now had about thirty of us to pull guard duty, fatigue detail, *and* KP.

The thirty-some yardbirds in the 89th were mostly from Washington and Idaho, so they were really close to home. They came from all walks of life and a couple of them had prior service under their belts. We ranged in age from eighteen to thirty-five. The older recruits struck me as virtually elderly. I never asked any of them why they

---

[8] I paid faithfully on this policy until 1961, at which time I collected $1,200.00 in cash.

had signed up because it really made no difference to me. We were all there for the same purpose, faced the same challenges, and shared the same hardships irrespective of chronological age.

Advance Training

It was not long before we were issued US Army Air Corps olive drab (OD) coveralls to work in as we trained for war. Our training consisted of close-order drill, familiarization with the Colt M1911 .45 caliber pistol, Army Regulations and Articles of War, General Orders for guard duty, aircraft nomenclature and characteristics, and group and squadron operations. Our curriculum was straightforward, not too demanding, but barely qualified us for any specific tasks or specialties. There were no kitchen police (KP) or latrine cleaning duties while we were in recruit training.

We were all assembled in front of our new shelters, when we were introduced to the Squadron First Sergeant (Acting). A Staff Sergeant in reality, he was a redheaded, whiskey-voiced, and wizened looking character. Somehow, despite his outward appearance, he struck me as an administrative type. Of course, I knew that a First Sergeant had five stripes, three up and two rockers with a diamond in the middle. For some reason, in those days the 89th Reconnaissance Squadron lacked a genuine First Sergeant.

There were also Master Sergeants (Grade 1/3 stripes up, 3 down) and Technical Sergeants (Grade 2/3 stripes up, two down) in the outfit, but they were serving as Supply Sergeants and Section Chiefs, not administrative types. As long as I was with the 89th, we never had anything but an acting First Sergeant. I never did learn why this was the case. On the other hand, I really did not much care because there were always plenty of NCOs to tell us what to do. "*Frog-throat*" gave us the word about what we were and were not to do. He also told us that we would be assigned to our proper sections at a later date.

In the meantime, we learned there was more training and drill in store for us under squadron NCOs. Along with the other members of the squadron, we were also to have more close-order drill and briefings on squadron operations and its aircraft. We were told about the rosters for KP, fatigue duty, guard duty, passes to town, when we would be issued our Class A uniforms, and the *"Articles of War."* Back in the day, the *"Articles of War"*, all the rules and regulations which governed the lives of Army personnel, were read in their entirety to every man every six months. There were more than 100 of them.

Section Assignments

When I first reported for duty at McChord, I knew very little about the nuts and bolts of various aircraft and even less about the art of aviation. I had never flown in an airplane of any kind, so I was really impressed by the variety of the squadron's different types of airplanes. At the time, we were allowed to 'look and touch' but not to ride in them.

Within 7–10 days of our arrival at McChord, we were assigned to our various sections. There were several of these: Maintenance (Mechanics, Propeller Specialists, sheet metal repair, bomb sight repair, etc.); Technical Supply (strictly aircraft parts and items); Supply (food, gasoline, clothing, etc.); Motor Pool (vehicle Drivers and Mechanics); Photography (the heart of a reconnaissance squadron with cameras, camera repair, photo processing in a fully equipped portable photo laboratory); Mess (Cooks and Bakers); Administration (personnel, records, and correspondence, etc.); Ordnance (armaments, ammunition of all kinds, and bombs, etc.); and Medical (Flight Surgeon and Medics with limited medical capability, e.g., bandages, salves, and drugs, etc.).

Aerial Photography Section
Assignment - Aerial Photographer

(MOS 640)

Owing to my high score on the US Army's General Classification Test (AGCT) and one year of college, I was assigned to the Photo Section with the Military Occupational Specialty (MOS) of 640, Aerial Photographer. At this time and throughout World War II, 640 was the highest MOS an enlisted man could attain. I guessed that my assignment as a 640 was due to the two reasons already cited above.

I'm not certain of the explanation, however, because the decision was never explained to me. On the other hand, I never actually questioned the classification. After all, in the pre-World War II Army, a Private never questioned anything or anyone of a higher rank.

In any event, about ten of us were assigned to this section. Of course, we all started right away to learn as much as possible about the details of aerial photography. We were taught the basic operational characteristics of the various cameras; camera maintenance; mathematical computations required to photograph specific areas from the air to obtain the desired results; and developing, printing, enlarging, mosaic overlays, and the basics of photo interpretation. It was generally understood that as openings became available, we were to attend the nine-month photographers' course at Lowry Field in Denver, Colorado, where we would become fully qualified in our designated MOS.

Familiarization Flights

Part of the training consisted of familiarization flights in squadron aircraft. They would gather up 15 or 20 of us and fly around for three or four hours. Since there were so many bodies in the plane, we couldn't move around. So, we laid around, talked, or slept.

Every now and then, the officers would let a couple of us sit in the nose in the Bombardier's area. Riding upfront was always a thrill to me. I felt like I was floating in space, all the while watching the world go by.

Opportunities to practice our newfound skills were few and far between, so we learned mostly through on-the-job training in the squadron. As it turned out, none of us ever made it to Lowry, the onset of the war saw to that particular detail. Much to my regret, our section training did not exempt us from KP, guard, or fatigue duty.

Issuance of Class A Uniforms

Our next big thrill came about with the issuance of our Class A uniforms. We were individually fitted for blouses, trousers, shirts, and shoes. Alterations were made at Uncle Sam's expense so that was a help. We each received one pair of OD gabardine slacks, one pair of high-top Garrison shoes for dress up, two cotton khaki shirts, two OD wool shirts, three pairs of cotton khaki socks, one black necktie, one khaki web belt with brass buckle, one leather-visor Garrison cap, one OD overcoat with brass buttons, and one pair of black leather gloves.

All uniform items were tailored to fit perfectly and looked great. I felt like a soldier for the first time. We were also issued an extra pair of Air Corps coveralls and a baseball style cap, which together served as the work and drill uniform. A brand-new item at the time was the short, green field jacket, which could be worn in lieu of the blouse. On the right collar of our blouse, we wore a solid brass U.S. insignia and on the left collar we wore the winged propeller Air Corps insignia.

The insignia, brass belt buckle, and the buckle on the Garrison belt were made to last through hundreds of polishing's, as were all leather items. Spit-and-shine was an integral part of Regular Army life and no one had to be told to do it. It was done out of pride in wearing the uniform as prescribed by Army Regulations – everything clean, pressed, and shined and all buttons buttoned. Any other way was out of uniform and subject to unit punishment – no *"ifs, ands, or buts"* about it.

Private Floyd R. Mulvany, Jr.
US Army Air Corps
17th Bombardment Group (M), 89th Reconnaissance Squadron
McChord Army Air Base, Tacoma, WA
April 1941

Fire Guard Duty

We had to pull Fire Guard duty during the night because Sibley stoves and tents were notorious for burning up – or down. I vividly recall one occasion when I was asleep alone in my tent and it burned to the ground. I didn't wake up until my fellow soldiers started throwing water on me. Luckily, I didn't get a scratch or a burn. This in spite of the fact that my rescuers didn't even know of my presence inside!

Fatigue Duty

Fatigue Duty ranged from picking up cigarette butts and discarded scraps of paper (*"policing the area"*) to moving furniture for officers, chopping weeds, painting fences and rocks, and hauling trash. We had a saying in those days: *"If it moves, salute it; if it doesn't move, pick it up; and if you can't pick it up, paint it."* It was a simple but precise explanation of the Army way. Because of the time I spent on KP, guard, and fatigue duty, I never did have the pleasure of cleaning the latrines at McChord Field.

Security Duty

When assigned to Security Duty, one of our special responsibilities was to guard a concrete vault in the main squadron hangar. It was within this structure that the soon to be famous Norden bombsight was housed. In 1941, this highly advanced device was one of America's most closely held secrets of the war. It was reputed to be the world's best bombsight and a technological marvel. There was no doubt that many countries would have liked to have had it in their own arsenals, especially the Axis powers, Germany, Italy, and Japan.

The vault itself was encased in a thick shell of reinforced concrete. The only way to access the vault was through a massive steel door that was secured by three iron bars and combination locks. The vault was approximately 12 feet square and seven feet in height. The guard post during daylight hours was a stationary one in front of the entrance. Physical access to the vault was limited to only two to four security-cleared personnel, who were always armed and customarily worked in pairs. At night, the security perimeter was defined as the entire interior of the hangar. All doors had to be checked every hour, including the vault door.

Vault guard duty was for 30 days at a time with six hours on and 24 hours off. No other duty was pulled during this 30-day period. While on duty, we carried a five round automatic pump-action, short barreled shotgun, and a .45 caliber pistol. We didn't know anything about the Norden sight other than it was highly classified. We had orders to shoot any unauthorized personnel who might try to gain unauthorized entry to the vault. It was just as well that we didn't know anything, since the less we knew the better off we were and the less trouble we could cause or get into.

In retrospect, it's amusing to recall how I got assigned to this security detail. One day during squadron training, an old Staff Sergeant asked if any of us wanted to learn to shoot skeet. Several of us, of course, raised our hands and thus allowed ourselves to be 'volunteered.' We spent a couple of enjoyable days on the skeet range and, of course, we all qualified. No one ever failed to qualify on a weapon of any type in the pre-war Army, because the quality of instruction was always very thorough. The day after we qualified, we were all put on 30 days vault guard duty. This was my first experience in learning about the importance of *never* volunteering for anything in the Army unless you really knew what you were getting into or really wanted the assignment for whatever reason.

I enjoyed guard duty because it taught me responsibility and was therefore worthwhile. Whatever was being secured, the responsibility for protecting it was mine and mine alone. There was no one else around to handle any situation that might arise.

Kitchen Police Duty

When not pulling guard duty, KP and fatigue duty came just about every other day. We pulled KP in a 5,000-man consolidated mess hall. All units stationed at McChord messed there, so all units provided KP personnel. Among other things, there was a steam tray washing machine in a small room that we called the *"China Clipper."* [9]

---

[9] The *"China Clipper"* referenced above is not to be confused, of course, with the *"actual"* China Clipper. In real life, the China Clipper was the Martin M-130 four-engine flying boat built for Pan American Airways by the Glenn L. Martin Company in Baltimore, MD. One of the largest airplanes of its era, it initiated its maiden commercial flight to the Far East on November 22, 1935. See: https://en.wikipedia.org/wiki/China_Clipper.

One man worked the machine to wash and rinse all the mess trays. The trays came in through a small window and had already been scraped clean by the user.

Specifically designated KP personnel pulled the trays in, stacked them, and then pushed the individual lots of dirty trays over to the actual 'clipper' to be washed. Once the cleaning cycle was completed, the individual clipper then pushed the clean trays out through a small window located on the other side of the room. As you might imagine, the steam was so thick throughout the room you couldn't see through either window. It was like being in a steam bath from 4:00 AM to 7:00 PM with your clothes on.

And then there were the pots and pans to clean. Army cooks had a habit of using the largest available pot or pan for mixing or cooking the smallest amounts of food. And why not? Plenty of KP crew were available to scrape, scrub, and shine them as soon as they were used. After a stint on pots and pans, I looked, smelled, and felt like a garbage pile. It was a rotten, stinking job.

Peeling potatoes wasn't too bad a job, just monotonous. Potatoes were usually served three times a day, so there was always a plentiful supply to be peeled – 90 percent of the time by hand. The mechanical potato peelers were not too good because they didn't remove the *"eyes."* I had potato duty so often that I ended up carrying my own personal peeler at all times while on the post.

Being designated the outside cleanup man was the most coveted job on KP duty. It consisted of keeping the garbage cans aligned, the garbage separated into various categories (edible, non-edible, paper, and metal, etc.), and maintaining the area outside the mess hall rear door. Usually, the first man to report for KP in the morning was detailed to this duty. I got the job no more than two times, even though I was first to report on numerous occasions.

Latrine Duty

Latrines were long trough-like affairs with 40 holes to a side and absolutely no privacy. The trough was made of wood lined with sheet metal. A large scoop-like bucket was located at one end – a sort of scupper device. Water ran into the bucket until it finally tipped over. The water then ran the full length of the trough and emptied out the other end. This sequence went on continuously day and night. The latrine was located inside a long, low, wooden building with Sibley stoves at each end (*what else?*). It had to be located inside a heated enclosure, otherwise we would have frozen to death especially in the dead of winter. There wasn't much snow, but there was always rain and fog. We lived in tents outside the main barracks, so those living in the barracks must have kept the latrines clean. It's a cinch that some number of anonymous Privates did, no doubt about that.

For the record, KP and fatigue duty were demeaning to me. It took me a long time to accept the fact that they were all a part of the Private's life in the Army. However, to this day I do not enjoy any aspect of food preparation or clean up afterwards. All those days on KP, in particular, really left their mark on me.

Pay and Benefits

After four months of active service, a Private's pay increased automatically to $30.00 per month. That was a $9.00 raise. Flying status was put on top of that, which at the time was 50 percent of base pay. For me that was $15.00 a month. So, my pay went from $21.00 to $45.00 a month. I felt like a millionaire.

In order to qualify for flight pay, an individual had to fly a minimum of four hours a month. It was considered hazardous duty and it was much of the time. With my newly found wealth, I could afford to go to town for a few enjoyments, like movies and dances. At the time, I still did not drink or smoke.

Prices were terribly low in 1941, but so were salaries. A dollar went a long way. Movie tickets cost $.20 each. Just $.25 got you into a dance. Hamburgers were $.05 or $.10 each, depending on their size. An ice crème soda only cost $.15. Only one Private in the squadron owned an automobile.

Off Duty Diversions

We rode buses to and from town. They were actually long trailers with standup room only that were pulled by truck tractors. About 75 GI bodies could squeeze into such transports at the cost of $.10 each way. Drunks were in no danger of falling down inside the trailer because the bodies were packed in too tightly. Before exiting the main gate, all drunks were made to take a prophylaxis to ensure that they wouldn't bring back any social diseases.

There were prophylaxis *("pro")* stations all around town. It was up to each man to obtain condoms if he anticipated *"going all the way"* with a girl. It was best that a soldier took such a precaution because the Army would not tolerate a man losing duty days due to having acquired a sexually transmitted *"venereal"* disease (VD).

Those that did were treated miserably. In the large mess, there was one table that bore a sign with only two letters: "VD". Any GI with a case was escorted to the table by two military policemen (*"MPs"*), whose responsibility was to stand guard over all transgressors while they consumed their meals. After eating their meals, the guards then escorted the miscreants out of the mess.

Soldiers were routinely court-martialed for this offense, reduced in rank (if he had one), and fined. No one wanted to be treated in such a humiliating manner, so visiting the nearest 'pro' station was a popular stop on the way to a night out on the town. "*Pro*" slips were seldom misplaced.

Going to town in Tacoma was not always a lot of fun, especially if you wore your uniform. Signs posted in various restaurants and shops read: *"Soldiers and Dogs Not Allowed Inside."* The local police also had a habit of harassing enlisted GIs in uniform. For no apparent reason, we might be stopped and asked what we were doing as if we had escaped from somewhere and had no right to be in town. I almost always wore my uniform which was always neatly pressed, properly worn, and shoes shined. My uniform items were all tailored to fit perfectly. This was my way of putting down the local clods who looked down on us.

Social Life

I dated a very nice local girl all the time. We never went to a bar or a night club. Instead, we went to movies, dances, the park, or wherever else nice people congregated. Her Mother accepted me, but I believe that her father always thought I was going to corrupt his daughter. I guess he never looked upon me as simply an 18-year-old young man from a good home who was away for the first time. The uniform made me a man of the world in his mind. Even though I was invited to their home many times, I never felt at ease with him. The girl got married in late 1941, before the war started, and probably lived happily ever after.

Entertainment

There were no USO shows or dances or large recreational facilities on post in those days. We made our own fun and games to pass our free time away. A GI blanket held by six guys was great for heaving someone up in the air and catching him. Everyone would take turns being tossed up and down. We also made our own music, since there were very few instruments of any kind available. Besides, no one could afford to buy them either. In any event, it would not have made much sense to own an instrument given that we lived in tents and couldn't have properly cared for them. Instead, someone would wrap toilet paper around a comb and hum into it to make a sound like a kazoo. Two spoons or dinner knives served as drum sticks and any hard surface filled in as the drum. I could cup my hands and make a whistling sound by blowing into them. Then, by manipulating my fingers up and down (like on a trumpet), I could play any tune I knew. With one or two combs, drum sticks, my whistling hands, and others humming or singing or clapping hands, we had some great jam sessions.

Writing letters was the number one pastime among the majority of us, for sure. I can remember only a few guys who didn't write an awful lot of letters. Writing them was good, but getting them was even better. All of us looked forward to mail call and really got ticked off if we didn't receive any. Not receiving any mail was downright disappointing.

I wrote to everyone I knew as frequently as I could. I figured that *as thou give'st, so shalt thou receive."* It worked, too. I seldom went without mail for any length of time.

17th Bombardment Group (M)
Four Squadrons: 34th, 73rd, 95th Bomber Squadrons and
the 89th Reconnaissance Squadron

April – May 1941

From its modest beginnings in 1918, the US Army Air Corps (USAAC) grew to about 20,000 personnel and 2,400 aircraft between 1939-41. Its successor organization, the US Army Air Forces (USAAF) expanded to roughly 80,000 aircraft and more than 2.4 million well equipped personnel between 1942-45. By the end the war, the USAAF was operating from more than 1,600 bases around the globe.

In February 1941, the entire 17th Bombardment Group (M) was flying B-18 *"Bolo"* and B-23 *"Dragon"* medium bombers. The B-18 made its maiden flight in April 1935. Its performance characteristics were nothing to write home about. The B-18 was slow, poorly armed, and could carry maybe 1,000 pounds of bombs. One .30 caliber machine gun in the nose and another behind the pilot comprised the only armament. A 150-mph cruise speed was its absolute limit. The B-23 made its maiden flight in July 1939. It was somewhat faster than the B-18 and primarily intended to fulfill a reconnaissance mission. Like the B-18, she was very lightly armed. Both aircraft were a good training platform for pilots since they were in the two-engine, medium size, and bomber class. I had to believe that they were only an interim training aircraft because they never would have survived in a combat situation.

In 1941, there was a practice bombing range at Moses Lake, Washington. It was a large expanse of wasteland that was ideally suited for bombing practice. The importance of this training was not lost on any of us, since even the yardbirds were aware of the conflicts already underway in Europe and Asia. Three of the four squadrons in the 17th Bombardment Group were bombardment types, so they received comprehensive bombing and gunnery training. In a reconnaissance squadron, of course, our top priorities were flying and photo efficiency though we too received a modicum of bombing and gunnery training.

Field Training
Camp Seven Mile
Spokane, WA

May – June 1941 [10]

Maneuvers were normally held in the summertime. In June, we left McChord for Spokane, Washington, by air and truck convoy. Air crews flew and the rest of us rode

---

[10] The United States Army Air Forces (USAAF) was established by an act of Congress on June 20, 1941. See: https://en.wikipedia.org/wiki/United_States_Army_Air_Forces.

in trucks. We took the B-18's and B-23's with us and operated out of Parks Field, a private airport. Geiger Field was not in existence until later in the war. We set up a tent city and simulated combat field operations.

We yardbirds learned photo developing, printing, and the making of mosaics. Mosaics were strips of film overlaid to give an overall high-altitude picture of a specific area. We only flew occasionally because the older, more experienced men were busy brushing up on their combat skills. So, often times, we yardbirds were not too terribly busy.

It was very hot that summer. Fortunately, the field was near the Spokane River, so we were able to swim and keep cool. Civilians came out each day to watch the big Army aircraft take off and land. We young ones enjoyed playing hero to the girls and telling them all about our lives of action.

The Photo Section Sergeants and Corporals were always trying to use us younger guys to get them dates with the local girls. Since they could leave camp at night and we couldn't, they encouraged us to fix them up. However, the young girls that showed up to swim were not there to talk to the Sergeants. As near as I could tell, they were interested more in the young men of their own age.

Once upon a time, a couple of Sergeants ordered me to swim out to speak with a couple of girls who were sitting on a rock in the middle of the river. My job was to ask them for a date on behalf of my superiors. I followed orders and politely told the girls what the Sergeants wanted. One of these *"innocents"* looked up at me and said, *"you tell those clowns to go piss up a rope!"* I hadn't heard this expression before, so it really took me a back – especially coming from a young girl. I asked her to repeat the message and got the same instructions again verbatim. Rather than swim back to the Sergeants, I stood up and hollered as loudly as I could, *"They said for you to go piss up a rope."*

Needless to say, I was told to get off the rock and report *"right now!"* I thought I had had it for sure. Luckily, I was able to convince the Sergeants that I didn't know for certain what the expression meant so they let me off and quickly lost interest in those particular girls.

Speaking of those two Sergeants, they were always on my tail for something. I believe it was because they were always trying to coerce me into to buy them beer or cigarettes though that was never my game. After all, I didn't drink or smoke and they made much more money than I did. There wasn't one good reason why I should waste my money on their ilk. Other Privates did, of course, occasionally cough up dough in the expectation of currying favor with others but not me.

About the only independence I exercised in those days was to decide how and what to what to do with my own free time and money. I also knew that those two Sergeants and the First Sergeant were resentful of the fact that I had gone to college for a year before enlisting. They were always referring to me as a *"smart ass college kid"* and volunteering me for extra duties.

I always obeyed their orders, without hesitation, while keeping my mouth shut. Their behavior never commanded my respect, even as I became wise to their motivations. At the end of the day, I benefitted from their abuse because it had the effect of teaching me valuable lessons about life that might have taken longer to learn on my own.

Later, we moved into another tent city at Fort George Wright, an Army post situated on a bluff overlooking Spokane's amusement park area. We could sit on the edge of the bluff and look over the entire park. Since there were always quite a few girls in the park, this activity quickly became yet another enjoyable pastime.

Application to *"Flying Sergeants"* [11] Program
Santa Ana Army Air Base, Santa Ana, CA

June – July 1941

In the summer of 1941, while based at Pendleton Airfield, I applied for pilot training through the *"Flying Sergeants"* program. This course taught qualified enlisted personnel how to pilot an aircraft and guaranteed an immediate rating of Staff Sergeant to all who graduated from the program. It was the enlisted man's equivalent to the *"Flying Cadets"* program, which almost everyone put in for so they could become instant officers.

My decision to apply to the *"Aviation Cadets Training Program" (aka, "Flying Sergeants")* seemed like a good idea at the time. However, this seemingly inconsequential decision had an outsized impact on the course of my early career in the US Army

---

[11] https://en.wikipedia.org/wiki/Aviation_Cadet_Training_Program_(USAAF).

Air Corps. In any event, I was one of several members of the 89th Reconnaissance Squadron who applied to the same program, at about that time, though not everyone was accepted.

Early on in the application process, it came as a bit of a shock to learn I was at risk of failing the required physical examination. While there was nothing wrong with my eyes (20/10 vision), ears, heart or lungs, it turned out I was at risk because the exam revealed my elbow was offset two degrees as a result of a childhood accident. The doctor who first examined me said he was *"not going to stick his neck out and let me kill someone"*, because I had a crooked left arm. Fortunately, the Squadron Flight Surgeon was present at the time. He immediately ordered me to step forward. He told me to pull him with my left arm. He then grabbed my upraised arm and tried to resist my pulling him. Satisfied with my performance, he told the other doctor there was nothing wrong with my arm and that he would sign a statement to that effect.

The Flight Surgeon's gambit worked, because upon returning from Gunnery School, another Sergeant Pilot candidate and I were ordered to the Army Hospital in Portland, Oregon, to take a final flight physical for pilot training. The final flight physical was rigorous in all respects and took place over a seven-day period. When it was over, we returned to Pendleton Airbase without knowing whether or not we had passed the exam. No one was going to reveal *anything* to two Privates, even though it meant an awful lot to both of us. They just let us sweat it out. We did, too.

Pendleton Airfield
Pendleton, OR

July – December 1941

We stayed in Spokane about six weeks and then returned to McChord. For some reason, which none of us understood, the government was building an airbase at Pendleton, Oregon. Pendleton was a famous old rodeo town situated on the northeastern border of Oregon. The town of Pendleton was the site of the annual 'Pendleton Roundup', located about 40 miles from Walla Walla, Washington. Walla Walla was home to several guys who had joined the 89th around the same time as me.

A couple of officers and NCOs, a cook, and one KP (me) were detailed to check out the base, because the entire 17th Bombardment Group (M) was to be transferred there at a later date. I had the dubious distinction of being one of the first members of the Group to set foot in Pendleton. Pendleton was some kind of town. It offered nothing but saloons, whore houses, and restaurants – something for every appetite. It catered to cowboys and tourists who visited at roundup time. Our inspection tour was successful in all respects, but as far as I was concerned most of the time spent in town was a complete bust, because I personally had neither any interest in drinking nor cavorting with prostitutes.

The barracks, runways, taxi areas, and some maintenance buildings on the base were finished. Wheat and weeds were still growing between the barracks and in all the other areas where there were no man-made objects. There wasn't a tree, shrub, or bush in sight, it was solid scrub country, good for rabbits and soldiers.

Our small group had no sooner returned to McChord when the entire 17th Bombardment Group (M) moved to occupy Pendleton Airbase. Getting settled at Pendleton required all our time during duty hours. We got passes at night and my best buddy, Jack Lowden, took me to his parents' home in Walla Walla. They were the nicest people – a happy family living in a very large house. Jack's younger brother and very pretty sister still lived at home, so it was great for me to stay there and be treated as a member of the family.

Although the thought might have crossed my mind, I never seriously considered getting involved with Jack's sister because she was so much like a sister to me. We soon dubbed Walla Walla *"Little Hollywood"* because of the inordinate number of beautiful girls who lived there. I fell in love with a different girl each time I visited the place. We always had good times with family and friends.

17th Bombardment Group (M)
Designated a "Priority One" Unit

July 1941

In the early summer of 1941, shortly after the Group relocated to the new Pendleton Airfield, the 17th Bombardment Group (M) was designated by the War Department as a "*Priority One*" unit. This certification meant that the 17th was combat ready and entitled to be issued all the equipment and supplies needed to maintain its readiness status. In August, we were the first outfit in the entire US Army Air Corps to take deliveries of the brand-new B-25B medium bomber. The B-25B officially went operational in January 1942.

North American
B-25 *"Mitchell"* (M) Bomber (12)
(1941)

The B-25B was far advanced over the B-18 and B-23, so we were required to engage in heavy transition training during the ensuing couple of months. All flight personnel were required to accrue many flight hours during May and June in order to reach prescribed proficiency levels. For some reason, during this period of intensive orientation and training there was no bombing or gunnery practice. This despite the fact the B-25 was designed to carry six 500-pound bombs. It was also armed with twin-guns (2 x .50 caliber Browning M1919) in the dorsal turret with a remotely-controlled, retractable ventral turret, and a pair of like 50's in the tail.

---

(12) The North American B-25 *"Mitchell"* is a medium bomber that was introduced in 1941. It was named in honor of Major General William "Billy" Mitchell, a pioneer of U.S. military aviation. See: https://en.wikipedia.org/wiki/North_American_B-25_Mitchell.

US Army Maneuvers [13] [14]
Nationwide War Games

June – November 1941

In mid- July, the 17th Bombardment Group (M) got orders to participate in the 1941 *"Louisiana"* and *"Carolina"* Maneuvers. At the time, the Louisiana Maneuvers were the largest peacetime maneuver ever held in the continental United States. Units from all branches of the US Army, viz., Regulars, Reserves, and the National Guard participated.

Ellington Field
Houston, TX

July 20 – September 10

The men of Major John A. Hilger's 89th Reconnaissance Squadron began departing Pendleton, Oregon on Sunday, July 20th. Air crews flew to our first destination, while most of the enlisted men travelled by truck convoy. The trip from Pendleton to Ellington was more than 2,000 miles.

Ground crews and personnel from all supporting arms were transported by trucks: ten men, each with a duffel bag, in the rear of a 2 ½ ton truck. This was to be our home for the entire trip. We traveled in convoy, stopping only along the road for pee calls and

---

[13] The Louisiana (August), Carolina (November), Tennessee (June), and Arkansas (August) maneuvers were a series of major U.S. Army exercises carried out throughout 1941. The purpose of such operations, which involved more than 400,000 troops, was to evaluate U.S. Army training, logistics, doctrine, and commanders. See: https://en.wikipedia.org/wiki/Louisiana_Maneuvers; https://en.wikipedia.org/wiki/Carolina_Maneuvers; https://en.wikipedia.org/wiki/Tennessee_Maneuver_Area; and https://www.jstor.org/stable/40027604?seq=1.

[14] Many of the US Army officers present at the maneuvers later rose to very senior roles during the Second World War. These included Dwight D. Eisenhower, Omar N. Bradley, Mark W. Clark, Walter Krueger, Leslie J. McNair, Joseph Stillwell, George S. Patton, John B. Anderson, and many others. War was already raging throughout Europe and in many parts of the Far East, so the time had come for the US Army to evaluate its training, logistics, war fighting doctrine, and its prospective field commanders.

meals. After about ten days, we enlisted types arrived at Ellington Field in Houston, Texas.

The rear of a 2 ½ ton truck was outfitted with stoves and kitchen utensils in which our meals were prepared as we moved along. At meal times, we stopped for one hour to eat and then proceeded on our way. Believe it or not, I was not detailed for KP at any time during the entire journey. I felt really good about this development, because it was no fun cleaning pots and pans – especially while on convoy.

It took us about ten days to get to Houston. Of course, the planes and crews were already there. If I remember correctly, we were assigned to the *"Blue"* team – the friendly-forces Army. We operated out of Ellington for four weeks, during which I pulled guard duty, KP, and fatigue duty.

During the time we were at Ellington, a hurricane, known to history as the *"Texas"* hurricane made its way up to Houston. It was the second hurricane of the season in 1941, a Category 3, with sustained winds in excess of 125 miles per hour. It formed in mid-September and its effects were felt for about ten days. Naturally, the aircraft and crews associated with maneuvers were evacuated, leaving us yardbirds and a few NCOs behind to wade in the rapidly rising waters. We were told to get in our barracks and stay there until the hurricane blew over. Being good soldiers, we did as we were told.

When the storm arrived, the winds initially blew 60 to 80 miles per hour but soon they increased dramatically. Rain was blown right through the side of the barracks, windows, and roof. The first floor was soon knee deep in water, so we all moved to the second floor. We had no heat, no lights, and no food. Near the end of the day, we were so hungry and thirsty that one man volunteered to try to get to the Mess Hall which was located about 100 yards away. The man's name was Ben Johnson. He was six-feet, three inches, tall and had a nose big enough to cover a caboose. When he stepped out the front door, he fell into water over his head. We had to fish him out and pull him back into the barracks.

Needless to say, we just stood down until the storm finally blew over. In today's Army, a situation like this would never have been allowed. In 1941, however, soldiers were considered to be men who could take care of themselves under any circumstances. Consequently, we never thought anything about it, there was absolutely no fear or panic among any of the men.

On occasion, we were given passes to go into town. Houston was a growing town with all sorts of attractions to visit, some nice and some not so nice, for a good time. I heard through the grapevine that the city had some of the best $2.00 cat houses in the United States. I knew nothing first-hand about the cat houses, but I did know from personal experience that the city had good restaurants and dance halls which catered to soldiers. We were also able to visit the San Jacinto Battlefield where Sam Houston skunked Santa Ana and won freedom for Texas on April 21, 1836. All in all, we enjoyed our time in Houston – it turned out to be a great place to be on maneuvers.

Next, we travelled to Georgia, to participate in the Carolina Maneuvers where we were to be in the "*Red*" or enemy army. Yes, we continued our journey in the back of 2 ½ ton trucks. I really learned how to live out of a duffel bag. I could pack two sets of khakis (summer uniforms) in my bag and retrieve them whenever I wanted with scarcely a wrinkle. Try it sometime, if you think it's an easy accomplishment to master.

The Texas to Georgia stretch of our journey marked my first visit to the Deep South. It took six or seven days to drive from Houston to Savannah. Our route took us through Texas, Louisiana, Mississippi, and Alabama, on our way. For some reason, stops were more frequent than had been anticipated on this stretch of the trip. Almost every night there was a dance sponsored by the locals in communities all along our route. Southerners had a soft spot for soldiers and we were always treated decently – like real human beings. The trip was a real education for most of us, too, and it was easy to develop a Southern drawl which still affects my diction to this very day.

As usual, the planes and crews had flown directly to our next destination Hunter Army Airfield. The squadron equipment was shipped by rail to Augusta. In addition to me, five other yardbirds were detailed to guard this train while the rest of the truck riders went on to Savannah in convoy. After ten days, we were picked up and taken to Savannah from whence the entire squadron operated until the end of October 1941.

Hunter Army Airfield
Savannah, GA

September 16 – October 31

Just prior to our arrival at Hunter Army Airfield, the regular Army Air Corps unit that had been permanently stationed at Hunter was ordered to the Philippines. As mentioned previously, all of these Air Corps types who were assigned to the Far East Air Force (FEAF), 24th Pursuit Group, were later to fight as Infantry on Bataan. Most of those who survived the initial assault by the Imperial Japanese Army (December 8, 1941 – April 9, 1942), though not all, were captured on Bataan. Survivors of the Bataan Death March spent the remainder of the war as prisoners of war ("*POWs*") in the custody of the Imperial Japanese Army.

Daniel Army Airfield
Augusta, GA

November 1 – 18

At the end of October, we moved to Daniel Field in Augusta, Georgia. As I recall, the aircraft parking areas were on the edge of the Augusta National Golf Club where the Masters Golf Tournament is now played. All our planes were parked in an area directly opposite Daniel Field and astride Highland Avenue. I vividly recall, in fact, civilians playing golf nearby while we were busy doing routine maintenance on our aircraft.

It was ungodly hot and especially humid while we were based at Augusta. Typically, daytime temperatures were in the high eighties and mid-nineties. The weather was hot during the day, but turned damp and penetrating cold at night. There was no snow, of course, just bone chilling cold. In fact, when I pulled guard duty at night, I was dressed in undershorts, a tee-shirt, long johns, fatigues, field jacket, scarf, heavy winter weather fleece-lined boots, pants, jacket, fleece-lined gloves, and my flight helmet. With all this clothing, I could just barely move and my pistol belt was out to the last notch. I was still cold.

On one stint, two or three of us were assigned duty some distance from the main camp for several days. I remember that a large tent was placed on the side of a hill fitted with only two Army cots inside. The bottom of the tent wasn't even pegged down as it normally would have been. Just outside the tent was a water spigot with an extension of pipe that stuck up in the air about seven feet. Of course, it was cold water only. This was our sole water supply – for drinking, washing, and showering, too.

We were issued two blankets each, but no pillows, pillow cases, mattresses, or sheets for the cots. This was my first experience being really miserable. It was so cold that it was impossible to sleep or to wash. The desire to eat was lost in the more urgent desire to get warm. Again, there were no complaints from us. In any event, no one would have listened if we had raised our objections. Just to be warm at the end of the duty was enough. I was surely glad when my daily turn in the barrel ended. While we were in Augusta, there was a power shortage because of a severe drought. Very few lights were on at night and little water was used. The town was not in a good mood.

During the same period, Camp Gordon, Georgia, was just being completed as an Infantry Training Center in late 1941. There were quite a few Infantry types already in and about Augusta. For whatever reason, the locals didn't care too much for *"Fly Boys"*, so it was difficult to avoid trouble with them whenever we ventured into town. The prevailing public sentiment seemed to be that there were too many soldiers around and thus the townspeople walked about as though in a perpetual state of ill humor.

One night a fight between some civilians and soldiers got out of hand and turned into a small riot. Several soldiers were arrested and put in jail, even though it was later proven that the civilians had initiated and escalated the fighting. The Commanding Officer (CO) of Daniel Field, a Colonel, went to confront the local constable. His opening gambit was to assert that if they were inclined to keep his men under lock and key, they would have to put him in the hoosegow as well. And, as God as my witness, the sheriff did just that!

When the Colonel was released from jail the next morning, he immediately issued an order placing Augusta off-limits to all troops under his command and attached to the airfield. Since the combined monthly payroll of the troops in late 1941 was about $2.0 million, the equivalent of about $20.6 million in 1994 dollars, this order really hurt the town's businesses. The local sheriff probably did not know (or care) how powerful a Colonel could be or that he had made a big mistake by putting the Colonel in jail.

After about two weeks of no soldiers buying anything, the town got a committee together to talk with the Colonel about lifting the restriction. I guess they apologized and the Colonel got the townspeople to do what he wanted because the troops were allowed back in town. Augusta was plainly not a welcoming place for soldiers, at least not prior to the attack on Pearl Harbor.

During our sojourn at Daniel Field, I reached the pinnacle of my Army career up to that time. I was made a KP *"Pusher."* I had pulled KP so often that I was now the one who saw to it that all things were done properly. Of course, as a Private, I had no authority whatsoever to give orders to anyone. The Mess Sergeant held those prerogatives. Everyone knew, however, that the Pusher was fully backed up by the Sergeant. My job was to see that his orders were carried out without question, period.

Throughout the Louisiana/Carolina Maneuvers, I did nothing but pull KP and guard duty. I never operated any cameras. I did not work in our portable photo laboratory. Very few of us Privates were tasked to do anything remotely associated with what we were supposed to be trained to do. However, just visiting all the different states and towns and meeting all sorts of people was an experience never to be forgotten.

Return from Louisiana/Carolina Maneuvers
Pendleton Airfield, Pendleton, OR

December 1–2, 1941

Combined maneuvers lasted until the third week of November. We then got on a troop train at Augusta and returned to Pendleton. It was a journey of about 2,500 miles and took almost two weeks. We arrived outside of Pendleton in the overnight hours between December 1st and 2nd. On December 2nd, an announcement was made that most of the squadron was to have a 16-day furlough commencing December 15th. All of us looked forward to going home because no Privates had had any leave since we joined up. Pendleton was cold, wet, and muddy. It started to snow. Our main job was to get all the equipment clean and repaired prior to the 15th. We didn't mind doing this because we knew we would be home for Christmas.

Attack on Pearl Harbor
A Day of Infamy

December 7, 1941

On the morning of December 7th, my pal Jack Lowden and I were on a weekend pass in Walla Walla. In the afternoon, we heard the news about the Japanese attack on Pearl

Harbor. All troops were to report back to their respective duty stations immediately. Needless to say, the news was quite a blow to us. A personal blow not because war had been declared, or because sooner rather than later we would be in it, but because all leaves had been cancelled.

We would not be going home for Christmas. All of us in uniform became instant heroes, regardless of our rank. I was still a Private, but the people of Walla Walla couldn't do enough for us and many asked what they could do to help, etc. All we could think of was that it would be helpful if someone could give us a ride back to Pendleton so that we wouldn't have to hitch hike the 40 miles. In any case, we didn't want to depart right away. There were simply too many girls to say *"goodbye"* to.

As it happened, we didn't get away until almost midnight. We knew there would be some soldiers who wouldn't report in until they had used up their three-day passes and nobody in authority could prove that they had not heard the order to report back immediately. We were pretty wise as to what we could and could not get away with even at this early stage of our Army careers.

Return to Pendleton Airbase
Monday Morning

December 8, 1941

There was utter pandemonium when we did get back to our base. While awaiting official word from our leadership, virtually everyone else was running around like a bunch of chickens with their heads cut off. There were at least a hundred rumors circulating any one time about what was going on in the moment and what would most certainly happen next.

The only ones who weren't especially excited were we Privates. We yardbirds were content to just sit around and wait for someone to tell us what was most likely to happen next and what was to be expected of us. When someone finally did deign to share some insider *"scuttlebutt"*, the story shared by higher ups was invariably something of a doozie.

There was, it was said, *"a Jap aircraft carrier reported off the coast near San Francisco and we were going to bomb it!"* All we had were some 100-pound practice bombs and very little ammunition for our .50 caliber machine guns. At this stage of the game, few of us had ever either qualified or fired the machine guns in the B-25's so ours was expected to be a one-way mission. To make matters worse, no one had a clue about who was assigned to which aircraft and crew, much less whether we any or all of us were to be part of a crew.

To underscore the urgency of the hour, we were all told to make out our *"Last Will and Testament."* Personally, that task wasn't hard for me to complete. I had literally nothing to leave anyone.

We later learned that there was no Imperial Japanese Navy carrier off the West Coast after all, so we stood down for the time being. After two or three days of being on alert, not having any sleep, and covering the aircraft wings with bedsheets to prevent freezing, things settled back down and into a normal routine. After a few more days, we even started getting passes again. War, what war?

With the attack on Pearl Harbor, nothing had really changed except there were no longer any furloughs. Christmas and the holiday season came and went in a flash. As 1941 drew to a close, the entire squadron got food poisoning, apparently from spoiled bread pudding served up in the Mess Hall. All enlisted personnel were out of action for the next two or three days.

We were off to an ill-starred start as the new year dawned. While the public health crisis was taking its toll at Pendleton, it occurred to someone within the ranks of higher leadership of the 17th Bombardment Group that very few, if any, of the enlisted men were qualified Aerial Gunners. Understandable, of course, since before the war we were too busy pulling KP, fire guard, and fatigue duty to receive any actual gunnery training.

As a result of this belated insight, a detail of men from each of the group's four squadrons was promptly returned to Camp Seven Mile at Spokane, Washington. Since our last visit to Camp Seven Mile in May, it had been converted into a ground armament school. It was there that we were to learn all about machine guns, bombs, and armament procedures. We had daily lectures, disassembled machine guns and reassembled them, and learned machine gun nomenclature by heart. For example, I learned exactly how many rivets and holes there were in a machine gun. Moreover, I have not forgotten the meaning of the term *"molecular cohesion"*, whereby a machine gun might not fire because the breech is frozen against the breech block cam.

We also shot skeet and fired at Jeep-pulled targets with the .30 caliber machine gun. It was a three-week school and competition among the various squadrons was keen. The boys of the 89th Reconnaissance Squadron wound up scoring the most hits on the machine gun range, so we finished the course with very high morale.

How about that!

CHAPTER 3

COLUMBIA ARMY AIR BASE, SC
(JANUARY – MARCH 1942)

US Army Air Forces
17th Bombardment Group (M)
89th Reconnaissance Squadron
American Theater of Operations (ATO)

The German Submarine Offensive
Against the Eastern Seaboard of North America

"Operation Drumbeat"
(January – June 1942)

Immediate Relocation Order
Destination Unknown

January 1942

When we arrived back at Pendleton in late December, we learned that the whole of the 17th Bombardment Group (M) was preparing to be relocated. Everything the group owned was packed or crated and loaded on flat cars, except for the aircraft. Aircraft flew out with a full complement of officers. Enlisted personnel travelled to

Portland in trucks, where we were taken to the local railway station and boarded troop trains. Each squadron travelled in separate trains.

Pullman sleeping cars were provided for us with two men to each berth, head to foot. This was much better than sleeping on benches or seats. We pulled out of Portland the week of January 25, 1942. I had just completed my first year in the service on January 23rd. I was still a Private, an ordinary yardbird, without any rating whatsoever.

We had been on the train maybe two days, when we discovered that we all had the crabs (pubic lice). What miserable little creatures, they spread like wild fire and drove us crazy. Like everything else, the Army had a remedy for this situation. It was to shave off all the hair from the genital area (scrotum) and our heads as well, then ordered us to apply KMn04, Potassium Permanganate, better known to us enlisted types as *Blue Ball Ointment*." It was blue in the bottle, blue on the skin, and blue so long as it was on one's skin.

As for myself, I refused to shave either my crotch or my head, declined the 'Blue Ball' treatment, and used Campho Phenique instead. I learned early in my enlistment about this latter compound from a medic. It killed lice without the need to shave off any hair anywhere. From then on, I carried a bottle of Campho Phenique with me for the duration of the war.

To be sure, there were an awful lot of bald, blue heads and scrotums on our train. As one might expect, the lice plague provided plenty of fodder for all manner of off-color humor throughout our journey. By the way, I subsequently learned first-hand under different circumstances that hair growing back on a shaved scrotum causes more intense itching and scratching than any lousy crab ever could.

Blackout conditions prevailed every night. The squadron's movements were classified as *"Top Secret."* This meant that there were absolutely no lights on in any car after dark or any open windows. No one was permitted to get off the train at any stops along the way to our final destination. Imagine, if you can, being cooped up with 50 others, all miserable, crab infested, unwashed bodies on a train with neither lighting nor fresh air in the dark of night.

None of us had any idea where we were going or how long it would take to get there. We were fed and watered three times a day. Happily owing to this set of circumstances, Praise the Lord, I was spared from pulling KP on the entire trip.

Columbia Army Air Base
Columbia, SC
American Theater of Operations (ATO)

February 5, 1942

On February 5th, we arrived in Columbia, South Carolina. We were badly in need of showers and clean clothes. First, however, the train had to be unloaded and work tents assembled. We learned that our new base was a former Army National Guard Airfield that had one small hangar and two runways. Since we were old hands at erecting tents, it wasn't too long before the squadron was in good operational order. Wooden floors had been obtained from somewhere so our sleeping tents weren't too bad. At least we didn't have to walk around on the bare ground.

We were eventually told that the entire 17th Bombardment Group (M), all four squadrons, had been ordered to Columbia to fly patrols off the coasts of North Carolina, South Carolina, Georgia, and Florida.[1] Our mission was to locate, fix, and destroy German submarines (U-boats) and, if unable to successfully engage such targets, to promptly report their last known coordinates to the US Navy. As previously mentioned, the 17th was the first US Army Air Corps unit to be equipped with the B-25B medium bomber. It seemed to us enlisted types that this was a strange mission for a reconnaissance squadron, but who gave a damn about what we Privates thought?

We spent the first several days shaking out our new airplanes, learning their flight characteristics, firing the 6 x .50 caliber M1919 air cooled machine guns, and becoming familiar with our designated patrol areas. Crews consisted of five members each: three officers (Pilot, Co-Pilot, and Navigator/Bombardier) and two enlisted men (Engineer/Gunner and Photographer/Gunner).

---

[1] From January to June 1942, Allied merchant shipping was being sunk by German U-boats at an alarming rate and within sight of U.S. shores. At the time, the German *Kriegsmarine's "wolf packs"*, commanded by Grand Admiral Karl Dönitz, were operating with impunity off the Eastern Seaboard, from the Canadian Maritime Provinces to the Gulf of Mexico. See: https://www.warhistoryonline.com/world-war-ii/operation-drumbeat-u-boat-happy-days-x.html.

Unexpected Visitors
Columbia, SC
February 17, 1942

Two distinguished visitors arrived at our base within a couple of days of our arrival in Columbia. Men from all four squadrons were assembled to hear a briefing about combat flying by none other than Lieutenant Colonel James ("*Jimmy*") H. Doolittle and Edward (*"Eddie"*) V. Rickenbacker. It was, of course, an interesting lecture, but at the time we didn't have a clue what was in the offing. In retrospect, however, it became clear their purpose had been to become acquainted with our leadership, personnel, and aviation assets. Major Hilger, my immediate commander, was later promoted to Lieutenant Colonel. He served as Doolittle's second-in-command during the daring raid over Tokyo, Saturday, April 18, 1942. [2]

At the end of February, I was promoted to Private First Class (PFC). This would be my very first promotion after having served 13 months in the Army. Two or three of the guys who were in boot camp with me were already Sergeants or Corporals. Almost everyone but me had long before made PFC, which just shows you what being a *"smart-ass college kid"* did for me. I was put on full-time flight pay as a combat crew member. Base pay of a PFC was $33.00 a month and flight pay added another 50 percent to one's base pay. Wow, I was going to be making $49.00 a month.

I felt like I was a millionaire as I hastily sewed my precious stripe on every uniform article in my possession.

Charleston Army Airfield
Charleston, SC
February/March 1942

Captain Greening's crew, which included me, and two others were detailed for anti-submarine patrol duty from Charleston Army Airfield, about 10 miles northwest

---

[2] The "*Doolittle Raid*", also known as the Tokyo *Raid*, was an air raid on 18 April 1942 by the United States Army Air Forces on the Japanese capital Tokyo and other places on Honshu during World War II. It was under the command of Lieutenant Colonel James H. Doolittle, USAAF. See: https://en.wikipedia.org/wiki/Doolittle_Raid.

of Charleston. We operated from a very small air strip that was equipped with two or three tents for sleeping, eating, aircraft maintenance, and armament. Very few military or civilian people realized that flying what was euphemistically termed 'coastal patrol' was considered combat duty. Odd as it seemed at the time, we were after all flying combat patrols while still being based in the United States.

In late 1942, members of the 17th Bombardment Group were awarded the American Campaign Medal, which was intended to recognize those military members who had performed military service in the American Theater of Operations (ATO) during World War II.[3] The award of this medal and its campaign star was recorded on my enlisted service record and was worth five points[4] towards discharge at the end of World War II. For reasons that I cannot recall, I never actually wore this service star. It was never referred to on any of my service records after I was commissioned as an officer on October 31, 1946.

Before departing Columbia in mid-March, our Squadron sponsored a farewell party for all the officers and enlisted men at one of the city's leading hotels. We rented a large ballroom and invited all the wives who were present (yes, *some* wives were in Columbia for the occasion.) as well as some of the leading local citizens. Cocktails and dinner were accompanied by local entertainment. It was quite the gala affair. Our Squadron Commander, Major Hilger, presided over the festivities. He was accompanied by his entire staff of squadron officers. Members of our squadron's Photo Section took numerous pictures of everyone, some of which are in my personal collection even to this day. We had just finished dinner and were getting ready for the entertainment when the doors burst open. In rushed a swarm of MPs who started pushing people around, which came as a surprise to all of the guests. We had neither been rowdy nor drunk and our civilian guests most certainly had been well-behaved and orderly.

---

[3] The American Campaign Medal is a military award of the United States Armed Forces which was first created on November 6, 1942, by Executive Order 9265 issued by President Franklin D. Roosevelt. See: https://en.wikipedia.org/wiki/American_Campaign_Medal.

[4] During World War II, members of the US Armed Forces were given one point for each month of military service and one additional point was given for each month of overseas service. Each battle star or decoration earned a soldier 5 points. See: https://en.wikipedia.org/wiki/Demobilization_of_United_States_armed_forces_after_World_War_II.

"On the beach near Charleston, SC"
March 1942

Members of the
17th Bombardment Group (M), 89th Reconnaissance Squadron
PFC Floyd R. Mulvany, Jr. (2nd from right)

Fortunately, Major Hilger took command of the situation by cornering the MP leader before any real trouble started. I never did learn why the MPs were called or by whom. Many of us felt that someone from hotel management had called them assuming that we were just a bunch of drunken soldiers, likely unaware that civilians, wives, and children were present.

It was almost like being in Augusta all over again.

Charleston Army Air Base
Charleston, SC

March 1942

I was still on patrol duty in mid-March 1942, when I received orders to report back to Columbia with all of my equipment. Several other guys in the squadron had been given the same orders. We all wondered what was going on. No one gave us any clues. No reasons were given. Upon reporting, we were told to turn in all our flying equipment and to standby. We were relieved of all duty while awaiting further orders.[5]

At the time, I had forgotten about having put in months before for pilot training. Even though all the papers had been approved, signed off, and forwarded to Army Air Corps Headquarters, I had not heard a word concerning whether I had been accepted to the program. This was easily understood, I supposed, given that the country was on a war footing and in light of all of our recent movements. Somehow, in the midst of being ordered to do nothing but hurry up and wait, my papers had come back approved. I was to report immediately to Santa Ana Army Air Base for further orders to begin pilot training. I was going to be stationed only 60 miles from my family's home in Los Angeles. At the time, this news was better than any furlough. What a surprise.

About the same time, I was also unexpectedly promoted to Corporal. My promotion to Corporal was a welcome surprise. With my promotion, I was now a Non-commissioned Officer (NCO) and this meant no more KP duty, and no more guard duty except as an NCO of the guard. I could not believe my luck. Overnight, my base pay jumped to $54.00 a month. Fantastic.

My parents were happy that I was coming home. I had not seen them for 14 months and we had a great reunion. I had a couple of days before I had to report in at Santa Ana, so I saw and did as much as I could in the time available.

This included being with my one true love, Margaret Johnson. I had been with her when I was in college and we had been corresponding ever since. I was overwhelmed by the very presence of this girl. She was the only one I really cared for and wanted to marry. At least at that point in my life. She was only 17, two years my junior, and she was still in high school. We truly believed that we were in love.

The world was my oyster, war or no war.

---

[5] Anecdotally, I did not learn why I had been relieved of duties until weeks later. I read in the papers about the Doolittle raid on Tokyo on April 18th. There on the front page of the morning newspaper were pictures of Major Hilger, my former Commander, Captain Greening, my former pilot, and several of the enlisted men with whom I had served in the 89th Reconnaissance Squadron. It was in that moment that realized that I too had been selected to participate in the Raid on Tokyo. Incredibly, the *"Fickle Finger of Fate"* had intervened before the fact and *my* career moved in other directions. Over the years, I have often wondered whether I would have survived that experience over Tokyo.

CHAPTER 4

US ARMY AIR FORCES
(APRIL 1942 – DECEMBER 1943)

**Aviation Cadet Training Program |
Advance Aerial Gunnery School | Armament School |
Bomber Aircraft Crew Training |
B-24 Crew Training/Certification/Orientation |
Advance B-24 Combat Crew Training |
Crew Assignment | Deployment**

*"I don't like work--no man does—but I like what is
In the work—the chance to find yourself."*

The Heart of Darkness (1899)
Joseph Conrad
(1857 - 1924)

I reported to Santa Ana to participate in the *"Flying Sergeant"* Training Program in early April. The place was full of civilian *"Flying Air Cadet"* candidates by the time of my arrival, but they were on the other side of the post from our enlisted quarters. This was just as well because they were neither enlisted nor non-commissioned soldiers. They were civilian cadets and only if they made it, they would be officers. If they didn't make the cut, they would be enlisted men and not necessarily destined to serve in the Army Air Corps.

Ground School
Santa Ana Army Air Base
Santa Ana, CA

April 1942

Santa Ana was a large base with an extra-large parade ground. Orange Coast College now occupies the site. As of this writing, some of the World War II era warehouses are still being used by the college.

It was a gathering place for cadets and soldiers like us who were waiting to be processed. Cadets received some pre-flight training and drill and were assigned to train as pilots, navigators, or bombardiers (depending on their tested abilities). About 99 percent of them wanted to be pilots and really bitched and moaned if they weren't selected to be pilots. Each candidate was asked if he would accept the training selected for him. He could refuse once, but if he refused a second time, he was promptly sworn in as an enlisted man.

This seemed fair enough to those of us already selected for pilot training. We didn't have three choices. We were either going to be pilots or we were to be washed out of the program. Actually, all we had to do every day was answer roll call in the morning and again at night. We got passes each weekend from 12:00 PM Saturday to 4:00 PM on Sunday.

Three Musketeers

I made a few real good friends at Santa Ana. One was Russ Snyder from California. Another was Floyd Hoover from Massachusetts. I found it interesting that both fellows had one of my two given names. Snyder had his own car, so we had no problems getting to Los Angeles on Saturdays. Of course, hitch hiking was never any problem during the war. Nothing was too good for soldiers in uniform. Most everyone would pick us up wherever we were to be found and cheerfully take us wherever we needed to go.

Medical Emergency/
Temporary Leave

Are you ready for this? Somehow, I had brought an infection with me from South

Carolina. It was an infection on the head of my penis just underneath the foreskin. I could scarcely walk. My penis was soon so swollen and caused so much discomfort, it kept me bent over much of the time. It appeared as though I was carrying a small bat around with a large ball on the end of it.

At the base hospital, the emergency room doctors said I needed to undergo a circumcision. I agreed to the procedure, of course, but before doing so the swelling in my penis had to be reduced. Accordingly, I had to soak the head of my penis twice a day in a fruit jar full of Potassium Permanganate (KMnO4), otherwise known as the *"Blue Ball Ointment."* I didn't have blue balls, but I did have a blue head and the stuff actually worked as advertised. The swelling dissipated after about one week and then I was skinned. They had to shave my entire scrotum to do it. That's how I discovered a shaved scrotum itches more than having crabs. *So, there you go!*

And there I was, at age 19, looking not a day older than 16 and having my penis circumcised as a young adult. All the nurses got a kick out of it and mothered me to no end. Naturally, my doctor warned me *"not to have any erections, no matter what, or the stitches might come out."* Well, the attending physician might as well have told me to fly to the moon. I did get them, frequently, and it was pure agony. Each time moans and groans emanated from between my clenched teeth, a nurse would appear to tap the side of my dink with a pen or pencil. Believe it or not, the involuntary erections went away immediately. I enjoyed all the attention I got since it was the first time, in a long time, that a female had taken care of me. Whenever I was able to walk on my own, I had to hold my pajama pants away from my *"pinkus"* to prevent inadvertent contact.

My parents came to visit as did Aunt Ella, who farmed about 20,000 acres of wheat not far from Newport Beach. Margaret also came down and I told her I got circumcised, so we could enjoy our married life much more. To this day, I'm not at all sure she understood what I meant. Actually, that's probably an understatement.

I spent ten days recuperating from the snip job. By the time I was released, most of the guys I had been serving with had departed for flight school. I remained in Santa Ana for another month, but did nothing except lay around and read. I went home every weekend and went out dining and dancing with Margaret. We did have good times. On Sundays at 2:00 PM sharp, my folks and Margaret drove me back to the base with a few stops along the way for a refreshment or two.

At 4:30 PM sharp each Sunday, there was a weekly parade for the four or five thousand personnel on the base. Without fail, the potential Sergeant Pilots like me brought up the rear of the formation. The parade ground was all dirt, so within a few minutes after everyone had started to march, a thick cloud of dust obscured everything and everyone. We were all just a bunch of bodies moving along in the dust. Some of these bodies were so intoxicated that they moved only by being held up by their buddies throughout the review. This really didn't matter because no one could see any of us individually anyhow.

As long as everyone showed up for the review, the brass did not seem to mind what condition we were in. I have always wondered what that gigantic moving cloud looked like to the spectators. For our part, we were covered from head-to-foot with dust afterwards.

Flight Training
Hemet/Ryan Flight School
Hemet, CA

May – July 1942

Late in May, I was finally shipped off to Hemet. Hemet is a small community about 85 miles east southeast of Los Angeles. In the summertime, the place is hotter than Hades to put it mildly. Russ Snyder and Floyd Hoover were there with me. Snyder brought his car along for the ride, too. This base was like a resort. There were three men to bungalow and enlisted personnel were mixed in with the civilian cadets. Everyone in the program had a mix of Army and civilian instructors.

Personally, I wondered why the civilians were not in uniform. If they were healthy enough to be qualified pilots, it was my opinion they should already have been in the service. But then, I always wondered why *any* civilian wasn't in uniform.

During the first two days at Hemet, we reviewed and were tested on the first year of college Algebra and Aerodynamics. If you didn't pass the tests, you didn't fly. At no time before this did any of us have any idea we would be tested in these subjects.

The rules and regulations at the school were designed for cadets who had no prior Army service and were, as a result, pretty juvenile. A single drop of water in the bathroom basin or shower stall during an inspection earned each man three demerits. Shoes out of line beneath the bunk were worth two demerits. Any demerits during any inspection meant no Sunday pass. We enlisted types went along with this charade because we wanted to be Staff Sergeants and get our wings.

I did fairly well the first month. I stayed in camp the first Sunday because I had a really bad case of jock itch in my crotch. I don't know where it came from, but I did know that the only sure cure was to keep it dry and let the sun burn it off. So, whenever the opportunity presented itself, I lay around naked with my legs spread apart to let the sun do its work.

I really enjoyed learning how to fly the Ryan all-metal P-22 monoplane. It was a hot little airplane that landed at close to 100 mph with full flaps. The first time I experienced a spin it really took my breath away. I was speechless. What a thrill!

Our instructors were very non-committal. We sat in the front cockpit and they sat in the back. They could speak to us, though we could not talk back. We could only shake our heads to indicate an affirmative or negative response. If one performed satisfactorily, there were no words spoken after the flight lesson. If one failed to properly execute the required maneuvers, you were told about it – once and only once. You were never to make the same mistake again.

Ryan Aeronautical Company
P-22 Monoplane Trainer
(1934)

I passed my seven-hour check ride with an Army instructor, so I thought I had it made in the program. My fortunes took a turn for the worse, however, when I was assigned to fly with a hard-assed civilian instructor. I did not like his attitude or the fact that he was a civilian. My attitude was, *"piss on him, he's only a G—D----- civilian."* As a result of my poor attitude, I became very careless in my flying which eventually led to my being washed out of the program.

Under the circumstances, I could not have cared less whether I continued in the program. Naturally, I never once thought about the fact that there was a war on and it only made sense to spend time with those men whose abilities to become a pilot were fairly evident. My potential as a pilot was limited, or so it seemed, but I didn't think about the matter in those terms at the time.

I did not challenge the Review Board findings. I left the pilot training program before the end of July. Of course, I immediately told my parents and Margaret. My parents didn't seem to mind, but Margaret certainly did. For this and probably other reasons, she told me she didn't want to see me anymore. After about two days, I actually didn't mind not seeing her anymore as well.

Advance Flight Training Center
Gardner Army Air Field
Taft, CA

August 1942

Russ Snyder could land a plane perfectly about 30 feet in the air, but not on the ground. Neither Snyder nor Hoover made it out of the program either – so at least I wasn't alone. All three of us were soon shipped out to Gardner Field in Taft. Taft Field happened to be a Basic Training (Phase 2) flying field. Since I was an Aerial Gunner/Photographer, I couldn't understand why I was sent to Gardner Field. After all, I had already flown on 'combat patrol' missions off the East Coast of North America.

We were assigned to a base squadron, a unit tasked to do all the housekeeping services for the base, that was under the command of a Reserve Major who had been a tire salesman before the war. What this gentleman did not know about being an Army officer would have filled a library. We did nothing for weeks but build sidewalks, drive trucks, swim, and go home on three day passes every week. On Saturday nights, Russ Snyder always drove Hoover and me to Los Angeles. He would ferry us back to the base on Sunday evenings. If we hadn't grown up in Los Angeles, we probably would have stayed on the base like most of the others.

The town of Taft was located just outside of Bakersfield, so it was fairly easy and quick to get to Los Angeles and back. No one ever had anything specific for us to do. It was a goldbrick's paradise. However, at 20 years of age and in the midst of a war, all I wanted to do was to get overseas and into combat. I was well-qualified to be a part of an aerial combat crew. I could not understand why I wasn't ordered to a suitable unit for assignment.

I repeatedly requested a transfer, but was repeatedly turned down. I ended up in the Motor Pool as a grease monkey and truck driver. Hoover went over to the MP detachment and Snyder was shipped off to parts unknown. I never saw or heard from Snyder again. Several others went to work in the PX and other places on the post.

I only wanted combat, so I turned down all offers since I was *asked* to 'accept' various assignments – not ordered. I grew tired of not doing anything constructive for the war effort. I grew weary of hauling around officers to their quarters off post and being cussed out by them. I grew bored driving a truck around town.

I got discouraged getting passes any time the urge struck me. Damn it, I reminded myself, I'm an Army Regular, a soldier, and not a half-witted personal valet. I was a well-trained and experienced non-commissioned officer (NCO). My talents were not being properly utilized.

I scored no points with my superiors, neither officers nor senior NCOs, by virtue of my persistence. I simply wanted to get away from the sink hole that was Gardner Field. In September, I finally succeeded in making my great escape.

Advance Aerial Gunnery School
Las Vegas Army Air Base

September 1942 – January 1943

I was transferred to the air base at Las Vegas, Nevada, where there was an Advance Aerial Gunnery School. When I arrived at the Las Vegas Army Air Base, I asked in what capacity I had been ordered to report to the facility. I was told that I would serve as part of what was termed a member of the base cadre, which meant I was to be assigned to the base but not specifically to the gunnery school.

I decided to accept the proposed transfer, reasoning that anything would be better than wasting more of my life back at Gardner Field. Much to my dismay, I found the situation in Las Vegas was worse than that at Gardner Field. Unbelievably, four of us enlisted types had an entire 50-man barracks to ourselves and none of us were assigned to any duties. Incredibly, in the midst of an all-out world war, no one even checked up on us. As a matter of fact, the only time anyone saw us was when somebody decided (infrequently) to take a roll call. I was getting two three-day passes a week and had Sundays off.

Best of all, I could go anywhere I wanted with no restrictions of any sort. In 1942, a good hotel or motel room in Las Vegas went for $3.00 a night. There was no shortage of restaurants, shows, and places to dance in Las Vegas. I never gambled because I could not afford such amusements. I soon met a local girl whose entire family worked at the Kaiser Aluminum Plant. The girl, her father, her mother, and her two brothers all lived and slept in shifts in a house trailer. Males were exempt from military service because they held priority civilian jobs. Weekly wages were about $85.00 for each individual.

I dated the daughter for a short time. We simply had a good time, whenever we were out on the town. Our affair soon grew to be quite serious, at least from her point-of-view. She wanted to get married and even took me to the Marriage License Bureau at City Hall one day. For my part, I didn't have any inclination to have a wife. My only desire was to find my way back into the war, something that somehow seemed to be slipping further away by the hour.

I soon became totally disillusioned with my circumstances. I was too young, healthy and conscientious to be content with doing nothing to contribute to the war effort. I asked my mother to send me my Gunnery School Certificate from the course at Camp Seven Mile (Spokane, WA). In the meantime, I went to the Orderly Room of the Gunnery School Squadron Headquarters every day to volunteer for overseas and combat duty.

No one offered any help and soon they tired of my petitioning. I told them I was already a qualified Aerial Gunner and had flown combat patrol, but they did not believe me because there were no entries on my service record to back my story up. I eventually obtained an interview with the Major who commanded the squadron. He proceeded to chew me out for bothering his staff and warned me to cease and desist.

By this time, I was fairly well known because of my refusal to work in the post exchange (PX), Motor Pool, and Orderly Room. I was never ordered to do so, I was only *"asked."* What a strange situation that was on lots of levels. When my prized Aerial Gunner certificate arrived, I immediately went to the vicinity of the Orderly Room in the hopes of catching the Major alone outside.

I got lucky one morning and bushwhacked the Major on his way into his office. I showed him my Aerial Gunnery certificate, but still had a devil of a time convincing him that I was qualified for combat crew duty. After hemming and hawing for several minutes, the Major stated that he could not ship me out on the basis of the certificate alone. He told me I had to be a graduate of a *"bona fide"* gunnery school.

He promised, instead, to get me assigned as a student to the aerial gunnery school on the base instead. About one week later, I received a transfer to the school and started re-training. It turned out to be a good school. All the elements of aerial gunnery were taught: how to sight and aim, machine gun nomenclature, functioning, aircraft recognition, and skeet shooting.

Skeets were shot at from the rear end of a ¾ ton truck travelling at 15 mph down a roadway. Along the side of the road, there were stations at regular intervals from which clay pigeons were released at all angles of flight. Prior to actually firing a .30 caliber machine gun from an aircraft in flight, we practiced with a mock-up .30 caliber gun that fired BBs by compressed air.

It was mounted on a single iron pole and could fire up, down, or sideways – a flexible 360-degree shoot. It was the only time I ever saw this type of mock-up used in the Army. It was a very effective teaching aid. In my opinion, it ought to have been a permanent inventory item.

While enrolled at the gunnery school, I learned that several of my former classmates from the Flight School at Santa Ana had received their wings. Several were flying gunnery missions for the school. Many of these fellows volunteered to fly me on my aerial gunnery missions.

This was a live fire exercise from a flexible .30 caliber machine gun mounted in the rear cockpit of an AT-6 *"Texan"* (advanced) trainer aircraft. The AT-6 cockpits were open with 360-degree visibility, more or less, from the gunner's perspective. Their targets were long canvas sleeves that were towed by another aircraft flying in front. My former classmates always took me as close as possible to the target sleeve, so my shooting scores were always pretty good on each training flight.

North American AT-6 *"Texan"*
Advanced Trainer
(1942)

We wore the seat-pack type parachutes. On one memorable occasion, in the excitement of the firing exercise, my parachute ripcord handle got caught on the machine gun mount. My chute popped open and deployed to the rear of the cockpit. Luckily, I had my safety belt securely fastened or I might have been jerked out of the aircraft with little hope for a happy landing. It took all the strength I could muster to pull the chute back into the aircraft so that we were able to make a safe landing.

With a little help from my friends, I received excellent scores on the air-to-air gunnery. I also did very well on the ground phases and written examinations. I graduated from the school in early January 1943. Upon graduation, I received my new and improved Gunner's Wings and was promoted to Sergeant. Now, I was fully qualified for combat and eligible to be assigned to a combat crew. There would be no more screwing around – or so I thought.

Brother, I was mistaken.

Armament School
Lowry Army Air Field
Denver, CO

January – March 1943

I was ordered to the Armament School at Lowry Field in Denver to become qualified for heavy bombardment aircraft. Just being a gunner didn't get it anymore. One also had to qualify in another job, such as Radio Operator or Engineer, in order to be part of a combat crew. I could just as well have been sent to Radio or Engineer school. I didn't mind going to Denver because I had lived there as a kid for several years and had some fond memories of the place. I arrived at Lowry Field in time to celebrate completing two years of service.

The First Sergeant of the unit I was assigned to was really a petty, small-minded, self-important individual. He had a highly inflated opinion of himself and, to no one's surprise, he was not qualified for flight duty. On this particular day, all of us reporting for duty were fresh out of Gunnery School. He didn't bother to check our service records in order to ascertain how long we had been in the service. He had no idea, therefore, whether we were Regulars or Draftees. Instead, he treated everyone as if we were draftees and had made Sergeant within the preceding six months.

On that first day, the First Sergeant got us together and asked if anyone had more than two years' service. No one spoke up. He then asked if anyone had more than one year of service. Again, no one spoke up. Several of us had two or more years' service, but we had learned long before never to volunteer an answer to such a question. Besides, all he had to do was screen our service records for any of the information he wanted to obtain.

This same First Sergeant had a penchant for punishing anyone for the slightest infraction. [1] If, for example, someone dropped a cigarette butt or a match stick on the

---

[1] I never understood how the First Sergeant got away with this sort of behavior. Even in those days, such actions were viewed as extreme punishment for a trivial violation of the rules. Evidently, the officers didn't want to know about his abuses of authority which in and of themselves had an adverse effect of good order and discipline. I recall thinking at the time that at it was degrading for any individual to be punished in this manner. Simply put, the punishment neither fit the offense nor reflected well either on the perpetrator or his superiors.

ground and was caught, the offending individual was required to dig a six-foot-by-six-foot hole about six-inches deep under the barracks, at night, and bury the butt or match stick in the hole. No questions and no excuses were allowed. That was it.

The armament school operated 24 hours a day. There were three consecutive, eight-hour cycles of instruction, underway all day every day. I attended classes from midnight to 8:00 AM, seven days a week. At 4:00 AM, we were fed either a late supper or an early breakfast – our choice. Anyone could eat in the mess halls at any time they wanted – all day and all night.

The instructor for my class was a young civilian woman about 25 years old. What she didn't know about machine guns, 20mm canons, bombs, and bomb shackles apparently wasn't of much consequence. All classes consisted solely of lectures – a potentially deadly method of instruction anytime – but especially when delivered in the wee hours of the morning. It was almost impossible to stay awake unless there was a lot of practical work to accomplish during class. If we fell asleep, as I did many times, she simply kept on speaking and teaching. She never made any effort to disturb the slumber of her students. We were not required to take notes, unless we cared to do so. There were no written examinations. Our only exams consisted of taking weapons apart and putting them back together again. We had no work to do outside of the classroom.

Responsible NCOs tried desperately to make us do some physical training, but this proved to be impractical in the dead of winter and on the graveyard shift. We did, however, have to walk around a 12-mile obstacle course occasionally. Frankly, discipline was generally lacking throughout the school, with the exception that we were required to be in class on time.

Denver was one of the best soldier's towns during World War II, so we went there as often as possible. There were so many girls, so many sights to see, and so many friendly townspeople with whom to socialize. I can remember being in town by 10:00 AM and not leaving until 11:00 PM on many occasions. Of course, I was young and in good physical condition. I could go on for weeks on as little as two hours sleep at night.

One of my classmates, Harry Clark, had his wife with him. She worked as a riveter in an airplane factory, so they could afford to have an apartment in town. Their home was my off-post base of operations for the entire time I was stationed at Lowry. This saved me a lot of money, which helped a lot, because it took quite a bit of money to be in town everyday even though you could get a hotel room for $.75 a night. Near the end of the month, I often had to pawn my watch and ruby ring for $5.00 in order to maintain my life style. I redeemed these items for $7.00 every payday.

On-post, our home was a typical World War II barracks that slept 80 men on 20 double bunks on each of two floors. Most of us were Sergeants with a smattering of Corporals and Staff Sergeants. While very different from each other, we all had one thing in common: we were all being trained to serve on heavy bombers in combat and we were doing all we could to enjoy life before being sent overseas to be shot at.

Observation Squadron
William Northern Airfield
Tullahoma, TN

March – June 1943

I finished school and was shipped out to Tullahoma. After all the training to become qualified as an Armorer/Gunner on heavy bombardment aircraft, I was shipped to an Observation Squadron where the largest aircraft was a Piper Cub. I simply could not believe my run of bad luck in finding my way back into the war.

Tullahoma had a population of about 2,000 folks. On one side of town was Camp Forrest with some 40,000 Infantry and Artillery types. In fact, both the 30th and 80th Infantry Divisions were training there at the time. The William Northern Airfield, now known as Arnold Air Force Base, with a contingent of about 2,000 Air Corps personnel was located on the opposite side of town. There I was, a qualified, well-trained, Armorer/Gunner who got sent to a Liaison Squadron on the 'other' side of town.

My new unit wasn't authorized any Armorer/Gunners, so I worked on any rifles, pistols, and so on that needed to be cleaned or repaired. Nonetheless, I was put on flight pay which helped with my finances. I even occasionally got some stick time in the Piper Cubs. I was also placed on guard duty and fatigue detail. In short, I was not a glorified prospective member of a combat crew, but a Sergeant (Grade 4) assigned to a rinky-dink backwater outfit. Our First Sergeant and his compatriots were Army National Guard types who had been called into the Federal Service for the duration of the war.

They all had more stripes than I possessed, but I was *Regular Army*. When payday arrived each month back in those days, everyone lined up to get paid in accordance with rank. Regular Army personnel, however, were always paid before anyone else regardless of rank. A Regular Army Private was paid ahead of a National Guard or Reserve Master Sergeant. I always made a point of never letting the others lose sight of this point.

I was fortunate to have found a nice room. It had a private bath in a single-family home in Winchester, located about 20 miles from the base. It meant having to get up every morning at 4:30 AM to catch a bus that departed at 5:00 AM and arrived at the base about 6:15 AM, which was just in time for morning roll call.

One morning the bus was late. A fellow Sergeant and I didn't make roll call. We were about ten minutes late. Our punishment was to clean the inside of field ranges (Army stoves) with paring knives. This was the sort of squadron punishment handed out routinely by the First Sergeant. We had no recourse but to do it or accept a Court Martial trial and lose our stripes. True, we were late, but it was not our fault. There were no 'excuses' in the Army. You either were on time for roll call, or you were late. It's only a guess, but I am pretty sure that I was one of very few Sergeants who ever spent a week inside a field range.

As for work, I really didn't have much to do. It was fun to fly the Piper Cubs and to holler out the window. We also enjoyed dropping flower sacks on the Infantry and Artillery cadres to simulate the dropping of bombs. After a few weeks, I was sent to a school on the base to receive instruction in Morse code with a beacon, first aid, photography, and so and so forth. The school lasted about ten days. I was then shipped out to Myrtle Beach Army Air Field in South Carolina.

After three months in Tullahoma, it was good to be reassigned to regular operating base.

Bomber Aircraft Crew Training
Myrtle Beach Army Air Field
Myrtle Beach, SC

June – July 1943

Myrtle Beach Army Air Field was a crew training center for a new high performance medium bomber designated the B-26 *"Marauder."* It was being manufactured by the Glenn L. Martin Company near Baltimore, Maryland. With this transfer, it finally seemed I was going to be assigned to a combat crew and get back into the war at long last. On my second day in Myrtle Beach, however, my hopes were dashed.

Pending my assignment to six weeks of advance gunnery training, I was temporarily put on KP duty and informed that while serving at the base I would not be paid. I wondered what could I possibly learn at Myrtle Beach Army Air Field, that I wasn't already qualified to do and how was it possible *not* to get paid?

After a delay of a day or two, I finally matriculated at the Advance Gunnery School. Unfortunately, I did not learn much that was new to me at all. The course material was quite familiar in every detail. By that point in time, I had to have been one of the most qualified Armorer/Gunners in the Army Air Corps. The school was not well organized and the courses were poorly delivered.

Actual gun turrets were mounted on the backs of 2 ½ ton trucks. Trucks were driven to a stretch of beach where we were ordered to fire into the water. Incredibly, there were plenty of civilian sunbathers and swimmers all around us.

The firing area was marked only by some red flags stuck in the sand. There were no targets, just water. Our instructors routinely ordered: *"Fire the .50 caliber machine guns all you want, because we've got plenty of ammunition!"* The barrels of these guns were so worn from so much use that all the lands and grooves had been burned out. The insides of the barrels were absolutely smooth. This caused the rounds to scatter to the right and left of the intended 'target' rather than to travel in a straight line. In short, the rounds did not go where one aimed them. It is a wonder that none of the civilians in the gallery were killed.

I couldn't get anything but outstanding grades on the written tests since I already knew all the correct answers. This made for quite a bit of goof-off time, because it was unnecessary to study. I took advantage of this situation by frequently travelling into town. For the time being, it seemed to me that no one was in a hurry to end the war. Six weeks passed and once again, I was deemed to be a qualified Armorer/Gunner – *and* latrine cleaner, fatigue person, and KP virtuoso.

Yes, Virginia, Sergeants in the US Army Air Corps did clean latrines, pull fatigue duty, and KP while attending the Advance Gunnery School at Myrtle Beach during World War II. I know. I was there.

I did *all* those things!

Crew Training/Certification
Kearns Army Air Base
Salt Lake City, UT

July 1943

I was shipped out of Myrtle Beach on July 14, 1943. From there, I travelled to Salt Lake City on a troop train pulled by a 1910 model locomotive which belched thick black smoke. Its coach class compartments were equipped with straight-back, rock hard seats, and 'ventilation' was provided through open windows. After just one night on this train, I looked like I had just pulled the swing-shift in a coal mine. Incidentally, we enlisted personnel were all dressed in khakis.

The only bathing facilities available to us along the way were the water hoses in the train yards where we stopped. We would all go out with soap and strip bare-ass naked then and there to wash off under the hoses. We were not near the main stations, but we were out in the yards, so no one cared what we did and neither did we. I say "*we*," because a group of soldiers always travelled together and, in some cases, even publicly bathed as a unit.

Whenever I was ordered somewhere, there were always others who were going to the same place. We stayed in the same coach with all the coal soot all the way to Salt Lake City. When we arrived, guess what? Yup, that's right, we were all going back to school again!

I could not believe it. Not again. What were they doing to me and why? It was unbelievable. By that time, I should have expected such an outcome, but I couldn't seem to get my head around the circumstances which led me from one dead end to the next. By the way, adding insult to injury, I was assigned to work in the Post Office until school started. I never did work at the Post Office, but I did pull KP duty.

The school was supposed to have been a review so that we could take one final overall test to determine how qualified we might be and for which assignments. It was a damn shame. After all, I was qualified as an Armorer Specialist/First Class on B-24 *and* B-17 bombers long before I sat for the 'final' examination.

Boeing Aircraft Company
B-17 Bomber (H)
(1942)

Consolidated Aircraft Company
B-24G Bomber (H)
(1942)

At any rate, I did take the final exam. Two days later I was ordered to report to the 302ⁿᵈ Bombardment Group, a B-24 training outfit located at Clovis, New Mexico. We left Salt Lake City for Clovis on another vintage troop train.

The trip took two days and two nights because the train broke down on both nights for several hours at a time. On this trip, however, we were permitted to eat in the dining car and the coal soot wasn't all that bad. Someone, I surmised, must have screwed up and put us on the wrong train.

B-24 Crew Orientation
302ⁿᵈ Bombardment Group
Clovis, NM

July – August 1943

Clovis was a nondescript town covered by lots of dust, heaps of sand, and many very drab looking houses. The townsfolk, however, were well aware of the war because most its young men were serving in the 45ᵗʰ National Guard Division when hostilities broke out in 1941. The 45ᵗʰ fought in the Italian Campaign, participated in the invasion of Sicily, the attack on Salerno, and later in Italy proper at Anzio and Monte Casino during 1943. After landing in the south of France during Operation Dragoon in August 1944, the 45ᵗʰ joined the drive into Germany in 1945. All along the way, the 45ᵗʰ had participated in fierce combat operations and taken heavy casualties.

The Army Air Base at Clovis was nothing to write home about. It was a transient base, which meant that guys like me came there only to be assigned to a combat crew, receive familiarization flying on B-24s, and then to depart for parts unknown following orientation. We enlisted men slept in tents with double bunk beds, six men to a tent. There wasn't much going on and we didn't have much to do, so we were permitted to visit the town of Clovis pretty much whenever we wanted to go into town.

The first and only time I took advantage of the opportunity to go into town, it was with one of my tent mates. We were sitting on a bench in the town square minding our own business and stone cold sober when a large, red faced, and ugly deputy sheriff wearing a cowboy hat and a Western-style six gun came up to us and said, *"Why aren't you two back in camp where you belong?"*

We replied that we had passes and, since there wasn't anything going on in town, we were just sitting and talking. The response we got was, *"Get the hell out of town or go to jail."* This incident didn't exactly make us feel really welcome in Clovis, as you can imagine, so we wasted little time in returning to the base.

While in Clovis, we attended lectures on the B-24 aircraft and saw, it seemed, a different film about one form or another of VD every day. I don't know why we had to see the films since we didn't have much of a chance of contracting VD in Clovis. Hell, we were there for nine days before we ever got near a B-24. When we finally did get time in a B-24, we had a short two-hour familiarization flight and one hour in the high-altitude pressure chamber which simulated flight conditions at 30,000 feet.

At long last, I was finally assigned to a crew. It was real this time. All the other crew members had come into the service after the war had begun. None of them were Regulars, but we were a crew and this was what I had wanted for more than a year. We were processed, given all our immunizations, and ordered to Biggs Army Air Field, at El Paso, Texas, for overseas training.

B-24 Crew Assignment
Biggs Army Air Field
El Paso, TX

August - December 1943

Biggs Army Air Field was one of the better Air Corps bases for quarters, mess, and training facilities, but during the first two days we were moved into different quarters four times. By all appearances, it seemed to us as though we were off to an unfavorable start. My arrival at Biggs came to pass on the occasion of my 21st birthday.

The next day, August 23rd, I had been in the Army for 31 months. It seemed more like 31 years after all the moving about and chicken shit I had been through during my time in service up to that point. Indeed, I was an old soldier compared to anyone on my crew and to most others in the whole training squadron.

We were part of the Hardison Provisional Group. It was named after Colonel Felix M. Hardison, Commanding Officer, of our particular unit. Training groups and squadrons had no numbers at Biggs Army Air Field.

Biggs Army Air Field
El Paso, TX
December 10, 1943

Hardison Provisional Group
Crew # 302-8-83

Standing left to right: 1ˢᵗ Lt. T. F. Ready (Pilot), 2ⁿᵈ Lt. R. J. Murphy (Bombardier), 1ˢᵗ Lt. Wm. (NMI) Lewis (Navigator), F/O L. R. Muldoon (Co-Pilot) | Kneeling left to right: Sgt. F. R. Mulvany, Jr. (Waist Gunner - R), Sgt. F. A. Carnes (Tail Gunner), T/Sgt. Wm. (NMI) Miller (Flight Engineer/Upper Turret), Sgt. W. B. Winkler (Waist Gunner - L), S/Sgt. K. A. Johnson (Radio Operator), and Sgt. E. J. Walters (Assistant Engineer).

Speaking of my first B-24 combat crew, perhaps I should introduce them:

Pilot: 1ˢᵗ Lt. Thomas F. (*"Bulldog"*) Ready. Bulldog was a National Guard Infantry officer who had gone through pilot training and then transferred into the Air Corps. He was one of those characters that thought he knew it all. In his mind, enlisted men existed only for being ordered around and nothing more;

Co-Pilot: Flight Officer [2] Laurence R. Muldoon. He was a nice guy, later 2ⁿᵈ Lieutenant, right in from civilian life and about my age. His rank wasn't enough to let him do much ordering around, even if he had wanted to;

---

[2] The rank of Flight Officer (F/O) was a temporary designation. It was abolished in late 1943. All such individuals so designated subsequently were made either Second or First Lieutenants.

92

Navigator: 1st Lt. William (*"Bill"*) Lewis, a good fellow, who couldn't find his hind quarters with both hands, let alone navigate an airplane;

Bombardier: 1st Lt. Robert J. (*"Bob"*) Murphy. He was a lazy Irishman who slept all the time except for those few minutes he was needed in order to drop bombs. He did not make much of an impression on me one way or another except that he *really* did know how to sleep circumstances be damned;

Flight Engineer: T/SGT William (*"Bill"*) Miller. He was a nice guy, dedicated to his job and had no intention of staying in the Army after the war was over. He operated the upper turret;

Assistant Engineer: SGT Edward J. (*"Ed"*) Walters. He was a good kid. He had a sense of humor, knew his business, and was a pretty good artist. He operated the ball turret;

Radio Operator: S/SGT Kenneth A. (*"Kenny"*) Johnson. More mature than the rest of us, he was about 27 years old. In spite of the fact that he was said to have a ruptured ear drum, he was selected to be a member of a combat crew;

Left Waist Gunner: S/SGT Warren B. *("Winkie")* Winkler. He was a good 'ole boy' from Arkansas, lacking in any pretensions whatsoever. I sure did like him a lot from the heart;

Right Waist Gunner: S/SGT Floyd R. (*"Russ"*) Mulvany; and

Tail Gunner: SGT Floyd A. Carnes. He was a young man who stuttered. Everything that happened always seemed to come as a surprise to him. We should have helped him more than we did, but at the time, none of us know enough about how to be better teammates.

No time was wasted in initiating our training regimen. We had classroom and practical work to accomplish. It was a twenty-four-hour-a-day, seven-day-a-week routine. Crews and planes flew at all hours of the day and night.

The B-24s used for training were mostly all early models. Every aircraft in our unit had far more than the maximum number of hours on the engines. Standard operating procedures mandated that engines were to be changed out after ~400 hours of flight time. I never witnessed this prescribed maintenance protocol observed anywhere. Emergencies and accidents were frequent, many planes crashed, and many men were injured or killed in the ordinary course of events. For example, we routinely made emergency landings with fire and crash trucks escorting us down the runway.

There were also many aborted take-offs either because of engine failure(s) or something else that had gone wrong with the aircraft while in actual flight. There were no set hours for flying or for attending training classes. It could be either during the day or at night and sometimes morning, noon, and night.

On our first flight together as a crew, three of the guys got air sick. "*Sickness*" was not a reason for landing once aloft. Every crew had to get in so much bombing and gunnery training, formation flying, night flying, and so on in order for a crew to become combat qualified. Training was carried out whenever the weather, planes, and equipment would allow. Some training flights were exclusively for officers, though one enlisted man always accompanied such flights in the rear of the aircraft in case of fire or some other emergency.

One such occasion occurred on a night time training flight. On the particular training flight in question, I was riding in the rear with the mission of pulling the pins from the bombs to arm them in order to enable the Bombardier to drop them. The bomb bay in the B-24 featured a narrow (8-inch wide) catwalk running down the length of its centerline fore to aft. Supposedly, the bomb bay doors were to remain closed until all the bomb pins had been pulled.

At an altitude of 20,000 feet, however, I was on the catwalk pulling the pins with a portable oxygen bottle strapped to my leg. I was all the way forward in the bomb bay, removing the last pin, when without warning the bomb bay doors opened. The blast of air caught me by surprise and threw me down on the catwalk. It also tore the hose on my oxygen mask from the bottle. Before I knew it, I was passed out on the catwalk with nothing standing between me and Mother Earth some 3 ¾ miles below – *except* 2 inches of cold steel.

Of course, I was supposed to be back in the waist by the time the bomb bay doors were opened so that I could report to the pilot that I had resumed my duty station.

When I didn't report on time, good 'ole' Ed Walters came forward and picked me up in a nick of time. I was really pissed that something like that had been allowed to happen. But for chance, I just as easily could have been sucked out of the bomb bay to my death.

On the home front, while at Fort Bliss, I lucked out and found a room in a house owned by a Sergeant of Artillery. He was a New Yorker and he and his wife were really kind to me. He was serving in Supply or some other cushy job at Fort Bliss for the duration of the war.

At this time, Fort Bliss was a training center for Artillery and, of all things, Pack Mule units too. I couldn't imagine why mules were there, since they were primarily intended for jungle and mountain terrain re-supply operations. At Fort Bliss, we were training in flat, desert country. They were there, however, and in abundance.

I had one room and shared a bath, but it was enough because most of my time was spent at the base due to the odd hours. I didn't have much money (which was nothing new), but it really didn't matter because Juarez was just across the border from El Paso.

I could enjoy a large steak dinner for about $1.00 American. Sometimes a steak dinner would be my breakfast and ham and eggs would be my dinner. Most of the time, however, all I could afford was doughnuts and milk.

We were all in the same boat. We did the best we could with what we had on hand. It wasn't easy, but few things came easy during the war years. At the end of September, we all got seven days leave. I decided to visit my folks in Los Angeles and once more I borrowed the travel money from my folks to pay for my visit.

After leave was up, it was back to training at full tilt. On at least two occasions, our pilot *"Bulldog"* nearly got me and the rest of his crew killed. On one particular occasion, the plane went into a right-wing slip from a vertical bank and Muldoon had to intervene to avoid catastrophe. We were nearly all the way down to the deck before leveling off and pulling out of our dive.

Bulldog was so marginally competent that all the enlisted men on the crew asked me to tell him that we were going to refuse to fly with him. In those days, a crew could do this and ask to be transferred or have another pilot assigned. The pilot would then either be transferred for another chance or disqualified if it proved necessary.

I spoke to Bulldog and told him how we all felt. Naturally, Lieutenant Ready did not want us to communicate our collective vote of no confidence to others up the chain-of-command. Muldoon was quick to assure us enlisted types that things would improve. We trusted Muldoon, so reluctantly we agreed to relent and let Bulldog off the hook.

On December 10, 1943, our crew was approved as being fully qualified for combat. It was my opinion that we could have learned and done much more to improve our combat effectiveness, especially with respect to our gunnery capabilities. All our firing was at target sleeves going in the same direction as our aircraft. This approach did not allow for any deflection practice. At the very least, we ought to have had the use of gun cameras to mitigate this shortcoming.

Also, we never experienced any simulated combat conditions such as fighters coming at us or anti-aircraft fire. At any rate, there was nothing more we could do inasmuch as out training time was up. Crews were badly needed in all theaters of operation. We were heading overseas.

We departed Biggs Field on December 15th by train for Tulsa, OK, where we were to pick up a brand-new B-24J, our flight equipment, and our overseas assignment. We all had thoughts about where we might be going – most likely someplace in the Pacific – but we really didn't have a clue. We would have to wait to find what fate had in store for us.

We arrived in Tulsa on December 17th. For the first time since I was in Flying School, I felt that someone really cared for us. We were treated really well. We had few duties and Christmas was just around the corner. Better still, I was able to obtain a pass almost every night. Kansas City, Missouri, where I had lived as a child, was only about 250 miles away. It was easy to hitch a ride to Kansas City and overnight with my Aunt and Uncle. They took good care of me and those occasions were memorable and pleasant.

After Christmas, I stayed on base. We got in some flying time testing out our new aircraft and sweating out our assignment. All crews were assigned to combat areas by number. Each crew at Tulsa had a number, after which was written the assigned combat area. When our turn came, there were only eight numbers on the blackboard.

The first four went to the Eighth Air Force in England. Ours was the fifth number and after it was Tenth Air Force followed by the letters "*CBI.*" The three remaining crews went to the Fifth Air Force in the Pacific. Not one crew member in the room knew what CBI meant, so we had to ask. It, the acronym, meant China-Burma-India. Not one of us had even heard of that theater of operations. We soon learned it was roughly a 15,000-mile trip and that we would fly our new ship all the way to India.

Our final destination was to be Pandaveswar Air Base in northeastern India. The 7th Bombardment Group (H), by then flying B-24s, was part of the Tenth US Army Air Force, the only Heavy Bombardment Group in India. We would operate from there against targets throughout the region.

No one we spoke with either at Biggs Army Air Field prior to our departure or at Tulsa seemed to have any knowledge of our prospective outfit and all our questions went unanswered. We did learn, however, that the flight would take us from Tulsa to West Palm Beach, FL and on to India by way of Trinidad, Brazil, Ascension Island, Africa, and Aden. It was going to be a long flight with many new things to see and learn along the way. It was a new year and a new adventure in the offing.

In all probability, the greatest adventure to date in our young lives.

CHAPTER 5

PANDAVESWAR AIR BASE (INDIA)
LATITUDE 23° 43' 0" E LONGITUDE 87° 16' 0" S
(JANUARY – JUNE 1944)

US Army Air Forces, Tenth Air Force,
7th Bombardment Group, 493rd Bomber Squadron,
China-Burma-India (CBI)
Theater of Operations

"You've never lived until you've almost died.
For those who have fought for it,
Life has a flavor the protected shall never know."

The Short Stories of M. Guy de Maupassant, Volume XI
Henri René Albert Guy de Maupassant
(1850 -1893)

THE "IMPATIENT VIRGIN'S" FLIGHT PATH
FROM TULSA TO PANDAVESWAR
January 11 - February 8, 1944

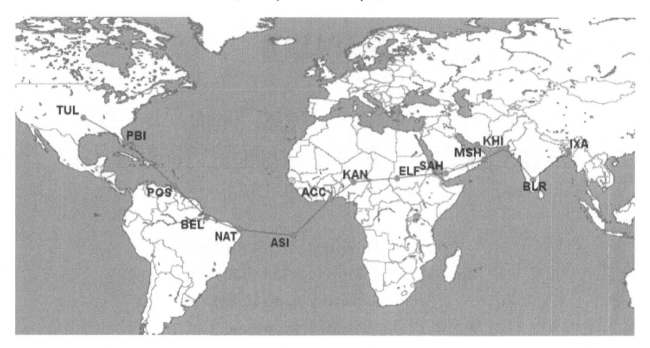

PART ONE: THE JOURNEY FROM TULSA TO THE TEMPLE OF MARS

LEG 1   11 January 1944 [Tuesday]

Departure: **Tulsa Army Air Base (TUL) | Tulsa, OK**
Destination: **Morrison Field (PBI) | West Palm Beach, FL**
Distance: **1,138 Statute Miles**
Duration: **8 Hours/15 Minutes**

We departed Tulsa Army Air Force Base in the early morning hours on the first leg of our long journey. After about 8 hours, we landed at Morrison Field near West Palm Beach, Florida. When we departed Tulsa, the temperature was about 10 degrees (F) below zero. When we arrived in West Palm Beach, the temperature was in the 80's (F).

The warm breezes were gently swaying the palm trees. It felt like home to me. We landed in our heavy winter flying suits. Everyone else on the ground was dressed in short-sleeve khakis. We were billeted in a transient barracks directly across from a dog racing track. We could see the stands and crowd and hear all the announcements from our windows.

We spent the next day checking our equipment and receiving our final briefings.

LEG 2   13 January 1944 [Thursday]

Departure:	**Morrison Field (PBI)	West Palm Beach, FL**
Destination:	**RAF Station - Piarco (POS)	Trinidad, British West Indies**
Distance:	**1,650 Statute Miles**
Duration:	**11 Hours/0 Minutes**

We departed Morrison Field before sunrise bound for Waller Air Force Base co-located with RAF Station – Piarco on the island of Trinidad, British West Indies. At the time, Trinidad hosted a joint training area for British and American troops which was a very nice place. Not a bad duty station either.

LEG 3   14 January 1944 [Friday]

Departure:	**RAF Station - Piarco (POS)	Trinidad, British West Indies**
Destination:	**Belem Airfield (BEL)	Belem, Brazil**
Distance:	**1,208 Statute Miles**
Duration:	**8 Hours/3 Minutes**

Our fight from Trinidad to Belem took about eight hours, before we landed at Belem Airfield. The air base was surrounded by thick jungle. It was my first glimpse of such terrain. Little did I know at the time, how familiar the jungle environment would become to me later in my career. The entire area abounded in strange sights, sounds, smells, and unlimited quantities of freshly cut pineapples and bananas. Fresh fruit was placed on tables everywhere around the air base. Brazil was one of the United States' staunchest allies during World War II.

We spent the night in Belem, gorging ourselves on bananas and pineapples. In addition to fresh fruit, there were also large quantities of and numerous varieties of mosquitos and other types of insects everywhere. It was there that I witnessed my first case of Elephantiasis (lymphatic *filariasis*), a disease which results in major swelling of the feet, legs, and scrotum. The only known cure at the time was to amputate the affected appendages. As far as I know, for some reason extremities above the waist were seldom affected by this disease.

As I learned years later, Elephantiasis is transmitted through the bite of a certain types of mosquitos which, in turn, transmit a parasitic *filarial* worm to its hosts. Though the disease can be treated, it is still widely regarded as a neglected health hazard. For obvious reasons, insect control was a major concern among public health personnel at the air base. An enlarged photo of a native afflicted with Elephantiasis of the scrotum was tacked up all over the base. The poor devil's scrotum had swelled so much that he had to carry it around in a wheel barrow. Needless to say, all the GI's practiced excellent insect control.

LEG 4   15 January 1944 [Saturday]

Departure:	**Belem Airfield (BEL)	Belem, Brazil**
Destination:	**Natal Airfield (NAT)	Natal, Brazil**
Distance:	**954 Statute Miles**
Duration:	**6 Hours/21 Minutes**

We flew down the coast to Natal to prepare for our hop across the Atlantic Ocean to Africa. On this fourth leg of our trip, we hit a terrific down draft that sucked the plane down about 1,200 feet in a matter of seconds. Winkler, Carnes, and I were sitting loose in the waist at the time. We all hit the top of the waist (about 8 feet) and were quickly and unceremoniously hurled back to the floor. Fortunately, none of us sustained any serious injuries, though the episode really shook us up.

The Natal Air Force Base (originally called Parnamirim Airport) was a good facility with beer, movies, and great food. It was the last spot in the Americas that crews would see for some time. For a lot of guys, it was the last of the Americas they would ever see.

We spent the entire day on January 16th, pulling a 25-hour engine check on our plane.

LEG 5   17 January 1944 [Monday]

Departure: **Natal Airfield (NAT) | Natal, Brazil**
Destination: **Wideawake Field (ASI) | Ascension Island**
Distance: **1,448 Statute Miles**
Duration: **9 Hours/39 Minutes**

We departed for USAAF Wideawake Airfield well before dawn. Ascension Island is in the middle of the Atlantic Ocean. It's more than 1,400 miles east of Natal, Brazil and about 1,350 miles southwest of Accra, Ghana.

Ascension Island is really nothing more than the top of a very tall mountain sticking out of the water, so it's not a very big place. A volcanic island, it was utterly devoid of flora and fauna. There wasn't a tree, bush, or shrub in sight. There was one artificial tree, however, which was planted in a large bucket and cared for by the U.S. Navy types who were stationed on the island.

Wideawake Airfield served as a refueling and rest stop for all aircraft flying to and from Africa. Water was obtained from a water tender anchored offshore that converted salt water into fresh (potable) water and then pumped it into storage tanks on shore. Its runway had been blasted out of solid volcanic rock and ran the entire width of the island. It featured a large hump in the middle that dropped sharply down to the leeward (windward or east) side of the island. Whether on its approach for landing or take-offs, a B-24 only had about 12 feet of clear space off either wing tip so all landings and take-offs had to be straight and true.

On the island, living accommodations and food were excellent. It was a good thing, because many of those guys had been there for over two years. It was difficult to muster any sympathy for the base personnel. They were far from any combat and lived damn well. There weren't any women, of course, but then there weren't any women to speak of in combat areas either.

LEG 6	18 January 1944 [Tuesday]
Departure:	**Wideawake Field (ASI)	Ascension Island**
Destination:	**RAF Station – Tokoradi (ACC)**
Distance:	**1,354 Statute Miles**
Duration:	**10 Hours/15 Minutes**

Early on January 18th, we departed for the Gold Coast of Africa. About two hours out of Ascension, roughly 250 miles into the 1,350-mile journey, we ran into a severe storm so it took more than 10 hours to reach RAF Station - Tokoradi at Accra. The base had excellent facilities – nice clean beds, good food, and beautiful scenery.

LEG 7	19 January 1944 [Wednesday]
Departure:	**RAF Station – Tokoradi (ACC)**
Destination:	**RAF Station – Kano/Mallam (KAN)**
Distance:	**743 Statute Miles**
Duration:	**4 Hours/56 Minutes**

We were scheduled to leave Accra at dawn, but generator trouble delayed our departure until about noon. As a result, we only flew about five hours and covered only about 743 miles on the way to RAF Kano Station – (Mallam) Kano, Nigeria. No one would ever argue that the B-24 was especially fast, but they were sure reliable. Well, pretty reliable *most* of the time.

We lucked out again because the British base there claimed to have the best food in all of Africa. We were waited on hand and foot by native workers. And the Brits were right about the food.

That night riding a bus back to the base from the movies, a thunderstorm struck. It featured thunder and lightning unlike anything I had ever experienced. It sounded like an artillery barrage. About halfway back to the base, the native driver got so scared he stopped the bus, hopped out, and ran away. We were left sitting there. One of the guys drove the bus back to the base. We never heard a word about the fate of our erstwhile driver.

LEG 8	20 January 1944 [Thursday]
Departure:	**RAF Station – Kano/Mallam (KAN)**
Destination:	**El Fashir (USAAF) Detachment (ELF)**
Distance:	**1,138 Statute Miles**
Duration:	**7 Hours/35 Minutes**

Before leaving RAF Kano, early on the morning of January 20th, we were advised to load our machine guns since our route would require us to cross the Anglo-Egyptian Sudan on the way to our planned destination near Sana'a, Aden (Yemen). We were so advised because it was possible that we could be forced down in the desert due to mechanical failure. Our hosts in Kano stated that those .50s might come in handy, since the local populations further to the east were not too friendly to outsiders.

Our flight plan was to fly from RAF – Station Kano (Mallam) to RAF Station – Khormaksar near Sana'a, a distance of approximately 2,407 miles and about 11 hours flying time. However, about seven hours after our departure from Kano and 1,100 miles into our flight, the No. 3 engine quit suddenly so we were forced to make an unplanned stopover.

As noted previously, no one would ever argue that the B-24 was especially fast, but they were sure reliable. Well, pretty reliable *most* of the time. Rugged too.

Safe Haven at El Fashir

Luckily for us we were quite near an emergency air strip that was manned by a small U.S. Army Air Corps detachment at El Fashir. It was a small village located about 500 miles southwest of Khartoum in the middle of the Sudan. We made it there safely and discovered that the engine had burned out and would need to be replaced. This would take some time because a new engine would have to be flown in from supply depots in either Libya (Benghazi), India (Bangalore), or other places unknown located somewhere in between.

Transient Quarters

The entire compound was small and every structure was white-washed inside and out to deflect the heat. Roughly fifty Air Corps types were stationed 'permanently' at El Fashir. Most personnel had been stationed there for about two years. Ground maintenance types didn't move around very much during the war. Once assigned to a particular station, it was normal for such individuals to remain in place for the duration of hostilities.

There was nothing we could do but sit and wait, so we unloaded our gear. We were shown to some rooms in a one-story adobe-type building where we were to sleep, two men to each small room. These rooms were designed to accommodate short-term visitors, since the air strip was configured for refueling operations and the occasional emergency landings. The only regular stops made there were by planes bringing in supplies and repair (spare) parts.

One day while I was walking around looking things over, I entered a room and found four or five GIs sitting cross-legged in the *"Lotus"* position making pillows. Not one of them spoke to me or even looked up when I entered the room. They were really intent on their sewing. It occurred to me that had I been in that place for two years, I might well be sewing pillows too.

Impromptu Sightseeing Tour

I wandered on and eventually ran into the detachment Medical Officer (Medic). He offered to show me the sights in and around El Fashir. We visited a village in the very heart of *"Fuzzy-Wuzzy"* [1] country. I had read the works of Rudyard Kipling as a student and knew that the Fuzzy-Wuzzies were the only African natives who had ever broken the British Square in open combat.

The Medic drove me around in an old Army sedan. Don't ask me where it came from because I never figured out the answer to the question. It seemed odd that there would be a sedan, rather than a Jeep or a truck, to ride around in the desert. On the way to the village, we passed a fort right out of the motion picture *"Beau Geste."* It was manned by black Sudanese troops and was surrounded by barbed wire, mine fields,

---

[1] "Fuzzy-Wuzzy" was the term used by British soldiers for Beja warriors who were supporting the Mahdi of Sudan in the Mahdist War. The term relates to the elaborate *tiffa* hair style favored by the Hadendoa tribe, a subdivision of the Beja people. See: https://en.wikipedia.org/wiki/Fuzzy-Wuzzy.

and lots of debris. My host told me there had been a '*helluva*' fight there a short time before between the troops and local natives. The troops held out and the fort was still in business. I was very impressed by what I saw, especially in light of the fact that this visit marked the first time I had actually witnessed the results of combat up close and personal.

We continued on past the fort and beyond where I recall seeing straw huts, wooden buildings with thatched or tin roofs, plenty of dirt, and filth. There were no paved streets, in fact, no streets at all, so we simply drove around the buildings. My friend told me that he would take me to see his girlfriend. I couldn't believe it. He had a girlfriend in this place? I could hardly wait to meet her. We stopped in front of a large thatched hut where six or seven colorfully dressed, very dark-skinned women were standing. A very tall one from the group ran up, hugged the Medic, and spoke in a language which I could neither understand nor comprehend in the least. When she smiled, I noticed that most of her teeth were gold and the others were blackened.

This was his girlfriend and we were visiting a native whorehouse. The Medic was very serious about all this and asked me if I wanted to come into the hut. I politely declined, so he went in and left me alone. Meanwhile, all the women were talking and gesturing. Although I did not know the language, I had a pretty good idea what all their chattering was about and had the impression that whatever it was it had to do with me.

These women really scared the hell out of me, because I was relatively young, inexperienced, and the only other damn foreigner in the neighborhood. After about 20 minutes, the Medic emerged from the hut with a very satisfied look on his face. I had to assume that his girlfriend had taken good care of him. So, this was my introduction to El Fashir. On reflection I concluded that living in such a place for more than two years could really dim one's perspective on a lot of things.

Professional Courtesies

Since our layover at the base was for a limited period of time and were on our way to a combat zone, the Captain in charge of the detachment, did what he could to make our stay pleasant and memorable. On one occasion, he even took some of us hunting in his Jeep. He had several shotguns and we had our service pistols. In the wide-open spaces around the base there were all sorts of animals: hyenas, giraffes, wild pigs, grouse, and several species of antelope. We managed to bag one grouse and a couple of gazelle antelopes. We brought our kills back to the mess hall. It was quite a thrill to go hunting in in the Sudan. I have never forgotten the experience.

"Tommies" in the Bush

There were also some British soldiers around El Fashir. I never learned any details about their mission or why they happened to be there, other than to note that the troops of the British Commonwealth were ubiquitous in that part of the world at the time. After all, they had fought many a battle in the Sudan and Egypt and governed large swaths of territory. The British weren't bad fellows. I shot the bull with them on many occasions as did other individual members of our crew.

Daily Routine

Most of our time was spent cleaning our plane and servicing our guns. The wind blew quite a bit of sand around, so everything and everyone got dirty quickly unless we took care to make sure both the aircraft and crew were properly covered. Since we really had no means to cover the plane, we labored hard each day to ensure our ship was kept clean. There were some movies to see and a few books to read, but unless we wanted to make pillows the only other alternative was to talk with one another.

A *"Tinseltown"* Cameo

One day a plane arrived carrying a group of civilians. There were a couple of females aboard, but I didn't pay much attention to them because I knew they would be off-limits to enlisted men. Later that day while I was hanging out in the recreation room watching the base pet, a Mongoose, nose around, I looked up and there stood Louise Rainer, the movie star. I had seen her in *"The Good Earth"* and several other pictures, so I immediately recognized her visage. I was so flabbergasted that the only thing I could say was, *"Hi."* She smiled and replied *"Hi."* in return before passing on through the building. I never saw her again and knew nothing concerning either her arrival or departure at El Fashir. Of all places to have met a celebrity, in the middle of the Sudan, while the world was at war.

Foot Loose and Fancy Free

I tried to see as much of the area as I could during our forced layover. I remember the day I saw my first native member of the warrior class. He wore indigenous garb, carried a shield, a two-handed sword, a couple of spears, and he was standing rigidly upright flamingo-style on one leg. In addition, he wore a couple of long, thin metal rods in his hair which were designed to take care of itching which was associated with the lice inhabiting his head and scalp.

He was the *real* McCoy, a member of the local Beja warrior class. I approached him to offer him some chewing gum, just as we had to other natives in the area. He not only declined to partake of the chewing gum offered, but he didn't even look down on me. I do mean 'down,' because he was six or seven inches taller than me. Throughout our encounter, he didn't move a muscle, so I beat a dignified retreat rather than run the risk of provoking some sort of an incident.

Harem Herding

Early every morning and again each evening, a large group of women were herded along by one man who carried a very long pole and they would walk by the air strip. They would be talking and laughing and would always wave to me when I waved at them. The man would also wave and shout a greeting that I never understood. In the evening when the group returned, the women would be carrying gigantic loads of grass on their backs. They carried so much grass that I could only see their ankles and feet. The man carried nothing other than a long pole which he used to keep the women on the path. It was plain the women, laden with their loads, could scarcely see where they were going. Whether this was the man's harem, I never got figured out.

Madcap Safari

Muldoon, Miller, Carnes, and I went hunting another time by ourselves. Muldoon drove the Jeep with Miller riding shotgun, while Carnes and I rode in back hanging on for dear life. We spotted a herd of gazelles which, of course, took off in a fright once we came into sight. Muldoon pulled out all the stops and promptly gave chase.

He literally put the pedal-to-the-metal and we were off at a pace which seemed to rival lightning speed. What a wild ride we had – zipping across the plains at about 40–50 miles per hour. At those speeds, it was hard enough trying to stay in the Jeep, let alone trying to shoot a graceful and fleet gazelle. In hot pursuit of our quarry, I fired my .45 caliber pistol right over Miller's head, which was, of course, a very dangerous stunt.

At one point, we actually hit a bump that caused Miller to bounce up just as I was firing a shot. The weapon discharged right next to his ear. An inch or two closer and I might well have blown his head off. Needless to say, Miller's ear was out of whack for some time after the fact. Muldoon didn't stop, though. He was determined to bag one of those poor little gazelles. Suddenly, the Jeep came to an abrupt stop and Carnes fell out the back end, Miller fell out the right side, and I was ejected forward over the hood. Fortunately, for all of us, the wind shield was folded down and locked in place.

The Jeep itself was standing upright at about a 45-degree angle because we had 'successfully' landed in a crater of some sort. Muldoon was slumped over the steering wheel. What a sight we must have made for the occasional passersby. Luckily, neither the Jeep nor any one of us were seriously hurt as a result of this fiasco. Except, perhaps, for Miller's ear drum which was disabled for several days afterwards as a result of my reckless antics.

It took us some time to extract the Jeep, but managed to do so without too much effort. Muldoon, however, wasn't quite ready to throw in the towel. On our way back to the base, he decided to give chase to a herd of giraffes. We must have been doing close to 40 miles per hour in order to keep pace with the herd. It was great fun because we were traveling on a grassy plain that had been baked so hard by the sun it was like driving on a concrete roadway.

We were so intent on the giraffes that we gave no thought to the effect of a red-hot muffler on the dry grass. We should have, by golly. Whenever we glanced back over our shoulders, we witnessed a straight line of fire following the tracks of the Jeep's trail as far as the eye could see. At this point, Muldoon decided it would be best if we were to just disappear since there was nothing we could do about the fire, except not make it worse.

You Gotta Pay the Band

To top off the day, when we returned to the detachment camp at El Fashir, the Captain who had loaned us the Jeep and weapons chewed us out royally for the expenditure of his ammunition. Since Muldoon was the ranking person of our small contingent, the chewing out was directed to him, the rest of us were regarded as simply dumb GIs. Our ride was never mentioned again – by anyone.

Third Anniversary of Enlistment

I spent the third anniversary of joining the Army at El Fashir. My initial three-year hitch was over. I was a veteran of sorts, but I never gave my status much of a thought since I had not yet tasted *true* combat.

Apparition Meets Killjoy

Walters, our Assistant Flight Engineer, was a pretty good artist. On his own one day, he started to paint a picture of a half-dressed girl on the side of the plane. We enlisted types had already dubbed the plane *"The Impatient Virgin"*, without soliciting any input from the of our officers. The image of the girl was intended to convey the fact that our aircraft was fresh off the production line and that our crew had yet to experience combat.

Walters had just about finished his masterpiece when 1st Lt. Thomas F. Ready came over and told us he didn't want any pictures on *his* aircraft. It was too late for us to do anything about his order to remove the image because there wasn't enough paint left to cover it up. Since a half image wouldn't do, Walters persuaded Bulldog to allow him to complete his artwork with the understanding that he would paint it over when we arrived at our final destination in India.

How Bulldog ever qualified as a crew commander was beyond us all. As previously observed, his flying skills were mediocre, at best, and it was self-evident that he had little respect for other members of the crew *especially* the enlisted types. As such, it was not difficult to understand why we, as a well-trained combat crew, never really gelled as a team. While every member of the crew respected his authority and position, everyone whether officer or enlisted types had a difficult time coping with his leadership style.

111

Arrival of Replacement Engine

Our replacement engine had arrived on Saturday, January 29th. It was promptly installed, tested, and thoroughly checked out. After our unplanned 10-day layover, we were eager to resume our journey.

LEG 9	31 January 1944 [Monday]
Departure:	El Fashir (USAAF) Detachment (ELF)
Destination:	RAF Station – Khormaksar (SAH)
Distance:	1,271 Statute Miles
Duration:	8 Hours/28 Minutes

We departed El Fashir on January 31st bound for RAF Station – Khormaksar in Aden (Yemen). Aden had it all – desert, heat, and flat terrain. It was about 110 degrees in the shade and there was no shade. Thank goodness we only spent one night in that place.

LEG 10	1 February 1944 [Tuesday]
Departure:	RAF Station – Khormaksar (SAH)
Destination:	RAF Station – Island of Masirah (MSH)
Distance:	1,028 Statute Miles
Duration:	6 Hours/51 Minutes

Early the next day, February 1st, we departed for the RAF Station - Island of Masirah in the Persian Gulf. It was such a short hop, we wondered out loud why we were scheduled to land in Oman. We never did resolve that question. Masirah was just another hot, flat, and featureless place hosting a British air base.

LEG 11	2 February 1944 [Wednesday]
Departure:	RAF Station – Island of Masirah (MSH)
Destination:	USAAF Air Transport Command/Karachi Airfield (BLR)
Distance:	602 Statute Miles
Duration:	4 Hours/0 Minutes

On February 2nd, we flew across the Indian Ocean and landed at Karachi Airfield in India. At the time, the USAAF Air Transport Command was headquartered at Karachi Airfield. Karachi was a major base of operations for both U. S. Army Air Force and U. S. Navy units in the CBI Theater of Operations. For every member of our crew, it was our first taste of India and we were more than curious about the place. Since we were scheduled to be in Karachi for a couple of days, the officers permitted enlisted personnel to go into town.

Sights and Sounds of Karachi

What strange new things there were to see: people, shops, camels, donkeys, and horse-drawn carriages, beat up cars and buses, garbage and trash, unpleasant smells, and red spots all over the streets and sidewalks.

The red spots were the result of people spitting out Betel nut juice. The Betel nut (Areca nut) is the fruit of the Areca palm tree which grows throughout the tropical Pacific, Southeast and South Asia, and in parts of East Africa. The nut itself was wrapped in a green leaf smeared with a white paste that was hotter than any chili pepper ever grown. You put the whole thing in your mouth and chewed it like gum. In fact, it occurred to me at some point that chewing the Betel nut was somewhat akin to our habit of chewing bubble gum. It seemed as though everyone chewed the Betel nut, meaning every man, woman and child. Chewing the Betel nut must have really agitated the salivary glands because people everywhere spat out red saliva in constant streams. Incredibly, spitting in public was common practice and it seemed there was no law against doing it.

Brass workers, jewelers, and rug makers were everywhere. The workmanship was beautiful and prices were very cheap. You could buy a good rug for 40 – 50 rupees. At that time, one rupee was worth about $.30 American. There were also any number of small-scale manufacturing outlets, e.g., producing fabrics, cotton mattresses, and straw mat shops. I later learned that such enterprises were commonplace in all the villages, towns, and cities throughout India.

There had to have been at least a million shoe-shine kids running around all over the place. They would swarm all over you and offer a shine for just two or three annas.

One anna was worth about $.02 American. Just one anna might buy a bowl of rice. These kids were so pesky, we had to constantly shoo them off. I didn't want a shine because I was too busy looking at everything and everyone in sight. Before I realized what was happening, one of these kids, whose services I had refused at least 20 times, finally went out into the street, scooped up a big gob of camel dung and smeared it all over my boots. He then fled into the crowd before I could catch him. As you might guess, I got a shine after all. From that moment on, I remained on constant alert for kids carrying camel dung. All the unfamiliar sights, sounds, and smells were fantastic, especially to someone like me who had never experienced anything like them.

LEG 12   5 February 1944 [Saturday]

Departure: **USAAF Air Transport Command/Karachi Airfield (KHI)**
Destination: **USAAF Air Transport Command/Bangalore Airfield (BLR)**
Distance: **1,059 Statute Miles**
Duration: **7 Hours/4 Minutes**

On February 5th, we learned that our final destination was to be the 7th Bombardment Group (H), a B-24 outfit stationed about 120 miles northwest of Calcutta at a place called Pandaveswar. Naturally, we thought we would fly directly there and get into the thick of things right away. Our crew was ordered instead to fly to Bangalore, in central southwest India, where there was another headquarters area even larger than the one at Karachi.

At Bangalore, we learned that there were several large commands located there, e.g., the primary British Army training camps, a number of Allied matériel supply depots, and storage areas for the entire China-Burma-India (CBI) Theater of Operations. Shortly after our arrival, we were ordered to leave our big beautiful ship at the depot. The handwriting was on the wall when we were informed that our good old *"Impatient Virgin"*, that brand spanking new B-24J model, was not destined to fly in combat after all.

This was very unwelcome news to us because we had grown used to her and figured, somehow, that *she belonged to us*. We later learned via the 'grapevine' that she

114

had subsequently been converted to the C-109 *Liberator* Tanker configuration. [2] As we were given to understand, she was employed in the cargo trade, flying the "*Hump*" between India and China. It was later reported, that she had crashed and burned somewhere in the Himalayas not long after she entered service as a transport.

LEG 13   8 February 1944 [Tuesday]

Departure:	**USAAF Air Transport Command/Bangalore Airfield (BLR)**
Destination:	**USAAF 7th Bombardment Group, 493rd Bomber Squadron, Pandaveswar Airfield (IXA)**
Distance:	**1,151 Statute Miles**
Duration:	**7 Hours/40 Minutes**

Upon our arrival at Pandaveswar, we enlisted types were greeted by the squadron First Sergeant (a non-flying type, of course). He got a kick out of pointing out the charred remains of two B-24s which had exploded on takeoff not too long before our arrival. This sight gave all of us pause and a big gulp, to be sure, because we had seen similar outcomes while in training at Biggs Field.

Our welcoming was not a long one. We turned in our service records, had our shot list checked and our flying equipment and gear inspected. Thereafter, we received a short lecture of the group's mission and operating procedures.

The journey from Tulsa to Pandaveswar covered approximately 14,743 statute miles, about 12,811 nautical miles. In terms of actual flight time, we logged almost 100 flying hours in transit start-to-finish. Our trip lasted twenty-eight (28) calendar days.

---

[2] At Bangalore, *"The Impatient Virgin"* (Ship # 42-51411) was converted to the C-109 *Liberator* Tanker configuration. She was assigned to the Air Transport Command, stationed at Dum Dum Airport Calcutta, British India. Aircraft crashed and burned near Jorhat (India) on May 12, 1944. Total number of fatalities unknown. See: http://www.joebaugher.com/usaf_serials/usafserials.html.

PART TWO: THE US ARMY AIR FORCES, CHINA-BURMA-INDIA (CBI) THEATER OF OPERATIONS, 1942 - 1945

A Brief Overview of the Theater of Operations China-Burma-India (CBI)

The CBI Theater of operations was at the tail end of the entire World War II supply chain throughout the war. It was given the lowest priority for every commodity imaginable. The European Theater received first priority, the Pacific Theater received second priority, and the CBI Theater was rated a distant third place in the supply chain hierarchy.

In practice, supplies sent to the CBI were the leftovers that could be spared from the other two war fighting efforts. Winning the war in Europe was priority number one. Winning the war in the Pacific was priority number two. The fight against the Japanese in China and Burma had to wait. Our task, plain and simple, was to do whatever could be done to stymie further Japanese inroads into Burma.

Truth be told, there were times when we had neither bombs nor enough aviation gasoline to fly planned missions. When we were able to fly, it was primarily at night with single planes taking off five minutes apart. Each aircraft and its crew would fly to the target alone. Crews had to depend on themselves because there was no immediate help to be had under any circumstances. Serving in the CBI Theater, there was no such thing as flying 25 or 30 missions and then rotating back to the States as was customary in the northern European Theater of Operations.

There were no 'automatic' awards of the Air Medal after each five missions or the Distinguished Flying Cross (DFC) after 25 missions. Such awards had to be earned the hard way. For example, when serving in the CBI, the Air Medal *might* be awarded after no fewer than 100 combat flying hours. As a matter of fact, it was not unusual for crews serving in the CBI to log 50, 60, or even 70 missions (well over 200 combat hours) before a DFC *might* be awarded. [3]

---

[3] See: https://www.afhra.af.mil/Portals/16/documents/Timelines/World%20War%20II/
WWIIDFCandAirMedalCriteriaChronological.pdf?ver=2016-09-16-111147-907.

In the CBI, it was not unusual to find combat crews which had served in theater for more than two years. If a member of a combat crew opted not to fly at some point, it was commonplace for that individual to be assigned to ground crew duty. He was relegated thusly to remain *in situ* for the duration of hostilities.

USAAF Tenth Air Force
7th Bombardment Group (H)
A Brief Unit History [4]

The US Army Air Corps (USAAC), 7th Bombardment Group (H), was activated in 1928. In late 1941, the War Department decided to reinforce the Far East Air Force then posted to the Philippines. The 7th was chosen to fly its B-17s out to the Philippines, while its ground echelons traveled by sea. Having departed San Francisco on Saturday, December 6th, elements of the Group famously arrived in the skies over Oahu in the midst of the surprise Japanese attack on Pearl Harbor on December 7th. Subsequently, it saw action in the Philippines and Java, before being evacuated to Karachi, India in early 1942, where it became the backbone of the Tenth USAAF.

The group had been operating out of Pandaveswar for nearly two years prior to our arrival. It was the only heavy bombardment group in the CBI theater at that time. Its missions covered a lot of territory, ranging from Burma to China, and as far afield as Indo-China. Under the best of circumstances, with maximum effort, the Group could put maybe 24 planes in the air at any one time. When you consider that the Eighth Air Force in Europe could pull off 1,000 to 2,000 plane raids, the 24-plane effort was pretty ludicrous.

At Pandaveswar, the 7th Bombardment Group (H) consisted of four squadrons: the 9th, the 436th, and the 492nd, and the 493rd. Each squadron was located about four miles apart from one another. The airfield at Pandaveswar had two main runways, 16/34 and 04/22, and numerous taxiways which had been hacked out of the surrounding jungle.

---

[4] For additional historical perspective, see:
http://www.historyofwar.org/air/units/USAAF/7th_Bombardment_Group.html;
B-24 *Liberator* Units of the Pacific War, by *Robert F. Dorr.*; and https://www.amazon.com/B-24-Liberator-Units-Combat-Aircraft-ebook/dp/B01DPPQ1MC, by Edward M. Young.

Each runway was about 5,000 feet in length, which was necessary for a fully loaded combat ready B-24 to make a safe takeoff.

**Tenth Air Force, 7th Bombardment Group, 493rd and 9th Bomber Squadron
Aircraft taxi into position for takeoff at Pandaveswar Air Base
Autumn 1943** [5]

A Brief Chronology of Combat Operations
7th Bombardment Group (H)
February 13 – May 31, 1944

During the period February 13 - May 31, 1944, the USAAF Tenth Air Force, 7th Bombardment Group (H), launched approximately 54 raids by its B-24s throughout Burma, Thailand, and Indochina from its base at Pandaveswar. Between February 13th and April 5th, I flew ten (10) missions as a gunner, either in the nose position (3) or from the tail position (7). Between April 23rd and May 20th, I logged five (5) additional combat missions from the tail gunner's position before returning the United States on June 20th.

---

[5] This photo was obtained from the U.S. National Archives and Records Administration in College Park, MD. Labeled a "Briefing at Pandaveswar." NARA # 18 CS 641 - Reels 1, 2, 3, 4 & 5 were filmed at Pandaveswar US Army Air Force (USAAF) Base (India) during August, September and October of 1943. It was filmed by the Tenth USAAF Combat Camera Unit, APO #886. It shows the Tenth USAAF, 7th Bombardment Group, 493rd and 9th Bomber Squadrons preparing for take-off on a combat operation.

General Physical Conditions
Natural and Unnatural Perils
Living on the Edge of the Jungle

Our squadron area was smack dab in the middle of a cleared-out jungle space rent with insects, snakes, jungle animals, and all manner of tropical diseases. Malaria, yellow jaundice, dengue fever, dysentery, and heat rash were common ailments. Heat was extreme everyday (110-115 degrees Fahrenheit) and it was always humid. Water generally, and fresh water in particular, was in short supply year around. Moreover, there were persistent shortages of good food, milk, beer, candy, and hard liquor. Nothing was too good for the troops and that's what we got, pretty much nothing. We enlisted men

Tenth Air Force, 7ᵗʰ Bombardment Group, 493ʳᵈ Bomber Squadron
Enlisted Men's hooches at Pandaveswar Air Base
Autumn 1943 [6]

[6] This photo was obtained from the U.S. National Archives and Records Administration in College Park, MD. Labeled a "Briefing at Pandaveswar." NARA # 18 CS 641 - Reels 1, 2, 3, 4 & 5 were filmed at Pandaveswar US Army Air Force (USAAF) Base (India) during August, September and October of 1943. It was filmed by the Tenth USAAF Combat Camera Unit, APO #886. It shows the Tenth USAAF, 7th Bombardment Group, 493rd and 9th Bomber Squadrons' Enlisted Men's Quarters and highlights the austere living conditions experienced by those serving at Pandaveswar.

lived in crew huts. Our quarters were either made of mud or an adobe-like substance with straw roofs. These hooches had no doors or windows, just open spaces where the doors and windows might have been installed. Each structure was just large enough to accommodate six crew members.

Typically, the only furniture provided for crew quarters was a rope strung bed, the same used by the local natives, meaning they lacked mattresses and pillows. There were no lockers, chairs, or furniture of any kind. Enlisted personnel had to buy bedding from the locals if we desired to acquire such amenities. Most of us shelled out for mattresses and pillows because it was almost impossible to sleep on a plain rope bed.

We were, however, issued mosquito netting for our beds – otherwise sleep would have been impossible. As time went by, we secured a few wooden crates which we used as makeshift lockers and writing surfaces. In addition, we used cardboard boxes to stow our few personal belongings. Finally, there were no electrical fans, air conditioners, and no natives manually waving Ostrich feather fans to keep us cool and dry. Ours was an absolutely Spartan existence.

The officers, naturally, were housed way off by themselves. In nice buildings with screened doors and windows and fans. Officers were also provided with a liquor ration each month. And on top of all that, they were typically furnished with individual man servants to care and clean for them.

We enlisted types, by contrast, had a single attendant by the name of Abraham, who cared for all six of us. Over time, we became very fond of Abraham. Each of us paid him something like 10 to 15 rupees a month. He was, therefore, so rich he could afford to keep three wives. I shared many a # 10 can of rice with him.

Abraham and I communicated with each other using an improvised method of sign language we developed together. There was not a lot for him to do, because we had so little in the way of possessions. He swept the floor, rolled up the mosquito nets each morning, let down the mosquito nets at night, and brought us water drawn from the water bag that hung from one of the porch rafters. His was a good and relatively easy life working for us.

The heat prevented us from doing much maintenance work during the day. The fuselage of the plane was made of aluminum which is a very good heat conductor. Inside the aircraft hull temperatures would often be in the range of 110 to 115 F. External hull temperatures frequently got so hot it meant the aircraft couldn't be touched with bare hands without risking severe burns.

Tenth Air Force, 7ᵗʰ Bombardment Group, 493ʳᵈ Bomber Squadron
Ground crew inspecting aircraft's No. 4 engine
Pandaveswar Air Base
Autumn 1943 [7]

In this connection, the squadron Flight Surgeon had a standing order that no one was to move around too much during the day unless it was absolutely necessary. Physical activity of any sort during daylight hours produced sweat, and sweat gave rise to heat rash, and could lead to heat exhaustion. Accordingly, all maintenance work on aircraft was conducted generally between sunset and sunrise. Showers were limited to one per week, provided there was enough water available. Water, of course, was only plentiful during the monsoon season.

---

[7] This photo was obtained from the U.S. National Archives and Records Administration in College Park, MD. Labeled a "Briefing at Pandaveswar." NARA # 18 CS 641 - Reels 1, 2, 3, 4 & 5 were filmed at Pandaveswar US Army Air Force (USAAF) Base (India) during August, September and October of 1943. It was filmed by the Tenth USAAF Combat Camera Unit, APO #886. It shows the Tenth USAAF, 7th Bombardment Group, 493rd and 9th Bomber Squadron personnel carrying out routine maintenance activities before sunrise.

Atabrine was the standard medicine prescribed by the U.S. military during World War II for the prevention of malarial diseases. It was issued in tablet form and each man was required to take one of these small yellow pills every day. Not surprisingly, our skin soon took on a faint yellow hue as a result of consuming the medication and to add insult to injury, hardly anyone successfully avoided contracting malaria.

Although it was not widely understood at the time, there are actually several variants of the disease. The most common type makes the victim shiver and burn up with fever. Eventually, its symptoms abate, only to return with a vengeance periodically. Other milder forms of the disease also are commonplace. The symptoms associated with these strains typically are limited a mild fever, which lasts a short time, and tends not to reappear.

There was also *"Cerebral Malaria"* which targets, as the name implies, the brain. During the war years, there was no known cure for this latter form of malaria. Anyone who was afflicted with this strain usually suffered an agonizing death, in terrible pain, as the brain was consumed by intense fever. Not a pleasant experience to *"sweat it out."* I contracted a moderate form of malaria in 1944 and last suffered an attack from the disease in 1965.

Dengue fever, which would strike without warning, was another commonplace tropical malady. You only knew you had it when you tried to move your body and it refused to comply. The only cure was absolute rest and if one was lucky, it was normally gone in about 24 hours. Contracting Dengue fever was just like being completely paralyzed. Luckily it was generally not fatal and, unlike malaria, it didn't seem to cause any lingering side effects. Almost all of us caught the fever multiple times.

Our food consisted primarily of "K" rations: Spam, powdered eggs, coffee and sometimes (real) meat when it was issued through supply channels. Generally, there were no fresh dairy products: no butter, no milk, and no desserts. Rations had enough vitamin content to maintain a soldier's physical well-being, but offered little more. "K" rations came in three varieties: breakfast, lunch, and dinner.

Breakfast consisted of a small tin of powdered eggs with specks of ham, powdered coffee, four saltine crackers, and a pack of four cigarettes (usually British). Lunch included a tin of cheese with four crackers, a "God-awful" lemon or orange powder, and a pack of four cigarettes (usually British). Dinner included a tin of corned beef, four crackers, a small chocolate or raisin bar, powdered coffee, and a pack of four cigarettes (yes, usually British). Of course, one could have dinner for breakfast, or lunch for dinner, or simply chuck it all and go hungry. Those three meals never varied either in quality or content. Their constituents could sustain life, but they never provided enough bulk to keep a belly full and free from hunger. Nobody ever got fat consuming K-rats, that's for certain.

When we did happen upon a hot meal, it was cooked in the mess hall but the serving line and eating places were out-of-doors. As hot as it was outside, it was simply too hot to be seated inside a building. We ate out of mess kits. On one such occasion, I had just filled my mess kit when I felt the flurry of wings beating about my face. Two seconds later, when I looked down at my kit, all my food was gone. It had vanished.

Tenth Air Force, 7ᵗʰ Bombardment Group, 493ʳᵈ Bomber Squadron
Typical Aircraft Revetment
Pandaveswar Airfield
Autumn 1943 [8]

It was customary not to tell any newcomers about the Falcons which snatched the food away from any uncovered mess kits. The Falcons were small, but very fast, so the trick was to cover your kit before the Falcons had a chance to strike.

---

[8] This photo was obtained from the U.S. National Archives and Records Administration in College Park, MD. Labeled a "Briefing at Pandaveswar." NARA # 18 CS 641 - Reels 1, 2, 3, 4 & 5 were filmed at Pandaveswar US Army Air Force (USAAF) Base (India) during August, September and October of 1943. It was filmed by the Tenth USAAF Combat Camera Unit, APO #886 at about dawn.

All enlisted crew members were responsible for pulling "*Fire Guard*" on all aircraft at night. Our planes were spread out in revetments near the air strip. The revetments were "*U-shaped*" berms which were generally about 15-20 feet high and open on one end. Such revetments were designed to protect the planes from bombing and strafing, but made the aircraft impossible to see in case of fire. Only flight crew members could pull fire guard, since they were trained to do whatever needed to be done in case of such an emergency. Fire guard was lonely duty, but not especially dangerous most of the time. There was no communication with anyone and the revetments were surrounded by thick jungle. Since this was a dusk-to-dawn tour of guard duty, it was often difficult to remain alert throughout the night.

In addition to the aircraft crew's which pulled fire guard, there were Gurkha mercenary soldiers who contemporaneously pulled camp and air field security in each

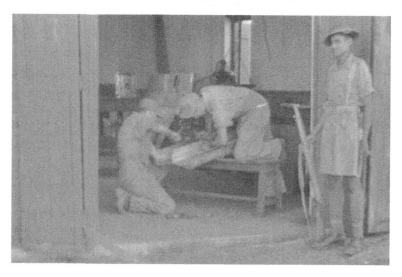

Gurkha Guard on Duty
Pandaveswar Airfield
Autumn 1943 [9]

---

[9] This photo was obtained from the U.S. National Archives and Records Administration in College Park, MD. Labeled a "Briefing at Pandaveswar." NARA # 18 CS 641 - Reels 1, 2, 3, 4 & 5 were filmed at Pandaveswar US Army Air Force (USAAF) Base (India) during August, September and October of 1943. It was filmed by the Tenth USAAF Combat Camera Unit, APO #886. It shows the Tenth USAAF, 7th Bombardment Group, 493rd and 9th Bomber Squadron personnel carrying out routine maintenance operations during an interval between missions.

designated Squadron area. If anyone knows anything about the Gurkhas, it is that they are brave, dependable, loyal, and excellent soldiers. At Pandaveswar Airfield, it was their duty to provide for the physical security of the jungle perimeter around each squadron to prevent infiltration and sabotage. They were always difficult to see or hear, but they were always there.

Several times while pulling fire guard, I would be tapped on the shoulder by a Gurkha who was just letting me know he was present and doing his duty. I'm sure he also told his superiors, who told mine that I was awake and alert. These sudden, silent shoulder taps always scared the hell of me, until I saw who was doing the tapping. Gurkhas tended to be very small, only about five feet tall, and they were renowned for their absolute fearlessness on and off the battlefield.

On one occasion, I witnessed one of them tackle a 12-foot-long King Cobra with nothing more than a big stick and an inward curving Nepalese khichuri knife -- which none of them were ever without. They always emerged from such fights victorious having cut off the head of the cobra. We had quite a few cobras around our squadron area, but seldom if ever were they to be found inside the perimeter, thanks to the Gurkhas.

Our life in the 493rd Bomb Squadron was, for the most part, a matter of trying to pass the time, staying as healthy as possible, and keeping mentally alert so that we were able to fly our missions. There were no USO shows, no liquor, no NCO clubs, and no sympathy from anyone. However, we were able to view an occasional movie, most of which none of us would have paid to see in the States. We didn't particularly care that the acting was terrible, that there was no plot, or that the movie projector broke down 10 to 15 times during the show. After all, our theater consisted of boxes and wooden benches in a clearing with no cover of any kind. We would just sit and watch, even in the rain, it was something to do and something of a link with home. The only times I can recall missing the opportunity to watch a film was when we were flying or I was physically ill.

Asansol was a fairly large town located between Pandaveswar and Calcutta, which hosted RAF Station – Asansol Airfield. It had a well-known restaurant called "Raffles", which served edible food and featured several varieties of ICE CRÈME. Now and then the squadron would get a 2 ½ ton truck and give passes to a few men to go there to partake of Raffles' hospitality. It was a 50-mile round trip ride. I only got to go there once. While there I consumed as much ice crème as could be eaten in a single sitting, lots and lots of ice crème.

We enlisted men were neither inspected nor subjected to visits by any of our officers. None of them ever came to either visit or inspect our area. The only time we visited theirs was if we were ordered to appear before them. They could have all died or been transferred and we would only have found out when it came time to fly a mission. I was summoned to the officers' area on only one occasion and then only for a few minutes. I never heard of an officer ever offering to share his booze or beer ration with the enlisted men. I would like to think that one or more of them had done so at some point, but if any of them did it would be news to me.

Our life in camp was almost completely sedentary. We were lethargic because of the unrelenting heat and humidity and due to the Spartan living conditions, which attended the life we led. No one ever took a correspondence course because there were none to be had. No one had any musical instruments or any inclination to obtain one.

We did, however, have a GI issued phonograph, but we only had one 45 rpm record. We played that record over and over a thousand times and more. Side one featured *"That's What You Think"*, written and sung by Carl Smith. Side two featured *"Sweet Kentucky Babe"*, sung by Robert Merrill and written by Adam Geibel. Understandably, these songs are probably unknown to any persons except those of us who heard them day-in-and day-out while serving in India.

I never knew much about the ground crew personnel stationed at Pandaveswar. Such personnel lived in an area separate from combat crews. In any event, we didn't have much in common with them since they didn't fly. We knew, however, that our lives depended on the quality of their work, i.e., keeping the planes in shape and getting us *"there and back."* Ground crews faced a difficult series of challenges each and every day. As mentioned, the weather was hot and humid and there were constant shortages of much needed replacement parts and equipment. By the time our crew arrived to join the 493rd in February, 1944, most of the planes in the squadron had been flying in combat for over two years.

ARMY PRO : A Memoir of a Soldier's Life

Priority maintenance activities such as mandatory engine changes every 400 flying hours of flying time simply could not be done because there were no replacement engines on hand. Somehow ground personnel always seemed to find a way to keep our aircraft flying. Such individuals did so through a combination of personal skill, ingenuity, and determination and in the face of chronic shortages of all types of spare parts. By way of example, our planes were actually so old that tail turrets were routinely cannibalized. Their tail turrets were installed in modified nose sections to become nose turrets in later models of the B-24 aircraft. In short, our ground crews stuck tail turrets in the noses of ships lacking them so that we would have the capability of firing forward.

In other Theaters of Operations, it was commonplace throughout the war for B-24s to come equipped with regular factory installed nose turrets. It wasn't until the autumn of 1944 that the *latest* model B-24Js were introduced to the 7th Bombardment Group (H). For those of us serving in the China-Burma-India Theater of Operations, we were damned for the duration of hostilities to be at the tail end of Uncle Sam's supply chain.

The Venerable B-24 Heavy Bomber:
Reputation, Rugged Reliability, and
Service Record in World War II

The Consolidated B-24 heavy bomber was designed primarily for long range missions such as those that existed in the Pacific and CBI theaters of operations. Her official maiden flight took place near San Diego, California on December 29, 1939. She went into active service in 1941. Between the years 1940-45, more than 18,500 of these beautiful birds were produced. The B-24 was sometimes referred to as the *"Flying Coffin"*, but this derisive reference usually came from the mouths of those who weren't flying in them.

The B-24 *"Liberator"* was never as well known as the B-17 *"Flying Fortress"*, probably because the B-17 was the primary heavy bombardment plane used over targets throughout the European Theater of Operations (ETO). As a result, the latter received a preponderance of publicity throughout the war. However, it should be noted that with extra fuel tanks in the bomb bay, a B-24 could fly missions lasting 15 hours or more. In other words, a B-24 carrying extra fuel could fly a round-trip of more than 2,500 miles with a 3,000-pound-plus ordnance payload.

In fact, while serving with the 493rd, we flew one particular mission (5 May 1944) from Pandaveswar to Koh Si Chang Island in the Gulf of Thailand, about 500 miles west northwest of Sài Gòn, laid our load of mines in the harbor, and returned to base unscathed. It was a roundtrip of slightly over 17 hours and covered roughly 2,750 miles round trip over enemy occupied territory. With all due respect to the *"Flying Fortress"*, there was not a single B-17 ever built which could have pulled off such a mission.

Cruising speed was typically 150 mph up to 30,000 feet. We hardly ever flew over 12,000 feet and quite often well below that ceiling. In order to avoid enemy radar on combat missions, for example, we typically flew just above the deck and far out to sea on the way to and from our targets and without the benefit of fighter escorts.

Our normal ammunition load was 1,200 rounds per gun. Extra .50 caliber ammunition could be carried, but it was difficult to reload while aloft. We were trained not to waste ammunition, since we could never be sure how much we might need for a given round trip. Since we usually flew at night, our ammunition expenditures were usually pretty low. Thus, the 1,200 rounds per gun were usually more than sufficient to complete the mission.

The basic armament on the B-24 was the same as that of the B-17, i.e., ten .50 caliber (12.7 mm) M2 Browning machine guns: two each in the nose, tail, upper and ball turrets and one single hand-held gun in each waist window. The upper and ball turrets could cover a 360-degree arc of fire; the nose and tail turrets could cover a 180-degree arc. The waist guns were restricted in terms of their arc by the wing and tail sections, but collectively the .50s covered the entire area around the plane.

In the China-Burma-India Theater of Operations, a 'normal' bomb load was generally 12 bombs, each weighing 500 pounds, hence we had a maximum 6,000-pound payload. Of course, the payload could be made up of a mix of bombs and explosives, e.g., two 2,000 pounders, clusters of fire bombs, and floating mines, etc. [10]

---

[10] Actual bomb loads varied based on a number of factors, viz., nature of targets, distances, cruising altitudes, prevailing weather conditions, etc. See: https://www.britannica.com/technology/B-24.

PART THREE: **COMBAT OPERATIONS IN THE CHINA-BURMA-INDIA THEATER OF OPERATIONS (CBI) FEBRUARY 8 – MAY 31, 1944** [11]

All pre-mission briefings were as thorough as possible. We had intelligence, Communications, Ordnance, and Tactical Officers imparting all the mission specific knowledge available to them. Following these briefings, the mission Commander would give his briefing and try to tie all the loose ends together. When it was over, everyone knew what had to be done, how to do it, the when, where, and why of it all, and what escape procedures to use if we were forced down for whatever reason. Even with all this preparation, there were things that could not be foretold and, when they happened, could not be thought of as the fault of anyone concerned.

First Mission [12]
Primary Target: Heho Airfield (Central Burma)
13 February [Sunday]

> ***This day in the CBI, 13 February 1944*** *- "BURMA-INDIA (Tenth Air Force): In Burma, 6 P-51s and a B-25 damage a road bridge and 2 warehouses*

---

[11] The information which follows documents the fifteen aerial combat missions in which Mulvany participated between 13 February and 20 May 1944. Apart from having recorded the dates of missions flown, the memoirist's papers did not always include narratives pertaining to each individual mission. Where the author's papers provided contemporaneous and original commentary relating to specific missions, such information has been incorporated into the text. In those instances, however, where pertinent contemporaneous recollections were not to be found in Mulvany's papers, it was necessary to rely on the *USAAF Worldwide Operations Chronology: Combat Chronology of the US Army Air Forces, China – Burma – India (CBI) Theater of Operations, 1941 – 1945"* to obtain relevant details concerning the scope of offensive operations in the field at the time. In this connection, please also see pertinent references cited in the endnotes at the end of this chapter.

[12] Actual distance to target *"as the crow flies"* was about 416 statute miles in each direction. Distances flown to and from a given target could vary significantly from day-to-day, depending on the nature of a specific target, availability of attack aircraft, type of mission, time of day, and prevailing weather conditions, etc. In the case of this particular raid, February 13, 1944, the estimated round-trip distance was about 1,040 statute miles. In addition, it's important to underscore the fact that most missions were flown at night in order to evade enemy detection and without fighter escorts. On the basis of the best evidence available, the shortest mission in which the author participated was just under ten hours, the longest was slightly over 17 hours, and by Mulvany's personal reckoning the average mission duration was between 14 and 15 hours.

in the Wuntho area; 32 P-51s and A-36s hit the supply area and radio installations S of Kamaing and blast bivouacs S of Walawbum;18 P-51s hit the road and railroad junction N of Sahmaw, a bivouac N of Kamaing and a camp between Tsumhpawng Ga and Walawbum; during the night, 16 B-24s bomb Heho Airfield."

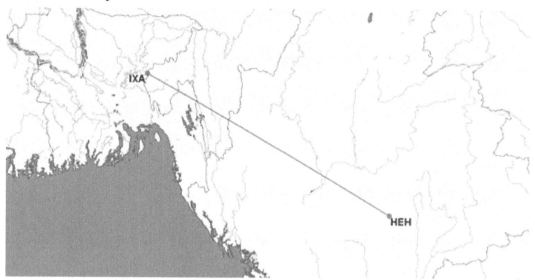

Notional fight path between Pandaveswar Air Base and Heho Airfield
Distance to target (direct) 416 statute miles
Initial heading 120 degrees (SE)

The raid on Heho Airfield was carried out by 16 B-24 aircraft during the night-time hours of Sunday, February 13th. The Pilot, Co-Pilot, Navigator, Bombardier, Engineer, and Assistant Engineer were all strangers, individuals who had originated with other replacement crews. They were complete strangers to those of us who had arrived in Bangalore (India) a week before with the *"Impatient Virgin."*

Shortly after arriving at Pandaveswar and joining the 493rd, we learned that it was standard operating procedure (*"SOP"*) that all new (replacement) crews were to be split up. New personnel were to be apportioned to more experienced crews in need of replacements. On my first mission, Carnes was in the tail, Walters was in the ball, Winkler was in the waist, and I was in the nose turret.

The incendiary bombs we carried were of the type whose main component was white phosphorous (WP). *"Willy Pete"* could burn through concrete and could not be extinguished by water. We were to fly out singly at night five minutes apart and bomb from an altitude of 20,000 feet. Heho, our main objective, was protected by anti-aircraft batteries and bathed in searchlights.

Consolidated Aircraft Corporation
B-24-J Nose Turret Assembly
Gunner's Perspective

I had never trained in a nose turret, especially one that was really a tail turret sitting out there all by itself. In order to adapt a scavenged tail turret assembly to the nose section, it was necessary to set the orphan turret out front of the nose and to Jerry-rig a 'door' for access and egress behind it to keep the wind from blowing into the cockpit. Once the door was shut, the individual manning the turret could not get out until someone in the cockpit deigned to open the door.

Everyone was anxious to get the mission underway. All the training and waiting were over. We were finally about to join the fight. One of life's biggest adventures – COMBAT – was about to happen. Nothing else could equal or surpass it, because there is no other experience like it.

As I recall, we did not take-off until it was absolutely dark. It was to be a seven-hour mission – 3 ½ hours out and 3 ½ back – about 425 miles each way as the crow flies. I never did like to fly at night. Even in training, I didn't enjoy it. I wanted to see where we were headed and what was happening at all times. In those days, this simply couldn't be done in the dark.

For the 7th Bombardment Group (H), the Bomb Line was the shoreline of the Bay of Bengal. This meant that all turrets were to be manned and all crew members were to be ready for combat when we reached the Bomb Line. At 10,000 feet or above, we always had to be on oxygen. Since it was only about a thirty-minute flight from our base to the Bomb Line, we were on oxygen and in our combat positions for all but an hour of the mission.

Sitting in a turret, my arms were the only part of my body which could move; my torso and thighs were strapped in by safety belts and practically immovable. I could only bend my knees upwards slightly. In short, it was very difficult to stretch or scratch and impossible to relieve oneself in place.

It occurred to me at the time it was odd that the only "relief" tubes were located in the waist section of the plane. We were required to stay in our combat positions at all times, except under the direst of circumstances. On many occasions, I was confined in a turret from eight to fifteen hours without any chance to get out to stretch, take a drink, or relieve myself. As you can imagine, I developed a strong pair of kidneys.

We all had flak vests to wear around our upper torsos and steel helmets for our heads. In practice, we usually sat on our vest to protect the family jewels. In the cockpit, the pilot's and co-pilot's seats were shielded with ¼ inch armor plates under their seats and on the backs and sides of their respective positions. Since there was no protection for them from the front, they wore their vests and so did the two waist gunners.

Our oxygen masks contained a small microphone. By plugging the microphone cord into the intercom system and pushing a button on the turret gun handle or on the microphone cord, we could all communicate with one another. When the masks came off, we all wore a throat microphone for the same purpose.

Each gunner had a specific responsibility to carefully scan his sector of the horizon for enemy aircraft. At night, visibility was usually significantly impaired so we generally were unable to spot enemy aircraft until they had already passed one's position and only then by the light of the enemy's fiery engine exhaust plume. On occasion, if one was lucky, it might be possible to detect the enemy aircraft when it was silhouetted against the night sky.

As our first mission unfolded, we followed the designated route along the coast. We all knew we had no friends below us and none beyond the still distant horizon. In 1944, the Japanese Army occupied all of Burma with something like 500,000 well- trained and combat tested troops. Naturally, we maintained strict radio silence throughout the flight to the target. We could speak with one another using the intercom because it couldn't be picked up by enemy radio detectors. We could not, however, communicate with other aircraft either in our attack formation or with friendly ground control stations.

Enemy radar could detect our presence, but because we did not fly on a direct course or over any large anti-aircraft batteries or airfields, the enemy had to wait and see where we were really headed. We knew this, of course, and being alone deep over enemy territory we sweated out the ride to our target all the more. It was inevitable we would be detected; the only question was at what point in the mission we were discovered and how much force the enemy could bring to bear against us on any given day.

Five minutes away from the target, the pilot turned control of the aircraft over to the Bombardier who flew it through controls linked to his bomb sight. Under control of the Bombardier, the plane could only fly straight ahead and level, so for at least five minutes we were at the mercy of anyone who was shooting at us with whatever they had in the way of anti-aircraft defenses. Only after our bombs had been dropped and bomb bay doors were closed did the pilot resume control of the aircraft and undertake measures to evade enemy actions.

All the safety pins in the bombs had to be manually pulled by a designated crew member just before arriving at the target. The procedure for accomplishing the task entailed crawling along a narrow catwalk in the bomb bay and removing the pins with the aid of a hand-held flashlight. All the pins had to be saved in case any bombs were not dropped. In such a situation, these pins would need to be reinserted to disarm them in order to make a safe landing at the end of the mission.

As we were flying along, we got the order to test fire our guns. This procedure was executed in sequence, starting with the nose, so the pilot would know whether all the guns were operating properly. Not long after we tested the guns, Carnes started stammering over the intercom. He was stuttering so badly that no one knew what he was saying.

While he was still trying to speak, the pilot, co-pilot, and I spotted the exhaust trail of a Japanese aircraft that had just crossed our flight path. Our pilot took immediate evasive action and we lost some altitude in the process. The enemy pilot had probably picked up our tracers from the test firing, but evidently, he had lost contact with us. After the single pass over, we were not bothered by that fellow again.

Nakajima Aircraft Company
J1N-S Model 11 *"Gecko"* Night Fighter – Burma
(1944)

As we approached Heho, we could see fires on the ground and searchlights in the sky. When Murphy took over the controls for our bombing run, we were picked up immediately by the enemy searchlights. The beams of light were incredibly bright [even] at an altitude of 20,000 feet.

I could practically see every detail in and around my turret. Suddenly, on both sides of the plane and to the front, I saw colorful explosions as if giant firecrackers were going off in all directions at once. It seemed as though there was flak popping up everywhere. It was all so exciting. I just sat there taking in the whole show. Calmly munching and gnawing away on one of the many pieces of fried chicken I had stuffed into my coveralls upon leaving the mess hall earlier in the day. Every plane in the entire Imperial Japanese Air Force could have flown by and I probably wouldn't even have noticed them.

Once over the main target, Heho Airfield, we could see scores of fires burning all over hell's half acre. These fires were the result of bombs dropped by those planes which had preceded us to the target. After our bombing run, the searchlights went out and the flak stopped. I suppose they must have been waiting for the next group of attackers to arrive. For whatever reason, the enemy neither came up to greet us nor pursued our formation on the route back to our base at Pandaveswar. We returned to the squadron area and were debriefed on the mission.

Debriefings, I soon learned, were held after every mission during which everyone reported on what could be recalled and what went on from start to finish. Frankly speaking once we had completed a mission, we GIs could not have cared less about the operation. For those of us who had tasted aerial combat for the first time, we were glad to have gotten this milestone behind us. After all we had just about run the gamut with flak, searchlights, and that close encounter with an interceptor high over enemy held territory. It's fair to say that the first mission was the most important mission of all, except for the one you knew in advance was to be your last one. In our world, there were no set number of missions to be flown before returning home as was the case in the European Theater of Operations (ETO).

Crews and individuals serving in the CBI Theater of Operations flew until they were either killed, wounded, or sent home for other reasons. No one ever really knew with any certainty when they might return stateside. An exception to this 'rule', of course, pertained to the ground crews who were fixed *in situ* for the duration of hostilities. For combat crews, this reality was not exactly a great morale builder. The combat crews of the 7th Bombardment Group (H) did not fly every day or night, since there were seldom enough bombs and rarely enough aviation fuel on hand to support sustained operations against the enemy. Moreover, all crews didn't fly every mission because often times one or more aircraft were temporarily out of service.

The same crew normally did not fly the same plane on successive missions. Crews flew whatever plane was available and assigned to them. As a result, few (if any) of our ships had either fancy names or slick, memorable, nose art adorning aircraft at this point in the war. We did, however, make a point of stenciling an image of a bomb on the Pilot's side of the aircraft each time a plane completed a mission. Some of the Group's aircraft actually had 50 to 60 stencils or even more. An understandable fact, considering that some of the aircraft in the Group had been in continuous use for more than two years, by the time I joined the fight.

Time between Missions

Between missions, we wrote letters, read, or played cards. I participated in Pinochle games that had as many as eight players, used four decks of cards, and lasted for three or four days without stopping. We also frequently played Hearts. No matter what the nature of the card game on any given day, the play was always cut-throat and in all ways. When games were convened, the first order of business was to check your 'friendships' at the door, before taking your place at the table. Playing cards was a good way of getting rid of the frustrations associated with our rotten existence and out of our systems.

There was no sympathy for anyone who complained about anything, because we were all in the same desperate situation. Flying missions was the only means available to break up the monotony. As a rule, due to the extreme heat and humidity, we neither engaged in games of physical exertion nor physical training. Looking back over the years, the time spent in India was the only period in my entire Army career I can remember being ordered to do *absolutely* nothing. It was just too damn hot.

While serving with the 493rd at Pandaveswar, I can only recall one occasion on which I visited another squadron area and even then, my visit lasted no more than a few hours. As I departed our sister squadron's area, it dawned on me that the 493rd was not the only squadron which '*practiced*' inactivity. As fate would have it, doing *nothing* was the only way to beat the heat when off-duty at Panda.

Royal Air Force (RAF)
Armada Road Airfield
Aerial Gunnery School

February 15th – 20th

Soon after my first mission, I was sent to the RAF's Aerial Gunnery School at Armada Road, located south of Calcutta, for a few days of crew training. Yes, I was sent to yet another gunnery school.

In a departure from usual practice, our leadership put together an entire composite crew to attend the school, i.e., a full complement of officers and enlisted personnel. As it turned out, I had actually flown with some of the guys on previous occasions. In addition, we took a plane with us since the officers were to instruct others in the group when we returned to our squadron.

Hawker-Hurricane MkIIa
RAF-615 Sqn-KWM-Croydon-Z270, England
(1941)

A composite RAF Spitfire and Hurricane squadron was stationed at the school to assist with our training on bomber tactics against fighter planes. Attending the school were pilots of all ranks, officers and NCOs from Australia, England, New Zealand, and South Africa. They were all young, typical fighter pilots, full of piss and vinegar.

Supermarine Spitfire Mk. XI
Photo Reconnaissance Aircraft, India
(1944)

It was a crazy bunch that knew and sang more rowdy songs than I had ever heard before or since. Individually and collectively, they could also put away enormous quantities of booze. We enlisted personnel ate in the British Sergeant's mess (we were all Sergeants, too).

This happened to have been my first exposure to British cooking – it was gawd awful. For breakfast, we had two sardines, a spoonful of beans, and all the tea we didn't want to drink. For lunch we had two sardines, a spoonful of beans, and all the tea, etc. Dinner was a goopy concoction of things unknown and all the tea, etc. All servings were small and we US types scarfed them down in two three bites. The English, however, would actually take up a single bean, cut it in two pieces, and consume each piece separately. We got so hungry, we requested that our officers send for some "K" rations for us to supplement our diet. Thankfully, the officers did so, for otherwise we might have been starved to death.

We did not fire live ammunition at this school at first. All our guns were equipped with movie cameras. 'Adversary' fighters would fly at us from all angles – front, rear, sides, bottom, and oblique while all the while the cameras were rolling. These aircraft and their pilots flew so close to us at times, we could see their faces clearly. Wild ass fighter pilots. They gave us a good show every time. My camera work turned out well.

Vickers-Armstrong (UK)
Wellington Mark III (M) Long Range Bomber

(1940)

While at the Gunnery School, I also got some flying time in a British-built Wellington Bomber. It was a metal "X" frame type aircraft with canvass covering on the fuselage and its wings. Shades of World War I, mates. It had two engines and a crew of three: pilot, navigator/bombardier, and tail gunner.

The tail turret was big in comparison to the B-24's. Unlike our gun controls which were only about ten inches apart, those in the Wellington were a full arm span apart. It was like guiding a motorcycle equipped with *"Monkey Bars."* I had a hard time operating the gun mount.

I gave Wellington crews all the credit in the world for flying combat in their *"Canvas Coffins."* One feature of the Wellington's tail turret assembly which struck me as a bit unconventional had to do the manner in which the gunner took up his position. Unlike bombers of American design and manufacture, the tail turret was rotated ninety (90) degrees to port and the gunner entered and exited the turret not from the inside of the ship, but through doors which opened and closed from the exterior starboard side of the aircraft.

The two photographs which appear directly below and at the top of the following page illustrate my point. Somehow, I always felt right at home manning the tail turret

Vickers-Armstrong (UK)
Wellington Mark III (M) Long Range Bomber
Tail Turret Assembly
Pre-Flight

in the B-24. I got more of a big kick out of seeing where we had been, rather than where we were headed.

Vickers-Armstrong (UK)
Wellington Mark III (M) Long Range Bomber
Tail Turret Assembly
In-Flight

After two days of *"camera gunnery"*, we started firing live ammunition at sleeve targets. Again, my shooting was rated above average. I managed to register over 20 percent hits, which was considered above the norm in those days.

I was complemented by the British instructors for my good work. I enjoyed attending the school and working with the British. My attendance at the Royal Air Force Gunnery School (Armada Road) was the first of what tuned out to be many opportunities to serve with them. Later I received a 'Certificate of Completion' from the school.

When we returned to Pandaveswar, I was permanently assigned as a tail gunner and promoted to Staff Sergeant. I was really feeling good about all this when, all of the sudden, I found myself in the hospital overnight suffering from Malaria. So much for the efficacy of the Atabrine tablets. All they had done was to turn me a nice shade of yellow all over (again!)

During World War II, the hospital cure for Malaria was to consume lots of liquid quinine (a terrible tasting medicine) and having an alcohol rub three times a day. More than anything, the best cure was our exposure to the nurses. They were real live American girls. They looked good, smelled nice, and were very kind to us. It was just seeing and talking to them. I actually really enjoyed my week in the hospital.

Second Mission
Primary Target: Airfields at Akyab and Dabaing (Northwestern Burma)
23 February [Thursday]

This day in the CBI, 23 February 1944 – "BURMA-INDIA (Tenth Air Force): In Burma, 14 B-24s bomb airfields and other targets at Akyab and Dabaing; 3 B-25s and 12 P-51s hit a radio station at Man Pang; 4 other P-51s hit warehouses at Chantha."

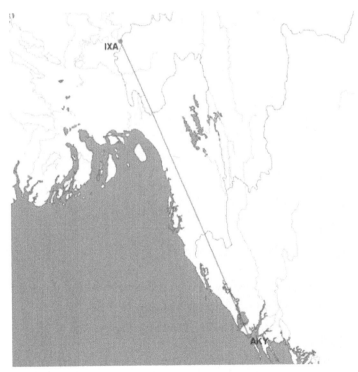

Flight path between Pandaveswar Air Base and Akyab Airfield
Distance (direct) 279 statute miles
Initial heading (S-SE) 159 degrees

Third Mission
Primary Target: Railroad marshalling yards at Mandalay (Burma)
28 February [Monday]

This day in the CBI, 28 February 1944 – *"BURMA-INDIA (Tenth Air Force): In Burma, 6 B-25s hit bridges and trains between Pintha and Kinu; 1 bridge is damaged and several boxcars are destroyed; 13 B-24s bomb the marshalling yard at Mandalay and targets of opportunity at Akyab, Monywa, and Pakokku; P-51s, A-36s and P-40s attack bridges, radio stations, supply dumps, bivouacs, troop concentrations, railroad by-passes, AA positions, and other targets at Seton, Sinkan, Ye-u,Kawlin, Loilaw, Namkwin, Shaduzup, and the Mogaung-Kamaing area."*

Flight path between Pandaveswar Air Base and Mandalay Airfield
Distance (direct) 338 statute miles
Initial heading 116 (SE) degrees

My third mission proved to be an unusually unpleasant personal experience. As previously noted, I flew my first three missions in the nose turret. On each of those missions, all of the makeshift nose turrets malfunctioned, e.g., either the guns would not fire or the turret would not rotate.

Curtiss P 40N *"Warhawk"*
Tenth Air Force, 80th Fighter Group, 'Burma Banshees'
(1943-45)

Before the mission, I decided not to wear the standard heavy fur leather jacket, trousers, and boots because it was so hot on the ground before take-off. I opted instead to wear an electrically heated suit, boots, and gloves. In comparison with to my normal flight gear, it was very lightweight and comfortable.

In fact, it looked like a pair of light blue long johns with wiring all over it. The suit hooked into a plug in the turret, the heat generated was controlled by a rheostat. It was a lot easier to move about than in all those heavy leather items of clothing.

Once we were over the target, my turret got stuck at a 45-degree angle to the left side. Shortly thereafter my rheostat stopped working and then my microphone went on the fritz. I could hear, but I was unable to communicate with other crew members.

We departed the target with me and my turret totally useless to the rest of the crew. Since I was located directly in front of the pilot, he could presumably see the turret and intuitively know that all was not well. Surely, I thought, either he or someone else up front would have noticed the turret was frozen at a 45-degree angle and inquire of me as to whether there was a problem.

No one either on the flight deck or below it seemed to have noticed the curious orientation of my guns. No one seemed to note the conspicuous silence from my position. I was dependent on either the Navigator or the Bombardier to open the doors in order to exit the turret.

I was alternately freezing and frying because the rheostat only worked on the "*high*" setting and nothing below it. I had to plug in the suit for a while to warm up, then unplug it to cool off. When I got so cold, I couldn't stand it, I plugged in the suit again until warmth returned to my body. I beat on the turret door with my .45 caliber pistol but to no avail. No one paid a damn bit of attention to me until we landed about four hours later.

Once I was free from the nose turret, I was so blind with rage that my temper got the best of me as I addressed the officers. I really blasted the officers for having failed to even inquire about what might be wrong with the nose turret. I didn't give a damn what they did with me, but I vowed then and there never again to fly in the nose turret. That was my final word.

When I removed my heated suit, my entire body was covered with thin red lines where the wiring burned me good. Understandably, perhaps, that was the first and last time I ever wore a heated suit in combat. Mercifully, I was never again assigned to man the nose turret.

Fourth Mission
Primary Target: Airfields at Lashio, Hsenwi and Loiwing
(Northeastern Burma)
3 March [Friday]

> ***This day in the CBI, 3 March 1944*** – *"BURMA-INDIA (Tenth Air Force): In Burma, 22 B-25s, some supported by Royal Air Force (RAF) Spitfires and Hurricanes, bomb the Ft White area; 10 B-25s and 4 P-51s pound airfields at Katha, Mawlu and Shwebo; 12 B-25s and 8 P-51s hit railroad targets and a warehouse at Kyaikthin and Kyunhla; 14 B-24s covered by 22 P-40s hit airfields at Lashio, Hsenwi and Loiwing; 70+ P-40s, A-36s, P-51s, and B-25s hit fuel storage, supply areas, roads, and other targets over widespread areas of Burma, including Shingban, Myitkyina, Zigyun, Mogaung, Manywet, and Washawng; 6 P-38s attack the Okshitpin bridge but the target is not damaged."*

Flight path between Pandaveswar Air Base and Lashio Airfield
Distance (direct) 418 statute miles
Initial heading 097 (E) degrees

The Tenth USAAF, 7th Bombardment Group (H), put on another magnificent effort having gotten 14 of our group's B-24s together in a single flight, six aircraft from the 493rd, four from the 492nd, and two each from the 9th and 436th respectively. Our raid was certainly a decent showing by CBI standards.

It was to be a daylight mission to the northeastern Burma to bomb airfields at Lashio, Hsenwi, and Loiwing. We were all looking forward to the mission. It was great to see the fighter cover for a change flying back and forth above us.

One of the primary reasons we did not perform many bombing missions during daylight hours had to do with the fact that we seldom had any fighter escorts. When fighter escorts were available, they tended to be either a few Curtiss P40's from the Tenth Air Force, 80th Fighter Group (based at the time near Shingwiyang in northern

Burma) or P-51's from the 14th Air Force, 311th Fighter Group, based in southern China.

As a general rule, fighter escorts were only made available when we flew missions near the Chinese border with Burma. It should be remembered that in 1944, the Japanese were in complete control of all of Burma on the ground, in the air, and at sea. It was simply too risky to fly unescorted missions and risk losing planes unnecessarily.

The P-51 was a long-range fighter. It had proven itself in the skies over Europe. Another reason we usually flew without escorts was the duration of our missions. In that era, most fighter planes simply did not have the range to go the distances required routinely in the CBI. In early April, however, we learned that a squadron of P-51 'Mustangs' had been stationed at Chittagong, a port town in India, close to the border with Burma.

North American P-51A
Fourteenth Air Force
311th Fighter Group – India/Burma
(1943)

I was the tail gunner in the lead plane of the 493rd squadron's six-ship formation. Ours was the second of four formations. From my perspective I had a great view of our planes and the escort fighters from the 14th Air Force.

Consolidated Aircraft Corporation
B-24-J Tail Turret Assembly
Gunner's Perspective

We approached the target at about 16,000 feet and found ourselves right over the runway lengthwise. There was a lot of flak thrown up at us, but to little effect. All of the sudden, the P-51s all took off like a flock of birds diving and strafing enemy positions from every angle.

I looked down and saw the runway and revetments full of parked aircraft. I also watched in disbelief as our bombs seemed to be hitting everywhere and everything below us *except* the runway and the revetments. Astonishingly, we dropped a total of 72,500-pounds of explosives (six planes carrying 12 x 500-pound bombs each) over the target, but failed to score a single direct hit either on the runway itself or inside any of the revetments.

Fortunately, the other three squadrons in our Group had better luck. Collectively, those three formations scored several hits very damaging hits on the target. As a result, the Japanese were forced to relocate their remaining aircraft to another airfield closer to their own interior lines.

When the raid was over, I could only hope and pray that when we returned to base the lead Bombardier would get his butt chewed out for (sadly) he was a member of my crew. As we headed home, the P-51s started coming in from all directions. Instead of flying cover, they tucked themselves right under our wingtips so we could guide them home. As it turned out, this had been their first escort mission. Some of them tucked so close, it was easy to see the pilots' faces and exchange hand signals with them. After parting company with us, they all landed safely at Chittagong.

North American P-51B
Fourteenth Air Force
311ᵗʰ Fighter Group – Burma/India
(1944)

Fifth Mission
Primary Target: Tavoy Airfield (Southeastern Burma)
9 March [Thursday]

> ***This day in the CBI, 9 March 1944** – "BURMA-INDIA (Tenth Air Force): In Burma, 6 B-24s bomb Tavoy Airfield and office area while 8 others hit the town of Mogaung; the town area, supply dumps and road bridge at Kamaing are pounded by 10 B-24s, 16 P-51s, and 10 P-40s; the bridge is knocked out; 10 B-25s score numerous hits on airstrips at Indaw and Katha; and P-51s, P-40s, and A-36s hit storage at Pyindaw, and support ground forces at Walawbum and Shaduzup."*

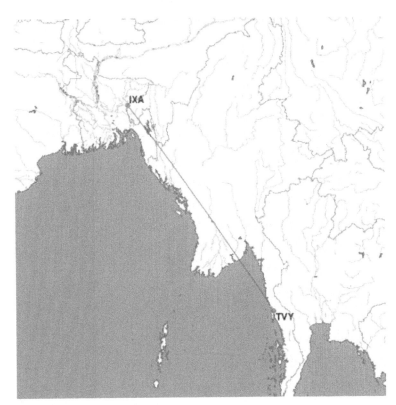

Flight path between Pandaveswar Air Base and Tavoy Airfield
Distance (direct) 812 statute miles
Initial heading 145 (SE) degrees

Sixth Mission
Primary Target: Enemy barracks near Bangkok (Thailand)
15 March [Wednesday]

*This day in the CBI, 15 March 1944 – "BURMA-INDIA (Tenth Air Force):
In Burma, 31 B-24s and 20+ Royal Air Force (RAF) Wellingtons and Beau
fighters pound supply dumps and targets of opportunity in the Rangoon area
while 8 other B-24s hit barracks near Bangkok, Thailand; numerous US
and RAF medium and fighter-bombers attack villages, Japanese positions,
ammunition dumps, tanks, and many other targets of opportunity in the Chin
Hills, at Chindwin, in the Mogaung Valley, and in areas around Mandalay."*

149

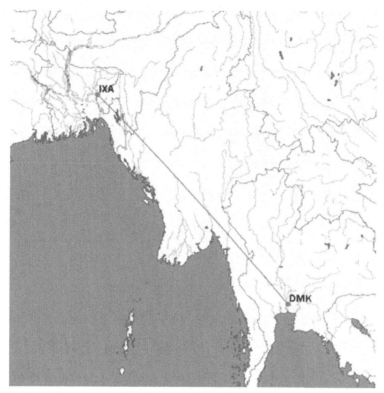

Flight path between Pandaveswar Air Base and Bangkok Airfield
Distance (direct) 919 statute miles
Initial heading 137 (SE) degrees

Seventh Mission
Primary Target: Moulmein-Siam Railroad at Martaban
Southeast of Rangoon (Burma)
20 March [Monday]

> *This day in the CBI, 20 March 1944 – "BURMA-INDIA (Tenth Air Force):*
> *In the Arakan area of Burma, 12 RAF Vengeance's hit Japanese positions near*
> *Kaladan and Buthidaung while 6 P-38s severely damage a bridge at Lamu;*
> *20+ B-25s and P-51s hit communication and transportation targets in the*
> *Katha area; 6 B-24s bomb the Moulmein-Martaban area; and 100+ fighter-*
> *bombers strike Mogaung Valley buildings and supply areas, and fuel dumps at*
> *Mogaung, Myitkyina, Sumprabum and Sahmaw."*

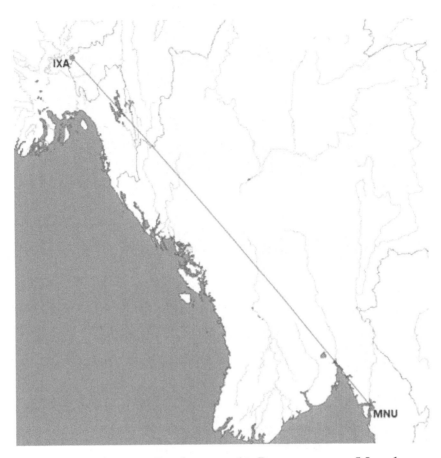

Flight path between Pandaveswar Air Base to target at Martaban
Distance (direct) 650 statute miles
Initial heading 146 (SE) degrees

Eighth Mission
Primary Target: Supply dumps at Kamaing near Mandalay (Burma)
27 March [Monday]

> ***This day in the CBI, 27 March 1944*** *– "BURMA-INDIA (Tenth Air Force): In Burma, 8 B-24s hit supply dumps at Kamaing, while about 50 fighter-bombers and 2 B-25s hit troops in in the Myitkinya area and support ground forces near Kamaing; in the Katha area 12 B-25s and 16 P-38s and P-51s hit a bridge and railroad facilities near Meza and a railroad near Kawlin."*

As part of an 8-ship formation, we flew a mission to Kamaing, near Mandalay, to hit supply dumps in the area. Mandalay is located on the east bank of the Irrawaddy River, in north central Burma. Approaching the target area, there were 42 known anti-aircraft emplacements in and around the town.

Flight path between Pandaveswar Air Base and Mandalay Airfield
Distance (direct) 338 statute miles
Initial heading 116 (SE) degrees

The outstanding recognizable feature of Mandalay, at least to experienced air crews, was a very large moat surrounding an even larger area which made up the central part of the municipality. The moat itself was in plain sight whether in daylight or in the light of the darkest night. We reached the target area and then started orbiting the town, round and round.

Our navigator that night was none other than *"Lewis-the-Dumb"*, the same fellow with whom some of us had trained with back in the States. All of us crew members in back were getting progressively more agitated and nervous as precious minutes passed with no indication as to when our bombing run would commence. What in blue blazes were we waiting for … that was the question. Why didn't we go in and drop our bombs?

There were no words spoken over the intercom for some time, until the pilot finally said to the navigator, *"What in the hell is the matter, where is the target?"* The Navigator,

First Lieutenant Lewis, responded that it was too dark to locate the supply dumps accurately. The pilot promptly ordered the navigator to *"get on with it"* because we couldn't afford to loiter over the target area all night.

After all there were other planes coming in behind us. There were plenty of enemy fighters prowling the night sky. And there were too many anti-aircraft batteries waiting to open up on us when we made our way free from the target.

At this point, believe it or not, Lewis came back to the waist with a very large map in hand and asked the waist gunners whether *they* could see Mandalay from the open waist windows. All of us had already seen the town several times within the past ten minutes. Apparently, Lewis had somehow missed the boat, or better said, missed the signature *moat* surrounding the town.

We were of one voice in orienting him and off he was to his position game to get on with his duties. Alas, we never did find the target. We didn't drop a single bomb. We didn't take one round of flak. We didn't get washed by the light of a single anti-aircraft battery.

Not a single Japanese interceptor came after us. Our luck was incredible, because every other aircraft on that particular mission was treated to the full range of options available to the enemy. As for me and the rest of the crew, we had to dump our bombs on the secondary target at Akyab, a town on the western coast of Burma which frequently experienced the unenviable fate of being bombed willy-nilly by every Allied ship that didn't drop its load on a designated primary target.

As you can imagine, Akyab really took a beating throughout the war.

Ninth Mission

Primary Target: Railway Station at Akyab (Northwestern Burma)

1 April [Saturday]

> ***This day in the CBI, 1 April 1944** – "BURMA-INDIA (Tenth Air Force): In Burma, 14 P-38s hit a freight train and damage a factory in the vicinity of Mandalay; near Rangoon, 16 B-24s hit a railroad station and bomb Akyab while 6 B-25s damage a railroad bridge near Nattalin."*

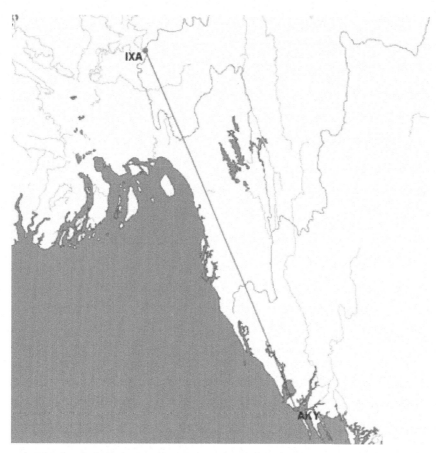

Flight path between Pandaveswar Air Base and Akyab Airfield
Distance (direct) 279 statute miles
Initial heading (S-SE) 159 degrees

Tenth Mission – "A Ditching at Sea"
Primary Target: Moulmein-Siam Railroad from
Moulmein to Kanchanaburi (Burma)

5 April [Wednesday]

> *This day in the CBI, 5 April 1944 – "BURMA-INDIA (Tenth Air Force): In Burma, 13 B-24s bomb the railroad from Moulmein to Kanchanaburi, destroying 3 bridges, damaging several others, and causing much damage to track and railroad cars."*

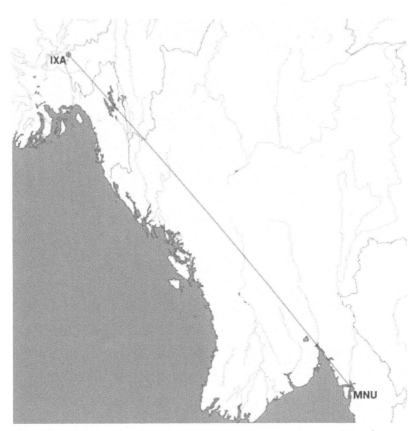

Flight path between Pandaveswar Air Base to target at Moulmein
Distance (direct) 650 statute miles | Distance (indirect) ~975 statute miles
Initial heading 146 (SE) degrees

The railroad, known as the Moulmein-Siam Railroad, was the primary supply route for the Imperial Japanese Army's planned invasion of India. It had to be put out of commission and the 7th Bombardment Group (H) was designated to get the job done. Special preparations had to be made, such as the development of a bomb especially designed (modified) to destroy railroad lines, both the roadbed itself and the overlaid ties which supported the rails. Its destruction was no ordinary mission.

The bomb selected to do the heavy lifting was a 100 pounder with a 24-inch long, 2-inch wide, steel spike fitted and welded to its nose. The bomb head had an 8 -11 second delay programmed into the detonating fuse. Bombs were to be dropped at very low altitude so as to strike the rail bed (hopefully) between the parallel rails. On impact with the ground, the spike would *theoretically* hold the charge in place. Bombs were designed to explode just above the surface of the ground so as to maximize the explosive effect and either blow the rails away or bend and twist them in a way that made it impossible for a train to pass over without derailing.

All participating aircraft were fitted with a 450-gallon bomb bay fuel tank. Such a tank would occupy one-half of the entire bomb bay, but allowed for the extra range necessary to successfully execute the mission. Fifteen of the specially fabricated spike bombs were carried in the remaining bomb bay area.

A total of thirteen B-24s were scheduled to fly the mission. The 492nd and the 493rd squadrons (three planes each) would carry the spike bombs. The 436th squadron (four planes) and the 9th squadron (three planes) would carry 1,000- and 2,000-pound bombs for hitting bridges, rolling stock, and buildings along the rail line.

Mission Briefing

The mission was scheduled for thirteen hours flying time round-trip, across the Bay of Bengal and back to Pandaveswar, at low altitude to avoid Japanese radar detection. We were to fly in three ship formations, each formation, separate and apart from the others. Each plane in each formation was to descend to its target alone and make its bombing run while the others remained aloft to provide what covering fire, they were able to and as circumstances might require.

When we gathered for the pre-flight mission briefing, we were shown the planned route for the day's operation and a collective sigh made its way throughout the room. The distance to be covered was so great that the string showing the way to and from the target was too short to make the ends meet. We knew then that this day was shaping up to be a special one, indeed.

We knew this for certain when someone began distributing a blank form entitled, *"Last Will and Testament"*. It occurred to me at that moment I might not make it back from this one. I had a good friend who was not slated to fly on the mission, so I asked him to write to my family and tell them what he could about what had happened to me. Naturally he agreed to do it for me, but *only* after I got back. My rejoinder was to urge him to do it any way. Right away, because I wasn't expecting to be coming back.

Knowing this to be the case, it didn't provide much comfort to us or serve to augment crew morale. It was rumored the Japanese offered bounties to the natives of

$100.00 U.S. currency for an American officer's head. A $50.00 U.S. currency bounty was offered for the head of any American enlisted man.

Special caches of food and supplies had been emplaced at various land locations along the route to and from the target areas. If we were forced down for any reason, we were to try to reach these rendezvous points and try to make radio contact via a predetermined 'special signal' to indicate we were waiting to be picked up. Some of these caches were located in the midst of Japanese controlled areas or in areas controlled by natives friendly to the Japanese.

Departure

We took off aboard a ship nicknamed "SNAFU" just after 10:00 AM on April 5, 1944. Our departure time would put us over the target before dark. The formation assembled over our group area, flew the Bomb Line at altitude, and then descended to fly on the deck. It was manual flying all the way, too.

The crew selected for this particular mission was a hand-picked composite one. Usually, the same crew flew together on all routine missions. This time there were six men who had flown together for quite some time as a unified combat crew and four others who were drawn from other crews.

The officers were: Our Pilot was Captain Robert G. Bailey (soon to be Major), Commander of the 493rd Bomber Squadron. Our Co-Pilot was Colonel Aubrey K. Dodson, Commanding Officer, 7th Bombardment Group, (H) (West Point – Class of 1930). Captain Henry P. Mitchell was Navigator and Captain James F. Duffy was the Bombardier.

The enlisted men were: T/SGT Royall E. Peterson, Engineer/Upper Turret Gunner; T/SGT Rolland D. Guffin, Radio Operator/Nose Turret Gunner; S/SGT Edward J. Walters, Assistant Engineer/Left Waist Gunner; S/SGT Warren B. Winkler, Armorer/ Gunner and Right Waist Gunner; CPL James H. Balma (six feet two inches and 200 pounds.), stuffed into the ball turret; and me S/SGT Floyd. R. Mulvany, Tail Turret Gunner.

Colonel Dodson flew with anyone he wanted to being the Group's *"Big Bird"*. Winkler, Walters, and I had trained together in the States. We had already flown several missions together. For their part, Balma, Duffy, Guffin, Mitchell, and Peterson had trained and flown combat missions together for quite some time as well.

Owing to the expected duration of the mission, projected to be 13 hours, we did not get into our combat positions when we crossed the Bomb Line. Instead, we were permitted to remain in the waist area for as long as possible in order to ensure we'd be fresh and fully alert when we approached the target area.

About half way into our flight, one of our three planes from the 493rd aborted due to a fuel leak and returned to base. At the time, we did not fully appreciate the significance of this development. It was only later, when it came time for us to make our bombing run that the consequences became clear to us.

Approximately twenty minutes before crossing the coastline, we gunners got into our respective combat positions and tested our guns.

Bombing Run

Our ship was designated to be first to descend to the deck to initiate the attack on the railway. Recall, if you will, the fact that one of our aircraft was forced to abort and return to base a few hours into the mission. Had this unfortunate turn of events been avoided, we would have opened *our* attack over a different section of the target area.

Specific sectors of the target area had been assigned to each squadron. Our sectors of the railroad line were from mile posts 6 to 11 and 20 to 24. Overall, the Group's aircraft were to hit targets along the route between miles 6 to 126.

Just as we arrived at the coast and started to climb to clear the coastal hills, a fleet of Japanese supply barges was sighted. The squadron immediately behind us (the 9th) fired on the barges as they passed over their position. I only caught only a look at this action in passing, but the fire seemed to have been effective.

As we climbed over the hills, I got my first glimpse of the terrain below, a rich green landscape dotted with many golden temple domes scattered throughout the jungle and soon enough our bombing runs commenced. From the tail turret I could not see much of the opening action, but I could see quite clearly how straight the railroad tracks were laid out.

There wasn't a curve in sight. The prisoners-of-war who had built the railroad had done a terrific job constructing the rail line, though many of them had died doing it.

158

As we flew onwards, we began taking fire from Japanese installations dug into the hills.

We were hugging the deck as we progressed northwards, so low (well below 500 feet) the enemy was actually firing down on us in some places. Nevertheless, we had to play the hand we had been dealt. No sooner had we started our bombing run, I spied the faces of numerous Japanese looking up at us while shooting at us.

I remember asking the Pilots for permission to return fire, but one of them denied my request on the basis that in doing so I would give away our position. Truthfully, I wasn't ready for *that* answer, because it could not have been too difficult for anyone to observe a B-24 flying straight and level down a railroad track in broad daylight at an altitude of about 300 feet. I attributed the nonsensical response from the cockpit to the kind of stress that invariably arises during intense combat.

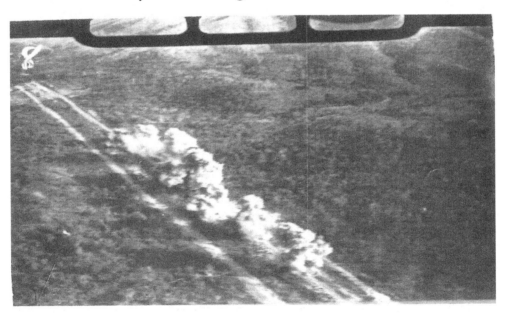

Moulmein-Siam Railroad [13]
Bombs on Target
between Anankwin and Thanbyuxayat
View to the South
April 5, 1944

---

[13] Photo shot taken by camera mounted on Mulvany's tail turret gun mount.

Moulmein-Siam Railroad
between Anankwin and Thanbyuxayat
View to the South
April 5, 1944 [14]

I had a movie camera mounted on my turret. I started the camera and made running commentaries to the Pilot about bomb hits. Jim Balma had climbed out of his ball turret to take some still photographs from the waist windows and the open hatch at the bottom of the waist area. He had placed his flak vest near the open hatch, so he could readily alternate his photographs from the two waist positions.

Sound and Fury

Suddenly, it sounded as if a huge load of gravel had been thrown at us. Simultaneously, I saw what I thought was Balma's body falling from the lower hatch as smoke was streaming from the starboard side of the aircraft. What had sounded like gravel was actually a combination of 20mm antiaircraft, machine gun, and (probably) small arms fire peppering the side of the ship.

---

[14] Photo shot taken by camera mounted on Mulvany's tail turret gun mount.

What had appeared to be Balma's body was really his flak vest and hand-held camera falling out of the hatch. What at first had appeared to be smoke was actually a stream of gasoline being emitted from the right-wing fuel tank. I had to put on my oxygen mask in order to avoid breathing pure gasoline fumes.

'SNAFU' (Ship #42-73442) shortly before ditching. [15] [16] [17]

As I peered into the waist section, I saw Balma and Winkler lying on the floor. Balma appeared to have been hit in the buttocks. Winkler was lying in a pool of blood. Walters had gone up to the cockpit. Captain Bailey gave the order to shut off all electrical and hydraulic circuits to prevent a spark from igniting the flowing gasoline.

---

[15] Observe the No. 4 engine is feathered. Moments later the No. 3 engine stopped cold. SNAFU ditched about 30 miles southwest of Foul Island.

[16] It is believed a member of Captain Allan Kass' crew, flying wing for Bailey, was responsible for having taken the above photo.

[17] According to the official "Flight Intelligence Report", dated 5 April 1944, and filed by Captain Alden L. McMurtry, Intelligence Officer (S-2), 7th Bombardment Group:

"Captain Bailey's plane was last seen at 1910 hours at a position of 16° 36' N – 93° 45' E at 3,000 feet on a TC [true course] heading of 341 degrees, with intentions of making an emergency landing at Chittagong. At 1930 hours and 1945 hours his ship was heard weakly calling Chittagong and at this time was believed to have been heading for Foul Island." "Capt. Allan Kass (Ship #44) was Capt. Bailey's primary wingman."

"Ship #44 made a call to Chittagong for Ship #42 at 1910 hours."

A Death in the Afternoon

I got out of my turret as quickly as possible and hastened to Winkler's aid. He was holding his oxygen mask to his face. As I bent over him, he told me he was doing okay. I pulled out a first aid kit when I saw he had been hit in the left knee. It appeared as though a 20mm cannon shell had exploded nearby and nearly severed his leg. A few moments later Winkler died, still holding his oxygen mask over his nose. I'm sure he bled to death.[18] I have never seen so much blood drain from a man as it did from Winkler. Balma and I had applied a tourniquet to his leg, but it did not seem to do much to staunch the flow of blood. However, the morphine we gave him probably helped to smother his pain and mitigate his suffering.

Damage Report

The hits we had taken had knocked out the No. 4 engine over the target. The No. 3 engine was leaking oil and seemed to be fading fast. Captain Bailey had banked left (west) coming off the railroad line the instant we were hit, since we had already dropped our last spike bomb.

At this point, we had started throwing out everything we could to lighten our load. We threw out machine guns, ammunition, flying gear, radios, tools, flak jackets – everything but our parachutes and life vests. We even tried to dislodge the ball turret assembly. In theory, it was supposed to come out by unscrewing three bolts, but one of the braces attached to the turret had been shot off. We never did get the damn thing loose.

Our crew was well-trained. No one was in a panic, everything which needed to be done got done in a calm, efficient manner. We did what we knew had to be done. Everything which could be jettisoned was thrown out. In short order, Walters retuned from the cockpit to report that the No. 3 engine was starting to fail and would have to be feathered.

---

[18] The death of S/SGT Warren B. Winkler marked the first occasion on which Mulvany lost a close personal friend in combat. Whenever Mulvany spoke of Winkler's death, he expressed regret about the fact he was unable to save him. Later, he lamented his inability to extricate Winkler's remains from the ship. Ultimately, Mulvany's grief gave way to resignation.

Command Decision

We were over the Bay of Bengal flying on three engines. It was getting dark and we had been in the air for over seven hours. A B-24 could not be flown very far on two engines. We all knew that for a fact.

Captain Bailey asked us if we wanted to bail out or ride it down and ditch in the Bay. Since it was dark and we were past swimming distance to shore, no one wanted to bail out. In preparation for ditching, Guffin, the Radio Operator and Captain Mitchell, the Navigator, joined Balma and me in the waist section. We piled our parachutes against the bomb bay bulkheads, laid down with our life vests on, and clasped our hands behind our heads.

We were all apprehensive, but everyone remained cool, calm, and collected. There wasn't anything we could do to possibly improve our situation, so giving in to panic would not have helped at all. Up in the cockpit, Peterson, Walters, and Captain Duffy braced themselves against the Pilot's and Co-Pilot's armor-plated seats.

Descent to the Sea

Captain Bailey, with the able assistance of Colonel Dodson, executed a flawless descent to the sea. Having decreased power to the No. 1 and 2 engines, they physically muscled the crippled aircraft into a series of gentle turns to port, spiraling the aircraft downwards from an altitude of approximately 3,000 feet. As the aircraft approached the surface of the sea, Captain Bailey straightened out the glide path in the final moments of flight.

Our ship skipped across the water tail first and shuddered to an abrupt halt. By the time we hit the deck at approximately 8:15 PM, we had been in the air just over ten hours. Coming to my senses after impact, I saw a thousand bright stars (or so I imagined) and then found myself floating in and swallowing salt water inside the waist section of the ship. No one else was there, except Winkler, and he was dead.

Somehow, I was able to gain my footing and found myself standing in the right waist window. I tried desperately to pull Winkler's body out the window, but to no avail. I was exhausted and incapable of mustering the strength to lift his corpse up and over the sill and free of the fuselage.

Overlay Map [19] [20]
Planned Flight Path Versus Actual Route of Retreat

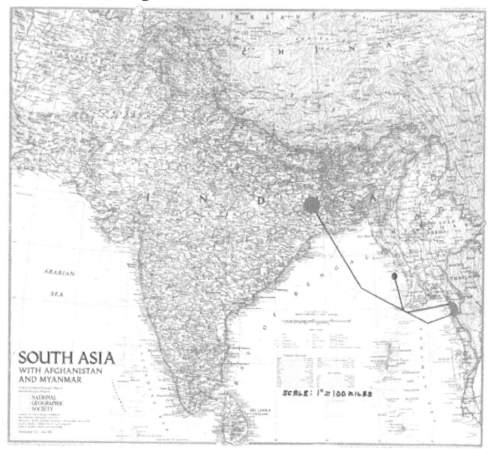

**Flight to Target Area from Pandaveswar Airfield and
Retreat towards Dohazari Airfield near Chittagong (India)
Tenth USAAF, 7th Bombardment Group, 9th/436th/492nd/493rd Squadrons
Mission #1962 | Thirteen B-24s | 5 April 1944**

Survival Instincts

Instantly it dawned on me that the ship was starting to break up. I felt the left side of my life vest being pierced by jagged edges of aluminum as the tail section of the

---

[19] Map overlay drawn to scale by former USAAF Captain Henry P. Mitchell (July 1993)

[20] Base map image courtesy of the National Geographic Society.

plane was drifting away from the fuselage. I took one last look at Winkler as I fell out the nearest window. Because the wing mounted fuel tanks of the plane were almost empty, the front half of the ship floated on the surface of the water for several minutes.

Once free from the ship, I began swallowing more salt water. I tried to move my arms, but they refused to budge. I was simply floating, unable to swim. Soon I felt the suction of the sinking ship as it began to pull me under. I did my best to flail my arms in an effort to get away, but I was helpless to do any more than simply float on my back.

How much time transpired from the moment of our ditching to the point at which I heard someone call out *"swim over here."*, *"swim over here."* is anybody's guess. Again, I tried to swim, but lacked the strength to move much at all. Slowly, I managed to distance myself from the aircraft, but I was too exhausted to do much more than float on my back.

Race for Life

Straight away, I heard someone's voice loudly repeating, *"Swim over here." "Swim over here."* As hard as I tried, I just couldn't seem to move very well. Straightaway, the voice bellowed, *"swim, dammit, if you want to save your life."* It was at that moment; I saw a dinghy with Captain Duffy aboard. He pulled me to safety and I just laid there in the bottom of the raft vomiting sea water. I was *"out of it"* for a good while, before coming to my senses as dawn broke on the morning of April 6, 1944.

How Duffy's dinghy came to be in the right place at the right time is quite a story. All the aircraft in our Group had ditching and survival equipment on board because so many of our missions took us over the water. The equipment included two ten-man dinghies, each outfitted with two paddles, small cans of water, sugar candies, first aid kits, and a hand-cranked signal transmitter.

All this equipment was stored in two separate overhead compartments in the cockpit above the pilot and co-pilot's seats. Each compartment had a handle that, when pulled, released and automatically inflated each dinghy. There were also handles on the exterior of the compartments that, when pulled, produced the same result.

Each exterior facing handle had a circle of luminous paint around it in order to make them visible in the dark. God bless the persons who thought of this idea, because there had been no time to pull the internal release handles before we ditched. After we ditched, the nose of the ship broke off and began to drift away from the remaining aft sections of the fuselage.

Captain Duffy and Peterson got to the top of the forward section of the fuselage through the top hatch. Captain Bailey was under water, still strapped in his seat, but managed to break free and climb to the top of the fuselage as well. Between the three of them, they managed to pull the handles which released and inflated both dinghies. Duffy and Peterson got into one dinghy. Bailey climbed into the other. Captain Duffy kept shouting in hopes of locating survivors. Mercifully, voices answered him back.

Walters had a dislocated shoulder and was found clinging to a floating parachute pack with his good arm. He kept whistling so we could get a fix on his position relative to our own. Colonel Dodson was in bad shape. Personally, I thought he had bought the farm because he was unconscious when we got to him.

Both he and Captain Bailey were pretty well beaten up, especially in and about their faces. Bailey's lower lip was hanging down below his chin. All of us were cut up, banged up, and tired. After lashing the two dinghies together, we all tried to rest and sleep as well as we could under the circumstances.

Two Dinghies in the Bay of Bengal
Adrift roughly 50 miles south-southwest of Foul Island
Off the Western Coast of Burma
April 6, 1944

Taking Stock

As the sun came up, I remember awakening, taking off my shoes, and bailing water out of the dinghy. All the while, I was whistling and singing though I cannot recall the name of the tune. Truly, it seemed as though I had contracted a case of the *"shocks."*

We took stock of ourselves and administered first aid to our cuts and bruises. Captain Bailey kept a close watch over Colonel Dodson (39), since he was quite a bit older than the rest of us. Colonel Dodson was, after all, *the* Commanding Officer of the 7th Bombardment Group (H), the only Heavy Bombardment Group in India.

Frankly speaking, Colonel Dodson was considered a very important person in the CBI Theater of Operations. As for the rest of us, other than being alive, we didn't have too much going for us. We were lost at sea bobbing about in the Bay of Bengal in a couple of flimsy life rafts and drifting perilously close to enemy held territory off the coast of Burma.

We did not know our exact position. However, we were pretty confident that no one else did either. The two ships which had caught up with us and flew alongside us after leaving the target area had to head for home as soon as darkness fell. We went down after they had departed for home base.

For our fellow combatants, returning to base at Pandaveswar was of paramount importance to the prosecution of the war effort. But before heading for home, they remained over our position as long as possible to obtain a good fix on our final position. It was this preliminary information that was soon thereafter passed along to the Air & Sea Rescue team.

Waiting Game

Colonel Dodson suddenly awoke. His first words were. *"How do you take a crap in one of these things?"* 'Tough Old Bird', I thought to myself. Bailey and Mitchell helped him crawl onto the edge of the dinghy and held his hands. Colonel Dodson then proceeded to defecate in the Bay of Bengal. With that business done, he laid back down and slept.

At about this time, Balma told me he had a terrific pain in his neck. I examined his neck and noticed a piece of wood protruding from it. It was so close to his jugular vein that it had to come out. Since my hands were pretty useless to grasp it, Captain Bailey pulled it out. It turned out to be a piece of plywood about an inch long that appeared to have come from one of our bomb bay doors. We poured a whole packet of sulfa powder into the hole in Balma's neck. We then secured his handkerchief over the open wound to limit any further loss of blood. By this time, everyone's clothing was saturated with warm salt water which seemed to have had a healing effect on everybody's open wounds.

It soon became quite warm and the next thing I knew, I had the *"dry heaves."* At least I had spit up all the salt water I had swallowed. We checked our supply of canned water. Inside all of the cans was a green seaweed like substance. It didn't look too healthy, so we decided to save the water until we really needed it.

We also had some Charm sugar candies, so some of us sucked on them to agitate our saliva glands and help to ward off thirst. Then there wasn't anything else left to do except to float around, rest, and think about fate. I didn't believe we had much chance of being rescued before we were discovered by the Japanese or dead from exposure. I knew then and there it had been right to ask my friend to tell my family what had become of me.

Every dinghy was equipped with a rubber sheet azure blue on one side and yellow on the other side. There were also several packs of yellow, purple, and green sea marker dyes and a flare gun with about eight to ten flares per dinghy. These were intended for use in air-sea rescue operations. The sea markers could easily be spotted from the air and would indicate that there was a dinghy in the vicinity.

The rubber sheet was large enough to cover an entire dinghy. For rescue, the yellow side was displayed topside. To hide from enemy planes, the blue side which matched closely the color of the sea was displayed. The dinghies themselves were yellow. Whenever we heard the sound of an airplane engine, the blue sheet went up because we knew that in all probability the plane was an *"unfriendly"* type.

Hope on the Horizon

Mid-morning on April 6th, shortly after 10:00 AM, we observed the silhouette of an aircraft approaching from a great distance. It was flying just barely above the surface of the water and appeared to be heading directly towards our position. It was flying so low, in fact, it could not possibly miss seeing us if it continued on its course.

We pulled the blue sheets over our dinghies and anxiously waited. For several minutes, we watched the aircraft approach when, almost as if on cue, we all seemed to recognize it as a B-24. There was no mistaking it and sure enough she kept coming towards us. As the plane passed over our position, we recognized its British (RAF) insignia. As soon as the aircraft was confirmed as a *"friendly"*, Captain Bailey fired two flares. As it began to circle overhead, we all cheered and waved our arms in celebration.

The crew of the British aircraft took photographs of us in the dinghies and dropped us some water and a medical kit wrapped in a note that read: *"HELP COMING SOON – "M" 354 SQD."* They continued to loiter over our position for more than two hours, probably intent upon getting a reliable fix on our position and angle of drift for an eventual rescue. At around 1:30 PM, however, our new found friends abruptly departed.

Message dropped to Bailey's crew with survival rations from
RAF *Liberator* Mark VI (B-24G) Reconnaissance Aircraft
Piloted by F/O Robert Banks (Canada)
April 6, 1944

Once again, we were alone and on our own.

It was long after our return to squadron duty that we obtained a partial explanation as to why the RAF crew had hastily withdrawn from our position. It was reported the Japanese had detected the presence of the RAF aircraft and sent an interceptor out to investigate their presence. Rather than to compromise our position, the RAF Pilot decided to pull up chocks and lead the Japanese off in another direction.

The crew the *Liberator* which located us was attached to RAF Squadron No. 354 based at RAF Station – Cuttack (India). It had been on a routine reconnaissance patrol over the Bay of Bengal in the early morning hours of April 6, 1944. According to Pilot F/O Robert ("Bob") Banks, at about 8:15 AM, he received an M.F.B. which stated:

> *"Look out for Dinghy, Position unknown".* [21]

Banks' After-Action Report (AAR) read: "At 10:30 AM, the Dinghy [*sic*] was sighted with 8 [*sic*] live men in it about 50 miles S.S.W. of Foul Island. Base was informed and given a weather report. Contact was maintained and at 12:14 PM, [another] M.F.B. stated "Resume Patrol. Check position of Dinghy [*sic*] before returning to Base." The Dinghy [*sic*] was left at 1:33 PM and course was set for Foul Island. Fifteen minutes later an Enemy Aircraft was sighted 2,000 yards away on the Starboard Bow and identified as a *"Betty."* It chased us to Chadura Island but was unable to close range and no engagement came to pass. Our *"Betty"* broke away at 2:06 PM and disappeared. At 2:20 PM, three *Liberators* in formation were sighted. At 2:25 PM, an M.F.B. stated "Return to Dinghy, signal when contacted." Wide-Wide on 500 KCs, homing aircraft C/S h721. At 3:31 PM a message was sent to Base stating "Insufficient Petrol, last position dinghy XPHX0627." The Captain (Banks) set course for home at 4:16 PM and landed at RAF Station - Cuttack at 6:20 PM. (The crew of the Dinghy [*sic*] were subsequently rescued by a PBY "Catalina" at 10:00 PM app.)."

In a cruel twist of fate, F/O Robert Banks and his crew perished on the return leg of an *"ill-fated"* mission over the Malay Peninsula on the night of May 7, 1944.

Salvation at Hand

Several hours past. We just laid in the dinghies in the hot sun watching the sharks and turtles swim by. At one point in the late afternoon, I saw a mirage of a very large chocolate malted milk shake sitting on the horizon.

---

[21] After Action Report (above) was published in a two-volume report entitled, "354 Squadron RAF, 1943 – 1945, A Record of Their Operations", RAF SF 540, 6 April 1944, page 77, by Robert G. Quirk, Winnipeg, Manitoba, Canada [Draft Edition – 2003]

At twilight, we could barely make out the silhouette of a plane circling far off as if her crew were searching for something. Was our unidentified visitor a friend or foe, *that was the question?* We could not tell, so we watched and waited.

The mystery aircraft on the distant horizon flew back and forth, seemingly following a certain search pattern, when we finally made it out to be a PBY, a Catalina Flying Boat. It was still a long distance away from us and, regrettably, not apparently headed in our direction. Daylight was fading fast, so Captain Bailey fired one flare and then a second one.

Signal Flares aloft over
Two dinghies (right of center) in the Bay of Bengal
April 6, 1944

There was no immediate acknowledgement from the crew of the PBY. By this time, we were more than a little edgy because if it got too much darker before they saw us, they would have to leave the area. Bailey fired another flare for good measure. Finally, the PBY turned in our direction and eventually landed very close by. We were fortunate that the PBY crew spotted us when they did, because the prevailing winds were picking up and the currents probably would have taken us to shore before dawn – Japanese held territory.

Soon we were transferred from the dinghies into the PBY with the aid of those on board. Everyone moved as quickly as possible so we could take-off without undue delay. One of the crew gunners sank our dinghies with a .50 caliber machine gun. The PBY-5 Catalina 'Flying Boat' was piloted by Captain Thomas C. Schiebel. Schiebel was a former member of the 492nd Bomber Squadron at Pandaweswar. He was also a veteran of 48 combat missions with the 7th Bombardment Group (H). Manning the PBY was a crew of four, plus four medical personnel. Since there were nine of us survivors, it meant there would be a total of 17 people on board.

Consolidated Aircraft Corporation
PBY-5 Catalina *"Flying Boat"*
(1943)

So much weight necessitated a very long take-off run. We taxied for at least 45 seconds before taking to flight. As soon as we were airborne, the medics got busy with Colonel Dodson first and only then did they turn their attention to Captain Bailey. Once our senior officers were stabilized, the medics turned their attention to the rest of us.

I recall having been almost overtaken by thirst once aboard the PBY. It seemed that I consumed more than a gallon of water without stopping during the flight back to Pandaveswar. It was then that I noticed my wrist watch and ruby ring had disappeared. Searching my body, I realized that my dog tags and my St. Christopher's medal were still around my neck. My .45 caliber pistol was tucked away securely in my shoulder holster. Funny, but I had not noticed these accoutrements all the time I was in the dinghy.

As my slow self-inspection progressed, I noticed that my flight suit had stretched rather than shrunk. After all we had endured, I could scarcely believe my good fortune inasmuch as my coveralls were now at least three sizes too big. This meant I could readily secure new ones at the base.

It happened that the RAF crew were on routine reconnaissance patrol when they spotted and followed a series of green dye slicks which made a path directly to our dinghies. Captains Bailey and Mitchell alternately had dumped the dye in the water every so often throughout the day. Fortunately for us, the Japanese apparently had not spotted the slicks.

Imagine what our plight might have been had the RAF reconnaissance patrol not chanced upon our trail and followed those slicks to our position. Later we also learned that our Group had sent up a three-plane search mission to the area of our last known position. We were nowhere to be found in that vicinity, of course, because the prevailing currents were driving us ever closer to the Japanese-held Burmese coast.

By the time the Group's search patrol reached the designated coordinates, we had already drifted miles away from our ditching point. Regrettably, I cannot recall much about the return flight to Calcutta, except to observe it took quite a while and I slept soundly most of the way. A few days later, members of Captain Scheibel's crew visited us in the hospital and told us how the RAF B-24G crew had found us.

Arrival at Dum Dum Airport (Calcutta)

When our rescue flight arrived at Dum Dum Airport, site of the USAAF's regional unit of its Air Transport Command, I recall we were greeted by several dignitaries, including Major General Howard C. Davidson, Commanding Officer, USAAF Tenth Air Force. He was accompanied by members of his staff. In addition, there were also some British officers on hand as well. There were quite a few photographers there to record the homecoming ceremony. Ambulances were standing by to transport us to the hospital.

At this point, the officers and enlisted men went their separate ways. With perhaps a single exception many years after the war, I don't believe I ever laid eyes on any of the officers again. We enlisted men were shuttled off to a hospital that had at one time been the palace of some local potentate. It was a very nice place with rose colored marble floors and other elegant appointments.

The best appointments of all, of course, were the American nurses. I was 21 years old, but I looked 16, so I was mothered quite a bit and I didn't mind it at all. With my hands all bandaged, there wasn't much I could do to help myself, so the mothering was only natural and well-intended. On perhaps the second day of our hospitalization, Major General Davidson and several of his senior staff visited us at the facility.

General Davidson came into our room and presented each of us with a Purple Heart Medal. He then looked around the room and said in a loud voice for the benefit of the hospital staff, "*If these bastards don't take good care of you, just let me know!*" Needless to say, the care we received was great.

Stars and Stripes

The raid on the Burma-Siam railway line had been an important one and worth the effort, despite the fact that we had been shot down and one other crew member was killed. Our efforts had made an important contribution to thwarting the Japanese invasion of India. Our mission was reported in the Stars and Stripes newspaper (CBI Edition) as follows:

> "*On 5 April Major General Howard C. Davidson's Strategic Air Force took its second sweep at the Burma-Siam Railroad within a month. U.S. Heavies attacking from low –level, destroyed three bridges, probably destroyed five more, blasted tracks at more than thirty-five points, destroyed three trains and an additional locomotive, and burned-out track installations to thoroughly snafu this vital line of supply and communications. Just to vary the program, they also destroyed a Jap motor ship and barge.*"

For about ten days in the hospital, we were all heroes and were treated as such. Also, we were one of the very few crews that had any survivors after being shot down in the CBI Theater of Operations. We were a very lucky crew.

Enlisted Quarters

Following our release from the hospital, we returned to our squadron at Pandaveswar. Upon our arrival, it came as quite a shock to discover that everything Winkler and I owned, except our bed frames, was gone. No one had wanted to sleep in Winkler's bed, so why the frame was still there I didn't understand. For my part, I visited every crew member in the squadron collecting my socks, boots, pictures, and so on. I cursed everyone who had taken anything of mine. At the time, it struck me as unthinkable that such a thing could happen.

All personal belongings of men missing in action (MIA) or killed in action (KIA) were supposed to be collected and sent to his next-of-kin. I recovered all of my possessions, though what I recovered really didn't amount to much. It was just the idea that my stuff was taken in the first place.

Mandatory Liberty

After a couple of days back in the squadron, all of us enlisted men who had been shot down were summoned to the Orderly Room. The First Lieutenant Squadron Adjutant told us we were all going on leave for two weeks. We certainly appreciated this expression of concern for our well-being, but unanimously said that we did not want to go anywhere.

Why? Because we had all tried very hard to forget about the real world with all its good things: females, ice crème, dames, soft beds, and girls. We didn't want to be exposed to them and start all over trying to forget about them. It was just too hard to do. Just seeing those nurses in the hospital set all of us back quite a bit. The sight of them was almost worse than the pain and suffering which attended our wounds and injuries. No, sir, we did not want to take leave.

The Lieutenant informed us that we had to go, that there was no way around it, and that we all had better inform him on the following day where we were headed. WE were free to go anywhere in India we wished wherever there were U.S. facilities for GIs on leave: Lahore or Darjeeling in the cool mountains to the north, Bombay, New Delhi, Karachi, or Calcutta. Those were the choices. Three fellows chose Darjeeling. Balma and I decided on Calcutta. Calcutta was closest to our base. Moreover, it offered everything a GI could want.

All Aboard

Orders were cut and we were given passes to ride on the railroad. First, however, we had a thirty-mile truck ride to Asansol to catch the train. If one is unfamiliar with riding Indian trains, then riding one for the first time can best be described as an experience of a lifetime. The cars had individual compartments with plain bench-type hard wood seats. There was no glass in the windows – thus passengers were exposed to the elements. Anyone could be seated anywhere they fancied. No, we didn't have first-class tickets.

When the gates opened, to board the train, there was a mad rush of Indians trying to board the train with all manner of bundles, baskets, rolled rugs, kids, food, live chickens, ducks, and whatever. Since we were taller than most Indians, we made it inside a compartment first. After three Indians joined us in our compartment, we fought off all others so we could at least breathe a bit.

Most Indians had a sickly-sweet odor which was offensive to unseasoned Western noses. Their breadth, as well, typically did not smell anything like fine perfume. We were still shooing and kicking out interlopers up until the time the train started rolling. Although the distance to Calcutta was only about 122 miles, it took the better part of the day to get there owing to the fact that the 'local' train stopped at every little wayside along the route.

Local Accommodations

When we finally arrived in Calcutta, the only place for us to stay was at the Red Cross Center. It happened that The Red Cross had taken over a large building and installed about 150 to 200 Army cots in a single large room. Fortuitously, this facility featured really western-style toilets and showers. The cost was a princely $.50 per night. The facility was intended only as a place to clean up and sleep. It was not meant to serve as a rooming house or hotel of any sort. There were a few Red Cross girls around, but *too* few, indeed.

We plunked down our shaving kits and then took off to get something to eat, mainly ICE CRÈME. We visited Raffles Restaurant, one of the finest in town. It had marble floors, ceiling fans, silver settings on white tablecloths, and plenty of Indian waiters. It took quite a while to convince our waiter that all we wanted to order was ice crème and lots of it. From our waiter's point-of-view *a lot* meant two to three scoops. For Balma and me, "*a lot*" meant two to three gallons – all in one bowl so we could dig in and get full. Believe it or not, the waiter brought out a punch bowl filled to the brim and graced with two large spoons.

We then proceeded to consume every last ounce of ice crème without taking a break. wow, it sure was delicious. At the time, we thought eating ice crème was better than having sex. Besides breakfast, lunch, and dinner each day, we had our bowls of ice crème, too.

Out on the Town

Balma and I visited several nightclubs around town, some of which featured orchestras, floor shows, and movie theaters. And, of course, we were not the only ones out on the town every night of the week. We crossed paths with British, Indians, Gurkhas, and other Allied forces troops besides all the other American GIs.

One evening we heard that Teddy Powell, an American band leader famous for his hit song "*Goodbye Mama, I'm Off to Yokohama*" (1941), would be appearing with his orchestra at a nearby club. When we arrived, Powell's band was really knocking out some popular big band tunes. The joint was full of soldiers including a large contingent of Scottish types, none of whom were taller than five-feet in height.

I had never seen so many short Caucasian soldiers before in one place. One of them came up to me, looked at my ribbons, and pointed to my Good Conduct Medal. He inquired, *"What's that one for?"* I answered it was for my sister, who was serving in the WACs. To this he responded in a loud voice with some wisecrack, which I couldn't understand for the life of me.

At about the same time, about 30 of the *"wee ones"*, started pushing and shoving everyone around. Without a doubt, the little Scots were a belligerent lot. The ruddy buggers began jumping up and swinging at everybody within reach. I do mean "*jumping up*", literally speaking, because they were so short, they actually had to jump in order to hit most others in the chin.

Neither Balma nor I had any desire to spend the rest of our leave in the stockade. We quickly decided to exit the premises without undue delay. It was clear a fight was in the offing and that the MPs would be summoned soon to restore peace and tranquility. As we made our retreat, there were dozens of U.S. GIs, Aussies, and Limeys swinging at one another and throwing things about willy-nilly.

Teddy and his band answered by playing their music real loud apparently in the hopes that in doing so the brawl might soon subside. His strategy didn't work and the melee only intensified and soon the band itself disappeared. Shortly thereafter, legions of MPs descended on the club blowing whistles and swinging Billy clubs.

We ducked out of the bar entrance and made our escape in a horse drawn carriage. It wasn't until 1979 that I learned the little Scots were actually called *"Bantams"* and had been a part of an all-Bantam Regiment in India. Every member of the Bantam's outfit was under five-feet, three inches tall. Good little fighters. Excellent soldiers.

Calcutta Street Life

Eating, drinking English beers, and frequenting nightclubs took up most of our time. Balma and I did do a fair amount of sightseeing too. Never in my life, before or since, had I ever seen such a wide variety of life styles as those that were presented in the streets and back alleys of Calcutta. I witnessed people competing with dogs, cats, and rats for food from garbage piles.

Piles of rubbish lined the streets and by-ways of the city and such heaps were often three to six feet high and 60 feet long. Frequently, adjacent the trash piles were magnificent homes and palaces adorned with marble. It was not uncommon to encounter ordinary souls afflicted with Leprosy and Elephantiasis, pus oozing from their eyes, running sores all over their bodies, and skin spots which resembled chicken pox.

Bodies were strewn all over the sidewalks. It was virtually impossible to tell whether these persons were dead or alive – until the cadaver collectors came and took away the corpses for burning. Burning pyres lined the banks of the Ganges River and its tributaries and the fires burned constantly day in and day out.

The sidewalks and streets were red with Betel Nut-stained spittle. Cows roamed wherever they pleased – in the streets, on the sidewalks, in stores and shops, and in hotel lobbies. Cows could neither be touched nor molested in any way because they were considered sacred by practitioners of Hinduism. Cows were fed and watered by the people, even when food and water were scarce and people were starving.

Food was always available for the cows. Members of the Hanuman sect worshipped the Hindu monkey god, too. Like the holy cow, monkeys and other non-human primates also rated the royal treatment in some parts of India.

In the mid-20th century, basic sanitation practices were unfamiliar to the average Indian. Human defecation and urination took place whenever and wherever a person happened to be at the time – on the ground, in the streets, or out an open window, whatever. Naturally, many preventable diseases ran rampant and the average life expectancy at that time was about 32 years of age.

It was not uncommon for both sexes to mature, marry, and procreate by the time they were no more than ten years old. I saw many girls aged 8-10 who had fully developed breasts nursing their own offspring. I saw women stop work in the fields, grab a large banana leaf, squat down, give birth on the spot, and return to work in the fields. In addition to all this, I also never quite got used to the sight of women standing to urinate and men squatting for the same purpose.

There were countless villages outside the urban areas. It seemed that India, practically speaking, was one very large rice paddy. One's entire life could be spent within the confines of a single village growing and harvesting its rice crops. With so many paddies, the mosquito populations were staggering in their proportions. Malarial diseases were a leading cause of death amongst the general population.

Rat populations were probably second only to mosquitos when it came to the spread of diseases, e.g., Hantavirus Pulmonary Syndrome, Leptospirosis, Bubonic Plague, Rat-Bite Fever, Salmonellosis, and Lymphocytic choriomeningitis, etc. In addition, water borne diseases were also commonplace, e.g., bacterial diarrhea, hepatitis A and E, typhoid fever; vector borne diseases like dengue fever, Japanese encephalitis, malaria, and animal contact diseases like rabies.

Each village usually had a pond which was used for washing dung off of water buffalo butts, defecation, urination, and water for cooking and drinking. Incredible, perhaps, but it just might explain why life expectancy was so damn short. Another feature of Indian society which caught my attention at the time was described as the Indian caste system.

Caste System

Indian society was rigidly structured. Among other considerations, its organization mandated that a son follow in his father's occupation, no matter how capable he might be of doing something else much better. By far, the largest caste was known as the *"untouchables."* These were the people who did all the dirty, menial, tasks that society had to offer, e.g., street sweeping and cleaning latrines. A person from any other caste could not touch or even allow the shadow of an untouchable to touch their shadow without performing an elaborate purification ceremony afterwards.

Men and women of half-Indian and half-British birth were known as *"half-castes."* Such persons were not acknowledged as being of either heritage. I did not understand all these things at the time, but later in life it became clear to me the English never really did much to correct these evils during the entire time they ruled India. In retrospect, I can certainly understand the socio-economic circumstances that led to periodic uprisings through the centuries and finally led to end of British rule in 1947.

Return to Duty

When our leave was over, Balma and I reluctantly returned to the great nothing which was our base at Pandaveswar. Nothing had changed during our absence, of course, so we started all over again dealing with the mundane aspects of life we led on the base. For the first time ever, though, I somehow actually had begun to dread the prospect of flying another combat mission.

At the time, right or wrong, it was my thinking was that I used up all my luck by surviving and coming back from being shot down. I couldn't seem to shake the fear of flying and being shot at again. By this time, all the guys who had been shot down with me were gone. Where they had gone, I did not know. Shortly after Balma and I returned from our leave in Calcutta, he shipped out without ceremony. I never saw him or any of my former crew mates until many years later.

Winkler's bed was eventually filled by a new man who had been assigned to our unit. He was a qualified Paratrooper and had his Jump Wings. He had somehow wrangled a transfer to the Air Corps and completed Aerial Gunnery School. It was highly unusual at the time for a single replacement to be assigned to a combat crew. Someone asked if he was superstitious about sleeping in Winkler's bed. He said he wasn't given to superstition and that was that. For some reason, I cannot recall either the name of this fellow or what ever happened to him.

As for myself, I resumed flying missions again. It was not easy, but the job had to be done and someone had to do it. I somehow managed to get in another five missions before wrapping up my tour.

Eleventh Mission
Primary Target: Railroads and jetties at Moulmein and Martaban
Southeast of Rangoon (Burma)

23 April [Sunday]

> *This day in the CBI, 23 April 1944 – "BURMA-INDIA (Tenth Air Force): In Burma, 24 P-51s, 8 B-25s and 51 RAF Vengeances attack Thetkegyin, Manipur bridge, Tiddim road and Japanese positions at Indaw. 12 P-38s hit Kangaung Airfield near Meiktila; and 21 B-24s bomb railroads and jetties at Moulmein and Martaban."*

Flight path between Pandaveswar Air Base to target at Moulmein

Distance (direct) 650 statute miles

Initial heading 146 (SE) degrees

Twelfth Mission
Primary Target: Supply Dumps at Prome (Burma)

29 April [Saturday]

This day in the CBI, 29 April 1944 – "BURMA-INDIA (Tenth Air Force): In Burma, 21 P–38s hit airfields in the Heho area and claim 8 aircraft downed in combat; 25 P–51s and B–25s bomb several buildings at Meza; 19 B–24s over Prome blast supply dumps in the area."

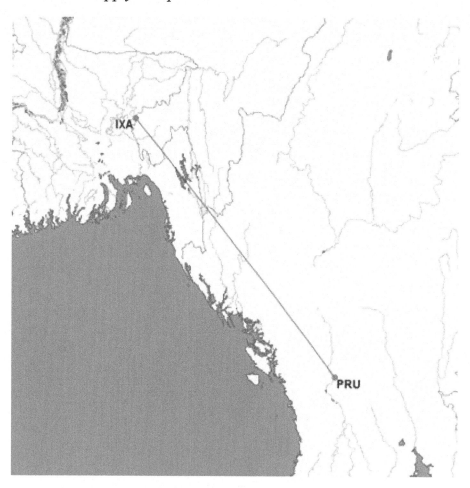

Flight path between Pandaveswar Air Base to target at Prome
Distance (direct) 555 statute miles
Initial heading 146 (SE) degrees

Thirteenth Mission
Primary Target: Mine laying in the harbor off Koh Si Chang Island (Thailand)

5 May [Friday]

This day in the CBI, 5 May 1944 – "BURMA-INDIA (Tenth Air Force): In Burma, 15 P-38s hit targets along Tiddim road; 3 B-25s bomb the Thayaung Airfield area; 80+ P-40s, P-51s, A-36s and B-25s carry out support of ground forces, hit gun positions and supply dumps, attack troop concentrations and blast numerous targets of opportunity throughout the Mogaung Valley; 3 B-25s and 6 fighter-bombers hit an ammunition dump N of Mohnyin; and 12 P-38s bomb a large warehouse E of Monywa. 6 B-24s lay mines in the harbor off Koh Si Chang Island, Thailand."

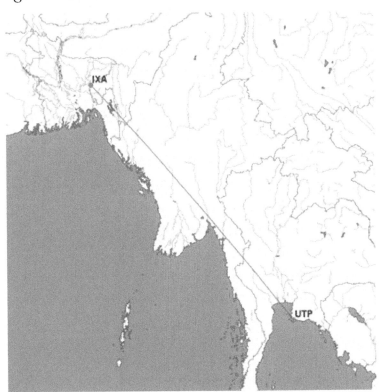

Flight path between Pandaveswar Air Base and Koh Si Chang Island
Distance (direct) 1,002 statute miles
Initial heading 139 (SE) degrees

Fourteenth Mission
Primary Target: Railroad Station at Maymyo (Central Burma)

11 May [Thursday]

> ***This day in the CBI, 11 May 1944*** *– "BURMA-INDIA (Tenth Air Force): In Burma, 70+ B-25s, A-36s, P-51s and P-40s, attack the Myitkyina and Pinbaw areas, Sahmaw, targets NW of Kamaing, gun positions at Nsopzup and targets of opportunity along the road from Inkangahtawng to Kamaing; 24 P-51s attack the airfield at Meiktila, Anisakan and Heho, shooting down 13 aircraft in the area; 14 B-24s pound Maymyo railroad station; 12 B-25s attack the railroad in the Shwebo–Sagaing area; and 12 other B-25s knock out bridges at Pyu, Thawatti, Ela and 7 mi (11.2 km) S of Ela."*

Flight path between Pandaveswar Air Base and Maymyo (near Mandalay)
Distance (direct) 338 statute miles
Initial heading 116 (SE) degrees

Fifteenth Mission
Primary Target: Pakokku Airfield and Akyab (Northwestern Burma)
20 May [Saturday]

This day in the CBI, 20 May 1944 – "BURMA-INDIA (Tenth Air Force): In Burma, 100+ A-36s, P-40s and P-51s pound gun positions, attack bridges, bomb troops and hit numerous targets of opportunity in areas around Myitkyina, Kamaing, Nanyaseik, and Nsopzup; 16 RAF Vengeances and 2 P-38s hit targets in the Arakan area, including a signal center SE of Buthidaung, gun positions SE of Maungdaw and a jetty at Akyab; about 40 B-24s and P-51s hit oil installations at Yenangyaung and Chauk, airfield at Pakokku, and town of Akyab. In India, HQ 1st Air Commando Group moves from Hailakandi to Asansol; the group consists of the following sections: bomber (B-25s), fighter (P-51s), light-plane (L-1 & L-5), transport (C-47), glider (CG-4) and light-cargo (UC-64); the bomber section is eliminated and after converting from P-51s to P-47s, the group begins a training program; a detachment of 9th Photographic Reconnaissance Squadron, 8th Photographic Reconnaissance Group, operating from Dinjan since Sep 43 returns to base at Barrack pore with F-5s."

Flight path between Pandaveswar Air Base and Pakokku Airfield
Distance (direct) 303 statute miles
Initial heading 125 (SE) degrees

Bulldog's Last Dance [22]
Pandaveswar Air Base

24 May 1944

Following what turned out to be my last mission with the 493rd, I was standing out in front of our hooch looking towards the airstrip one afternoon. A B-24 crew was practicing continuous landings and take-offs (*"touch-and-goes"*). This procedure was often done to check out a plane after it had an engine change or some other form of major maintenance or simply to maintain and improve a cockpit crew's proficiency.

On about the third go around, the plane suddenly veered off the runway, skidded along the ground, and exploded in a huge fireball. Flames and smoke filled the air and live ammunition exploded all over the place. I could tell the plane was going to be a total loss. I wondered who was flying and why the accident happened.

I knew for sure that someone had most certainly 'bought the farm', which is to say, died as a result of the crash. A short time later we learned that *"Bulldog"*, our former pilot, and another pilot with his same demeanor were checking out the plane. Apparently, one of those at the controls wanted to land and the other wanted take-off at the same time. As inconceivable as it might seem, this tragedy was not surprising to those of us who had flown with Lieutenant Thomas F. (*"Bulldog"*) Ready.

We learned all this from the Flight Engineer who was riding with them. He was thrown out of the plane through the co-pilots window after having been hit by the nose wheel which came up through the cockpit floor when the plane blew up. We interviewed him in the hospital where he told us what had transpired in the cockpit. He survived the crash, but he was severely hurt and lost one leg in the aftermath.

All that was found of 1st Lt. Ready and his co-pilot were the respective remains of their waist sections still strapped in their seats. And that was what we buried. Not one man who had ever flown with the Bulldog was surprised to learn of his death or the circumstances surrounding his last dance.

---

[22] Aviation Safety Network, Consolidated B-24J *Liberator*, Serial #42-73314, catastrophic crash with two confirmed fatalities at Pandaveswar (India), 24 May 1944. See: https://aviation-safety.net/wikibase/.

Back to the States

On or about June 1ˢᵗ, I was summoned to the Orderly Room where I received word from the Group Adjutant that orders were being cut to return me to the States to go on a War Bond tour. I couldn't believe it. Why me?

I was also told that if I chose not to return to the States and agreed to stay on, I could expect another stripe (i.e., promotion to Technical Sergeant). He gave me until the next day to mull the offer over. Having been an enlisted man for over three years and a Sergeant for half that time, I was somewhat skeptical (maybe even a tad cynical) about the prospects of receiving another stripe anytime soon.

I reckoned there was only a very small chance for an Armorer/Gunner being both a Technical Sergeant and a member of a combat crew. On the one hand, I also felt I would be welching on the rest of the crew I had come overseas with, even though we seldom got to fly as a part of the same crew. After all, they would have to remain either for the duration of hostilities or until they were maimed or wounded seriously enough to be shipped home. On the other hand, none of them had been shot down as was my fate.

Heading into the summer months in 1944, things were starting to heat up in the CBI Theater of Operations. The vanguard of a B-29 outfit was already in the CBI and British forces were making headway in retaking Burma. While I knew the theater could use all the experienced hands it could recruit and retain, I was soon to be a father for the first time and decided against rolling the dice one more time.

End of Tour

I decided it would be better to return home and go on tour. Simple as that, I decided to accept the Adjutant's offer, orders were cut, and I was ordered to leave for Calcutta and return to the States. I was promptly taken off flight status and turned in all my flying gear.

Peterson had been transferred to Karachi and completed his tour in a non-combat role. He never flew another combat mission, but it must be noted that Peterson was flying his 73ʳᵈ aerial combat mission (yes, it was his 73ʳᵈ mission.) the day we were shot down. For my money, Peterson had earned his twilight tour on the ground and behind the lines.

T/SGT Royall E. Peterson (l) and
S/SGT Floyd R. ("Russ") Mulvany (r)
April 20, 1944

T/SGT Roland D. Guffin
Radio Operator/Nose Turret Gunner
March 1944

At the time, it seemed as though everyone else in the 493rd was wise to the policy which precluded airmen who had survived the downing of their aircraft as a result of combat action from being reassigned to flight status. Except for yours truly, of course, and it also might explain why I was *"offered"* the opportunity to return home to do the bond tour. In retrospect, it seemed to me that the offer was part of a *"cover your ass"* (CYA) exercise on the part of higher authorities because it had been a mistake to send me back into combat that spring.

Shortly before I separated from the 493rd, a certifiable *miracle* happened. There was a special delivery of ice crème delivered to the base. Someone confided to me that henceforth, ice crème was to be a regular-issue item from that point forward. Yup, I had struck out again.

D-Day Invasion

I arrived in Calcutta on the morning of 6 June 1944. I took a carriage from the train station to the hotel. I was cleared to return home. As I approached the entrance to the hotel, a British Major rode by on a bicycle and hollered, *"Have you heard, they've invaded Europe?"* All I could think to say was, *"So, what?"* My response didn't please him too much as he struck a *"put out"* pose in reply to my tepid response to his news.

At that moment, I couldn't have cared less what the Major might have thought of me. Up to that day, I felt, the European Theater of Operations had received everything it needed and now it was their turn to feel the heat. For those of us who had been serving in the CBI, there was little compassion for our brethren in Europe who were about to be heavily and hotly engaged.

Stateside Rendezvous

I left Calcutta on 7 June and returned to the States by the same route by which we had come over with the *"Impatient Virgin."* On this trip, I was simply a passenger hitching a ride aboard a C-47 transport. When my plane landed in Agra, home of the Taj Mahal, it was 119 degrees in the shade. From Calcutta, we flew to Karachi, where we boarded a C-87 aircraft a couple of days later bound for home.

The C-87 *Liberator Express* was the cargo/passenger variant of the B-24. Its inside had been gutted and seats were installed. As I recall, my seat was in the bomb bay area. The whole way home, I had an uneasy feeling that I was about to be dumped out at any moment. Mercifully, that didn't happen. I made it back to West Palm Beach about 10 days later no worse for the wear.

Endnotes

(1) In the years following war, Mulvany actively supported the efforts of Mrs. Lucy Winkler, mother of the deceased, to obtain financial redress from the US government. In spite of sworn eyewitness testimony and affidavits filed attesting to Winkler's death, the War Department officially listed Winkler as "missing-in-action" (MIA) for several months following the date of his actual death. His mother, Mrs. Winkler was therefore, arguably, entitled to collect his monthly salary allotments until such time as his status was changed from MIA to "killed-in-action" (KIA). Once declared dead, Winkler's mother was entitled to collect the $10,000.00 proceeds from his GI life insurance policy.

In a letter addressed to the Commanding General, Army Air Forces [sic], Washington 25, D.C., dateline Wilmot, Arkansas, dated July 12, 1944, Mrs. Winkler wrote:

> *"Dear Sir,"*
>
> *"I can't understand why I get a message of Warren's death, then missing in action and no one of his crew knew of his disappearance when Warren's friends wrote us, we know it must be true about his death and I don't know why there should be a letter stating missing in action when the men, members of his crew, were witness to his death.*
>
> *It just makes it more pain and agony to get these messages of hopes and then to go over it again and suffer.*
>
> *I have received no allotment in two months and it is working a hardship on me.*
>
> *Please give me more facts if you can.*
>
> *Yours truly,*
>
> */s/Mrs. Lucy Winkler"*

It is unknown whether Mrs. Winkler ever obtained any of the benefits due from the War Department. In connection with the Winkler affair, please see also the final few paragraphs of endnote (9) below.

(2) In 1988, the author was reunited with Royall E. Peterson, Flight Engineer on the fateful mission of April 5, 1944. It was through this encounter that he learned that a crew member who had been shot down, survived, and returned to duty were by regulation not supposed to fly any more combat missions. No wonder, the author remarked, *"I never saw Peterson or others after we were released from hospital. For whatever reason, I was returned to the squadron. While there, I was afforded the 'opportunity' to fly at least five more missions before someone noticed I no longer belonged to the tribe."*

(3) In 1990, the author attended a reunion of the 7th Bombardment Group (H) in Las Vegas, NV, where he renewed his acquaintance with his former Pilot Major Robert G. ("Bob") Bailey.

(4) Information contained in this chapter concerning missions flown, days, dates, and results related thereto was derived from the "USAAF Worldwide Operations Chronology: Combat Chronology of the US Army Air Forces, China – Burma – India (CBI) Theater of Operations, 1941 – 1945." Published online by Jack McKillop USAF, based on original work completed by Kit Carter and Robert Mueller (1973), it is referenced here as a research aid for all those interested in the activities of the USAAF in World War II.

See: http://aircrewremembered.com/USAAFCombatOperations/Mar.45.html

See: http://www.afhra.af.mil/ Maurer, Maurer. "Air Force Combat Units of World War II." Maxwell Air Force Base, Alabama: Office of Air Force History, 1983. ISBN 0-89201-092-4

(5) Unless otherwise noted within the body of the text, it is to be understood that all photographs contained in this work are drawn either from the author's private collections or the public domain and none are subject to any known copyright restrictions.

(6) Map of Southeast Asia with flight path overlay by former Captain Henry ("Hank") P. Mitchell, US Army Air Forces, Tenth Air Force, 7th Bombardment Group, 493rd Bomber Squadron, Navigator, Mission #1962, April 5, 1944. Image courtesy of the National Geographic Society.

(7) Original sketch included in the Captain H. P. Mitchell's After-Action Report, entitled "A Ditching in the Bay of Bengal", filed 10 April 1944 in connection with Mission #1962.

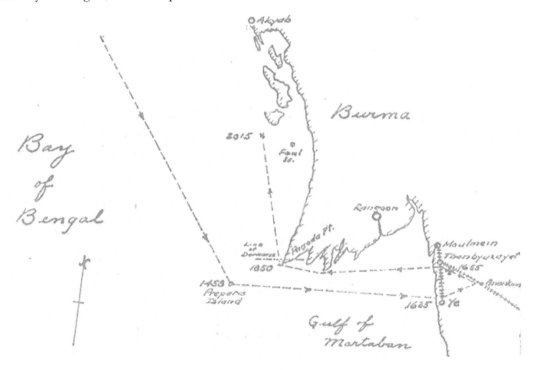

(8) Original maps, sixteen (16) in number, were generated by the Great Circle Mapper © online tool kit (http://www.gcmap.com/). Copyright © 1995-2011, 2014, 2015, 2018, Karl L. Swartz. Permission requested by editor on behalf of author via email to Swartz on 2019.10.05; permission granted to author by Karl L. Swartz on 2019.10.16.

(9) In the early stages of editing and fact-checking the author's manuscript, I was intrigued to learn that neither the author nor any of his fellow crew members had ever learned much about the RAF unit responsible for their discovery and eventual rescue. It was known to be the "No. 354 Squadron", but there was a war going on and no one ever quite got around to looking up their whereabouts. On several occasions, Russ had confided that he sure wished it would have been possible to have met those fellows and personally thanked them for their favor.

In May 2018, I decided to surf the Internet for clues concerning the origins and fate of the No. 354 Squadron. It took about one week to track down the unit and to identify pertinent historical resources, viz., a two-volume manuscript entitled ***No. 354 Squadron RAF – SEAC '43 – '45, "A Record of Their Operations"***, by R. G. Quirk [Draft Edition - 2003]. Volume I weighed in at 300 pages. It was an unadorned chronological operational history of the unit, a compendium of verbatim after-action reports (AARs) drawn from the Royal Air Force's [Standard] Form 541, from the date of the formation of No. 354 Squadron at Karachi (Drigh Road) on 06 July 1943; its arrival at Cuttuck (Odisha) on 01 August 1943; and its disbanding at Cuttack on 18 May 1945. RAF Station Cuttuck was located roughly 300 statute miles (490 km) south of the USAAF, 7th Bombardment Group's HQ at Pandaveswar Air Base (West Bengal). Volume II weighed in at about 250 pages. It was a collection of photographs of everyday life taken by the many amateur photographers serving with the No. 354 Squadron during its sojourn at Cuttack.

On the evening of Monday, May 18th, I noticed that the copyright page of the unit history made reference to the fact that Robert G. Quirk, was living in Winnipeg, Manitoba, Canada at the time of the initial publication of the work [2003]. On a lark, fully expecting to draw an empty lot, I made a virtual visit to Manitoba and started vetting the local press, public library, and other sources for clues as to the possible whereabouts of the illustrious R. G. Quirk. At some point late that evening, I literally stumbled upon an email address ("robert@") which seemed too good to be true – particularly in light of the fact that Quirk himself was a World War II RAF veteran likely over 90 years of age and possibly deceased.

Around midnight, I composed an email to "robert@" introducing myself and inquiring as to whether he might be the author of the unit history. Much to my amazement, the following day I received a reply to my email query. His reply was, in essence, *"c'est moi, c'est moi."* While Robert was unable to be of assistance in providing additional contacts, especially with respect to F/O Robert Edward Banks and his crew, he expressed satisfaction that his work had benefited researchers like myself. It was owing to Quirk's scholarship that we were able to learn a bit of the backstory on RAF Squadron 354.

Subsequently, on Wednesday, May 20th, I placed a call to Russ to tell him all about my interaction with Robert Quirk. He was delighted by my news, but quickly added: *"so guess who I heard from on Sunday evening (May 17th)?"* Well, I replied, I have no idea so "hit me with your best shot, pal."

Russ proceeded to tell me that he had received a call from a complete stranger living somewhere in Arkansas. When Russ answered the phone, the caller asked "is this the same Russ Mulvany who was shot down over the Bay of Bengal in April 1944?" Russ replied, yes, who's this? As it turned out, the caller was the nephew of S/SGT Warren B. Winkler.

The younger Mr. Winkler, in his late 70's at the time, was planning to visit Russ in June (2018), but owing to his own health problems cancelled his visit days before his planned arrival in Indian Wells. Russ was really looking forward to meeting Winkler's nephew. We were both hoping to learn how Lucy Winkler's life had played out.

(10) Group Photograph – No. 354 Squadron RAF, Cuttack Air Field, Odisha (Undated)
Courtesy of the Australian War Museum

(11)   Photograph of RAF Flight Officer (F/O) Robert Banks (Canada)

Requiescat in Pace
F/O Robert Banks and Crew
7 May 1944

F/O Robert Banks and his crew were attached to RAF Squadron 354 based at Cuttack Air Field (Odisha). While returning from a routine reconnaissance patrol over the eastern Bay of Bengal, on 6 April 1944, it was Banks who discovered the survivors of the Bailey crew adrift off the western coast of Burma. Banks loitered at the scene for more than 2 perilous hours before being forced from the area by approaching enemy patrol aircraft. By his courageous actions, Banks ensured that USAAF Air-Sea Rescue crews got a good fix on the position of the downed crew and thereby ensured Bailey's crew would live to fight another day. Ironically, thirty-one days later, Banks and his crew were killed/missing in action returning from an *"ill-fated"* mission over the Malay peninsula.

CHAPTER 6

US ARMY AIR FIELD, LAREDO, TX
(JULY – AUGUST 1944)
|
MARCH FIELD, RIVERSIDE, CA
(SEPTEMBER 1944 – APRIL 1946)

**Turret Instructors Course/Aerial Gunnery Instructor/
Training Instructor/Supply Officer/Duty Sergeant/
Aerial Photographer/Applicant-in-Waiting (OCS)**

*"Though a soldier in time of peace
Is like a chimney in summer
What wise man would pluck down his chimney
Because his almanac tells him 'tis the middle of June?"*

Robert Chambers
(1802 – 1871)

I arrived at West Palm Beach on June 20, 1944. It was plain not much had changed since the last time we passed through the Morrison Field (PBI) heading in the opposite direction. My fellow returning service personnel and I were subjected to a debriefing at the hands of some high-nosed First Lieutenant attached to the US Army Air Forces (HQ) Intelligence staff. During my debriefing, he confiscated all my identification cards and related items without offering any explanation. When I asked him why it was necessary to surrender these papers, the essence of his curt reply was that they might be of help to the enemy if they ever got a hold of them. This action only added to my bad feelings about the so-called *"Officer Class."*

The replacement depot in West Palm Beach was a transit facility for servicemen returning from overseas. Support personnel assigned to the depot seemed more intent on moving as many people as quickly as possible, than actually matching individuals with openings related to their respective military occupational specialties. I was assigned as a Turret Instructor to the Army Air Base at Laredo, Texas. There I was, a combat-qualified Aerial Gunnery Instructor, about to become a ground crew member at a base were there were no aircraft.

To add insult to injury, in those days there was almost nothing one could do to get an assignment changed. It seemed to make no difference to them whatsoever that I knew next to nothing about the *inner workings* of gun turrets. Their theory, it seemed, was that I could learn whatever I needed to know at Laredo!

US Army Air Forces
US Army Air Field
Laredo, TX

July – August 1944

The only good thing about the situation was that I had 15 days leave before I had to report. This didn't mean that I had 15 days of actual leave, because it included travel time to Laredo. In any event, I immediately set out for Los Angeles, to visit my parents. About one week later, I set out for March Field in Riverside, California, where I remained until departing for Laredo.

Laredo was a very small border town. As it happened, the base there also hosted an Instructor School for Air Corps enlisted men. Although I was not assigned to the Instructor School as such, my orders actually vaguely indicated that I was to be officially attached to the base cadre. Upon arrival, I was interviewed and informed my interlocuters that I had been told in Florida that I was to go through the Instructor School. My reception committee didn't bother to check my orders thoroughly, so I actually *was* assigned to the school after all. Much to my chagrin, I soon learned that the school's Commandant was the same Major who had given me such a hard time at Las Vegas, before I attended Gunnery School at that airbase (September 1942 – January 1943).

A small world, indeed. *Oh yes*, and he remembered me too. I'm sure he told his instructors to pay close attention to my performance. I had no problems, though, because continuing education had always been a priority from my point-of-view. I really enjoyed learning and it probably showed.

The Turret Instructors Course was a three-week course, which I passed with high marks. Once qualified, we were to be shipped out to become instructors in our own right wherever we were needed. Just before our orders were published, the officer-in-charge of our detail assembled my entire class for a briefing.

S/SGT Floyd R. Mulvany, Jr.
US Army Air Forces
Summer - 1944

During the briefing, the Major announced that he had just received some special orders pertaining to our pending assignments. Anyone who had been classified as an *"Evadee"* from enemy capture was allowed to pick any duty station he wanted. All of us who had been shot down on April 5, 1944, were designated "Evadees" since we had not been captured by the Japanese while floating about in our dinghies.

The Major then asked if there were any such personnel present. Three of us raised our hands. The Major looked directly at me and declared he would thoroughly check our records and then declared, *"If I find any of you SOBs to be lying, I'll have your ass."*

Undaunted by his remarks and a threat that any good officer would not have made to a group of enlisted men, I selected March Field as my next duty station. It was only about 65 miles from my parents' home in Los Angeles.

Aerial Gunnery Instructor
March Field, CA

September 1944 – January 1945

After about five weeks of schooling in Laredo, I arrived back at March Field in September 1944, assigned as an Aerial Gunnery Instructor, and I was put back on flight pay. I flew with crews on B-24 combat training missions at all hours of the day or night. Aerial combat operations were increasing all over the world in the fall of 1944. There was great demand for well-trained crews to off-set persistently high and increasing casualty rates especially in the skies over Europe.

Training was conducted around-the-clock, 24 hours per day, and seven days per week. On average, we lost a B-24 while training every five or six days. Our bombing and gunnery range was in the desert east of Palm Springs, about 70 miles away, in the area that is now known as Indio in the Coachella Valley. It offered nothing but great expanses of tumble weeds and sand. Naturally, all the crews were eager to finish their qualification training as soon as possible so they could get into combat. To do so, there were different types of bombing and gunnery missions they were expected to be able to successfully complete.

We Instructors had the final say-so on gunnery missions – whether they had been successfully completed or not. There were occasions when I flunked the Gunners. Of course, they resented this because it meant they had to re-fly the mission, which could set them back a week or more. Crew officers would occasionally chew me out for my actions. Some would even complain about my performance to my superiors. I didn't mind the complaints, but in some instances a crew would be retroactively marked as *"passing"* when I had failed them. My attitude was that if they were later killed, wounded, or captured, I didn't want it to be my fault. I had seen what had happened to Bulldog, because he had been rated *"qualified"* as a pilot and never, ever, should have been placed in such a leadership position.

In August, I became violently ill with Yellow Jaundice. Evidently, it had been coming on for quite some time. When I returned from India, I weighed 140 pounds, only one pound more than I weighed on the day of my enlistment. I turned yellow from head-to-toe. You couldn't tell where my khakis stopped and I began. I couldn't do anything, so they slapped me in the hospital for three weeks. I was put on a special restricted diet which included no fried foods or alcohol for the next two years. Not having alcohol didn't bother me much, since I didn't drink before that time and still don't to this day.

Following my release from the infirmary, I continued to instruct on B-24s for about six months. With the rank of Staff Sergeant and flight pay, I was earning the magnificent sum of $244.00 a month. Still, I had no car and no money in the bank.

Training Instructor
883rd Bombardment Squadron (H)

February – September 1945

I was transferred to 883rd Bombardment Squadron, a B-29 outfit, which was training combat crews for the war in the Pacific in early 1945. The first time I saw a B-29 close up, I thought it was too big to ever get off the ground. It was the biggest bomber at the time and a very good aircraft.

We had to undergo transition training – ground school first and training flights thereafter. It was commonplace for the B-29, once aloft, to fly for a minimum of seven hours before landing, except for *real* emergencies. It was nothing to fly from March Field to Seattle, Washington, to Phoenix or Tucson, Arizona, and back to March Field. The B-29 was entirely pressurized, except for bomb bay spaces. If necessary, a man could crawl into the wing sections to make repairs to generators, hydraulic systems, and so on during the flight. There was a 40-foot-long tunnel (tube) which stretched from the cockpit to the waist over the bomb bay.

Boeing Aircraft Company
B-29 *"Superfortress"*

(1944)

Individual crew members could transit through the tunnel on a wheeled trolley by pulling along by ropes. There was no way anyone could go into the bomb bay when the aircraft was pressurized. Pressurization could cause problems occasionally in the event that a window or door happened to blow out in flight. If this happened, there was a very good chance that a person would be sucked out unless properly strapped in. For this reason, it was standard operating procedure (SOP) to be strapped in at all times except when traversing the tube. If an individual was in the tunnel when a window or door blew, one would be propelled through the tube like a speeding bullet. In such cases, serious injury was taken as a given and death was a real possibility. Unfortunately, there were a number of cases with gunners being sucked out, hanging outside the aircraft secured only by a safety belt, while being slammed against the fuselage before being hauled to safety. Life threatening dangers were ever present in military aviation, even in peacetime.

S/SGT Floyd R. Mulvany, Jr. (r) and

S/SGT Willy (*"Put 'in on the Ritz"*) Waldman (l)

Reunited – October 1945 [1]

I remember one flight, in particular, when we were repeatedly just landing and taking off (aka, *"shooting landings"*), better known as *"touch-and-goes"* today. We had just landed when the tires on the right-side landing gear blew out. Rubber shards flew all over the place and gigantic sparks sprang from the wheel rims. This might have caused one nasty explosion, but for the fact that we managed somehow to cheat the hangman. We made more landings accompanied by engines which were aflame than I care to recall or recount.

---

[1] While serving with the Eighth USAAF, Waldman's B-17G, was disabled during a mission somewhere over Germany in late 1944. Lacking the capability to make it back to its base in England, Waldman's crew made an emergency landing in neutral Switzerland. He and his crew mates were interred as prisoners of war (POWs) and lodged at a 'nice' hotel in the Alps until May 1945. Once the *'cat was out of the bag'*, Waldman became a frequent target of good-natured ribbing from his former gunnery mates at March Field for ... *"Put 'in on the Ritz"*.

On May 8, 1945, we had just taken off on a training flight when word arrived over the radio that the war in Europe was over. Would we be permitted to go around and land so that we could join in the celebrations which had already broken out on the ground? No way, instead, we were compelled to log our mandatory seven hours in the air, before we were granted permission to land. By the time we returned to March Field, the celebrations were pretty much over and done.

In the weeks that followed, we ferried a few B-29s from March Field to Davis-Monthan Air Base at Tucson, Arizona, where there were already several B-29 squadrons. On one trip, there were several WACs heading to March Field and we were ordered to ferry them with us on our return trip. In those days, it was all but taboo to fly with a female aboard a combat aircraft. We enlisted men objected to this order because we were thoroughly indoctrinated in the notion that having females on board was a bad omen. Our objections were overruled and so we made the best of the situation.

All of the WACs wore skirts and the only parachutes we had for them were the seat pack type. We had a ball fastening the leg straps on them with their skirts hiked way up. All of us tried our very best to keep straight faces. For their part, the WACs were so serious about it all that they never realized either how they appeared to us or how much fun we were having at their expense. We had impressed upon them that they could not move around once they were onboard and that all we had were relief tubes built for males, not females. They dutifully got on board wearing their chutes and sat motionless until we reached March Field. Since we made it back safely, so much for female 'bad luck.'

As it turned out, it was the only time I ever flew with women during my entire time in either the US Army Air Corps or US Army Air Forces. [2] Once the war was over, I was fortunate to have been able to stay at March Field and in the US Army Air Forces. In early 1945, the manpower situation for the Infantry in Europe was so desperate that stern measures were taken to corral enough bodies to fill out the thinning ranks. A

---

[2] The United States Army Air Forces (USAAF), successor to the United States Army Air Corps (USAAC), was established by an Act of Congress on June 20, 1941. Its successor, the United States Air Force (USAF), was established as a separate branch of the U. S. Armed Forces by an Act of Congress, with the passage of the National Security Act of 1947, on September 18, 1947. For a thorough overview of all USAF antecedents, see: https://en.wikipedia.org/wiki/United_States_Air_Force.

great many enlisted men were transferred from March Field to the Infantry at Camp Anza across town, given two weeks of Infantry training, and then shipped to Europe as replacements for troops repatriating for discharge stateside.

These men were of all ranks, from Master Sergeant to Private. I was not transferred because I was declared to be essential to the Air Corps training mission as an Aerial Gunnery Instructor. In the process of rationalizing the Army's force structure, the entire Air Corps was being hollowed out, including the Aviation Cadet Program. There were just simply too many cadets and too few Infantrymen. I continued to instruct on B-29s until the war ended on September 2, 1945.

With the surrender of Japan, everything having to do with the massive war effort came to an abrupt halt. With respect to my own duties, no more crew training was required and so my position was made redundant. In practical terms, I was immediately taken off flight status and summarily my pay was reduced to around $177.00 a month.

Supply Clerk
Squadron Supply Group

October 1945 – January 1946

Since there was no longer any flying to do, they had to find some form of work to keep us occupied. I was assigned to inventorying and maintaining life rafts (perhaps because I was intimately acquainted with their maintenance, deployment, and use?). Subsequently, I was assigned to the Squadron Supply Group, where we were kept busy processing all the clothing and equipment being turned in by the men being discharged.

It was a big operation, especially in light of the fact that the American Army had long been known to quickly disband once the hour of national crisis was past. Being Regular Army, I was in for the war plus however long the government felt I was needed. For the time being, at least, I did not have to worry about being discharged. At the same time, the tens of thousands of draftees were leaving the Army, literally in droves. We had tens of millions of dollars' worth of clothing and equipment that had to be sorted, inventoried, packed, and either stored or declared 'surplus' and shipped out.

In 1945, I was told my enlistment was up. By that time, I had served four years and ten months. Since I was in for thirty years, I immediately re-enlisted and received $815.00 in re-enlistment bonus money. I made good use of the windfall. I had never seen that many bucks at one time in my entire life. I was also given a 90-day re-enlistment furlough.

Naturally, I had signed up for duty at March Field again, because it was located so close to where my immediate family were living. During my re-enlistment furlough, I managed to find a temporary job with United Parcel Service (UPS) making deliveries in the Los Angeles area. I had worked for their messenger service in Hollywood prior to my enlistment, so I also enjoyed some seniority, in addition to having priority as a veteran. I made $50.00 a week, which came in real handy.

Duty Sergeant
420th Air Base Squadron

February – March 1946

I returned to duty in February 1946 and was assigned as Duty Sergeant in the 420th Air Base Squadron. Officially, I was a "pencil pusher." It seemed to me that almost everyone who had re-enlisted in the Army had joined the Air Corps. Suddenly, we were being taken over by people from every other branch of the Army. What all these newcomers were going to do was beyond my comprehension. Since there were almost no Privates or Privates First Class (PFCs), this meant that Corporals, Sergeants, and Staff Sergeants were soon being assigned to KP, fatigue detail, and guard duty.

From my perspective, this reality gave rise to a totally unsatisfactory situation which had an immediate and decidedly negative impact on good order and discipline. When NCOs are treated as Privates, then morale and discipline are bound to suffer. It is impossible for an NCO to command the respect of Privates when he is pulling KP and hauling garbage with him. I didn't like my job or anything about it because, for one thing, I was the one who had to replace those NCOs on such details.

Fortunately, I still possessed my photography MOS which enabled me to soon be transferred to the newly organized 1st Jet Group as a Photographer. This jet group was the first ever in the US Army Air Forces. Jet planes were a brand-new item in 1946.

Aerial Photographer, 1st Jet Group/
Applicant-in-Waiting, Officer Candidate School (OCS)

March – April 1946

Although I was unable to get on flying status, being a photographer again sure beat being in a clerk in the base squadron. I soon learned, however, that there were five Master and Sergeants First Class in the Photo Section to whom I would be subordinate. Before long, I also figured out that I had more time on active duty than any of them. Moreover, I soon discovered not one of them had ever been in combat or served as part of a combat crew. It quickly became clear that I would probably not get promoted for a very long time (if ever again). Still, I was determined to give my new assignment a run for its money.

After two months in the 1st Jet Group, I made up my mind that I'd have to take a chance on something else if I was ever to rise above the rank of Staff Sergeant. My only option at the time appeared to be Officer Candidate School. As fate would have it, it was an especially good time to go for a commission. At this stage of my career, attendance at the US Military Academy at West Point was no longer an option. Nevertheless, in the immediate post-war years, so many officers had been discharged, there were a great many openings for Second Lieutenants. In fact, it seemed as though Second Lieutenants were as scarce as Privates.

There was never any doubt in my mind that I could meet all the required standards to earn my commission. I knew I could surpass all the mental and physical requirements. It meant a long hard pull, but I was confident in my ability to make the grade. When the time came, I applied for Officer Training in the Infantry, Armor, and Army Air Forces Administrative. Applicants had to specify three choices, by order of preference, whether they liked it or not.

The First Lieutenant to whom I presented my paperwork made a snide remark about my brain needing an examination for putting in for the Infantry ahead of the US Army Air Forces Administrative. I answered by stating that if I couldn't fly, it made little sense to remain in the Air Corps. In fact, I told him that the only *real* Air Corps was the flying one. At that point, it must have dawned on him that I hadn't really appreciated his smart aleck commentary.

The Lieutenant then proceeded to tell me that I would have to pass a mental acuity test with a score of 110 or above. Subsequently, I would have to be interviewed and approved by a board of high-ranking officers. Finally, I would have to pass a rigorous physical examination. I do believe he was trying to impress me with the fact that it was not easy to become an officer and that not just *anyone* could do it. I listened to all his jazz without being the least bit impressed. I had been in the Army much longer than he had. I was a combat veteran and he was not. In my early years, I never failed to wear my Purple Heart Medal when called upon to interact with overly pretentious and officious types.

A few days later, at the appointed hour, I was handed a sealed envelope which contained my OCS mental acuity test. I was escorted to a room where I was to be locked up alone until the exam was completed. What they failed to tell me was that there was a construction crew at work in an adjacent room creating quite a racket. Hammers were pounding, saws were buzzing, drills were whirring, and their banter was loud and boisterous. My powers of concentration were sorely tested, but it was not long before I had completely tuned out the distractions.

I don't know whether I was placed in that particular room on purpose, but in the end it really didn't matter. My final test score was 134, one point higher than my I.Q. score of 133, and 24 points more than the 110 points necessary to qualify for OCS. On top of that, it turned out that the fitness board was chaired by the same Colonel Felix M. Hardison who had commanded my B-24 training group at Biggs Field (August – December 1943).

When Colonel Hardison learned that I had trained in his former command at Biggs Field, I could do no wrong. There was no way I could fail to pass muster with the board. In fact, I sailed through the entire interview process without any hitches. When it was over, all five of its Board Officers endorsed my fitness to attend OCS. Colonel Hardison shook my hand and wished me well.

With two obstacles out of the way, I prepared to take on the third, my physical examination which didn't worry me a bit. I had successfully passed many such tests simply to remain on flight status. This one turned out to be no different than any others, there was nothing wrong with me, and I passed with flying colors. Within

30 days, I received orders to report to the Infantry School at Fort Benning, GA. All my friends at March Field immediately started treating me differently. To them, I was already an officer. They did not even think about me having to take 17 weeks of training and guff and passing all my tests before I could *actually* become an officer.

From that point onward, it was "*hello*" Infantry and "*goodbye*" to the US Army Air Forces.

PART III

US ARMY SERVICE
OCTOBER 31, 1946 – AUGUST 1, 1972

"I offer neither pay, nor quarters, nor food;
I offer only hunger, thirst, forced marches, battles, and death.
Let him who loves his country with his heart, and
Not merely with his lips, follow me."

Giuseppe Marie Garibaldi
(1807 – 1882)

CHAPTER 7

FORT BENNING, GA
(MAY 1946 – APRIL 1947)

Officer Candidate School
(May – October 1946) |
Tactical Officer/Instructor, Army Officers Course
(November 1946 – April 1947)

"Here lie the bones of Ranger Jones: A graduate of this institution.
He died last night in his first firefight, when he applied the school solution."

Saying at U.S. Army Ranger School

I caught a train for the long ride to Columbus, Georgia and ended up in a car full of sailors from the West Coast In general, members of the armed forces of all stripes who were returning home for discharge traveled by train. Aboard this particular train, it seemed that I was the only Army type around.

We started playing blackjack and didn't stop until we arrived in Kansas City, Missouri, two days later. By the time we arrived, I had cleaned them out. I had suggested two or three times that we quit while they still had some bucks in their pockets. They opted to continue playing, betting they had a shot to get even with me at some point. None of them did. By the time I got off the train in Kansas City, I walked away with over $300.00.

I was met at the station by my aunt and several local girls with whom I was socially acquainted. My new found Swabbie pals couldn't believe that one guy could be so lucky: heading off to OCS, winning all their money, and being met at the station by so many females. To be honest, I couldn't believe my good fortune any more than anyone else. The money and the girls were a complete surprise to me, but admittedly a welcome one. I was only changing trains in Kansas City, so there was scarcely enough time to kiss all the girls 'hello', chit chat a bit, and hug and kiss each of them goodbye. As it happened, my aunt was the only one of that group I ever laid eyes on again.

From Kansas City, we traveled to Chicago, Illinois. During the layover in Chicago, I visited the USO Center located across from Grant Park where I found everything which was available was free to servicemen. I washed up, ate, drank, danced, and had a fantastic time before resuming my cross-country trek bound for the Deep South. I arrived in Columbus at night, which compelled me to spend the evening in town.

I spent the night at the best hotel in town, the Ralston, and was treated like any ordinary enlisted man at a General's party. It was clear the hotel manager could not refuse me a room because I was White and had the cash money in-hand to pay in advance. It was equally not difficult to see, however, that enlisted men were not among their preferred clientele. Such an attitude on his part only stiffened my resolve to be served properly. I pulled my $300.00 wad of cash out of my pocket for effect, then tossed the necessary amount on the counter before scooping up the key to my room. I departed for Fort Benning early the following morning.

In 1946, Columbus was a small nondescript rural town which was heavily reliant on Fort Benning for its economic survival. Local inhabitants made no secret of their red-necked attitudes, their hatred of colored folks, as well as their suspicion and distain for outsiders. Police were a menace to anyone hailing from out-of-town. Bullying, clubbing, hitting, and the shooting of strangers and undesirables was commonplace.

The fact that Columbus was heavily reliant on Fort Benning for its economic well-being appeared to have little effect on local attitudes towards outsiders. In general, soldiers of all stripes, especially we enlisted types, were treated rather poorly. Officers were treated somewhat better, as a class, because they were regarded as so-called gentlemen. It was a relief to know that I wouldn't be required to spend much time in Columbus.

Officer Candidate School
OCS Class #543
May – October 1946

My class at OCS was #543, the 543rd OCS class to train at Fort Benning since the school was opened in 1942. We were the next-to-last class to actually receive 17 weeks of combat Infantry training in order to earn our commissions. Training was 98 percent tactics and two percent administration. This meant, of course, it would be necessary for us to acquire our administrative skills later through on-the-job (OJT) training. There was something like 283 men from all branches of the Army in my class. Twelve of us were NCOs and only seven of those had served in combat.

Everyone at OCS was a volunteer. Most candidates in my class were draftees putting in their two years of service. If one were required to serve, then why not do so as an officer? Draftees typically came in for two years active-duty service and, if qualified, they could apply for a commission. If successful, such individuals would be required to serve an additional two years from the date of their commission. Graduates of the Military Academy at West Point, on the other hand, had to serve only five years, but then consider the education they received essentially 'for free.' If they chose to extend their respective tours, that decision was at their sole prerogative.

Naturally, we NCOs gravitated towards one another as old soldiers are wont to do everywhere. We knew we were in for some chicken shit and kid's stuff because that's the way the game was played. As NCOs, we understood the situation and could handle the challenges well. On the other hand, draftees were at an inherent disadvantage. Many found the environment difficult to cope with effectively. The saying was, *"If you want to give orders, then first you must learn how to take them."* Because everyone was a volunteer, if you didn't like it, you could volunteer to quit the program.

Our Company Commander and Platoon Leaders were combat Infantry veterans to a man. We respected them. As it turned out, I was one of only two candidates who were from the Air Corps. One of the few who had been awarded a Purple Heart Medal, too. Both considerations earned me the added respect of others.

When I reported for duty, I weighed in at about 175 pounds. During the previous year, I had grown a bit pudgy, especially while doing supply and photography work at

March Field. However, the excess weight soon disappeared as at OCS, whether you moved one foot or one mile, every movement was executed *"double time"* (i.e., running). Nobody walked anywhere, unless we were marching in ranks.

The first day of formal training, for example, we ran two miles without a break. We did a minimum of one hour of physical training every day in addition to running, bayonet drill, obstacle courses, and close order drill. If one failed to keep up with the physical demands of the daily regimen, one was simply 'boarded out.' We lost many individuals because they lacked the physical endurance to keep pace. Infantry OCS was no picnic. The Infantry was very physical because it had to be that way. An Infantry Officer had to be in as good or better physical condition than any man in his unit, especially young lieutenants whose job it was to bear most of the hard work in the field.

We had inspections every day on every piece of our bedding, books, clothing, and equipment. There existed, of course, a prescribed method of arranging everything (books, clothes, boots, equipment, and bedding). There was the only one acceptable way to get things done. Any other way was wrong and demerits were the reward for screwing up. Three demerits on any inspection bought the transgressor extra duty (physical, of course). If required to make an explanation in writing explaining why things were wrong the only correct answer was *"No Excuse, Sir"*. In any event, one's explanation was required to guarantee that the same transgression would not be repeated – *ever* again.

The first two weeks found nobody without some specific job. This was done deliberately in order to teach us in detail how tasks were to be accomplished and to impress upon each of us that there could be no excuses for anything an officer did wrong. These gigs were later disregarded in the reckoning of one's overall demerits, but we didn't know this at the time. Needless to say, those of us who were determined to earn an officer's commission worked our butts off. No excuses.

To say the very least, it was disheartening to work two or three hours cleaning one's rifle only to have the inspecting officer look through the bore and announce for all the world to hear, *"dirty butt plate."* It was equally disheartening to return from a very long, hard day in the field, to find all of one's clothes, books, blankets, and sheets, dumped out on the floor; along with the entire contents of one's footlocker. In addition to cleaning, one's rifle, boots, and other equipment, everything had to be cleaned, folded, and squared away before *"lights out."* Rare were the times when we were in bed before 1:00 or 2:00 AM. This, in spite of the fact, that taps had been sounded at 10:00 PM. It was harassment, to be sure, but such aggressive intimidation served its purposes.

Could a man take all this crap and still perform the duties which were required of him? Would an individual hold up in the face of adversity? If a man could not deal with such travails in the rather tranquil confines of peacetime, how in the hell could he possibly do so in combat where the lives of others would depend upon his orders and actions?

We lost many who either could not or would not accept this kind of treatment. No one missed them or ever worried about them when they were gone. Some left of their own volition and it was not held against them. Others really tried to perform, but just couldn't hack it. Often, such men were sent back to the ranks as presently unqualified to perform in a commissioned capacity. Later, of course, some of them may have received battlefield commissions in Korea or even as members of the National Guard or Reserves. It was possible.

We had one man in our class, who like me, had begun his Army career in the Air Corps. He was serving in the Philippines when the Imperial Japanese Army attacked the Commonwealth in 1942. Fighting on Bataan as an Infantry soldier, he was bayoneted, captured, and held as a prisoner of war (POW) for the duration of hostilities which ended in September 1945. The fellow suffered from recurring attacks of malarial diseases and nightmares which arose as a result of his years of imprisonment. He really wanted to become an officer and, naturally, we helped him all we could within the bounds of reason and professional ethics. We would offer him support and encouragement and never reported his struggles to the Medics. All the strenuous physical activity had the effect of wearing him down physically and mentally. Eventually, it got to the point that he either had to go to the hospital or die. Once hospitalized he was unable to return to us, though he gave OCS his best shot despite falling short of his goal.

Another man contracted a severe case of poison oak. It affected one of his arms, which swelled to three or four times its normal size and resisted cure. He had it treated, bandaged it up, and tried to carry on with the program. Finally, it got to the point where he was at risk of having the arm amputated. He, too, had to withdraw from the program. Of course, there were other men who gave it all they could, but ultimately, they too were forced to drop the course and return to the enlisted ranks. I am convinced my ROTC training and almost 5 years as an enlisted man made my success at OCS possible. Some individuals, however, were unable to think through a solution on their feet or give a proper order. They simply were not cut out to join the officer ranks.

After a few weeks at OCS, the level and intensity of physical activity stripped away all the excess body fat accumulated during the previous year. I shed roughly twenty pounds, weighing in at a svelte 155 pounds. Within the first few weeks, I had increased my physical stamina and mental toughness. I never had any difficulty giving a command loud enough to be heard and clear enough to be well understood. Many of the younger men had difficulty giving loud commands. On any given night, these young people could be heard out in the woods giving orders to the Georgia pines.

Our Platoon leaders were tough on us, but they were also fair 99% of the time. All of them had had combat commands, so they knew first-hand what it took to be an officer and a leader of men in the field. It often seemed as though all of our Platoon Leaders could run all day and scarcely break a sweat or suffer from shortness of breath. If anyone fouled up or was caught talking when they ought to have been listening, or otherwise doing whatever improperly, our Platoon Leaders would take all of us out on a *"speed march"* to shape us up.

A speed march entailed double timing with all of our equipment (i.e., steel helmets, rifles and bayonet works, packs, clipboards and books, etc.) for as long as they thought it necessary to command our undivided attention. At times, I saw men collapse on speed marches with their tongues the color purple and literally hanging out of their mouths. It was a wonder that no one ever died from exhaustion, because Georgia in the summertime is often hotter than blue blazes. Several men did end up in the infirmary and some never returned to the company. Personally, I never really felt such marches served any really good purpose and the costs associated with such activities seemed to outweigh any benefits.

As an officer, I never imposed such a routine on the men under my command – unless, of course, ordered to do so. It didn't take long for me and the other NCOs to come to terms with what we thought were superfluous exercises. Examples of which included: polishing the soles of one's boots; retrieving dirt from the cracks in the floor with a tooth brush; shining the inside of our rifles even though the parts would not be seen; and tightening the blankets on our bunks so a coin flipped upon them would bounce on contact.

Each man had to have at least one written report on him every day. These reports were characterized as *"observations."* Observation reports were used as the primary means for determining if a man was proper officer material. We were given a different leadership assignment every three days, e.g., Squad Leader, Platoon Sergeant, or Company Commander, etc. Whatever the assignment, one was held responsible for taking all actions and giving all orders necessary to ensure the accomplishment of a given mission.

We were rated on our ability to effectively lead and command, to solve problems, and to devise solutions to any challenges which might arise in the course of the exercise. We were also graded on military bearing, command voice, and our ability to supervise the proper execution of our orders. In total, there were 22 tactical exercises as well as practical tests and written examinations. Such proficiency exercises covered weapons, map reading, scouting, patrolling, etc.

We learned to call in artillery fire, adjust artillery pieces, drive a 45-ton tank, operate radios, and operate, maintain, assemble, and disassemble all weapons in the Infantry's arsenal. Weapons training included pistols, carbines, M1 rifles, sub-machine guns, 57mm and 75mm recoilless rifles, 60mm and 81mm mortars, various types of hand and rifle grenades, and water- and air-cooled .30 caliber and .50 caliber machine guns. We fired and employed them all tactically. We learned what they wanted us to learn and gave it back to them.

I went through all of OCS without receiving any demerits after those first two weeks. Our Platoon Leaders were not after us, rather they respected us as NCOs, especially those of us who had been in combat. Our Platoon Leaders *knew* we NCO-type OCS candidates *knew* the score. They took care to teach the inexperienced draftees what they would need to learn the hard way, but in spite of their efforts a few draftees made it through OCS, who probably should not have made the grade. We knew who they were, but we never could quite figure out how they managed to meet the standards for graduation. Our class, OCS # 543, started out with 283 men in June. In October, on graduation day, only 87 men were left standing. Fewer than one man in three made the grade and went on to receive their commissions in the United States Army.

At the end of two months' training, I was in absolutely prime physical condition. I could run 5 to 10 miles with full equipment without breathing hard, do 72 sit ups in less than two minutes, crawl 40 yards under barbed wire on my elbows and knees in less than 12 seconds, do fifty pushups on two hands or 20 on either one hand or the other, etc. Whatever was demanded of me, I could easily accomplish, with one exception: I could only do six pullups. I never did understand this limitation. Six was all that was required, but to my amazement I could barely make this minimal fitness standard. Later while serving as a Second Lieutenant at Fort Benning, I was finally was able to increase my total to 12 pullups.

Commissioning as a Second Lieutenant
Thursday – October 31, 1946

Fort Benning, GA

On October 31, 1946, the 87 of us who remained were commissioned as Second Lieutenants in the Infantry. My new serial number as O (for officer) 1341355. I was now a hot-shot 2nd *"Louie"* with over $400.00 worth of new uniforms.

2nd LT. Floyd R. Mulvany, Jr.
Fort Benning, GA
November - 1946

In those days, there were several different types of uniform which were authorized. First, there was the *"Pink and Greens."* This was an everyday duty uniform which consisted of pink (taupe) colored slacks, green (OD) blouse with matching cloth belt, OD colored brown billed service cap, brown shoes, and khaki shirt and tie. What a snappy looking uniform. Next, we had all *"Greens."* This uniform consisted of a dark green *"Ike"* jacket with matching slacks and overseas cap, a khaki shirt, green tie, and brown shoes. Then we also had the all *"Pink"* uniform with matching slacks and shirt.

All the uniforms were handsome and, of course, mine were all tailored and properly fitted. We had a $200.00 allowance to buy uniforms, but I spent over $400.00. I also purchased a Pink overcoat. I can testify to the fact that these uniforms never wore out or frayed during the ensuing eleven years they were authorized for wear. One cannot make the same claim about the Army Green uniform which replaced them.

Ours was the next to last 17-week OCS class. Thereafter, the course lasted 26 weeks and became a basic officer training and indoctrination course rather than one restricted to the Infantry arm. All Army Officer Candidates matriculated in this course to learn basic Infantry tactics. If they successfully completed this school, then they went on to their branch basic school, e.g., Artillery, Armor, Signal Corps, Quartermaster/Supply, Ordnance, etc.

Post-Graduation Celebration and
Transition Days

October – November 1946

Following our graduation, we had a company party to celebrate our shared success in making it through OCS on Friday, November 1ˢᵗ. It was a big affair which was held at a wooded lodge some distance from Columbus. There was plenty of booze, food, women, and music.

Everyone was transported to and from the site on buses provided by the school. No one wanted to run the risk of anything going amiss with any of us so close to our pending commissioning. It was anticipated there would be more than a few of us consuming a few too many during the festivities. As things played out, the party was a dandy, a good time was had by all, notwithstanding the lingering after effects of 'one too many' on the part of a few. As it happened, the whiskey being served that evening was real rot gut.

All stages of inebriation were reflected in the long list of casualties, from mild to severe. Eyeballs could be observed peering in all directions and revolving anywhere from 45- to 360-degrees. Tongues had the thickness of tundra. Speech was widely impaired. Words were unintelligible by varying degrees. 'Blackouts' were commonplace among the celebrants as bodies were gradually rendered supine. Some stumbled out the doors in search of fresh air, only to tumble down the slopes towards the lake below. Others became entwined with one another under the tables, over porch railings, and in the grass. Alas, even the bus drivers got stoned and passed out.

Three or four candidates who claimed they were not *"out-of-it"* volunteered to drive the buses back to our barracks. Company officers had little choice except to permit them to do so. It really was a scramble to round up all of the troops and get them loaded on the buses. Once on the buses, we were soon weaving our way down the road. Several men were gripped by the heaves and so it was to the windows with them. Since no one was eager to hold their heads while they heaved, their heads were simply shoved out the windows with their chins propped up beneath their forearms. Why no one choked to death is anybody's guess.

Thank God the following day was a holiday, because 95 % of out graduating class would not have made it out the doors of the barracks. Oh, and one body was found to be missing when an impromptu head count was taken. He was found the next morning under a bush down by the lake – still passed out.

Tactical Officer/Instructor
Army Officers Course #1

November 1946 – April 1947

Five of us from my class were assigned as Tactical Officers to the first six-month class. Two of us were assigned to the same company. And, believe it or not, my platoon of candidates was assigned to the same barracks which I had lived in all through OCS.

At the time, there were several changes made for the 26-week course. First, the curriculum included many more administrative subjects such as supply, food administration, military justice, records, and reports. Second, a successful graduate could choose his branch of service rather than automatically becoming an Infantry Officer. This latter change was a necessary step since all other Army OCS schools had been dissolved. Henceforth, Fort Benning was to train OCS officers for the entire Army. Third, candidates could come directly from either induction or through enlistment in the Army.

Newcomers to the Army, right-off-the-street, no longer were required to have even one day of duty in a unit before putting in for OCS. All a man had to do was volunteer to attend OCS, either at the time of his enlistment or when he received his draft notice. This last change made for a real difference in the type of men who came through OCS. There were quite a few, in fact, who had no idea of what the Army was all about. Many of these same individuals did not care to learn. If they had to serve, they would be officers, not enlisted men. There were also some men who had served anywhere from one to ten years before putting in for a chance for a commission. We even had two Warrant Officers in this first class – AOC #1 or, Army Officers Course #1.

Since the centralized concept of OCS training was new, there were a lot of bugs to be ironed out so procedures could be established for the classes which would follow. It was a great opportunity for me to learn the administrative policies and procedures from the ground up, which heretofore we had not been formally taught, and to review all manner of tactical problems and weapons systems, etc. I was very fortunate to be one of the five individuals selected to run the incoming candidates through the new course.

One thing was certain, we Tactical Instructors knew what needed to be done and how to get things done because we had already successfully navigated the process ourselves. Plus, I knew every inch of the platoon barracks. I knew where all the dust and dirt collected and the best means of cleaning everything. After all, I had literally *"done it all"* before by the sweat of my own brow. Then as now, I felt a commission was not something to be given away. It had to be earned.

I made no bones about my position, thus anybody who couldn't hack it would be recommended for elimination and returned to the ranks. I eliminated a total of

42 men whom I determined were not deemed to be officer material. All men up for elimination were brought before a Board of Officers who made the final determination as to whether such individuals could stay in the program or would be returned to the ranks. None of my recommendations for dismissal were ever reversed.

In the first two weeks of the class, we lost the two Warrant Officers. Neither of them really wanted a commission. Their warrants were really good enough for a career. No one was *"Boarded Out"* during the first two weeks because it was not enough time to determine whether an individual really had the right stuff. There were some, however, who just quit because they discovered that it wasn't going to be easy to make the grade.

As a Tactical Officer, it was my job to observe each man in my platoon every day and note in writing at least one observation per day. Another part of the job was to offer practical advice and encouragement where appropriate, and to advise others when it was time to consider quitting the program because they were unlikely to be able to go the distance and make the cut. On the other hand, we bent over backwards for some men who had the potential and only needed a little encouragement to bring out the best in them. I was a tough task master, a hard grader, but always strived to be fair. The Army had been whittled down to peacetime strength. We had to ensure that it was the best it could be in order to survive under peacetime conditions.

Second Lieutenants have always been the life blood of the Officer Corps. As Instructors, we were guided by the principle that only good ones would be of any value to the Army. Our hours were very long every day. All our reports and other paperwork had to be completed after regular duty hours were over. As young Lieutenants, we stuck together since our rank was not very high on the Army social scale. We made our own good times and stayed late at parties, so we could cut loose after most of the older officers retired from the scene.

Since I had over five years of active duty at the time of my commission, I drew a First Lieutenant's pay right away -- $225.00 a month. Nobody ever said I'd get rich in the Army. I didn't.

CHAPTER 8

REPUBLIC OF PANAMÁ
CANAL ZONE (CZ)
(MAY 1947 – APRIL 1950)

33rd Infantry Regiment, Regimental Aide-de-Camp (May 1947) | Company A – Rifle Platoon Leader (June – August 1947) | Headquarters Company – Intelligence & Reconnaissance (I&R) Platoon Leader (September – October 1947) | Company D – Heavy Weapons Section Platoon Leader (November 1947 – June 1948) | Company C – Rifle Platoon Leader (July – October 1948) | Company B – Rifle Platoon Leader (November – December 1948) | 1st Battalion, Headquarters Company Platoon Leader (January 1949 – October 1949) | Company A - Intelligence & Reconnaissance (I&R) Platoon Leader (November 1949 – April 1950)

"Before, I didn't even know how to spell "Officer."
"Now, I are one."

Saying at U.S. Army Officer Candidate School

In April 1947, I received orders to report to the 33rd Infantry Regiment in Panamá. This was a choice assignment. I was sent to Camp Le Roy Johnson in New Orleans to await my passage to Panamá. I had no duties to perform, so this was more or less a vacation for me. Camp Johnson was an overseas replacement center for all troops going to the Caribbean. Every morning at 6:00 AM, the Post band paraded through the entire base. This was reveille at its very best. Three of my OCS classmates also received orders and we were to travel there together. In addition to the four of us, there were several other officers going to assignments in Panamá and other Latin American countries.

Voyage to Panamá – New Orleans to Cristobal Island
Aboard the USS *St. Mihiel* AP-32

May 1947

We were scheduled to sail on the USS St. Mihiel, AP-32, and an US Army Troop Transport Ship. It regularly plied the U.S. Eastern Seaboard from the Port of New York picking up personnel along the way to the Panamá Canal Zone (CZ). I had never been on a large ship before, so I was looking forward to our voyage. Launched in 1919 she had seen active service before and during World War II, but after the war she was only used on the Latin American run.

During our time in New Orleans, I ate fresh shrimp served *"as is"* on a piece of newspaper with a bottle of ketchup and a box of crackers at a nondescript fish house on Lake Ponchetrain. I visited the French Quarter and strolled up and down Bourbon Street to hear the likes of the Preservation Hall Jazz Band, Louis Armstrong, and Billie Holliday. I also visited several famous restaurants, including Broussard's, Chez Antoine's, and the Court of the Three Sisters. I really had a great time.

When we boarded the ship, we learned there was an entire company of WACs on the deck below us. Naturally, we were told they were *"off-limits."* As if there was any need to remind any of us newly minted junior officers. The most memorable part of the trip was the ride from New Orleans down the Mighty Mississippi to the sea, a distance of about 120 miles. During the voyage, we saw flying fish and dolphins, and enjoyed the warm sun and brilliant moonlight. I was happy to be there in that place and at that time.

The ship's crossing of the Gulf of Mexico was uneventful. As we neared the Isthmus of Panamá, we could smell the jungle long before it came into view. It gave off a marshy, damp, and fetid smell, which was a product of thousands of years of accumulated rotten vegetation. It was an odor which, even with the passage of years, would prove difficult to forget. We disembarked at Cristobal Island, located on the Atlantic Coast side of the Isthmus of Panamá.

Soon thereafter, we boarded a train bound for Panamá City, on the Pacific Coast, a journey of about 45 miles. For most of our journey, the railway paralleled the course of the Canal itself. Reflecting on its monumental proportions, I could not help but wonder about the human sacrifices which were made to build the railroad and construct the canal. Taken altogether, these facilities were marvels of engineering and construction on a massive scale.

The 33rd Infantry Regiment
The *"Triente-Tres"*

Panamá's Own

The 33rd Infantry Regiment was nicknamed *"Panamá's Own"*. It was formed in the Canal Zone in 1916 and remained on active status until 1956. The 33rd was a regiment with a good reputation. It was liked and respected by the Panamánian people. Everyone knew the *"Triente-Tres"* Regiment. In the summer of 1941, the regiment was transferred from the Panama Canal Department to the Caribbean Defense Command.

On September 6, 1941, the 1st Battalion was sent to Trinidad (Fort Read), with some elements of the battalion later being transferred to Surinam to guard bauxite mines and protect the Dutch government in exile. Other elements were later sent to guard the border with French Guiana which was governed by Vichy France. Eventually, the 2nd and 3rd Battalions were later also sent to Trinidad. The 1st Battalion was withdrawn from Surinam and relocated to Aruba in June 1943. In March 1944, the entire regiment departed Trinidad for New York. Its arrival marked the first occasion on which the regimental colors arrived on Continental American soil. The regiment was assigned to Camp Claiborne (Louisiana) and attached to the Fourth United States Army. The 33rd Infantry Regiment was inactivated on June 26, 1944. It was reactivated in the Canal Zone (CZ) at Fort Clayton in February 1946.

In 1946, *"Old Army"* customs and manners were still being observed in the 33rd. There were written and unwritten rules governing almost every aspect of an officer's life, socially and militarily. An officer's word was his bond. Lying, cheating, and stealing were unheard of and would not be tolerated from either an officer or his spouse. Orders were to be obeyed and questioned only after-the-fact. Immediate and unquestioning obedience was the order of the day. Protocol was strictly regulated and observed.

A Second Lieutenant was at the bottom of the totem pole. Everyone above him was more than willing to help him learn, usually the hard way. He was routinely treated as though he knew nothing and had everything to learn. All extra details were assigned to and supervised by Second Lieutenants. Such duties included, but were not necessarily limited to, accompanying enlisted men whenever they were permitted to go swimming on the weekends, inventorying at the Post Exchange (PX) and Commissary Stores, and patrolling the downtown off-limit areas at night looking for drunken soldiers who were sent back to the post so as to avoid arrest.

33rd Infantry Regiment, Headquarters Company, Headquarters Command, Regimental Aide-de-Camp Fort Clayton, CZ

May 1947

At Fort Clayton, I was assigned to Headquarters Company, Headquarters Command, which consisted of an Armored Calvary Squadron (attached to the 33rd), a Regimental Communications Platoon, an Intelligence and Reconnaissance Platoon, motor pool, and regimental staff personnel. An additional Infantry battalion was stationed at Fort Gulick, located on the Atlantic side of the Panamá Canal near Fort Davis, on Gatun Lake. My quarters consisted of a small room in the Bachelor Officer Quarters (BOQ), which was located in a very large building at the end of *"Officer's*

Row", i.e., Married Officer Quarters. My single room was actually situated on the veranda, had no doors, no windows, and it was open on all four sides. No one, it seemed, stole anything from anybody in those days.

Misplaced Expectations

I was really looking forward to my first assignment as a Platoon Leader in a Regular Army Infantry regiment. When I reported to the Regimental Adjutant, First Lieutenant Elmont, he told me I was not going to be assigned as a Platoon Leader. According to the First Lieutenant, this was because I had no previous Infantry experience. I could scarcely believe the words coming out of his mouth. In reply, I noted that I had successfully graduated from Infantry OCS as a qualified Infantry Officer and Platoon Leader. At this point, First Lieutenant Elmont confided the order had come from the Commanding Officer of the 33rd Infantry Regiment, none other than Colonel Normando A. Costello.

First Lieutenant Elmont, someone with seven years in grade, reiterated in no uncertain terms that I would be serving as the Commander's very own Aide-de-Camp. Lieutenant Elmont proceeded to inform me in a very friendly manner there was only *one* Commanding Officer of an Infantry Regiment in the entire Caribbean. As a practical matter, this meant Colonel Costello could pretty much do as he pleased. This despite the fact that a Colonel was not authorized an Aide of any rank. While it wasn't quite according to regulations, I *was* going to be the Commander's Aide-de-Camp come hell or high water. In stark contrast to my circumstances, all the guys I had traveled with to Panamá were assigned to lead Platoons. Only one of them had ever served in the Infantry. As for me, I was assigned to be an office flunky, serving with three enlisted men, and working full-time in the commanding officer's office.

As my conversation with First Lieutenant Elmont was wrapping up, a Lieutenant Colonel, the Regimental Executive Officer (XO), our second in command, came in and confided that CO had commanded a regiment in Europe during World War II. Colonel Costello's unit had been inadvertently bombed by B-24s from the USAAF Eighth Air Force based in England. Even though it had been a grievous error, the CO harbored a deep dislike of the Air Corps, in general, and a distain for its personnel ever since. As a result of his war time experience, Colonel Costello was of the opinion that anyone who had served in the Air Corps probably wasn't worth a damn under any circumstances anyway.

Duties as Aide-de-Camp

What an inauspicious start to my career as an officer. Right then and there, I figured the odds were stacked against me and that it would be essential to proceed with caution or face the possibility of being returned to the ranks. Elmont told me my desk would be in plain view of Colonel Costello's office. This latter revelation was the final blow, inasmuch as every working hour my actions would be under close scrutiny.

My duties as the Colonel's Aide included setting up and coordinating visits and inspections of units in the regiment, checking our many and widely scattered guard posts, and other odd jobs. I never handled any paperwork because the Colonel had an entire staff to handle it. I also never had to make any social affairs because the Colonel had his wife and three enlisted staff to take care of that business. I never figured out how Colonel Costello got away with having a full-time enlisted staff, especially since everyone seemed to be aware of this fact and its very 'irregular' nature. I hated being a flunky, but there was nothing I could do about it except to grin and bear it. No one was willing to lend a hand in reversing my misfortune because everyone was afraid of our Commanding Officer.

As time went by, I gradually learned more about our regimental commander's command experience and leadership style. During World War II, he had served with the 87th Infantry Division, as Commanding Officer of the 346th Infantry Regiment, in the European Theater of Operations (ETO), from October 22nd to December 15th 1944. His regiment was stationed in the Ardennes region of Wallonia in eastern Belgium, northeast of France and Luxembourg, on the eve of the Battle of the Bulge -- which might very well explain his units' brush with those wayward B-24s.

A 'Better Idea' Carries the Day

Early one morning as we were returning from checking guard posts, I suggested to the Colonel that we dress up the helmet liners we wore everyday by putting a regimental insignia on each side. He didn't like the idea at first, stating there was no place for such frills in a Regular Army regiment. Whenever the opportunity presented itself, I would mention how distinctive the regiment would be if each man's liner displayed our insignia. Eventually, the CO agreed to my proposal and ordered me to prepare a single liner – his own. So, I took his liner, painted it with a glossy OD (olive drab) paint, and had the insignia hand-painted on each side. It really looked great and he wore it every day thereafter. Everyone thought it was a good idea, so it wasn't very long before all helmet liners looked the same as the Colonel's. Instead of hand-painting them all, we had decals printed and distributed throughout the regiment. It was a first in Panamá and a small victory for the Colonel's right-hand Second Lieutenant.

Prevailing "Old Army" Customs

Colonel Costello required all his officers to practice the prescribed traditional customs. An officer was a gentleman at all times. An officer was never expected to deviate from the strict rules which applied to his conduct and demeanor. If one fell short of these lofty expectations, he was no longer going to serve as an officer in the 33rd. As time went by, it became clear that Second Lieutenants were particularly vulnerable to the CO's capriciousness if they didn't play the game all the way *his* way.

Within a matter of days of our arrival, all us new officers were invited to the homes of more senior officers. Such invitations were an *"Old Army"* custom designed to allow everyone to learn who we were and find out whether we were single or married. There were no secrets in a regiment. Someone always knew all about you.

This didn't mean people were nosey or overly interested, it was simply the way it was within the immediate community-at-large. To some observers, a Second Lieutenant was so low on the social scale he could neither help nor harm anybody. What we had going for us was we were young, healthy, and for the moment on our own.

Temptation in the Tropics

There was something about the climate in Panamá which seemed to arouse the desires of certain women to the point that customs and social mores were often set aside. Some women were very aggressive about securing a hot, young body, and highly desirable side man. Others were less overt in their intentions, but were also often times in the hunt as well so to speak. Personally, I neither condemned nor condoned such behaviors. It was apparent, however, from the get go that such games had the potential to place newly minted junior officers in a precarious position.

Our careers were only just beginning and most of us were planning to spend the next 20 to 30 years in the Army. Generally, most of us new arrivals were self-aware enough to avoid trouble and play by the rules. None of us were particularly interested in becoming involved in extracurricular activities especially with more senior officer's wives. Most of us soon became adept at sidestepping some very gracious offers without offending the women involved.

Those who succumbed to temptation and got caught, were unceremoniously sent back to the States at the next sailing of the St. Mihiel. The CO would make me read the efficiency reports he had written on these officers despite the fact that such papers were supposed to be confidential. At the time, efficiency reports used a scale from 1 to 7 to rate officers, 7 being the highest grade. Several of the reports I read had ratings of minus 2, 4, and 5 with the written recommendation by the Colonel that the officer in question be discharged upon arrival in the US for the *"Good of the Service."*

Regrettably, there were also some good officers sent home because their wives had been caught fooling around. Since a soldier of any rank was responsible for the conduct of his dependents, there was no excuse for a spouse's wrong doing and both husband and wife were punished equally. At the end of the day, the careers of these Officers were adjudged over and without any recourse. It plainly did not pay to play the field, especially within the confines of Army garrison life. There were some who broke the rules, were not caught, and so they were not punished. For most of us, breaking the rules, any of them, simply was not worth the risk.

A Night to Remember

One evening the regiment held a dance at the Officer's Club. All officers and their wives were in attendance. Each officer wore his ribbons and decorations. I decided to wear my Air Corps Gunner's Wings, because I was really proud of them. As circumstances turned out, this move on my part was a *faux pas* of the first order. While dancing and having a good time, I heard my name called out in a very loud, angry voice. It was the Colonel ordering me to *"get your ass over here, now!"*

Colonel Costello proceeded to thoroughly chew me out in front of everyone for wearing Air Corps Wings in an Infantry regiment. Needless to say, I was thoroughly embarrassed, especially when he ordered me to remove them at once. Remove them I did and never again wore them at any time during my remaining 25 years of service.

Talk about low morale. I didn't have any left over. Privately some of the staff tried to cheer me up, by reminding me how the Colonel felt about the Air Corps. While well-intentioned, their encouragement didn't really do much to lift my spirits.

Heat of the Night

Not long after this incident, the regimental Executive Officer called me into his office one morning and asked, *"Mulvany, don't you know that discretion is the better part of valor?"* I replied that I did. He then said, *"What's this I hear about you and Mrs. Maloney being in a parked car in front of the hospital last night?"* I was aghast.

I had no idea what he was talking about. I told him I didn't even know Mrs. Maloney. He expressed skepticism, but assured me that nobody else knew and wouldn't find out from him. I remember thinking to myself, someone else must have known otherwise how else did he find out? He warned me to be more careful where I parked next time. Suddenly, all those negative efficiency reports I had seen passed through my head.

Somehow, the thought crossed my mind that I could be returning to the States very soon. Rumors tended to make the rounds, even baseless ones, regardless of whatever assurances were made to the contrary. Before leaving the XO's office, I told him again that the man seen with Mrs. Maloney was not me. He then said, *"We don't mind you getting a little now and then, but you really need to be more discreet about it. That's all, dismissed."*

After this admonition, no one ever mentioned anything about the alleged incident again.

A Scourge: Sexually Transmitted Diseases [1]

One thing that really concerned every CO was the venereal disease (VD) rate in the regiment. It might sound strange now, but VD was a very serious problem in the *Old Army*. I knew (personally) of Commanders who were relieved of their commands for having what was considered to be excessive rates of sexually transmitted diseases in their units. In my early Army days, condoms were issued free to everyone on request. There were 24-hour prophylaxis stations open to all military personnel to aid in the prevention and spread of VD.

There were training films galore on the subject and some of them were among the raunchiest on record. Quite a few young soldiers got physically ill when they viewed them. Some even swore off all sex for at least the ensuing five minutes. In Panamá, VD ran rampant among the natives, so extra precautions were routinely taken by the military. Officers and senior NCOs were designated frequently to patrol the "off-limits" red light districts to ensure that soldiers were not in there doing what comes naturally and picking up VD in the process.

The CO was probably thinking about making General. He didn't want anything like the regiment's rate of VD infections to hamper his chances for his next promotion. What he wanted was a chart that would communicate the VD rate in any given unit within the 33rd at a glance. No one had been able to come up with such a chart, a fact that he was highly put out about. The CO turned to me (perhaps out of desperation) and said that if I could come up with a satisfactory solution then he would assign me to lead a platoon. In taking up his challenge, I simply said, *"When do you want it, Sir?"*

Colonel Costello gave me one week to solve the problem. As luck would have it, I had an officer friend in the Army Topographical Engineer Unit stationed nearby. His unit was mapping parts of the Panamánian jungles, most of which had never been mapped. He and his team possessed all the equipment required to make very fine

---

[1] Outbreaks of sexually transmitted diseases in World War II brought interest in sex education to the public and the government.

See: https://en.wikipedia.org/wiki/World_War_II_U.S._Military_Sex_Education.

maps. I sat down with my friend and we came up with a knockout idea for a chart that would please even the *"Old Man."* My friend was happy to lend a hand because he knew how much it meant to me to trade my flunky billet for platoon command.

My friend understood the challenge perfectly. He put his people to work and within five days, they produced the most beautiful multi-colored chart which mapped the prevalence of VD within the regiment to specific units, etc. His team gave me the chart and I gave them a fifth of booze. I placed the chart on the Colonel's desk, when I was sure he would be out of the office. I then made myself scarce until I knew it was likely he had had a chance to study it. Well, the CO was delighted with the results of my work. He informed his staff that it was the kind of work they should have been able to produce, rather than forcing him to prevail upon a mere Second Lieutenant.

Company A, Rifle Platoon Leader

Fort Gulick, CZ

June – August 1947

Two days later, I was ordered to Fort Gulick as a Rifle Platoon Leader in Company A. I was thrilled, because I was finally getting a shot to do what I had been trained and commissioned to do – to be a Platoon Leader. As quickly as possible, I moved myself lock, stock, and barrel into a great room in the BOQ.

I was really happy in Company A. Its Company Commander, Executive Officer, and most of the NCOs were World War II combat veterans. I knew this was an opportunity for me to learn a great deal serving with them. They loaded me with classes to teach and I was as happy as a pig in a slop bucket. My first class on map reading was given to the whole Company. The whole lot of them sure had a good time with their new instructor. To a man, they were really coming after me with their asinine questions, to which they already knew the answers. They were testing me in a good-natured way.

I also taught a weapons class (mortar firing), which I thoroughly enjoyed. I thought, at long last, I had finally found a home. But it was not to be.

Company A, Intelligence and Reconnaissance (I&R)
Platoon Leader
Fort Clayton, CZ

September – October 1947

Less than two weeks into my service with Company A, I was ordered back to Fort Clayton. I really didn't understand why, so I called Lieutenant Elmont and requested an explanation. Lieutenant Elmont told me that I had been selected to take over the Intelligence and Reconnaissance (I&R) Platoon. The I&R Platoon performed jungle rescue operations in Central and South America. I told Elmont I was very happy in Company A and expressed my preference to remain there. I carried on and on until a voice interrupted and said, "*Since when does a Second Lieutenant dictate the decisions of this regiment?*" "*Now get yourself back here by tomorrow without fail, do you understand?*" It was, of course, the Regimental Commanding Officer, Colonel Costello. I assured him that I understood his order clearly.

Awards Ceremony | Fort Clayton, CZ
S/SGT D. Stammer [l] Silver Star Medal and
2nd LT. F. R. Mulvany, Jr. [r] Distinguished Flying Cross
October – 1947

As ordered, I reported for my new assignment the following morning. I reported to the First Lieutenant who commanded the Headquarters Company, of which I&R Platoon was a part. He was tall, skinny, and square-jawed, wore thick glasses, and walked humped over.

The First Lieutenant was not my idea of an Infantry Officer, especially a Company Commander. He, too, knew I had served in the Air Corps and never let me forget it. I had mistakenly thought that by then that nonsense was over and done, but not so. I hated his guts from the get go. If I hadn't been a Second Lieutenant, I probably would have gotten into trouble because of my attitude. I subsequently learned that Colonel Costello had personally selected me for the job, *a good sign*, so who was I to question either *his* judgment or motivations?

The platoon had special equipment to be used in jungle operations. At the time, no other outfit in the Army had any of this equipment. Our job was to evaluate the usefulness of the equipment in jungle terrain. We had canvas-top, leather soled boots that were the forerunners of the famous Việt Nam era jungle boots. We had special cooking stoves, compasses, aluminum containers, etc. I had a lot to learn and so did some of the men. Again, I was tested by some of them. I made it clear to them that, having been a Sergeant for quite some time in my own right, I knew a good deal more than they might suspect and if I had any disobedience of orders, I'd personally bust their asses. It was an uphill battle that I soon won, because they understood I had come up from the ranks and had served in the enlisted ranks longer than any of them.

My commission from OCS was as Second Lieutenant in the Army of the United States of America. "Army of the United States" (AUS) was the wartime title of the huge Army we raised to fight World War II. The title was still in effect in 1946, when I graduated at Fort Benning. There was also the Officer Reserve Corps, which was comprised of those Officers who were in the US Army Reserves (USAR).

AUS was a temporary title, while USAR was more or less a permanent one. Many NCOs had Reserve Officer Commissions and were called to active duty when needed. I knew a full Colonel in Panamá who I saluted each time our paths crossed. It wasn't too long before he was saluting me because he had reverted back to his permanent rank of Master Sergeant.

I put in for an appointment in the USAR. I also applied for a Warrant Officer's rating in the United States Regular Army. A Warrant Officer ranks between the highest NCO rank and the lowest commissioned officer rank (Second Lieutenant). Warrant Officers are specialists in their chosen field, usually one specialty which they perform throughout their careers.

If I couldn't be a Reserve Officer, I wanted to be a Warrant Officer. Either way, I would not have to go back to being a Sergeant when the Army was reduced in size. Reductions in force were a commonplace occurrence in peacetime. I lucked out however and was appointed Second Lieutenant USAR, though I was turned down on the warrant since I had no specialty yet. So, I was now USAR, rather than AUS, and thus was assured of a longer time in the Officer Corps.

Company D, Heavy Weapons Section,
Platoon Leader
Fort Gulick, CZ

November 1947 – June 1948

In November 1947, I was assigned a set of quarters at Fort Gulick and transferred to Company D. Company D was the Heavy Weapons Company of the battalion (82mm M1 mortars and .50 caliber machine guns). I was to take command of a machine gun platoon. That really pleased me since I had had quite a bit of experience with heavy machine guns in the Air Corps.

I drilled the men in regulation close-order drill and improvised movements and ended up beating all others, including the rifle platoons. Best of all, the final contest for the trophy was between my platoon and Lieutenant *"Hunchback"* from Headquarters Company, 33rd Infantry Regiment, at Fort Clayton. It was a pure joy to have had the opportunity to administer a proper whipping to him courtesy of yours truly -- an Air Corps type.

Fort Gulick was a one-battalion post and all the officers lived in close proximity to one another. The Officers' Club was perched on a hill in the midst of our quarters. My

33rd Infantry Regiment | Awards Ceremony | Fort Gulick, CZ
"Best Drilled Platoon"
Company D, Heavy Weapons Section
1st LT. Floyd R. Mulvany, Jr. [Far left], Commanding Officer
February 20, 1948

abode was right on the edge of Gatun Lake and only about 20 feet removed from the jungle. It was a great setting on a small and beautiful post. We had honey bears, sloths, iguanas, and snakes in our yards and never gave their presence too much thought. At night, we could hear the alligators barking in the lake.

The only drawback that attended out domicile was the fact that my next-door neighbor (our quarters were two story duplexes) turned out to be my new Company Commander. Really rotten luck. Like his predecessor, he too was a tall and skinny fellow, with a huge Adam's apple and a narrow moustache. He thought he had a superb singing voice, but in reality, when he sang it sounded as though his gonads were being pinched by a pair of pliers. We did not hit it off terribly well, in part because he had a habit of giving me orders through his wife. She would come over and tell me he wanted me to do this, that, or the other thing. I couldn't believe it.

It quickly became apparent to all who interacted with him that he did not know the first thing about either employing heavy weapons or running a company. Besides giving me orders through his wife, he pulled at least one other brilliant move which stands out in my memory. He put out an order that officers were not to eat any ice crème in the mess hall because it was just for the enlisted men. The Mess Sergeant offered us ice crème anyway, because he was an old hand and wouldn't think of depriving us young Lieutenants of anything.

Having a cup of coffee or a snack was an accepted thing in any Army mess. It was part of Army life, too. But no, he said, NO ice crème. Why this matter was of such importance to him was anybody's guess, but I for one was extremely fond of ice crème. In any event, it was not long after his announcement that the Mess Sergeant and I opened the walk-in ice box door and found our Company Commander – sitting on a stack of boxes consuming a large bowl of ice crème. He said nothing and neither did the two of us.

What's Past is Prologue
An Annual Records Check

January 1948

In January 1948, in the course of verifying my awards and decorations during an annual records check, it was discovered I had been awarded the Distinguished Flying Cross (DFC). It was awarded for actions in connection with a mission flown on April 5, 1944, when our aircraft was crippled by anti-aircraft fire in the midst of a bombing raid along the Moulmein-Siam Rail Line southeast of Rangoon. A few hours later, we were forced to ditch our ship in the Bay of Bengal. For some reason, I had never been notified of the award and it had never been entered on my service record. In 1947, the DFC was pretty high on the list of decorations. It was also one of three awards in the Army that paid an extra $2.00 a month to enlisted men to whom it had been awarded.

Not only was I entitled to about 2 ½ years of back pay, but the War Department directed that the medal be awarded to me at an *appropriate* ceremony. Unless I am mistaken, the presentation of awards was made by Major General Joseph Cowles

Mehaffey, U. S. Army Corps of Engineers, Commanding Officer, US Canal Zone, and included a pass-by review of all the troops stationed on the Pacific side of the CZ. Talk about retribution for all the crap and insults I had taken for having served in the Air Corps.

Awards Ceremony | Fort Gulick, CZ
33rd Infantry Regiment
June - 1948
1st LT. Floyd R. Mulvany, Jr.
(Far right)

In the above photograph, Major General Mehaffey is standing at attention on the far left. Best of all, none other than Colonel Normando A. Costello, Commanding Officer, 33rd Infantry Regiment can be seen standing immediately behind Mehaffey in the photograph. Earlier Colonel Costello had marched at the head of the troops of the 33rd Infantry Regiment during the review.

All the hubbub must have really gotten to the Commanding Officer, Company D, because he subsequently gave me an efficiency report (ER) which ought to have resulted in my separation from the Army for inefficiency. There was something like 50 traits on the ER to be rated. Notably, I received a rating of "worst" on all 50 of them and a "1" (the lowest rating) for efficiency.

Fortunately, the Battalion Commander did not particularly care for my company CO and endorsed me as being fully proficient as a Second Lieutenant. His endorsement stated, in part, *"Any young officer develops only with proper leadership."* Shortly thereafter, my company CO was relieved of command and we never heard from him again. It is a good bet that he was among the first to go when the Army got around to reducing its ranks. In my opinion, the Army was much better off without him and others of his ilk.

Our new company CO was a real gentleman, a mentor, and a leader of men. This did not mean, however, that he made my life as an officer an easy one. He, too, did not take to Army Air Corps types. In his case, I had the impression that he had probably tried to get into the Air Corps but didn't make the grade and ended up being drafted during World War II.

Company D, Mess Officer
Temporary Duty Assignment
Fort Gulick, CZ

June 1948

Upon my return to Company D, I was temporarily designated Mess Officer. This assignment worked out well for me, because the old Mess Sergeant made a point of always making me look good. As fate would have it, I was soon sent off to the Mess Officers School at Fort Clayton. It was a four-week course. Among other things, I learned how to open a can of sardines with a meat cleaver and how to bake cinnamon rolls for a company of 150 men. And that was about all I learned.

Social Life, Accommodations,
And Friendships

As a group, we young Lieutenants never mingled socially with Captains or above unless it was a prescribed affair. We kept to ourselves and made our own fun on our meager pay. The Army provided us with steel frame beds, mattresses, dishes, utensils, and a dining room table and matching chairs. Furnishings in such quarters were modest, mostly made from boxes and crates that often times had been left behind by the preceding tenant. In my case, I paid the previous Lieutenant $40.00 to leave everything he had used in place.

Army wives were very good at fixing up a set of quarters at little or no cost. Target cloth, a type of cloth *literally* used for targets on the rifle ranges, could be used for drapes, table cloths, chair and sofa covers, etc. It was usually available from the Post Quartermaster. Some of the most memorable times spent in those quarters, were spent playing penny-ante poker at home with four or five sets of friends at a time. A $3.00 pot was considered something to write home about.

Soon after returning from Mess Officers School, the Lieutenant who lived across the street from me and attended the school at the same time as I did, asked me to come over to show the ladies how well we could cook. We decided to make some cinnamon rolls. The only recipe we had was the one in the Army cook book that fed 150 men. We started out nicely, but things soon got out of hand.

We had all the wives in the neighborhood bringing us flour and sugar. The kitchen got so hot, we stripped down to our aprons and cook hats – nothing underneath. Boy, we were really putting out the rolls. Needless to say, we ended up with so many of them that even after distributing them to everyone we knew, we still had enough left over for at least 50 more people.

That was my first and last attempt to cook anything on such a grand scale. My only regret is that no one took any photographs of us on that occasion, because it was an event I'll always remember. Sadly, the Lieutenant with whom I made the rolls died of a heart attack soon after the occasion.

Garrison Duty

Duty in Panamá was pleasant. Training exercises were conducted from 7:30 AM to 12:30 PM daily. The hours from 1:30 to 4:30 PM were reserved for maintenance of weapons and equipment. Regular maintenance was essential in the tropics in order to ensure readiness.

Mildew and rust were a constant concern. All clothing and leather goods, for example, had to be stored in a cool, dry place. Small lights were left on in closets 24-hours a day to mitigate the growth of mold and mildew. Metal objects had to be coated with oil to prevent rust. Motor vehicles had to have a heavy undercoating of rust resistant paint.

Private vehicles really rusted out quickly unless they also were properly maintained. A friend of mine learned this the hard way. He should have had his first clue when the running boards of his car fell off. He disregarded this omen since he had no intention of taking the car back to the States when his tour was up. One day while I was driving along, he put his foot on the brake, pushed down, and the floor board collapsed. He had one hell of a time stopping the car.

Some of the quarters for civilian workers in the housing areas were built during the days when the French were attempting to dig the canal (ca 1879). Constructed about 70 years before our arrival, these quarters were all built upon piles which had the effect of elevating living spaces roughly ten feet above the ground. Apart from reducing the risk of flooding during the rainy season, this construction technique also served to reduce the prevalence of various creepers and crawlers as well as mitigating the prospect of dry rot.

Our quarters on the post were built in a similar manner, except that the core of each duplex had a 'ground' floor with a washroom and maid's accommodations. On one occasion during 1947, a civilian worker was taking a shower when the entire floor of the shower room gave way and dropped him to the ground – stark naked and soaking wet. It probably wasn't amusing to him, but it certainly was to those who saw it happen. Civilians were always telling stories about spiders, centipedes, and other critters popping out from their shower heads.

Fort Gulick did not have a swimming pool, so we frequently visited the site of the US Navy's Officers Club at Coco Solo to sun and swim. There were also several golf courses and tennis courts in the area. I did not play much golf, because it required too much of an investment of time. I did, however, play tennis almost every day and swam too.

It was commonplace to dine like locals. For whatever reason, I always suspected that a lot of the chicken we ate in town was actually Iguana meat. Iguanas were considered the chickens of South America, especially when it came to feeding the masses.

Booze was probably the least expensive commodity available in Panamá. A bottle of the finest rum cost no more than $.75 a fifth. Rum and Coca-Cola with lemon and sugar was the drink of choice in this part of the tropics. Each service, except the Army, had its own dance band.

Dances were held every Saturday night at one of the Navy or Air Force's Officers Clubs. We enjoyed good dining and dancing at an affordable price. In addition, there were numerous Panamánian clubs in town which offered drinking, gambling, Latin music and dancing. Such clubs were open every night, so there was no lack of entertainment. We spent many nights watching floor shows, eating, drinking, and watching the sun come up before returning to the post and getting ready for the day's work. It was fun while it lasted. Everyone had a good time.

True to the practices which were prevalent at the time, all officers had several different uniforms to wear to fit whatever the occasion required. We had cotton khakis for everyday wear, khaki gabardine blouses and slacks for informal wear, and dress whites for formal wear. I never cared much for the whites because they were so heavily starched and required a white shirt, black tie, white shoes with black socks, and a white/black-visor service cap. The best thing to do in this latter uniform was to stand still in one place, because one bend of the arms or legs would break the creases and cause a completely rumpled look.

The gabardine blouse and slacks were a great looking uniform. It was worn with a light weight cotton khaki shirt, black tie, khaki service cap with brown visor, and brown shoes. Remember, this was still very much the *"Brown Shoe Army."* Our cotton khaki shirts and trousers were starched absolutely stiff and were supposed to look that way all day, regardless of how much we moved around.

As a result, I had 22 sets of cotton Khakis. It was regular practice to change uniforms two or three times a day so you would always appear freshly starched. For a short time, at the order of our Commanding General, all officers had to wear the cotton khaki uniform with khaki tie, button our sleeves, and tuck our trousers in our boots even while marching and training in the jungle.

On reflection, it was like working in a sweat box. Of course, we were also wearing our steel helmets and field equipment too. There was no way to properly ventilate your body. It was an impossible situation dictated by an old Commanding General who spent all of his time either in an air-conditioned office or automobile and who had never served in the Infantry.

His Staff Officers inspected us even when we were out on jungle maneuvers to ensure that we wearing our ties and had our collars buttoned. Anyone who broke the rules were put on report. We could not understand the situation and, predictably our complaints fell upon deaf ears.

The Mission of the 33rd Infantry Regiment:
Physical Defense of the Panamá Canal and the

Surrounding Canal Zone

The primary mission of the 33rd Infantry Regiment was, first, to guard the Canal, and second, to guard the Canal Zone. The Canal Zone was a ten-mile-wide swath of land, five miles to either side of the Canal itself, which ran the length of the isthmus, a distance of about 52 miles. Since we had only one Infantry battalion, we were in reality an under strength regimental combat team. The Armored Calvary Squadron could only operate in open terrain. It was of no use in the jungle. In order to guard the Canal, we established guard posts on all three locks, located respectively at Gatun, San Miguel, and Mira Flores.

This arrangement would, in theory, prevent anyone from getting into these areas to jam the gates, blow down the retaining walls, or blow up the control towers. Any of these things could have been done by dedicated, properly trained and equipped, people with nothing more than mortars firing from positions in the jungle. However, I was only a Second Lieutenant with orders to carry out and no mandate to speak out or ask any questions.

The Officer of the Guard (OG), usually a young Lieutenant like me, was required to check each guard post every two hours. There were 20 to 22 guard posts situated on each lock. The distance around each lock was about three miles, so it took a full two hours for the OG to make his rounds. This meant the OG was constantly on the move for the entire time he was on duty.

There was, of course, some satisfaction in performing his duty. Our mission was frequently interrupted and occasionally impaired whenever large passenger liners transited the locks. It was commonplace for passengers to speak with us as we stood by while the ships were lowered or raised some 80 feet to sea level.

Geopolitical Importance,

Local Politics, and

Other Considerations

I, for one, certainly met some very interesting people while on duty. Occasionally, a ship registered under the flag of the former Union of Soviet Socialist Republics (USSR) was permitted to transit the Canal. Whenever this happened, the whole regiment was turned out for lock duty. Troops were also stationed on board the ship as it was shepherded through all the locks on a priority basis to avoid any trouble.

The political situation in Panamánian society was volatile. In the aftermath of the Panamánian general elections on May 27, 1948, for example, there were three different Panamánian presidential candidates claiming to hold the office at the same time (viz., Domingo Diaz Arosemena, Arnulfo Arias Madrid, and Jose Antonio Ramón Cantera) each professing to be the legitimate head of state.

During the two or three weeks it took to resolve this political impasse, the 33rd Infantry Regiment was on round-the-clock alert throughout the Canal Zone. We encountered no trouble within the Canal Zone during this period. The official position of the US government was that whatever the Panamánians did outside the Canal Zone was their business and theirs alone.

The US Army was not involved in local politics of any kind until the late 1960s. Up to that point, it was an unwritten rule among service members serving abroad never to discuss matters relating to either politics or religion, etc. In addition to lock and guard duty, we trained regularly as an Infantry unit.

For open terrain tactics, we had a maneuver area at Rio Hato, located 80 miles northwest of the Canal Zone along the Pacific Ocean. Rio Hato was a permanent US

Army base which had been fully occupied during World War II. It had all the facilities one would expect to find anywhere else: barracks, mess halls, BOQs, clubs, and so on, as well as a beautiful white sand beach that was free of fleas.

The enlisted men really liked Rio Hato because there was an entire company of WACs stationed there on a permanent basis. To this day, I do not know understand why the Army chose to station WACs at such a remote post. There were also about 15 female government workers stationed there who lived next door to the US Army Officers Club.

Talk about a bachelor's paradise. Ocean swimming at night was beautiful. The water was so florescent that the swimmer's bodies were illuminated and the water dripping from them was like watching cascading stars.

Panamá: Jungle Training Laboratory
And Proximity to other Training Areas

In the Caribbean Basin

The jungle was always available for training. We only had to march down the back road of the Fort to be in the thick of it. The weather was almost always hot, humid, and it rained nearly every day. There were times when it would rain on one side of the road and be perfectly dry on the other.

Twice each year, the entire outfit moved out for range firing. We set up a tent city adjacent to the range and remained there until everyone had qualified on basic weapons: rifles, carbines, and pistols. We also fired our mortars, machine guns, and bazookas. There was plenty of ammunition of every type and description left over from World War II.

The War Department encouraged all units to fire as much ammunition as desired. This allowed our people to become very proficient with their weapons. It was one of the few times in the service when I encountered a situation where there was a surplus of stores to expend for training. More often than not, there was never enough of the stuff needed for proper readiness training.

War Maneuvers Ordered
Vieques Island, Puerto Rico

February 1948

In February 1948, we were ordered to conduct war maneuvers in Puerto Rico. It was amphibious warfare training. We loaded our equipment and ourselves onto an attack transport and sailed off to Vieques Island east of the main island.

The main town on the Island of Vieques, Isabella Secunda, had a Spanish fort which was built in the 16th century. At one time, the fort was apparently a prominent one, because Queen Isabella of Spain was said to have remarked that surely it was made of gold since it had cost so much to construct it. From our point-of-view, the fort didn't look like much of a facility. In 1948, it was however a principal tourist attraction. Second, in fact, only to the island's beautiful white sandy beaches and warm emerald waters in popularity.

We staged a mock invasion of the island which turned out to be a very successful training operation. The 65th Infantry Regiment, an element of the Puerto Rican National Guard, acted as the enemy. Beyond any doubt, we learned a great deal about amphibious operations.

Garrison Life
During Maneuvers

As a general rule, whenever our outfit moved out of the post, the wives and children often doubled up and stayed together in one set of quarters. It was customary to leave some men behind to provide security and assistance to families whenever it might be required. As a general rule, Infantry wives were a very resourceful group of individuals and being on their own was second nature to them.

They always managed to get things done that had to be done, whatever the circumstances. I'm not sure, however, any of them ever quite got used to iguanas looking in the door, sloths hanging on the clothing lines, raccoons and honey bears invading the trash cans. In addition, few if any of them ever got accustomed to the annual migrations of millions of ants rolling out of the jungle in living, swarming balls, which could only be stopped by setting them afire and 'controlled' by pouring gasoline into the gutters hanging from the house.

I'm also certain they never got used to the annual migrations of millions of beetles which ended up dying all over the windows and stairs forming layers seven- to eight inches deep. No, I don't believe they enjoyed such things, but they did put up with them. The barking of alligators in Gatun Lake wasn't hard to take, but the heat and humidity were the source of considerable year-round discomfort. It was hard on women to live in that environment.

U. S. Army Reorganization:
Throwing Down the Gauntlet and

Testing the Mettle of the Junior Officer Corps

In June 1948, The Department of the Army announced that it was implementing a program to procure officers for Regular Army Commissions from personnel on duty either on an AUS or USAR status. It will be recalled that the Army had been cut to the bone in the aftermath of World War II. Many fine Reserve Officers were *"pink slipped"* (terminated) from active commissioned status in order to align its manpower with peacetime requirements, along with a fair number of deadbeats and strap hanger types.

As usual, in those days the government was not concerned with being prepared for future threats to our national security. Rather, its number one priority was reducing the absolute headcount of the armed forces. We had only recently won a great war, so the conventional wisdom at the time was that the country no longer needed to maintain a large standing Army.

One notable consequence of such cutbacks was the shortage of Regular Army Second Lieutenants. When the impending cuts were announced, there were about 700 Regular Army Second Lieutenant Billets available for appointments. The Army's program was to be known as a *"Competitive Tour."* In theory, qualified personnel were to compete for the vacancies by being observed and rated for a period of one year.

From the time I was first commissioned, I had tried several times either to obtain an extended active-duty Reserve Officer status or a Regular Army commission. This information was a part of my official Army records. So, the Department of the Army was well aware of my efforts to remain in the Regular service and to retain my status as an officer.

The entrance requirements for participation in the Competitive Tour program was very tough. For example,

- No one with more than five years of commissioned service or above the grade of Captain could apply;

- An applicant was required to have completed at least two years of college credits (This requirement could be waived in lieu of passing a two-year college equivalence test prior to going on tour.); and

- Applicants had to be in excellent physical condition, deemed be of high moral character and whose integrity beyond considered reproach, and recommended by at least three senior officers – two immediate-past Commanding Officers and another next higher Commanding Officer.

Once accepted, an applicant had to serve in four different units under a minimum of four different Commanding Officers and be rated individually by each of them. As a practical matter, this meant a transfer every 90 days over the course of 12 months.

These were very difficult requirements to meet, but I felt this program was the only chance I had to obtain a regular Army commission and thereby be assured I would be able to serve as an officer until I retired. I did not hesitate to apply. I was recommended by my company CO and the battalion CO, since I had done a good job for them. And I had received some outstanding awards for meritorious service on their watch. One was the Distinguished Flying Cross (DFC) and more recently for having the best drilled platoon in the 33rd Infantry Regiment, Company D, Heavy Weapons Section, Platoon Leader.

I was in excellent physical condition at the time. I also had one full year of college credits under my belt, so I was confident in my ability to pass the two-year equivalency exam. My only real concern was about the rotten ER I had received from my first Company CO at Company D. As it happened, that ER was expunged from my records at the time of my promotion to First Lieutenant in May of 1948. A total of six individuals from the 33rd put in for the tour (myself included). Four of us had to take the two-year college equivalency test. We all passed the exam and embarked on our tour on July 15, 1948.

Second Lieutenants form the base of the officer rank pyramid, just as Privates are for the enlisted ranks. The need for Second Lieutenants is especially acute in the months immediately following the cessation of hostilities, since in general a military career was not viewed as a particularly desirable profession in peacetime. Invariably, however, there was always an acute shortage of Second Lieutenants in the Army. The reason for this situation is fairly easy to explain. Either not enough junior officers remained in the service after their service obligations were up (e.g., four years for West Pointers and two years for everyone else), or they were killed in combat, or they were promoted. As the largest of the services, it is natural the Army is targeted for the largest personnel cuts in terms of absolute numbers.

Company C, Rifle Platoon Leader
Fort Gulick, CZ

July – October 1948

I was transferred to Company C and given a rifle platoon. The CO was a hard-headed Irishman, like me, except that he had absolutely no sense of humor. This was probably because he had been a First Lieutenant for over six years. He lasted 60 days before being shipped out. On his way out the door, he gave me an Efficiency Report (ER) which said, in part, that I was dogmatic in my dealings with enlisted men. Fortunately, my good friend and next-door neighbor, a First Lieutenant, then took command of the company. He was unable to give me a complete ER, because he was soon transferred to the Artillery. A Captain whose name I can no longer recall, took over next. I was supposed to have been transferred at the end of three months, but the transfer did not happen on schedule since I had not received a complete ER from Company C. It seemed to me they were stretching the rules a bit by delaying my transfer. My fear was that I would be penalized for the inaction of my superiors.

Company B, Rifle Platoon Leader
Fort Gulick, CZ

November/December 1948

On November 15th, I was finally transferred to Company B after serving four months in Company C and having received three partial ERs. At this point in the game, I was not at all optimistic about my chances of being selected for the Regular Army. In Company B, I served under Captain Roberts, a combat-wise veteran, with whom I got along famously. After 60 days, he was replaced by another great Captain. Before he left for his next assignment, Captain Roberts gave me a terrific ER, as did his replacement another 60 days later. Once more, I had spent four months in a company, but I had come away with two great 60-day (not 90-day) ERs. Eight months of my tour had passed. I was transferred to Battalion Headquarters Company as a Platoon Leader under another fellow who (you guessed it) had no use for *"Air Corps"* types.

1st Battalion, Headquarters Company
Platoon Leader
Fort Gulick, CZ

January – October 1949

From my earliest days serving with the 33rd, I was hopeful that all the anti-Air Corps biases would eventually pass into history. I was decidedly mistaken, of course, because that fact had been made clear to me right up front. Once again, I had the sinking feeling there would be no Regular Army Commission for me because there was no way to overcome the pervasive prejudices which infected the leadership ranks vis-à-vis my Air Corps pedigree.

Since I was the only other officer in the company, I was assigned 16 additional duties besides those that attended my role as a Platoon Leader. I humped and jumped in an effort to do everything possible to satisfy the demands and expectations of my new CO. In order to avoid unnecessarily antagonizing him, I avoided the CO like the plague while trying to maintain a positive outlook and remain focused on the tasks-at-hand.

My efforts earned me an ER of "2" with the observation that my time in the Air Corps had not properly prepared me to be an Infantry Officer. His comment was the lowest blow yet. I spoke with my CO about the ER and told him his report was grossly unfair and did not accurately reflect upon my performance. I also respectfully reminded him that I had been serving as an Infantry Officer and Platoon Leader for almost two years. Furthermore, it was noted that I had been on tour for ten months and that in the interim was promoted to First Lieutenant. He responded by stating, in brief, that *"that was the way he saw it, and that was it, nothing more or less."*

A new captain soon came to the company and I remained to wrap up my tour with the platoon. Over the past 12 months, I had been assigned to three different units (not four) and had served under seven different Company Commanders. My last ER was excellent, but I feared that the anti-Air Corps type(s) might have done me in. My 'tour' was over, but we would hear nothing for at least 90 days because the Department of the Army had to evaluate the ratings of all those men who had been on tour. While I was pleased with my performance while on tour, I continued to be very concerned there would be no Regular Army Commission for me despite my best efforts and owing to my mixed efficiency ratings.

During my year on tour, quite a few changes occurred in the old 33rd. First, the regiment was deactivated. Overnight, our battalion became the First Infantry Battalion, Ranger, in June 1948. We wore the Roman numeral "I" above our crossed rifles. The 33rd, which had served since 1916, was no more. The Panamánians who knew and respected the regiment couldn't understand why it no longer existed. It was difficult to explain to them the US Army was being reduced dramatically in terms of manpower and sheer size. The peacetime Army was no longer able to support a regiment unit in Panamá. While our mission did not change, we were called upon to deliver more with less. Thus, we resolved to do whatever needed to be done with one battalion instead of a reduced Regimental Combat Team.

In July 1949, the 1st Battalion designation was changed to the 7475th Service Unit. This was the lowest form of degradation – a Regular Army Regiment reduced to the status of a service unit. What in the hell were those idiots in the Pentagon thinking about when they cooked this one up? Evidently someone got the word to the resident *"illuminati"* in Washington, DC, because in October 1949, we were re-designated the

33rd Infantry and relocated to Fort Kobbe on the Pacific side of the Isthmus of Panamá. Forts Gulick and Clayton were turned over to other units. For the first time in a long time, the entire regiment was together in one place.

Company A, Intelligence and Reconnaissance (I&R)
Platoon Leader
Fort Kobbe, CZ

November 1949 – April 1950

In October 1949, I received a most pleasant surprise. I could not believe my good fortune. I received a telephone call direct from the Pentagon informing me that I had been selected for appointment in the Regular Army. I asked that the message be repeated twice to make sure I had heard it correctly. In fact, five of six from the 33rd had made it. I later learned that my *"I hate the Air Corps"* type CO had either reconsidered his rotten ER or had been told to reconsider it. In any case, justice was served when he submitted a second report which wiped out the original one.

In November 1949, I again took over the Intelligence and Reconnaissance (I&R) Platoon. This was the same one I had led as a Second Lieutenant. This time, however, emphasis was on I&R training rather than jungle rescue, although we continued to train for both missions simultaneously. I was confirmed as a Second Lieutenant Regular Army with a date of rank of January 1, 1948, and a new serial number: RA 060459. All Regular Army Officers had a five-digit serial number which set them apart from AUS and USAR and National Guard types. I was finally a member of the Officer Corps for good. It had been a struggle, but it was all worthwhile. All I had to do was work my butt off, stay out of trouble with the ERs, and get promoted. It was easy to say and hard to do.

Fort Kobbe was a former United States Army Coast Artillery Corps post located in the Panamá Canal Zone. Its 16-inch coastal guns were still in their original emplacements when the 33rd Infantry took over the base in late October 1949. It was located adjacent to Howard Air Force Base, where USAF operations drew down during the summer and all training ceased by mid-October 1949. We were able to make good use of their large hangars to house our motor pools, storage, and recreational areas. It was great because everything was out of the weather. If the need arose, we could even train, hold close order drills, and even parades inside those mammoth structures.

The I&R Platoon under my command was used to test communications equipment and jungle operations techniques. It was a small platoon with only 17 enlisted men out of an authorized strength of 33 personnel. What we lacked in quantity, we more than made up for in quality. We had a tremendous maintenance challenge before us. We were responsible to properly maintain a fleet of 11 Jeeps, numerous and various types of radios, two ten-men boats with 50 HP outboard motors, and our individual weapons and machine guns. Each one of us carried a machete and our own individual cook stove whenever we were in the field.

The men were well-trained. They responded well to jungle operations. I developed, designed, and wrote all our training schedules, which called for two weeks out of every four in the jungle. As a unit, we became very proficient going cross-country over jungle terrain, mapping uncharted areas, using boats, and making camp in virtually any jungle area and in any terrain.

33rd Infantry Regiment, Company A,
Intelligence & Reconnaissance (I&R) Platoon
1st LT. Floyd R. Mulvany, Jr., Commanding Officer
November 1949 – April 1950

We had individual hammocks which, I believe, were the best such devices ever issued by the US Army. Briefly speaking, these hammocks featured a large rubber top which extended beyond the sides of the hammock, such that the sides were sheltered, and the whole hammock was enclosed in mosquito netting. A pair of two one-inch-thick ropes extended from either end of the hammock, which when securely tied to opposing pairs of trees, gave more than enough strength to provide support and stability. Each man carried an individual mattress cover to crawl into once inside the hammock. We could hang our boots off the bottom of the hammock and above the ground – free from insects and other jungle critters. These items were well designed, easy to use and maintain, very functional, durable and reliable. Why I never saw or heard of them again is anybody's guess.

We traversed all of Gatun Lake and became very familiar with much of the terrain in and around the Canal Zone. We made many trips up and down the Chagres River across the Isthmus of Panamá to Fort San Lorenzo on the Atlantic side. The Spanish built Fort San Lorenzo between 1587 and 1599 in order to protect the approaches to the mouth of the Chagres River. The English buccaneer, Henry Morgan, ordered the fort sacked in 1670, soon after he had sacked and burned Panamá City. Later Morgan was said to have crossed the Isthmus of Panamá via the Las Cruces Trail.

Operation PORTREX
Amphibious Warfare Operations
Commonwealth of Puerto Rico

February – April 1950

In February 1950, the 33rd Infantry Regiment was designated as the aggressor force in "Operation PORTREX." This was to be the largest amphibious operation to be conducted since World War II. The Army's Third Division and other units participated with elements from the US Air Force, US Marines, and US Navy. These units were to make a massive amphibious landing on Vieques Island. The operation was to last over two months. Once again, we loaded all our equipment on a cargo vessel and we set sail for Roosevelt Roads on the eastern end of the Island of Puerto Rico.

San Juan, Puerto Rico (PR)

We had some time off during the training, so we were able to visit San Juan, the island's capital city. Fort Brooke was a US Army Post situated at the edge of El Morro. El Morrow was a famous old fort built by the Spaniards which had long guarded the entrance to San Juan Bay.

On the base, there was a golf course and, of course, an Officers Club. Next to the 'O Club' stood the nurse's quarters for Fort Brooke Hospital. San Juan was a swinging tourist mecca with night clubs, floor shows, and dancing all night long. We had to go everywhere in our uniforms, so we rather stood out from the crowd, as I recall. None of the personnel from the 33rd got into any trouble, since everyone was fairly well indoctrinated in what to expect if they did violate standing behavioral protocols.

The *"Old Brown Shoe Army"* wasn't inclined to coddle its soldiers. Everyone was treated like a man. Each individual was expected to act like a gentleman at all times and without exception.

St. Thomas and St. Croix, Virgin Islands (VI)

During another break in our training, several of us officers got into a small Chris Craft and sped off on a 68-mile jaunt across open waters of the Atlantic to St. Croix in the US Virgin Islands. We made good headway at an average speed of about 14 knots. I was wearing khakis, so in order to avoid breaking starch, I stood for the entire five-hour voyage while most others did not.

Many got sea sick, but I managed to stand tall and maintain my sea "legs". We were lucky to have a young US Army Captain with us who knew the islands well because his father had retired in St Thomas some years prior to the date of our visit. A Navy Underwater Demolition Team Detachment, forerunner of the S.E.A.L. teams, was stationed on St. Croix (rough duty), so we were able to secure billets with them. We ate, danced, and saw the sights as much as we could. We visited the warehouse where Alexander Hamilton, a native of St. Croix, had clerked as a young man.

We also visited what I believe was (and still might be) the largest liquor store in the world. It was a large three-story warehouse with only a ground floor located down on the docks. Clerks used stairwells to access shelves that ran all the way up to the roof. On a table near the entrance, sat a bottle of 1815 vintage Napoleon Brandy. Next to the bottle was a sign which declared: *"Any customer who did not find the liquor he asked for would get the bottle of Napoleon Brandy for free."* Some confidence, huh?

There's no way to know for certain, but I'm willing to bet the bottle never left the store. All military units in the Caribbean and on the east coast of the US seemed to procure their liquor through this outlet. It was said that plane loads of it flew out every day because it was so cheap. No customs duties were paid in the islands, so booze could be purchased in great quantities and shipped pretty much anywhere with impunity.

Roosevelt Roads, (PR)

When we made it back to Roosevelt Roads, I was invited to participate in a tour of the battleship *USS Missouri* (BB-63), "BIG MO", whereon the Japanese had signed the unconditional surrender on September 2, 1945. The Lt. Commander Gunnery Officer, whose name I can no longer recall, was our tour guide. He took us on a lengthy tour to virtually every corner of the ship.

As a former Gunner/Armorer, I was fascinated by her impressive array of fire power. *Missouri's* main battery consisted of nine 16-inch (406mm)/50 caliber Mark 7 guns, which could fire 2,700-pound (1,200kg) armor-piercing shells some 20-miles (32.2km). Her secondary battery consisted of twenty 5-inch (127mm)/38 caliber guns in twin turrets, with a range of about 10-miles (16km).

All the loading and firing of the 16-inch guns was fully mechanized, with the exception of one operation. Located in one corner of each turret was a small platform from which one man visually checked the breeches of each gun between firings to positively ensure they were sealed. At the last instant, this individual would duck out of the turret before the guns were fired. All wadding, powder bag residue, smoke and the shell itself were blown out of the barrel. Nothing came out of the breeches when they were opened to receive a new charge and shell.

Our tour ended in the Officers Ward Room, which to my eyes looked almost as large as one of the hangars at Howard Field. I must confess, this tour was an incredible experience for a young US Army Infantry Lieutenant.

Commencement of War Games

During Operation PORTREX, Vieques was to be bombarded and attacked by combined amphibious forces. The 33rd and 65th Infantry were to defend the island. My platoon was the aggressor's reconnaissance force. We were to operate independently of our higher command.

The 65th had spent months shoring up the fortifications on Vieques. Many beautiful Palm trees were cut down in order to build bunkers and create obstacles on the beaches. The beaches themselves were strung with barbed wire everywhere. Pill boxes and gun emplacements, constructed of Palm logs and cement, were dug out and placed in such a manner as to optimize killing zones by ensuring overlapping fields of fire. The southern half of the island below Isabella Secunda was designated a live round impact area. It was in the live impact area that all artillery shells, naval gunfire, and aerial bombs were to be targeted. It later became a permanent US armed forces training and live fire zone.

Once beautiful Vieques Island was never again to be the same tropical paradise. All invasion troops temporarily retired from the scene, only to return for their landing on Vieques Island after about 24 hours. My platoon and the 65th remained behind to await their return and the opening of the battle. Before the amphibious attack commenced, we learned that a battalion of Paratroopers from the 82nd Airborne Division from Fort Bragg, NC was on its way to make a jump behind the invasion beaches. The 82nd Airborne was tasked to secure the high ground overlooking the beachhead. When the 65th learned of the planned maneuver, they scattered stakes, vehicles, booby traps, and mines all over the drop zone. They also deployed machine guns and rifle men to cover the area.

The mines and booby traps were not real, but the stakes, obstacles, and vehicles were real. At this point, the 65th lined up their Regimental Tank Company (15 tanks) on a ridge overlooking the drop zone. My platoon and I were already positioned on this particular ridge. Since we had no part in this phase of the exercise, we simply remained in place and waited for the action to get underway. Unfortunately, the wind was blowing in from across the sea at a rate that rendered it unsafe to jump, i.e., in excess of 15 mph.

This fact did not affect the planned jump and out of the planes dropped something like 800 Paratroopers. As the troopers reached the ground, they were warmly greeted by both the wind and the 65th. As I recall, there were 42 injuries on that jump, which was reasonably viewed as excessive. In the end, the exercise umpires ruled that the entire battalion had been wiped out in the assault on the drop zone. Although I was not airborne qualified at the time, I learned a valuable lesson about airborne operations that day. It was to make damn sure the drop zone is safe and the wind is not blowing too hard at the time of the drop.

My orders were to harass the Third Infantry Division in any possible way, at any time, and in any place of our choosing. We were traveling light, so we carried no radios, and a limited supply of food, water, and ammunition. For this exercise, we wore the aggressor uniform of dark green khakis and we were armed with M-3 sub-machine guns.

We roamed the entire exercise area foraging for food, water, and [blank] ammo. I kept in touch with the aggressor command only by intermittent personal contacts. We screened beaches and attacked supply dumps. On one occasion, we found ourselves in the middle of a battalion from the famous 15th Infantry Regiment as it was about to cross over its final line of departure and join the fray. We blasted the hell out of them and were neither seen nor caught.

Their attack was thoroughly disrupted. For our part, we rested whenever we got too tired to carry on, always with at least one sentry always pulling guard duty. We stayed where the trees and grass were the thickest, so that we might see but not be seen and thus avoid detection. For eight days, we never washed, shaved, or had a change of clothes. We smelled like swamp water and looked like something the cat dragged in from a rubbish pile.

The final act of the 33rd Infantry Regiment's Intelligence and Reconnaissance (I&R) Platoon required that we link up with a tank company from the 65th. With lights flashing, sirens blaring, and guns blazing, we stormed a battalion of the Third Infantry Division in an attempt to capture their supply dumps on the beach. The battalion was so surprised by our actions, they didn't fire a single shot at any of us and we took the beach easily. It was then and there, however, the umpires declared we had all *actually* been captured.

This action was taken, of course, in order to save face for the battalion. Our part in Operation PORTREX thus came to an abrupt end. Personally, I felt bad for the 3rd Division because they did not fare well in the exercise. Their tactics and conduct of operations left much to be desired. When I recall the fact that the entire Division was shipped to Korea to fight a real war later in the year, I can only hope they were better prepared for it than they appeared to have been while participating in Operation PORTREX.

As prisoners, my entire platoon was confined to a small grass hut. We were told we were out of the exercise, so we decided it was time to take off our boots and wash up a bit. When the boots came off, three guys flew through the sides of the hut. What a dreadful smell. We really did smell like swamp water. The odor was so overwhelming, everyone went outside to sun their feet and dry out. It's a shame that no one had a camera handy on that day.

We were really grubby and proud of it, because we looked the part of genuine Infantry soldiers in the field. Our appearance that day remains embedded in my brain even to this day. It is as clear now as it was more than 65 years ago. Our entire platoon received glowing commendations from Major General Edwin L. Sibert, US Army (OP4 Commander Operation PORTREX), down through channels to the Company level for its performance during Operation PORTREX. All our hard work had paid off.

Return to Panamá
Fort Kobbe, CZ

April 1950

While we were away, the ladies on the post had been worried by someone who kept stealing a single shoe and a single pair of panties from several of them. Nothing else was ever taken – only women's underpants and the odd shoe. As mentioned, in general, no one locked their doors on the post because entering someone's quarters without being invited simply was not done.

Such a breach of protocol was a serious violation of long-standing custom, which is precisely why it caused so much consternation. Apparently, this bizarre activity had been going on for some time and continued after our return to the base. The MPs had no success in tracking down the culprit and had developed few leads in the case.

My entire platoon was detailed as a security force. One man armed with a .45-cal. pistol was placed in each set of quarters where a theft had been reported. The occupants of these quarters left the premises, so that it would appear as though no one was home.

As often happens in such cases, the thief eventually went beyond swiping shoes and panties. One night the thief entered an Officer's quarters when his wife was home alone and without a security guard on duty. He entered the bedroom and was standing over the Officer's wife when she awakened, saw him, and screamed. Her next-door neighbor heard her, came running to her aid, and saw a man running across an open space towards the post chapel. The MPs were called, they surrounded the chapel and took the suspect into custody.

The culprit turned out to be an individual attached to a support unit on the post. In the belfry of the chapel, the MPs found barracks bags full of single shoes and panties. This was the only instance of its kind reported during my three years in Panamá.

Final Days in Panamá

My last job with the 33rd was the construction of an obstacle course located in the jungle close to Fort Kobbe. I did not know it at the time, but this facility was the forerunner of the soon to be well-known Jungle Warfare Training School. We designed and built various obstacle courses and other ancillary facilities, which included a live-fire hand grenade range. As I stated before, my small 17-man platoon was well-trained and able to execute any assigned mission. When completed, the course was rated as excellent by higher command. It would probably last a good five to ten years.

I remember personally testing the live-fire hand grenade range. I had three or four grenades and tossed them into the impact area from behind a six-foot wall. All but one grenade exploded. The method for detonating an unexploded grenade was to wait 40 to 60 minutes, then cautiously approach it carrying another grenade and a sandbag. You then placed the live grenade next to the unexploded grenade, pulled the pin, dropped the sandbag over both grenades, and hauled ass out of the area. As I was approaching the unexploded grenade, the damn thing exploded. I was not ten feet from it. Believe it or not, I was not hit.

I consider this a minor miracle because an exploding grenade throws off about 70 fragments of steel and has a killing radius of 30 to 40 feet. How I walked away without a scratch, I'll never know. It was just one of the many occasions I came close to *"buying the farm."* If I had been killed or wounded, there would have been no one around to render me medical aid.

Rotation Back to the
Continental United States

April 1950

In late April 1950, I was scheduled to rotate back to the continental United States. When my orders arrived, I learned I had been assigned to the 14th Infantry Regiment at Fort Carson in Colorado Springs, Colorado. At the time, the 14th was the only regiment in the Army which had been trained in mountain warfare. I thought it would be a great assignment. After three years of jungle operations, I could now learn about mountain operations. What a switch.

I was somewhat sad to leave Panamá because my three-year tour had been full of lessons learned which would serve me well in the years ahead. I had finally become an officer, a leader of men, and shaken off the last vestiges of all those years spent in the enlisted ranks.

I finally felt, too, that I could take my place as a member of the Regular Army Officer Corps and make a real "go" of my career.

After all, this is exactly what I had always hoped to do with my life.

CHAPTER 9

FORT CARSON, CO
(JUNE 1950 – FEBRUARY 1951)

14th Infantry Regiment
1st Battalion, Headquarters Company
Pioneer and Ammunition (P&A) Platoon -
Platoon Leader

The Korean War and the Price of Unpreparedness:
It was "*déjà vu … all over again.*"

Anonymous

I reported to the 14th Infantry Regiment [1] at Fort Carson, CO on June 10, 1950. Stationed at the post was also the only (and last) Quartermaster Pack Mule Company in the US Army. QM pack mules had been a big thing in World War II, especially in Italy and the China-Burma-India (CBI) Theater of Operations. Since the 14th IR was trained for mountain warfare, it was only natural in 1950 to support it with pack mules and pack mule Howitzers. Each mule could carry approximately 300 to 400 pounds

---

[1] See: https://en.wikipedia.org/wiki/14th_Infantry_Regiment_(United_States)#Korean_War,_1950%E2%80%9353.

of ammunition, water, and rations, etc. A Howitzer (75 mm short barrel) would be broken down into a three-mule load. The officers in this outfit wore riding boots and breeches as did the enlisted men in the Howitzer Unit. The *"mule skinners"* wore fatigues like everyone else in the Army.

The motto of the 14th was *"Right of the Line."* This nickname was earned at the Battle of Chickamauga, during the American Civil War, when the 14th was placed at the extreme right flank of the Union Army and refused to retreat when the rest of the line wavered. The regimental crest was a golden dragon, which derived from the regiment's service in China during the Boxer Rebellion (1900). The 14th IR was also one of the three US Army regiments which possessed a ceremonial *"China Bowl."* The bowl reputably was made from melted Chinese silver dollars. The Bowl, along with silver cups for each officer, was used on special occasions and at formal social gatherings. The other two regiments with bowls were the 9th and 31st, both of which had served in China into the 1930s.

Fort Carson is a large post spread out over about 137,000 acres covering parts of Pueblo and Fremont counties. It afforded ample space for rifle, mortar, and artillery ranges. It boasted a large hospital, commissary, a Post Exchange (PX), as well as warehouses with railroad sidings, motor pools, and, of course, stables for the mules. Mountain training consisted of climbing, rappelling, and skiing, etc. Since the 14th consisted, in the main, of leg Infantry, we generally had to walk to wherever we needed to get to come rain or come shine. Training was also conducted on Cheyenne Mountain, which now houses the headquarters for the North American Aerospace Defense Command (NORAD), formerly known as the North American Air Defense Command. NORAD is a combined organization of the United States and Canada which provides aerospace warning, air sovereignty, and protection for the North American continent.

The Officers' Quarters consisted of converted hospital wards. During World War II, the building had been a regional medical facility for recuperating wounded GIs. It was a very large facility, much larger than required in peacetime, so the spaces were converted to officers' living quarters. Walls had been built to divide the wards into quarters that included bedrooms, a living and dining room, and kitchen. The floor support posts, however, had not been removed. These quarters were not too bad by

Army standards of the day, but none of them were ever likely to have been featured in either *"House Beautiful"* or *"Town & Country"* magazine. Very little landscaping had been done to enhance the appearance of the properties. There was virtually no grass, there were no trees, no shrubs, and no sidewalks – but plenty of dirt.

The regimental Adjutant called me in for a briefing and meeting with the regimental Commanding Officer. Captain Charles Tyson was the Adjutant. He and I hit it off right away. Through him, I learned there was an immediate opening in the 1st Battalion for a Platoon Leader in the Pioneer and Ammunition (P&A) platoon. From my point-of-view, I didn't mind taking on this assignment since I had already served in a similar capacity with the 33rd IR in Panamá. Charlie had confided to me that the platoon was in need of some real leadership. That evening, he invited me to dinner and that marked the beginning of a life-long friendship.

14th Infantry Regiment, 1st Battalion,
Headquarters Company,
Pioneer and Ammunition Platoon (P&A)
Platoon Leader

June 1950 – February 1951

The Battalion CO was a short, rotund, Lieutenant Colonel whose looks and gentle nature might have had him mistaken for either a Preacher or soft-sell type salesman. Throughout the regiment, there were several graduates of the US Military Academy at West Point (USMA), Class of 1946. Headquarters Company, 1st Battalion, 14th Infantry Regiment was commanded by a Captain, formerly a Sergeant, who had been called to active duty during World War II. The P&A Platoon had been run by a Master Sergeant for some time before my arrival. I am certain he was very unhappy about being removed from the top spot because the platoon only rated a Sergeant First Class as Platoon Sergeant. He was a doer, rather than a leader, and it did not take him long to understand there was only room for one Platoon Leader.

The Platoon was responsible for all the battalion's engineering requirements, mine field laying and removal, ammunition requisition, storage and disbursement. As such, the platoon had a heavy load of assorted tools, equipment, and supplies – none of which had been either well organized or adequately controlled. Drawing on my experience with the 33rd Infantry P&A, it took only a short period of a few days to plan, build bins, boxes, and racks to organize our affairs and implement a standard set of policies and operational procedures.

On June 21, 1950, eleven days after my arrival in the 14th, the Korean *"Police Action"* commenced with the outbreak of hostilities. It was not the first time that the US armed forces were caught unawares by the sudden advent of war. Our post-World War II political leadership, in its haste to return America to a peacetime economic footing, oversaw the rapid decline and weakening of all branches of the United States military.

By the summer of 1950, the standing US Army, Navy, Marine Corps, and Air Force were decimated to the point where virtually all units were understrength and undermanned. Between 1946 and mid-1950, the remaining US Army divisions were down to two regiments rather than the standard three. Likewise, regiments were reduced in strength to two battalions from the authorized three.

When North Korean troops flooded across the 38th parallel to attack the Republic of Korea (ROK), the US government scrambled to mobilize enough combat effectives to halt the onslaught. Within days of the attack, the US Army formed *"Task Force Davis"* at Fort Carson. The task force was cobbled together by forming and equipping one full strength battalion from *all* the battalions in the 14th Infantry Regiment.

This unit, the 3rd Battalion, would be supported by a full Tank Company (18 tanks) and one Artillery Battery (four to six guns). It underwent a crash two-week combat training course at Fort Carson, before shipping out for the Far East in early July. Of course, organizing and equipping the task force was given priority over all other activities. It was to be outfitted with everything needed to sustain combat operations at the expense of all other units. We worked our butts off to help them out.

On July 21, 1950 the 3rd Battalion, 14th Infantry Regiment was reassigned to the Far East Command and subsequently attached to the 1st Cavalry Division where it was re-designated as the 3rd Battalion, 5th Cavalry Regiment. Unlike other units that had been cobbled together at the last minute, the 3rd Battalion, 14th Infantry was at full strength and as a result of its rigorous training in mountain warfare -- well prepared to fight in the mountainous terrain characteristic of the Korean peninsula.

Following the departure of the 3rd Battalion, those of us attached to the 1st battalion finally had time to take stock of what was left. Most of the P&A equipment was gone. Most of the battalion's vehicles had been taken as well. What remained in the motor pool required a lot of work and plenty of spare parts. The better NCOs and Privates were gone. I was left with the Master Sergeant and 10 to 12 other ranks. Our remaining manpower fell far short of a normal complement of about 40 NCOs and men and six to seven vehicles. At that point-in-time, we were unable to carry out all of our assigned duties, but we didn't have to worry about that for very long.

Fort Carson was designated as an Infantry Training Replacement Center (ITRC). The idea was that we were to train our own recruits and draftees in order to refill our own regimental slots first. In effect, we were to recruit manpower, provide them with basic training, then provide individual advanced training in each man's assigned military occupational specialty (MOS). In other words, this was to be the mother of all on-the-job training exercises.

Yardbirds started arriving almost immediately. In the 1st Battalion, the NCOs greeted the men, assigned their equipment and bunks, and conducted most of their training. While awaiting the recruits, I was assigned the mission of building a regimental obstacle course. The course was of a standard design common to all Infantry Training Centers in the US Army. It was to be built from matériel already on hand. This presented few problems, since the surrounding mountains were flush with plenty of trees of various sizes. All we had to do was find the trees, coordinate with the Forestry Service, cut the trees down, trim them, and have them delivered to the construction site located at the base of the Rockies about 20 miles away.

At the site, we pitched our pup tents, set up camp, and got on with the project. While acting as chief architect and engineer, it took our construction gang about two weeks in total to assemble all necessary matériel, lay out and erect the obstacle course, one obstacle at a time. We built it with the tools we had on hand: one chain saw, several hammers and hand saws, thousands of nails, and a few axes. We soon devoted all our energies to the goal of recruiting and training necessary manpower. I was placed in charge of all physical training.

At an altitude of over 5,800 feet, it was a real challenge for many recruits to run and exercise for any length of time. Understandably, many recruits had a hard time breathing until they became accustomed to living and working at this sort of elevation. Anyone who has ever been through basic training knows how challenging it can be to meet necessary physical standards, even under the most favorable circumstances. The daily regimen involved keeping up a breakneck pace for 15 to 16 hours a day. At times, it could be enormously frustrating, difficult, and satisfying to take raw recruits and transform them into soldiers – especially Infantry soldiers.

Our training went beyond the standard Army manual specifications because we had all those mountains and cliffs to use instead of flat terrain. We routinely ran them up and over the mountains and took them straight up cliff faces in all types of weather day and night. Not everyone tried as hard as was expected, so a certain amount of ass-kicking was occasionally required to ensure that each recruit measured up to expectations and passed the course.

The weather at Fort Carson was unusual during the late winter of 1950. During the months of February and March 1951, for example, the mean temperature was normally 20.9 degrees (F). However, during the winter of 1950-51, the weather was highly variable with temperatures swinging wildly between unseasonably warm and extremely cold. At one point, during February, we recorded a temperature of -20 degrees. At Denver Stapleton Airport, that same month, the official temperature hit -25, which is still the coldest temperature ever recorded in Denver. When it was cold, it was at least a dry cold, which therefore did not unduly impair our ability to train. Training exercises continued irrespective either of the weather conditions or temperatures.

I can recall conducting one class on 'Stream Crossing Expedients' inside a vehicle repair facility. There was no stream to cross, of course, but the principles were taught as if there were one. My assistant instructor was Verlin E. ("Lew") Jenkins, a Sergeant First Class, who saw action in Italy and France in World War II as a member of the US Coast Guard. Lew had once been the light-weight boxing champion of the world (1940). I was as surprised as the next guy to learn he was in the Army. He was a very good fellow and a fine NCO. In fact, Lew was awarded the Silver Star for his actions while serving in Korea with the Second Infantry Division, 23rd Infantry Regiment, at *"Bloody Ridge"* (August 18th to September 5th, 1951).

Speaking of boxing, it was during this time that I physically tangled with an enlisted man. It was the only time in my entire commissioned career that this sort of thing occurred. He was undisciplined, insubordinate, and rapidly becoming a threat to unit cohesion. I took him to the shed, so to speak, and behind closed doors administered a proper whipping, which got his attention. In the end, he acknowledged the error of his ways. He soon became an exemplary soldier. Before leaving the regiment, I recommended him for promotion to Corporal.

In late September or early October, a National Guard Division which had been activated reported for duty at Fort Carson. They had every bit of equipment they were supposed to have, but the troops had little or no idea either how to use it or maintain it. We were ordered to get them squared away, organized and trained. It was my first exposure to the Reserve Components.

In early December, I decided I was going to volunteer for airborne training. I wanted to try jumping out of air planes, because it was something I had never done and felt it might be one more way in which to advance my career. It also promised to pay an additional $110.00 a month in hazardous duty pay.

One of my good friends at the time was Lieutenant Arnie Smith. He and I put in for airborne training at the same time. We started our own physical training program while still at Fort Carson in order to be sure of our ability to pass the much-vaunted requirements of the Airborne School. As I recall, the test consisted of pullups, sit-ups, pushups, and running the 200-yard dash in a specified time. I was in such good physical shape that I actually passed the test with plenty to spare. Arnie got his orders almost at once, went off to school, got qualified, and returned to the regiment before my departure. Arnie was a Reserve Officer, but it was a different situation for me because I was Regular Army. My original request to attend the Airborne School required 13 separate endorsements between the 14th Infantry Regiment and the Pentagon.

The final result was that I was transferred to the 11th Airborne Division at Fort Campbell, Kentucky, for airborne training with a temporary duty assignment (TDY) at Fort Benning. This was a complete and also very pleasant surprise.

For my work at Fort Carson, I received what undoubtedly turned out to be one of the very best ERs of my entire US Army career – and the personal best wishes of the Battalion and Regimental Commanders.

CHAPTER 10

AIRBORNE SCHOOL

FORT BENNING, GA
(MARCH – APRIL 1951)

"I become a Paratrooper.
Airborne. Airborne. Have you heard?
We're gonna' jump out of' a big ass bird."

Airborne Cadence Chant

I left Fort Benning for the Panamá Canal Zone in May 1947. Returning to Fort Benning in early 1951, I discovered the place had changed very little during the previous 46 months. What had changed during the intervening years had everything to do with me. When I last served at Fort Benning, I had been a member of the enlisted ranks for more than 5 ½ years. On October 31, 1946, I graduated from Officers Candidate School (OCS) and received my commission as a Second Lieutenant in the US Army. When I returned to Benning, in March 1951, I had been an Officer for about 4 ½ years. I still felt like a Sergeant at times, but I certainly no longer *acted* like one.

Airborne School

Airborne School was conducted over a five-week period and open to qualified officers and non-commissioned officers (NCOs) from the top three grades.

The basic airborne course consisted of three phases: Week One – Ground Training; Week Two – Tower Training; and Week Three – Jump Training. Its purpose was *"to qualify students in the use of the parachute as a means of combat deployment and to develop a sense of leadership, self-confidence, and an aggressive spirit through mental and physical conditioning."* In addition to the basic airborne course, two more weeks of training were provided: Week Four – Aerial Delivery of Heavy Equipment and Week Five – Jump Master Training and Certification.

There were eight Officers and about 200 enlisted men in my class, which was designated #34. We Officers were taken aside on the first day. We were told that *"Officers do not fail the Airborne Course."* It was that simple. We had passed the qualifying tests, we had volunteered to become airborne types, and we *would* pass the airborne course come hell or high water. After all, by definition, Officers could not be failures at anything. That was it, period.

The first two weeks of training were purely physical. The body had to be toughened to be capable of carrying 42 pounds of parachutes (one main and one reserve), plus field equipment (sometimes as much as 100 pounds), and to withstand the shock of the parachute when it fully deployed and suddenly opened on a jump. The speed of one's descent could vary slightly from one jump to the next, but there was never quite enough time to prepare for a text book landing – you simply had to make it happen instinctively if you expected to live to jump another day.

In 1951, the main chute was the T-7 model. It had a 15-foot static line which was attached to a rigid steel cable running the length of the aircraft's interior. One jumped from the plane with the opposite end of the static line attached to the T-7. When the static line was fully extended, it pulled out the main chute and the jumper's body weight instantly extended the shroud lines attached to the body harness.

This sequence of actions had the effect of literally jerking the jumper's body like dead weight when the shroud lines were fully extended. After accelerating to about 60 mph during the free fall phase of the jump, the jumper came to a sudden full stop and instantly transitioned to a controlled descent. At the risk of citing the obvious, the human body was not designed to take this kind of abuse, which explains why such a premium is placed on top flight physical fitness and mental acuity within airborne units.

The ability to instantly transition into a controlled descent was dependent upon one's mastery of jump techniques, e.g., how to control the chute while in the air in order to avoid collisions and to land and absorb impact with your entire body, and how to use the reserve chute in case the main chute failed. It was essential to learn and master these techniques if one wished to remain healthy, whole, and alive. For this reason, daily physical exercise sessions routinely consisted of a set of 12 prescribed (mandated) exercises the Army had developed to ensure that every body muscle was used every day.

While training, we went from five sequences of *each* exercise to sixteen sequences within three weeks. This meant, for example, that with respect to some of the exercises such as pushups where four pushups were part of a single sequence – we actually performed 64 pushups without stopping. We also did a lot of running, which is to say that all movements from one place to another -- whether the distance was one foot or one mile -- was done in double time.

The first day of school, we ran one mile. We repeated this one mile run daily for five consecutive days. The next five days, we ran two miles each day. In the third week, our endurance was tested by scheduling a four-mile run. Anyone who failed to complete this endurance run was deemed to have failed the physical training. Individuals guilty of an infraction of the rules or an unsatisfactory performance of any kind were punished (usually) by being assigned to perform extra pushups.

It can to be taken as a given that when one jumps out of an airplane at 1,200 feet and your chute operates perfectly, the parachutist can be confident of reaching the ground in 46 seconds, give or take a few seconds, depending mainly on how much equipment is being borne by the jumper. If the chute does not function as it should, one's velocity of descent increases to 125 mph almost instantly and reaction time is reduced to about 12 seconds. Again, this is why it was so important to learn to react to orders at once and without hesitation. One's failure to react in this manner, all but guaranteed the jumper was either dead or seriously injured. After all these years, I still remember *everything* I was taught to do to ensure a safe descent.

Week One – Ground Training

During the first week, ground training featured an introduction to the mock tower. It is an imposing structure which stands 34-feet tall, a kind of simulator designed to teach students individual airborne skills, prepare them to make a parachute jump, and land safely. Students train on the mock door, the 34-foot tower, and the lateral drift apparatus (LDA). The mock tower has a reputation for separating the men from the boys. From the base of the tower, individual harnesses are attached to a trolley by a cable, then students climb up the stairs to the top of the tower, and each in turn takes his place in the mock door (which simulated an airplane door) and, on command, each student jumped up and out. Jumpers slid down the cable a distance of about 100-feet to a sawdust mound where they would be greeted by a pair of ground personnel.

Since one of the human mind's greatest fears is that of free falling into space, quite a few candidates froze in the door atop the tower and either could not or would not jump. In all fairness, the 34-foot tower *looked* to most of us to be more like 340-feet in elevation. Those who did not jump out the door were made to walk back down the stairs while all the others were waiting in the queue and were under orders to report to the Officer-in-Charge. At this point, such individuals were eliminated from further training. All were shipped out from Fort Benning within 24 hours. None was allowed to mingle with their former classmates while awaiting their departure.

Week Two – Tower Training

During the second week, tower training was aimed at refining the individual skills learned during the preceding week, while teaching new skills promoting team efforts and introducing the concept of mass exit jumps. The apparatuses used this week are the 34-foot towers, the swing landing trainer (SLT), the mock door for mass exit training, and the suspended harness. In order to advance to actual airborne jump training students had to qualify on the SLT, master the mass exit procedures from the 34-foot tower, and pass all PT requirements.

Jumps were made from the 250-foot so-called *"free"* tower. Individual jumpers were hoisted vertically to the top of the tower and attached to a 22-foot diameter, fully deployed parachute. The chute then was released and the jumper descended to the ground like on a real jump. Jumpers were graded on how well they made use of all the previous instruction received. Four satisfactory jumps from the 34-foot tower and the 250-foot tower, and a student was adjudged to be ready for the real thing.

Week Three – Five Jumps

Finally, during the third week, we began making jumps from actual airplanes. Five airborne jumps were required to qualify as a Parachutist. Each jump differed from the others in some respect. For example, the first three were made from an altitude of 1,200 feet. The final two jumps were made from 1,000 feet. Exits were made from the right door of the aircraft and then from the left.

The third jump was made with a full complement of combat gear. My third jump was especially memorable, inasmuch as I was knocked unconscious by my rifle when the chute deployed. To the best of my recollection, I limply floated all the way down unable to move my arms and thereby steer the chute. Upon landing, I suddenly regained consciousness, got up smartly and walked away with a satisfactory grade.

The last two jumps were mass exits – 16 men to a door. All our jumps were during daylight hours. No night jumps were made at the school in those days. Malfunctioning chutes were very rare at the school because they were packed and inspected very thoroughly – more so, perhaps, than in an Airborne Unit. Our class, however, did have one young Sergeant whose main chute did not open on the first two jumps he made and on the very same day. His chute didn't work on the morning jump and it did not function properly again that same afternoon. This sort of incident was virtually unheard of but certainly not unprecedented. That young Sergeant was some kind of man, because he went on to make his last three jumps and won his Parachutists Wings. No mean feat given the circumstances.

All eight officers in my class qualified for their Wings as did roughly 80% of the enlisted men. Ten percent quit for whatever reason and another 5% to 10% failed to qualify either due to illnesses or injuries. I had a friend who got through the course all the way up to the 250-foot tower phase. As he was being hoisted up the tower, the chute released prematurely and dropped him about 30-feet to the ground. He broke a leg and was sadly unable to finish the course.

At the graduation ceremony, we wore our Paratrooper boots with our trouser bloused in them and the Paratrooper Patch on our overseas caps. I also had the 11th Airborne Division Patch on my jacket since I had been assigned there before being sent off to attend the Airborne School. Each man's Paratrooper Wings were individually pinned on him by Major General John H. Church, Commanding. It was a proud day and the first day of what has never ended -- being a Paratrooper and a member of the US Army Airborne.

Week Four – Airborne Operations Training

The following week, Week Four, consisted of learning how to prepare for all phases of an airborne operation, including the planning, preparation, and conduct of aircraft inspections, equipment, and personnel. We were also taught how to jump into unmarked drop zones, which were zones that had not been prepared for drops and had no guides concerning where to jump. On my second such jump, I was #1 to exit the door only to discover through observation that the winds were blowing very hard over the ground below. In fact, the furiously blowing sand over the ground's surface was obscuring the drop zone.

I was told to go. I followed the command. It turned out I had jumped at what appeared to be the extreme end of a very large drop zone. As I passed through an altitude of 1,000 feet, the wind was blowing really hard. My old T-7 chute popped open so violently, I was swinging around and bobbing about like a cork in the sea.

There was no way to either control my chute or manipulate my risers and thereby the speed and direction of my descent. I was carried (driven?) by the wind for what I reckoned must have been at least a minute – horizontal to the ground. I finally started to steadily descend but it was hardly a controlled descent.

When I got close to the ground, I was still struggling to gain control of my chute. As the ground rapidly approached, I noticed a gigantic Georgia Pine which appeared to be about six feet in diameter looming to my rear. All I could think to say was, "Oh boy!" because there was no way I could miss hitting a tree that large. Suffice it to say I somehow managed to land at the base of the tree. My head was no more the two-feet removed from its centerline.

So hard was my landing, I was sure my neck was broken. Momentarily, I could not seem to move at all. I laid on the ground for several minutes until someone in a Jeep pulled up and asked if I could walk. I told him *"no"*, so he dismounted and came to my assistance. Once seated in the Jeep, he asked me a second question: *"Why did you jump?"* According to this fellow, ground control had told the plane to call off the jump because the winds were well above allowable limits. But here's the kicker, the plane only got *"the word"* after I had hit the silk. No one else jumped that day.

For the next week or so, I could not stand up straight though walking was in the cards. My backside was black and blue from top to bottom. When I landed it was on my tailbone or so it seemed. As things played out, this was just one of many such incidents that took place over the ensuing 21 years. When I had to return salutes, all bent over, scarcely anyone thought anything of it because they could see my boots, Patch, and Wings.

They knew damn well what ailed me. I successfully completed the prescribed five weeks of training at the Airborne School, wrapping it up with seven jumps to my credit, and soon departed Fort Benning, Georgia for my new assignment at Fort Campbell, Kentucky.

CHAPTER 11

FORT CAMPBELL, KY
(MAY 1951 – JUNE 1953)

**11th Airborne Infantry Division,
188th Airborne Infantry Regiment (AIR), 2nd Battalion,
Company H - Machine Gun Platoon Leader (May 1951)
2nd Battalion, Motor Pool Officer (June – September
1951) | 188th AIR, 1st Battalion, Company B –
Commanding Officer (September – December 1951) |
188th AIR, Regimental Service Company - Commanding
Officer (December 1951 – June 1953)**

*"On the eighth day God created the Paratrooper
And Hell cried, "Airborne."*

Airborne Folklore

Fort Campbell is a very large military post. It covers more than 164 square miles and 105,068 acres. Located between Hopkinsville, Kentucky and Clarksville, Tennessee, it straddles the state border pretty much equally between Tennessee and Kentucky.

Division Headquarters and two of its three regiments were located in Kentucky. My regiment, the 188th Airborne Infantry (AIR) was billeted in Tennessee.

Three of my OCS classmates were already stationed at Fort Campbell at the time of my arrival. As a relatively senior First Lieutenant, I was #12 on the list to receive family quarters. It was one of the few nice things about having seniority or date-of-rank as a Lieutenant. Otherwise, Lieutenants were a dime a dozen and generally treated as such. While awaiting permanent quarters, I lived in the 188th Bachelor Officers Quarters (BOQ).

My initial impressions of the 188th were not especially favorable. Its facilities consisted of typically beige-painted two-story barracks, single story orderly rooms, a mess hall, and a supply room. A typical company area consisted of a combination orderly/supply room, mess hall, and four two-story barracks buildings. All companies and battalions of the regiment were in close proximity to each other.

In 1951, a US Army Infantry Division had three Infantry Battalions, each with three rifle companies, a heavy weapons company, and a headquarters company. Each rifle company had three rifle platoons of three squads each and one weapons platoon with two light .30 caliber (7.62 mm) machine gun squads and one 60 mm mortar squad. Heavy weapons companies had .50 caliber (12.7 mm) machine gun platoons and 81 mm mortar squads. Headquarters companies had a communications platoon, motor pool drivers and mechanics, mess hall personnel, and administrative personnel who worked in the battalion headquarters.

The 3rd Battalion of the 188th had all Black NCOs and enlisted men and all White Officers. Segregation was still prevalent across the US Army in the early 1950s. A standard battalion had about 850 officers and enlisted men. The 3rd Battalion, however, had a complement of more than 1,100 officers and enlisted personnel.

During this period, all buildings on the base were heated by coal stoves. There were large coal bins located throughout each company area. Naturally, these bins were always being whitewashed and the coal piled so as to conform to military standards of appearance. Coal smoke and soot covered the entire post area in the winter months. Our beige colored buildings always looked dirty and had to be hand washed for inspections.

11th Airborne Infantry Division, 188th AIR, 2nd Battalion, Company H, Machine Gun Platoon Leader

May 1951

I was assigned to H Company, 2nd Battalion, 188th AIR as Platoon Leader, Machine Gun Platoon. This was the same job I held in D Company, 33rd Infantry Regiment in Panamá. Each company in the battalion had a letter designation, except for the Headquarters Company.

**11th Airborne Infantry Division, 188th AIR, 2nd Battalion,
Company H, Machine Gun Platoon
1st LT. Floyd R. Mulvany, Jr. [Second from left] | Platoon Leader
Fort Campbell, KY
May - 1951**

When I reported for duty with H Company, the only person I ran across was a Warrant Officer Junior Grade (WOJG, pronounced WO-GEE), who appeared to be reading a set of regulations. When he stood up to greet me, I noticed there was a comic book concealed behind the regulation's pamphlet. This was my introduction to the one and only Herbert L. ("Jack") Evans. I always referred to Jack as *"Hood Head"* and he always returned the compliment. We became lifelong friends, last having served together years later during my first tour in Việt Nam (June 1962 – December 1963).

Jack had been a Paratrooper since 1943, had served with the 11th in the Pacific, was one of the first 'troopers' to occupy Japan, and had only 13 jumps by the time I made his acquaintance. He had also been one of the first enlisted men to become a Warrant Officer after the program was inaugurated following World War II. When we met, he was the Company Unit Administrator. A former Company First Sergeant, he was always right at home in the Orderly Room. We hit it off from the start. He helped me in many ways to do a better job in the regiment.

The 1st Battalion always had A, B, C, and D companies; the 2nd Battalion had companies E through H; and the 3rd Battalion had companies I through M (aka the "MILK, Battalion). The letters D, H, and M designated heavy weapons companies. This same organizational framework applied to every Infantry regiment in the US Army.

None of the regiments in the 11th Airborne Division was up to fully-authorized strength in 1950. When the Korean Conflict broke out, rather than send a regiment assigned to the 11th, *per se*, the Pentagon elected to place levies on each regiment and formed the 187th Airborne Regimental Combat Team. Some of the best NCOs and young officers were sent to the 187th.

Since units in Korea had top priority for men and equipment, as surely ought to have been the case, the 188th was rendered just shy of ½ strength as the first year of the conflict came to a close. In my heavy machine gun platoon, for example, I had under my command 20 men out of an authorized complement of 42. Vehicles of all types were in short supply but, being Airborne all the way, we thought nothing of walking seven or eight miles to a training area carrying our machine guns and all other equipment on our backs. God knows all of us were lean, mean, and physically fit.

When I arrived at Fort Campbell, the Commanding Officer of the 11th Airborne Infantry Division was Major General Lyman L. Lemnitzer. General Lemnitzer had been highly decorated during WWII for, among other things, reputedly having slipped into North Africa in a dinghy to convince the Vichy French to surrender to the Allies. How he ever or why he ever became a Paratrooper was beyond my powers of comprehension. My hunch was that it was all about getting that *command time* ticket punched, hence his promotion to command the 11th Airborne Division.

Unfortunately, on Lemnitzer's watch, I cannot recall during my entire tour, a single combat readiness inspection, any record of rigid adherence to discipline, and few (if any) personal appearances in any regimental areas. Moreover, it also boggled my mind to think the 11th had been written off as a mere replacement unit for the 3rd Battalion, 187th Infantry Regiment, then serving as already noted in Korea as the 187th Airborne Regimental Combat Team.

11th Airborne Infantry Division, 188th AIR, 2nd Battalion Motor Pool Officer

June – September 1951

In May 1951, I was unexpectedly appointed the Battalion Motor Officer. I mildly protested the assignment, because I really knew very little about vehicles and felt I was not really qualified for the job. My preference, if given a choice, would have been to lead troops instead.

I quickly learned that motor pool personnel were living in a world apart from the troops of the line. Typically, they were Mechanics, Drivers, and Dispatchers. It was fortunate that the Battalion Motor Sergeant was an experienced motor pool type who knew the *'ins'* and *'outs'* of the operation. He was very resourceful, probably the best damn scavenger I ever came across during the entirety of my Army career. For my part, I knew what I didn't know but thankfully he did too.

While I worked to learn as much as I could as fast as possible, my limitations gave him a chance to actually run the whole show. It was shaping up to be a challenging assignment, since all our vehicles were in need of lots of repairs and maintenance. In retrospect, it was clear that I had been tagged with this assignment because of my reputation as a problem solver. It turned out that a recent round of inspections showed that the average deficiency rating for each vehicle in our inventory was thirteen (13). At the time, 3 or more deficiencies was considered unsatisfactory. It was determined that the only way to correct the situation was to come up with a plan to rotate all vehicles through the shop on a regularly scheduled basis. This meant we had to take them away from individual companies for up to thirty days. As a practical matter, it was the only way to properly and efficiently address required maintenance activities.

The battalion inventory consisted of the following types of vehicles: Jeeps (¼ ton); weapons carriers (¾ ton); and trucks (2½ tons) in each company. I requested permission from the Battalion Commander to get this program underway without delay. It was imperative to start as soon as possible, because the entire battalion was scheduled to travel to Fort George G. Meade, MD, in June to conduct training for ROTC Cadets. It was unlikely that many of the vehicles could make the trip in the shape they were in at the time.

11th Airborne Infantry Division, 188th AIR, 2nd Battalion, Company H
1st LT. Floyd R. Mulvany, Jr.
Annapolis, MD
July 22, 1951

To make a long story short, our Battalion Commander endorsed our plan and permission was granted to schedule and initiate necessary repairs. Within days, we had begun to bring in vehicles, tear them down, and make necessary repairs. We worked day and night, seven days a week for about a month. A re-inspection at the end of the repair cycle revealed we had achieved an overall of three major deficiencies per vehicle. We had pulled off a minor miracle in record breaking time and learned a lot in the process, which ultimately resulted in a round of *"atta boys"* from the Battalion leadership team.

Temporary Living Quarters

I only had to wait about four weeks before I secured a set of quarters on post – if a converted company mess hall could in any way be construed to be suitable quarters. God as my witness, the grease sumps were still embedded in the floors, the floors were bare cement, and so were the walls, to say nothing of the fact that there were no partitions between "*living*" spaces. A drape, of a sort, separated the kitchen from the other "rooms." I couldn't believe it. I was a senior First Lieutenant with more than ten years' service. Here I was living in a converted mess hall. Fortunately, the "*Old Army*" spirit prevailed in me and with my confreres. We were told these quarters were temporary, until the new Wherry Housing Project was finished and available for occupancy in the next three to four months. That news came as a great relief.

Surplus Jump Slots

Since the outfit was understrength, we had no trouble making parachute jumps. There were plenty of chutes on hand. The second day after reporting for duty, I was placed on the jump manifest for the next morning.

There were several drop zones (DZs) on the reservation. The largest was named Yamoda DZ. It was nice and soft and relatively safe with few, if any, stray obstacles or other hazards. It was a 60-second DZ. As the term implies, this meant an aircraft had a full 60-seconds to drop troopers before clearing the DZ. Many troops can be dropped in 60-seconds time. There were smaller DZs where only one or two men or between five and ten could drop at one time. Some of these smaller DZs had not been cleared of artillery shells, barbed wire, and fox holes.

The first drop I made was at a battalion DZ often used by the 187th, which formerly had been a field training area. It was covered with trees, bushes, rocks, and strewn with barbed wire entanglements, shell craters, fox holes and the like. When I hit the ground, I landed within a foot or so of six barbed wire entanglements surrounding a pile of artillery shell casings which had been thrown into a hole. On the other side of me was a thorn bush about three feet in height. Luckily, I landed in between these impediments and avoided injury. I remember wondering at the time why the command would run the risk of dropping four to five hundred men into this kind of terrain. Within a few days of my own experience, this particular DZ was placed temporarily off-limits. This action permitted demolition teams the time necessary to clean up the area and make it safe to use.

Our Battalion Commander was Lieutenant Colonel Sam Walton. He was nicknamed "*Stuttering Sam*" because he stuttered frequently, despite the fact he tried hard to avoid doing so at all costs. He was a good fellow and able commander. As a Paratrooper, he is fondly remembered for an odd habit – every time he jumped, he would without fail, pull the reserve chute whether or not it was necessary. He was easily spotted in the air, because he invariably came down on two chutes.

After completing Airborne School, staying healthy and maintaining top physical condition remained our #1 priority. Every man in the division, except one duty Cook and a Fireman in each company area, fell out for physical training (PT) every morning at 7:00 AM. Our PT consisted of running three to five miles followed by the Army PT test. The PT test entailed pullups, pushups, squat jumps, and running. Normally, every soldier took this test at six-month intervals. Paratroopers made it a part of their daily routine.

11th Airborne Infantry Division, 188th AIR,
1st Battalion, Company B,
Company Commander

September – December 1951

In November 1951, Major General Wayne C. Smith had relieved Major General Lyman L. Lemnitzer as Division Commander. Smith's body was pear-shaped, so he was often referred to as "*Shape Charge*" Smith. A "*shape charge*", as one might infer, is an explosive device shaped like a pear. Its small end was designated the head, which when in use was attached to the object to be blown up.

Major General Smith was an irascible fellow, supremely arrogant, and completely lacking in self-awareness. Despite such limitations, generally he was regarded as a capable commander -- but hardly someone who was likely to be held in high esteem by his subordinates. A single anecdote will suffice to illustrate my point.

Whenever the Division was massed on the parade grounds, Major General Smith would arrive in his soldier-driven sedan, exit the car on the troop side, and *require* his driver to blouse the Commander's own trousers over his boots in front of the entire 15,000-man assemblage. He would occasionally elect to *"troop the line"* from a helicopter, which would be flown directly over and in front of each unit blowing dirt, dust, and grass all over the troops who were standing at attention.

11th Airborne Infantry Division, 188th AIR,
Regimental Service Company,
Commanding Officer

December 1951 – June 1953

In January 1952, Major General Ridgely M. Gaither succeeded Major General Smith as Commanding General, 11th Airborne Infantry Division. Major General Gaither was a lean-faced, slightly built man, whose outward appearance masked his inner toughness. One of his first actions was to personally inspect every unit's area on foot.

He covered every square yard of territory and examined every structure. Shortly after his arrival at Fort Campbell, he leaned on a stair rail while entering a barracks, the rail collapsed, and he took a fall. Although [then] Brigadier General Gaither was not seriously injured, this incident might very well explain his insistence on complete inspections of all facilities and prompt repairs of all facilities at the company level. Brigadier General Gaither also instituted a 24-hour, seven-day-a-week Summary and Special Courts Martial Board to ensure swift and just sentencing of any enlisted man who violated any standing division, regiment, battalion, or post order or regulation. To his credit, the new Commanding General's actions quickly restored good order and strengthened discipline which had been eroded through neglect under Lemnitzer and Smith. Summary court fines for those found guilty were an automatic $25.00.

We learned to respect Gaither and his efforts because such actions had the effect of making the division a better one. In July 1952, Major General Smith took over as Commanding General, 7th Infantry Division in Korea. Shortly thereafter, he became infamous for planning a daylight attack, having seats installed on a hill overlooking the action, and having had programs printed and disseminated for the members of the international press who had been invited to cover the affair. He never changed.

Temporary Duty – ROTC Training
Fort George G. Meade, MD

April – May 1953

During the latter stages of my stint as the Battalion Motor Pool Officer, we were scheduled for temporary duty at Fort Meade for about two months. ROTC Cadets from colleges all across the East were receiving their annual two weeks of required summer training. On the morning of our departure from Fort Campbell, I noticed that all of the battalion's vehicles were freshly painted and lined up in good convoy order – except for two ¼ ton trailers which had disappeared from our motor pool the previous night. There wasn't enough time to solve this mystery, so I told the Sergeant we had to have the two trailers back within the hour. Otherwise, we would be unable to get under way on time.

Convoy Protocols

Well, as anticipated, the trailers soon took their proper place in the caravan in a nick of time. Both trailers were sporting a fresh coat of paint and their new serial numbers were stenciled on the rear ends. As mentioned, the Sergeant was truly a first-rate scrounger and a remarkably resourceful NCO. Scrounging was a way of life in the Army. On occasion it rose to the level of an art form. Everyone knew about it and virtually everybody engaged in the practice at some point. Thievery was never condoned, but scrounging was essential to a unit's survival in those instances when the supply system failed to function as expected.

Military convoy travel was governed by set procedures. Vehicles traveled on highways at 100-yard intervals so as to avoid hindering civilian traffic. The lead vehicle in a convoy carried a large sign which read *"Convoy Ahead"* and traveled at about 25 mph, irrespective of the prevailing speed limit. Radios were interspersed throughout the convoy to facilitate good and timely communications. Fuel trucks and wrecker vehicles brought up the rear. Specially modified 2 ½ ton trucks outfitted as mobile kitchens provided meals at regular intervals along the route of travel. It was all well organized and very military. When appearing in public, it was customary to make sure all units put their best feet forward for the sake of good order.

We stopped each evening at preselected locations, e.g., at local armories, State Parks, or campgrounds, etc. Pretty much any location would do as long as it was safe and out of public view. Generally, passes were made available to enlisted personnel for those who wanted them. Normally, passes were good for 24 hours. Our first stop was at a small town in eastern Tennessee at which a carnival happened to be playing. Carnivals were big events in small towns across America and small Southern towns were no exception. I was serving as Officer-of-the-Day, when word reached me that some of our troops had been raising a ruckus at the carnival. I promptly headed into town to investigate the matter.

What I found was a crowd of about 100 locals and roughly 12 – 15 soldiers milling about. I asked our people for an explanation concerning the affair. It was reported that several of the enlisted men had paid to see a stripper perform, but she was a no show once they had been lured inside one of the tents. Some of our people proceeded to tear apart the wooden stage and the locals took exception to their actions. Being alone and unarmed, I decided to take the *"Irish"* way out. I repaired to the ticket booth at the main entrance and declared to those inside that I was placing the entire carnival off-limits to all military personnel and that it would be deemed a federal offense to sell a ticket to anyone in an Army uniform. Everyone heard me because I made a point of speaking loud enough to be heard. I was backed up by my troopers. We were then subjected to verbal abuse by several civilians.

One civilian, in particular, a small skinny-faced fellow who sported an enormous Adam's apple, was especially vocal. I told him to shut his mouth and come forward. Fortunately, he declined to do so which gave me time to mull over how best to defuse the situation. I ordered my men to leave the area, telling them the money they had paid for the stripper show, which did not go on, would be used to pay for repairs to the stage they had damaged. I told the carnival barker there would be no extra charges brought against my people. I reminded the carny barker that I could hardly be held responsible for any further damage which might result if a bunch of angry and aggrieved Paratroopers were further provoked.

It seemed as though the operative term was *"Paratroopers."* The locals knew of Fort Campbell and could only imagine what sort of mayhem might ensue if circumstances got out of control. Few additional words were spoken by either side as we withdrew, though in a couple of cases it was necessary to give direct orders to those who insisted on responding to verbal barbs. In spite of our unfortunate interaction with the carnival crowd in eastern Tennessee, we did have a number of good stops as we made our way to Maryland.

The distance between Fort Campbell and Fort Meade was approximately 760 miles. At 25 mph, it took roughly slightly more than 30 hours driving time spread over four to five days. The drive itself took us through portions of Tennessee, Virginia, and Maryland -- some extraordinarily beautiful countryside. Much to our delight, we also found that the closer we got to our destination the more welcoming were the natives. One of our more memorable encounters took place near Roanoke, Virginia. A few of us young Lieutenants happened to meet the local US Air Force Recruiting Officer, a female Second Lieutenant, whose father was in the liquor business. She was kind enough to invite a few of us over to her family's home where she and her folks showed us a lovely time.

Fort Meade Debut

A couple of days later, we arrived at our destination without much fanfare. Our barracks area, mess hall, headquarters, and so on had been prepared by our advance party. Everything was in order, so much so it proved unnecessary for our travel party to even break a sweat getting our individual areas squared away.

At first it was not apparent to our hosts, all those *non-jumpers* at Fort Meade, that we were not just another outfit until the following morning. Our new Battalion Commander, Lieutenant Colonel Sam Petersen, had been on the cross-country team at West Point. He was tall and slender and could run all day without breathing hard. A member of the battalion staff had told Lieutenant Colonel Petersen we were a running outfit, right after he took over command.

On our very first morning at Fort Meade, Lieutenant Colonel Petersen had us out of the rack and ready for PT at 5:00 AM. We all lined up in a column of companies with the battalion staff front and center. We moved out on the double. Battalion had ordered tee-shirts for each company and every member to wear during our time at Fort Meade. Each shirt was white with the regimental crest and company designation emblazoned in blue letters across the front. There could be no mistaking it, we were the 2nd Battalion, 188th Airborne Infantry Regiment.

11th Airborne Infantry Division, 188th AIR, 2nd Battalion, Company H
1st LT. Floyd R. Mulvany, Jr.
Annapolis, MD
July 25, 1951 [1]

---

[1] 1st LT. Floyd R. Mulvany, Jr., is crumpled up in the extreme lower right corner of the above photograph. According to Mulvany, *"the Chaplain came over to read me the 'Last Rites'. It seemed everyone thought that I had been killed. Fortunately, I was only knocked unconscious."*

Each company also carried its individual Guidon. When we were on the move, we ran, and when we ran, we always chanted airborne slogans as we wound our way throughout the post. Since we were visiting a non-Airborne post where reveille wasn't sounded until 5:30 or even 6:00 AM, we made every effort to sound off loud enough to wake the dead.

No one could sleep through our chants. As we ran by the post barracks area, everyone had an early reveille and, of course, we were on the receiving end of plenty nasty jeers from the unwashed masses. "Leg"[2] types, including their officers, did not understand the airborne spirit. They were blissfully uninformed, so we did our best to spread the word. It wasn't very long before the insults became stronger and the threats more aggressive.

Clash of Cultures

Usually, young troopers went around together and avoided the "legs" because they knew they were cut from better stock. This ethos was ingrained in the volunteer Paratrooper types from the very outset of their training at jump school. In our book, one single paratrooper was worth any four to ten *legs* on any day of the week.

Two of our young men visited the Enlisted Men's Club one evening. They soon found themselves surrounded by 25 or 30 brave *legs*, many of whom were showering them with all sorts of derogatory names. The two troopers responded by throwing punches, but they really didn't stand a chance.

It turned out the bold group which initiated this action hailed from one of the engineer battalions on the post. Indeed, we learned this was the same outfit that had made a practice of heckling us from the relative safety of their own barracks during our early morning PT sessions. One morning after PT, the officers were assembled in an orderly room for a briefing.

By some strange coincidence, at the same hour as the Officers' Briefing, the Battalion Sergeant Major formed up all the enlisted men in their steel helmets and took them over to the engineer barracks. As a result of the Sergeant Major's unannounced "house

---

[2] The terms "leg types" or "legs" was used to describe infantry soldiers who were not airborne qualified, i.e., not paratroopers.

call", several engineer types were sent to the hospital as the MPs arrived to break up the donnybrook. Regrettably, a couple of the MPs were also laid out before order could be restored.

The upshot was that there was an investigation into the circumstances which gave rise to the brawl. It was determined that our Battalion Sergeant Major was the principal instigator of the trouble. He accepted sole responsibility for the actions of his troopers. Unhappily, the Sergeant Major was reduced one rank as a consequence.

For some reason, the MPs at Fort Meade felt it necessary to harass our enlisted personnel on and off the post. Battalion leadership, officers and enlisted men alike, soon found this situation intolerable. And so, it happened that on one particular morning, instead of engaging in our usual PT exercises, the Battalion Commander, Sam Petersen, addressed his assembled troops and asked how many boxers there were in the ranks.

Several hands went up, including a hand which belonged to a young Lieutenant who had held the welter-weight title at his alma mater. The boxers were interviewed and ten were selected to participate in an important mission. Once the necessary personnel were identified, Colonel Petersen paid a courtesy call of a kind to the Lieutenant Colonel in charge of the MP regiment and threw down the gauntlet.

Colonel Pete told the Commanding Officer of the MPs that we were ready to settle our differences once and for all by means of a boxing tournament. Each outfit would nominate ten individuals in various weight classes to square off against one another. While Colonel Pete's challenge might have come as a surprise to the Lieutenant Colonel, his polite refusal to square off against the airborne troopers certainly was not at all surprising.

ROTC Training Results

We were good at training ROTC Cadets. It was that fact that explained why we had been selected for the job. We delivered our training airborne style and the cadets responded well to the challenges posed. Some cadets even requested the opportunity to train at Fort Benning. We returned to Fort Campbell with many compliments from the ROTC Camp Commanders, all of whom were Regular Army Officers.

Missing Property

Unfortunately, our departure from Fort Meade didn't exactly come off without a hitch. Our battalion was accused by the post Office of the Deputy Chief of Staff for Logistics (G-4) of shorting the base some 2,000 bed sheets. The sheets had been issued to us over a period of several weeks, but all were to have been returned to the logistics operation prior our departure.

Having had advance notice of the apparent shortage, we investigated the matter and, sure enough, the sheets were missing. What explained the shortage was an administrative error on the part of our Battalion Supply Officer. He had had them shipped back to Fort Campbell with our advance party, himself included, so the sheets weren't really *"missing"* at all.

Given the circumstances, there was nothing that could be done to immediately resolve the matter. Nevertheless, the Post Commander ordered our Battalion Commander to line up all the officers because someone in the post G-4 office said he could identify the Lieutenant who had signed for the sheets originally. He would be held liable for paying for the sheets.

Of course, there was no positive identification that could be made because the offending party already had returned to Fort Campbell with our advance party. Moreover, a thorough inspection of our battalion's baggage train failed to turn up any sign of the allegedly purloined bedding. As far as I know, no one was ever brought up on charges and none of our people were out-of-pocket a dime. And the sheets eventually did find their way back to Fort Meade.

Airborne All the Way

Life at Fort Campbell was good. We were young and full of piss and vinegar. We were healthy, if not wealthy, resourceful, and thoroughly devoted to the professional Army.

We were also pretty well adept at keeping ourselves entertained. Regimental life was by its nature very closed. Seldom did we mingle either with other regiments or units on the post. About the only times we did were on the occasion of our monthly division review, where every outfit in the entire 11th Airborne Infantry Division lined up on the parade grounds for a gigantic march around.

Lining up 15,000 officers and men took time and a great deal of coordination. The division, on line, stretched for the equivalent of more than three city blocks. The Infantry marched by in review, followed by the Artillery and Armor units, and other supporting arms brought up the rear.

US Army | US Air Force
Joint War Games - "Exercise Snowfall"
Camp Drum, NY

February 1952

In February 1952, three Infantry regiments were ordered to participate in *"Exercise Snowfall"* at Camp Drum, Watertown, New York. Camp Drum was situated close to the Canadian border, where temperatures were colder than an Eskimo's ice box. Here we were taught to use skis and bear-paw snow shoes while engaged in simulated winter combat operations. During training we learned how to defecate in a paper sack, sleep soundly on a one-man sled, and keep our feet warm in rubber boots.

We learned survival techniques which enabled us to stay alive and combat effective even when the temperatures dipped below minus 50-degrees Fahrenheit. We also learned how to load and unload aircraft while dressed in a heavy hooded parka with a main and reserve chute on our backs. And to top it all off, we experienced the exhilaration of jumping out of airplanes in the face of howling 30 mph wind gusts with all manner of equipment strapped to our bodies and landing safely. As it turned out, this maneuver was good training for fighting in Korea, except for the skis and snowshoes.

We carried those damn things on our backs for two weeks before the maneuver got underway, even though there was no snow on the ground. Inevitably, we were ordered to turn the snow gear in to supply – and we did. You guessed it, the night before *"Exercise Snowfall"* commenced, it started to snow and didn't stop for about a week. During the exercises, I served as Commanding Officer, Headquarters Company, 2nd Battalion, 188th AIR. I had assumed command of this unit in October 1951. It was my first company command.

Racial Integration in the US Military [3]

In November 1951, the Army was ordered to integrate all its Black units into the segregated predominantly White ones. It was mandated that henceforth each unit should be made up of no less than 11 percent persons of color. The Army was in the vanguard of promoting civil rights long before there was a civil rights movement as we came to know the struggle during the latter 1950s and 1960s. Within the professional Army, especially within the Officers Corps, we really didn't give this directive much thought because most of us held the view that a good soldier was a good soldier irrespective of skin color. Certainly, this sentiment was not embraced by everyone all at once but it soon became the reality for the rank and file.

Promotion to Captain

In early December 1952, while still at work in my company headquarters, I was ordered to report to Colonel "*Poopy*" Connor, Commanding Officer, 188th Infantry Regiment. It was dark and cold as I walked over to the head shed. On the way over to his office, I was completely clueless as to why we were to meet. When I arrived, Colonel Connor was alone in his office. Well, believe it or not, the Commanding Officer opened by reading aloud the orders promoting me to Captain. He also presented me with a set of Captain's bars and pinned them on my person. He wished me good luck, then thanked me for all my hard work.

11th Airborne Infantry Division, 188th AIR,
1st Battalion, Company B,

Commanding Officer

The battalion was commanded by a senior Captain. It wasn't too long after receiving my promotion to Captain that I was transferred to the 1st Battalion, which was a battalion in name only. Each of the five companies had only cadre in them since there

---

[3] President Harry S. Truman signed Executive Order 9981 to end racial segregation and discrimination in the military on July 26, 1948. See: https://www.archivesfoundation.org/documents/executive-order-9981-ending-segregation-armed-forces/.

were no soldiers to fill the ranks. I was designated Company Commander, Company B, 1st Battalion, 188th AIR. Notwithstanding the fact that we were only cadre, we had to drill, undergo inspections, and participate in field exercises, etc., as though we were a regular company. It wasn't until the Korean War had been underway for a couple of years that the 11th began to fill up with soldiers.

11th Airborne Infantry Division, 188th AIR, 1st Battalion, Service Company,

Commanding Officer

About three months into my new command with Company B, I was again summoned to Colonel Connor's office. He asked me to do him a favor and take over command of Service Company. This company was composed mainly of vehicles and mechanics. Its inventory consisted of 72 2 ½ ton trucks, which were used to transport the entire regiment in the event it became necessary. Since the regiment was training troops at the time, these trucks were on the go 24 hours a day, and seven days a week.

Rarely were they ever in the regimental repair shops for routine maintenance and repairs, even though there were plenty of mechanics and tools on hand to take care of business. As it turned out, most maintenance had to be done in the field, in order to mitigate the possibility of interrupting training exercises. Also attached to this company were the men who operated the various boilers which produced the steam used to heat and service the regimental area. In addition, the personnel who worked in the regimental supply depot were also attached to the company.

Now, this was truly a service company. I really didn't want the job, but the Colonel told me it was a great opportunity for me to demonstrate my capacity to make the best of an unappealing set of circumstances. According to the Colonel, the service company was an embarrassment, the most run down in the regiment, and its morale had hit rock bottom. He felt I was just the man to turn the situation around. In a nutshell, Colonel Connor made me an offer which I could not refuse. He had been good to me, especially with respect to my ERs, so the obvious answer to the question was *"how soon can I start, Sir?"*

It didn't take long to come to the realization that Colonel Connor's appraisal concerning the state-of-the-company in terms of efficiency and morale was correct. In point-of-fact, matters were probably worse than had been at first imagined. For openers, the company lacked a comprehensive and proactive plan of action. Among other considerations, there was no system in place to govern how drivers were to be deployed to the field; there was no plan for either the scheduling or prioritizing of maintenance activities; there was no 'tool crib' to control system critical assets; the barracks accommodations were dirty and sub-par, and there was no day room where troopers could rest and recuperate throughout the course of the work day.

Plainly, I had my work cut out for me. My first priority was to come up with a plan of action which would ensure the proper alignment of the company's mission, the highest and best use of limited resources, and service-driven priorities. My second priority was to find someone within my command who could design and supervise the construction of a suitable day room. In this regard, I got lucky and quickly found an enlisted man who had been a carpenter in civilian life. With guidance from me, he designed and built a superb day room. His reward was being excused from all other duty while construction was underway. My third priority was to tackle the challenge of setting up a system through which to organize and control the enormous number of tools required to prosecute the work of the company on a day-to-day basis.

Working with the company Maintenance Officer, we conducted a thorough inventory of our stockpile of tools, set up a proper 'tool crib', and introduced an inventory control system to ensure that we always knew what we had to work with, who had signed out which tools, and when each piece out on loan would be returned to the shop. For the first time, the company Maintenance Officer had both the responsibility and authority over the tool crib. When mechanics either signed out tools or equipment from the tool crib, they were solely responsible for returning same to the crib upon completion of every task or project.

In a relatively short time, we were also able to address a fourth priority, which was to get a program in place to clean up and repair all barracks and ancillary facilities. Barracks were reassigned, so that each company section lived in a common set of spaces. With modest changes to standard operating procedures, we experienced a discernable uptick in morale throughout the company within a matter of weeks. Within three months, Colonel Connor was congratulating me and the men for our fine performance.

I had the pleasure of serving in command of the Service Company for about 18 months. During my time in command, I never did actually see or physically touch all the millions of dollars' worth of hardware entrusted to my care. This was alright by me, since it was all signed out to members of my team in whom I had full faith and confidence. My salary at the time was $425.00 a month, but I was still responsible for over $10.0 million worth of equipment and the well-being of more than 200 troopers.

Senior Parachute Wings, Thirty-two Jumps and a Few

"Prop Blast" Ceremonies

At Fort Campbell, I made no fewer than 32 jumps and earned my Senior Parachute Wings in the process. I also witnessed ceremonies at the battalion and regimental levels during which a man who had refused to jump was placed on a platform in a public setting, and had his jump boot laces slashed with a razor, his Parachute Wings broken in half, and was handed orders transferring him off the post the same day. I also witnessed *"Prop Blast"* ceremonies during which newly qualified Paratroopers were made to drink a concoction made from whiskey, beer, and champagne in a single gulp from a steel pot.

And so, it was too, that I became a bona fide member of the "Airborne Association," which is said to be good for a lifetime. I served as an S-3 Officer at the battalion and regimental levels. I grew and I learned and I received excellent efficiency reports (ERs). All of which is to say that from where I sit today, the 16-hour days were worthwhile and very rewarding.

During the three years I spent at Fort Campbell, I made many friendships and created a raft of memories which have been treasured throughout the ensuing years – in some cases for decades. Last but not least, I also received orders for Korea, which were cancelled at the last moment and changed to read: "Report to the Regular Army Infantry Officers Advance Course at Fort Benning, GA, (10AC#1)."

I was to report in June 1953.

CHAPTER 12

FORT BENNING, GA
(JUNE 1953 – MARCH 1954)

Infantry Officers Advance Course
Class 10AC#1

"A leader leads by example, not by force."

The Art of War (~500 BC)
Sun Tzu
(545 BC – 470 BC)

It was truly a pleasant surprise to learn that I was to attend the Advance Course before going to Korea. Attendance was a must for any aspiring young officer on the road to promotion. It was at the Advance Course where we learned how to be Regimental and Battalion Commanders and Staff Officers.

I had the privilege of attending the Advance Course with several notable individuals. These included: Colonel George S. Blanchard, who served as Commander in Chief, US Army Europe/Commander, Central Army Group (CINCUSAREUR/COMCENTAG) from 1975 to 1979.; Charles P. Murray, Jr., then an US Army Major, who as a First Lieutenant serving in France, won the Medal of Honor (1944), and retired as a full Colonel; Kenneth J. Houghton, then a Major USMC and "a Marine

Corps legend", later retired as a Major General; John E. Stannard, who served as a US Army Sergeant on Guadalcanal, later graduated from the US Military Academy at West Point and retired as a Brigadier General; and (best of all) Army Major Charles M. Tyson, who retired as a full Colonel, an old friend and comrade who had tried to persuade me to remain with the 14th Infantry Regiment and who had tried to talk me out of going Airborne. Our class also included officers from Italy, the Philippines, and Ethiopia.

The Advance Course required a significant amount of study after hours. Almost every class involved maps on which we were required to color-code terrain features prior to the class presentation to be conducted the following day. We studied all facets of command and staff functions. As part and parcel of the Advanced Course training, participants were required to author an original, independently researched, error-free, type-written staff study which was to be completed on our own time and submitted two weeks prior to graduation.

I elected to prepare a case study focused on the role of Intelligence and Reconnaissance (I&R) platoons functioning within an Infantry regiment. It was a topic of great interest and importance, especially since I had served for almost two full years as the leader of the I&R platoon with the 33rd Infantry Regiment in Panamá. As a result of my field experience, I recommended the Army develop an all-terrain, armored track vehicle capable of transporting a squad of 12 men who could fire their weapons from inside the vehicle. Such a vehicle was introduced by the Army in the late 1950s. Until that time, I&R platoons had to rely on less mobile, highly vulnerable, wheeled vehicles to conduct reconnaissance missions.

There was nothing easy about the Advance Course, but you could successfully complete the course if one was devoted to learning and refining their professional knowledge. Charlie Tyson and I frequently paired off for late night study sessions. As a rule, we studied each evening from about 7:00 PM to 1:00 AM. More often than not, we spent several hours on the weekends studying as well.

As an interesting feature of some classes, particularly those dealing with tactics, there were officers in the class who had participated in the actual operations being presented. On one occasion, one such officer had a heated argument with the instructor because he felt that the 'facts' presented were at variance with his experience. Ultimately, this interaction led to changes in the manner in which facts were presented and altered the thrust of 'lessons learned.'

I graduated in the middle of the class – 151 out of 297. My case study was graded as "Superior" and duly noted. Moreover, it was stated that my leadership "potential" was far greater than was evidenced by my class standing.

I got orders for Korea along with about a dozen others in the class. Successful completion of the Advance Course meant I had gotten my second *"ticket punch"* on my way to becoming a Full Colonel of Infantry someday. The first was, of course, my graduation from Airborne School.

CHAPTER 13

REPUBLIC OF KOREA
(JUNE 1954 – SEPTEMBER 1955)

**US Army, Armed Forces Far East (AFFE),
8097th Geographical Survey Unit,
Assistant Operations Officer, June – November 1954 |
7th Infantry Division, 31st Infantry Regiment,
2nd Battalion, Operations Officer (S-3), December 1954 –
January 1955 | 7th ID, 31st IR, Regimental Adjutant (S-1),
January – September 1955**

"Now, it is *not good* for the *Christian's health* to *hustle* the Aryan *brown*,
For the *Christian riles*, and the Aryan *smiles*, and
He weareth the *Christian down*;
And the *end* of the *fight* is a *tombstone white*,
With the *name* of the *late deceased*,
And the *epitaph drear*: '*A fool lies here who tried to hustle* the East'."

Solo from the Libretto of Naulahka (1918)
Rudyard Kipling
(1865 – 1936)

The Army granted thirty days' leave prior to the scheduled departure for the Republic of Korea. My time was largely spent preparing for deployment getting my personal affairs in order. In addition, I relocated from my quarters on post at Fort Benning to off-post temporary quarters in Columbus.

As mentioned in the previous chapter, upon completion of the Infantry Officers Advance Course in March 1954, eleven other members of our class were ordered to report to the port of embarkation (POE) at San Francisco to board a troop ship bound for Korea. The U.S. Army Transport *General Simon B. Buckner*, commissioned in January 1945, was a very large troop ship used for the Far East run. She could transport the equivalent of a battalion of soldiers (800). The ship's crew consisted of 38 officers and approximately 360 enlisted personnel.

Arriving at San Francisco on Saturday, May 15, 1954, we embarked and set sail for the Far East on or about Thursday, May 20th. When we boarded ship at the Port of San Francisco (Pier 35), we learned that we eleven were the only officers on board. We had the entire *"Officers Country"* to ourselves, a space designed to accommodate 280. The Officers' Quarters were on the top deck. Accommodations for members of the Women's Army Corps (WAC) and the Naval Reserve Women's Corps (WAVES) were one deck below. Accommodations for enlisted personnel, up to 4,430 troops, were mainly located below decks.

The voyage was uneventful. We did PT every morning, ate, slept, read, enjoyed the ocean view, and basically took it easy for the duration. After about ten days at sea, we docked at Yokohama, Japan on or about Sunday, May 30th. We reported to Headquarters, Armed Forces Far East (AFFE), in Tokyo for assignment on or about Monday, May 31st.

Three of us were told to report to Headquarters' command in Tokyo and the other eight were told to proceed directly to Korea. The three of us told to report to Headquarters were puzzled about our orders. Why would the Army want to keep three Infantry Captains fresh from the Infantry Officers Advance Course in Tokyo? It didn't take long for us to find out.

The following morning, we were told we were assigned to AFFE at Camp Drake, near Tokyo. Camp Drake was the site of the Headquarters for the First Calvary Division, in Japan. One officer accepted the assignment, no questions asked. Barney

Broughton and I objected to our assignment, however, on the grounds that we wanted troop duty in Korea. Broughton and I went round-and-round with our superiors for three days. Finally, the personnel types relented and granted our respective requests for immediate transfer to Korea.

Imagine our surprise when we got the word we were going to Korea. We never did discover why the brass at Camp Drake put up with our antics. While it was customary for an individual officer to express a particular duty preference, it was quite rare when one's objections to orders were taken into account affirmatively and orders were changed.

Captain Broughton was assigned to a line unit. I was assigned to an Intelligence outfit known as the AFFE 8097th, a Geographical Survey Group. Somehow the title of this unit struck me as odd, so I assumed it had to be a cover name. Add to this, the fact that I was not immediately told anything about the mission of the 8097th. What I was told is that I would find out what was up when the time was right.

Only later did I learn that several others from our group (Class 10AC#1) had already been assigned to the 8097th, a Special Operations Group. In any event, it made no sense to resist this assignment. I knew damn well what a stroke of good fortune it was to be leaving Japan, headed to the Korean Peninsula. Besides I also knew that after six months in country, I could request a transfer to a line unit.

I flew to Kimpo Airbase, designated by the US Air Force as K-14, which was located less than 10 miles west of downtown Seoul. As our aircraft approached Seoul from the east, our flight path took us directly over the ruins of the capital and its devastated suburbs. I remember thinking at the time that nowhere had I ever beheld the sight of such destruction and utter desolation. The evidence of heavy fighting was everywhere: blasted buildings, shell holes, remnants of vehicles, and every manner of battlefield rubble.

Momentarily, I felt my heart sink. Was it possible I really could serve 16 months in this place and emerge unscathed? As things stood in the spring of 1954, a tour in Korea was nominally 16 months because we were still at war living in a combat zone with only a [precarious] armistice in place. [1]

---

[1] The Korean Armistice was signed at Panmunjom (Korea) on July 27, 1953.

No peace treaty appeared to be in the cards. Up to this point in my career, I always seemed to be able to find some saving grace in war's death and destruction. In Korea there was no peace, no consolation, to be found anywhere in the aftermath of three years of savage combat.

When I joined the 8097th in late May, the unit was billeted on the grounds of Gyeongbokgung Palace in central Seoul. The palace grounds were originally constructed in the late 14th century, during the Chosun Dynasty (1392 – 1897), and consisted of royal residences and government buildings. During the Japanese occupation of Korea, 1905 – 1945, this royal complex was systematically deconstructed and repurposed by the Imperial Japanese colonial government as part of a larger effort to obliterate all traces of Korean culture.

Armed Forces Far East (AAFE)
8097th Geographical Survey Unit [(2)]
Assistant Operations Officer

June – November 1954

In the later stages of the conflict, the 8097th was among several American military units which took up tenancy on the site and in other structures adjacent to the palace grounds. In addition to office spaces, the palace grounds provided living quarters and an Officers Mess for the 8097th. The enlisted men's living quarters and mess were located in a nearby high school about 100 yards west of the palace.

Our initial briefing revealed that the 8097th was engaged in surreptitiously sending Chinese agents across the demilitarized zone (DMZ) for intelligence gathering on the Chinese Army. We also ran agent cells that had been established throughout North Korea for the same purpose. As near as I could tell, the majority of these agents (assets) were former Chinese Communist soldiers who had supposedly surrendered of *their own free will*" to escape Communism. Over time, I came to the conclusion that most of them had surrendered to get away from the fighting *and* the Chinese Army.

[(2)] For additional insight into the activities of Special Forces HUMINT units in the days following the Korean Armistice, see: https://arsof-history.org/articles/v8n2_tlo_line_crossers_page_1.html.

The 8097th had a number of subordinate units which were responsible for housing, feeding, indoctrinating, and training these Chinese and a more limited number of North Korean defectors. Such units were scattered across rugged mountainous terrain and among several islands off the northwestern coast of the Korean peninsula. In addition to US Army personnel, the 8097th hosted contingents of Army and Navy officers from the Republic of China (Taiwan).

And for good measure, the 8097th also hosted a highly skilled US civilian plastic surgeon who had been placed on temporary duty as a Lieutenant Colonel, Medical Corps. His job was to remove all telltale tattoos from the bodies of our agents before inserting them into no man's land. By the time I arrived, most of this gentlemen's work was completed. He was good at his trade, I thought, because one had to look very closely to find evidence of any former art work.

Our cover story was that it was a Geographical Survey Unit tasked to map the watersheds, rivers, and other hydrographic features throughout Korea. It had no other military function and, as such, no one working in the Group wore any sort of distinguishing patches, insignia, or unit identification on our uniforms. Likewise, our vehicles bore no special identification.

In fact, the 8097th operated a clandestine 'reproduction' center (e.g., tailor shops, print shops, and crafts shops, etc.) which enabled us to reproduce high quality counterfeit reproductions of any item of clothing, identity documents, etc., which the Chinese were issuing to their own cadres. We also maintained a stockpile of contemporary weapons, ammunitions, combat gear (e.g., radios, etc.), eating and cooking utensils, etc., in current use by the People's Liberation Army (PLA). We took pride in the fact we had the capability to completely outfit our agents as a member of any Chinese Army unit. It was quite an operation. The operational cells which had been established behind the Chinese front lines were in direct radio communication with the various field units. Intelligence on Chinese and North Korean units was gathered in the field, collated, and evaluated, before being forwarded to Headquarters, Combined Command Reconnaissance Agencies Far East (CCRAFE), in Tokyo.

Like the US Army, the US Air Force maintained its own intelligence unit in Korea, the 8040th, code name *Jack.* Naturally, Jack was organized and operated along the same lines as the 8097th. Every individual in the intelligence community irrespective of service branch carried on our person, at all times, a printed card stating we were authorized to travel and visit any area in Korea, at any time, and that no questions were to be asked about why we were there or what we were doing. It was a pass signed by the Commanding General, United States Eighth Army.

Captain Floyd R. Mulvany, Jr., S-3 (Acting)
8097th Geographical Survey Unit
Seoul, Korea
(1954)

The 8097th operated several safe houses in and around Seoul. These were inconspicuous looking homes and buildings where our agents could be securely housed with little likelihood of detection. Some facilities were also used as detention centers to house prisoners captured by our agents. Many such facilities were innocent looking enough from the outside looking in, but from the inside they were packaged like maximum security prison cells. On occasion, these facilities also served as places for officers to shack up for a few days of hard duty without anyone besides our trusted Korean security personnel knowing anything about it.

Officers of the 8097th were drawn from all branches of the Army: Artillery, Armor, the Signal Corps, etc. As an added bonus, some of them were actually drawn from the Intelligence Corps as well. Everyone was assigned an intelligence MOS while serving with the 8097th. For the most part, those with whom I served had little or no prior intelligence training or experience. While my own experience was limited at the time, I really didn't understand why the Army chose to operate in this manner. In retrospect, the explanation probably had everything to do with the prevailing assumption that any officer of any branch was capable of performing well in any assignment.

The reality was, of course, another matter altogether. On more than one occasion, it struck me that higher command was occasionally assigning some real duds to our outfit to mitigate the prospect they might do harm in a line unit. Hell, as far as that goes, the Commanding Officer of the 8097th was a Full Colonel on the cusp of retirement from active duty. During my entire time with the unit, I cannot think of a single occasion on which he ever made a decision on his own. Decisions were made by committee by cognizant staff and presented to the Colonel for his stamp of approval. It was a good thing he deferred to his staff. Much of the time, unfortunately, it seemed as though his biggest concern was whether or not this, that, or the other safe house would be available when his next tryst was to be scheduled.

I served in the 8097th as the Assistant Operations Officer and held a 'Top Secret' security clearance. It was my responsibility to know all about our intelligence operations on both sides of the DMZ. An important part of my job was to sift through reams of raw intelligence, analyze the data, write and disseminate monthly operational reports. Such reports summarized which initiatives were underway, their tactical and strategic relevance, and expected benefits, etc. Our intelligence estimates did not rely solely on third party inputs. Rather, I made a practice of spending as much time in the field as possible. Field inspections were carried out by helicopter, junk, and Jeep. We monitored the recruitment, indoctrination, and training of agents through regular field inspections. With the benefit of hindsight, it is clear we were a well-intentioned lot, reasonably well-funded, but neither very sophisticated nor particularly well led.

A few incidents, described below, will serve to elucidate this latter point:

Operation "Bulldog" – Democratic People's Republic of Korea (DPRK)

For several months in a row one of the agents within our intelligence network in North Korea, code named *"Bulldog"*, had been feeding us detailed information concerning the operational readiness of certain enemy units to our front. Everything we might have desired to learn, hoped to know, and coveted for its advantages was forthcoming. Naturally, Headquarters was elated by Bulldog's apparent audacity and perspicuity.

After a period of months had passed, certain repetitious patterns in Bulldog's reporting emerged which gave our analysts pause to reflect upon the possibility we were being played by the enemy. Growing skepticism triggered an internal investigation. It revealed Bulldog's true identity, which turned out to be a certain high-ranking General Officer serving in the North Korean People's Army. Bulldog was ordered to shut down his operation and return to Seoul.

Neither the general nor his minions were ever heard from again.

Insertion Operations – Demilitarized Zone (DMZ)

On another occasion, I was given a mission to send an agent disguised as a member of a Chinese Signals Unit which was located just across the DMZ, through the US lines opposite the [Chinese] Signals Unit. The agent was one of those dedicated former Chinese Communist soldiers who was ready to do or die for us. While coordinating the mission with the US line outfit, 2nd Battalion, 15th Infantry Regiment, 3rd Infantry Division, I learned the Battalion Operations Officer was Captain Earl S. ("*Tip*") Dye, Jr., a graduate of the US Military Academy at West Point (Class of 1946).

Tip was an old friend with whom I had served at Fort Carson and in Panamá. I briefed Captain Dye on the nature and scope of the planned mission. Captain Dye and I worked out the necessary logistical details and the insertion plan was set in motion. It called for my unit to temporarily swap out manpower with Dye's unit, in order for me and my team to assume temporary command of a certain outpost on a specific day, date, and at the designated hour. When arriving at the outpost, I would be accompanied by a small security detail and the agent who would be crossing over through our lines to infiltrate those of the Chinese.

Insertion operations were inherently tricky and fraught with danger. Such operations were highly classified and required approval all the way up the chain of command. Obtaining necessary approvals was very time consuming and could be frustrating as well. When the time came to escort our agent through the lines everything came off without a hitch.

Our agent was successful in crossing the DMZ. His mission was to 'join' the Signals Unit on the other side, observe for seven days, and return to the original point of departure at the same hour exactly one week hence. However, Tip contacted me within two days following the insertion and reported, employing a prearranged code speak, the agent had returned to his outpost. His premature return triggered lots of concern and gave rise to all sorts of speculation on the line.

Here was a presumed Chinese defector approaching an American outpost on the DMZ and asking to speak with me, by name, someone no one on the lines knew of and were not supposed to know anything about.

During our debriefing of the individual, he confessed that while crossing no man's land a change of heart led him to hole up short of his objective. When he ran out of food and water, he decided his chances for survival were best served by returning to the American side. All our effort had been wasted and worse, since this episode might easily have compromised other ongoing operations.

Insertion Operations - People's Republic of China (PRC)

In 1954, a significant number of Chinese Liberation Army (PLA) and North Korean People's Army (KPA) prisoners-of-war (POWs) were being detained on the island of Porum-do. It is located just off the coast of the Korean peninsula and south of the DMZ, in the Yellow Sea, approximately 33 miles west northwest of Incheon City and about 50 nautical miles west of Seoul. A small number of these individuals had been recruited to participate in an intelligence gathering operation on the Shandong peninsula (East China) about 250 miles west of Incheon City and roughly 95 miles due south of the Chinese port city of Dalian.

There had been no actionable intelligence collected about this part of the Chinese mainland for some time. From an intelligence gathering perspective, our objective was the covert insertion of a team of 'reeducated' former enemy combatants south of the port City of Yantai (Shandong Province). My responsibility was to oversee the selection of prospective insurgents, supervise their training, and oversee the procurement of necessary transport, supplies, and equipment to enable the successful execution of the mission.

It took more time than expected to find a suitable Junk type ship, more than two months, but finally we secured such a vessel. Once we had procured the necessary means of transport, we set about to properly have her outfitted with authentic flat ware, utensils, food stuffs, and fishing gear, etc., in a manner consistent with the customs of ordinary local Chinese fishermen. My recollection is that we spent about $250,000 mobilizing for the planned insertion. At the time of this writing (1994), our expenditure of $250,000 forty years ago would be the equivalent of $1.4 million in today's money.

Training for the mission began shortly after we had outfitted the Junk. Several trial runs were made at sea during night time hours to ensure the crew were well-trained in the operation of the vessel and properly indoctrinated with respect to their duties and responsibilities. When it came time to launch the mission, much to our dismay, our insertion cadre adamantly refused to board the ship and set sail for Yantai.

After a heated exchange, we finally told our 'friends' that unless they agreed to get underway immediately, they would be turned over to the tender mercies of our South Korean allies. With this credible threat on the record, all hands agreed to proceed on the condition that at least one American would accompany them on the mission. This was an impossible demand.

No American could credibly pose as a Chinese fisherman unless, of course, he was of Chinese ethnicity and spoke the local dialect. In any event, a compromise was reached in the interests of moving forward. A young US Army Captain was ordered to take the helm of our unit's 80-foot launch and tow the Junk and its crew halfway across the Yellow Sea, a distance of about 125 nautical miles, in the direction of Yantai on the coast of the Shandong peninsula.

Our compromise was a good deal for the insurgents, but a very risky proposition from our point-of-view. Certainly, the refusal of our insurgency team to embark on their mission with enthusiasm and alacrity did not inspire much confidence in their ability to deliver the results we were expecting. In any event, our young Captain upheld his end of the bargain.

When the launch reached the designated mid-point in the voyage, he dutifully released the Junk and bid the insurgents good luck as he turned and headed back to port at Porum-do. While still within ear shot of the Junk, the Captain looked back and saw the vessel was taking on water and sinking fast. It seemed as though our intrepid crew of would-be insurgents had scuttled the vessel.

Being an American, the young Captain felt compelled to reverse course and rescue the whole lot rather to see them drowned. When he returned to port, the insurgents were taken into custody. Soon thereafter they were turned over to the South Korean military authorities.

There were other examples of enemy infiltrations of our cells and refusals of our agents to infiltrate enemy units. Successful operations of this sort were few and far between, but that never seemed to impede access to funds for covert activities. I'm certain we must have scored a few wins, but I never had direct knowledge of such being the case.

Transition Planning

I began preparing for my departure from the 8097th in early October, during my fifth month with the unit. It took some time and effort, but I finally turned up some promising leads. My first outreach involved placing a call to Colonel John H. Michaelis, Commanding Officer, 27th Infantry Regiment.

A good friend of mine was serving on Colonel Michaelis' staff at the time. He had run some interference with his boss, which entailed a personal endorsement and his description of my desire to transition to a line unit. Believe it or not, I was able to speak directly with COL Michaelis. He told me there were vacancies and that he would "start the ball rolling" for my transfer.

In the end, my transfer to the "*Wolfhounds*" did not work out, because the 27th was scheduled to rotate back to Hawaii before my six months' service obligation would have been completed. Within days of learning my transfer to the 27th had fallen thorough, I was speaking with one of my former classmates from the Infantry Officers Advanced Course. Lieutenant Colonel John Pratt was serving as Regimental Executive Officer in the 31st Infantry Regiment.

All was not lost. LTC Pratt told me his regiment also had immediate openings. He assured me that if I applied for transfer to the 31st, I would be welcomed with open arms. With his assurances, I completed and submitted all necessary paperwork, packed my bags, and reported to my new unit at the end of November.

Back at the 8097th, my boss tried to talk me out of moving forward with my transfer, which was nice of him. He wasn't a bad fellow and gave me an excellent ER, but I was simply not comfortable with either his leadership style or my work. While I learned a great deal about covert intelligence operations, I was really pleased to have an opportunity to join a first-rate Infantry unit serving in a combat zone and on the front lines.

7th Infantry Division, 31st Infantry Regiment, 2nd Battalion, Operations Officer (S-3)

December 1954 – January 1955

The 31st Infantry Regiment, my new unit, was known throughout the Army for its colorful history. It bore several nicknames: *"Polar Bears"*; *"America's Foreign Legion"*; and *"Manila's Own."* It was activated in the Philippines in 1916; served as part of the Siberian Expedition of 1919; served in China alongside the 14th and 9th Infantry Regiments during the early 1930's; and in the early stages of World War II while serving in the Philippines (Dec 8, 1941 – May 8, 1942) the entire regiment was decimated by the forces of the Empire of Japan. Later the regiment became the only US Army regiment to be stricken from the rolls of the Army due to combat losses, i.e., killed, wounded, and captured.

I reported to the 31st Infantry Regiment in December 1954. The regiment had recently occupied Camp Casey, an area turned over to it by the 5th Marines. Camp Casey was a motley collection of tents and canvas huts situated just below the DMZ, about 40 miles north of Seoul.

The 31st Infantry Regiment, part of the 7th Infantry Division, was I Corps Reserve. Serving in close proximity to us were the US Army's 32nd Infantry Regiment, the Turkish Brigade, an Ethiopian Battalion, a reinforced company of Greek Army Regulars, and (nominally) a half-battalion of Filipino Army Regulars. It was a grab bag of Allied troops of uneven proportions and dubious combat capability and effectiveness.

Camp Casey | Korea | Demilitarized Zone (DMZ)
Headquarters – 7th Infantry Division
31st Infantry Regiment (Reserve)
December 1954

All of the aforementioned units were understrength and the 31st was no exception. Our regiment had an authorized strength of 133 officers, but on the day of my arrival only 55 were present for duty. Some companies were commanded by brand new Second Lieutenants. Over half of each company's strength were KATUSA's (Korean Augmentation to the US Army). KATUSA troops were integrated into each platoon and squad. At the time, only a very small percentage actually either understood or spoke English. KATUSA's wore our uniforms and were equipped with our weapons, supplied with our equipment, but were issued their own foodstuffs.

I was assigned as Operations Officer (S-3) for 2nd Battalion. I had been a Captain for less than two years, but was now filling a Major's billet. We had a good old USAR type Lieutenant Colonel serving as Battalion Commanding Officer (CO). We had a rather stiff, prickly, Regular Army Major serving as Battalion Executive Officer (XO). My guess was the only reason the XO accepted my presence at first had something to do with the fact that I (too) held a Regular Army commission and (also) had completed the Infantry Officers Advance Course. In any event, since the S-3 was appointed by the CO, there was nothing he could do about my appointment except to accept it.

Temperatures in Korea hovered around 15 degrees Fahrenheit during the last two weeks of November 1954. It turned out to be colder than the knob on an outhouse door. It was a bone chilling cold with plenty of wind and snow. In other parts of the country, especially north of the DMZ, temperatures in some places fell well below zero for extended periods of time. Officers and enlisted personnel were equipped with rubber boots ("*shoepacs*") with which a soldier had to wear two or three pairs of woolen socks to even achieve a modicum of warmth. We had parkas, heavy leather gloves, fur winter caps with ear flaps, and heavy woolen (OG) shirts and trousers. Each man was issued an artic-type (double thickness) sleeping bag with two GI blankets.

Enlisted men slept in regular Army Arctic tents, ten men to a tent. We all had a regular GI issue Army canvas cot on which we laid out our two blankets, our shelter half, and poncho to keep the cold from coming up through the cot. No heat was permitted at night for fear of fire. It was too cold to fight a fire any way. Besides, the water we would have needed to fight a fire would have been frozen – even if water had been available.

Latrines were canvas covered huts, one-, two-, and three-hole units, erected (usually) a fair distance from our living spaces. Each latrine contained an oil stove, a real creature comfort. With no heat at night and the latrines so far away, once we got into our sleeping bags and felt warm, no one wanted to visit the latrines no matter how stridently Mother Nature might have called. As a result, we all developed sensationally strong kidneys. We learned how to endure the agony associated with the urgent need to take a leak, but without succumbing to the urge to get out of bed in order to take care of business.

As the Battalion Operations Officer (S-3), I was in charge of operations planning. In this capacity, I was expected to anticipate unforeseen situations which might arise during combat actions. Moreover, I was expected to prepare standard operating procedures for addressing contingencies, handle any unforeseen circumstances, communicate pertinent plans, develop training course curricula, and routinely conduct training classes to ensure unit readiness at all times.

I had a good operations Sergeant. The fact that more than half of each company's manpower was KATUSA (i.e., Korean Augmentation to the US Army), this reality compounded the many challenges associated with conducting effective training activities. All training classes were, by definition, conducted in English and it was too often painfully clear that most KATUSA were in over their heads. All were tested combat veterans, courageous, and capable warriors, but very few had even a passing command of the English Language. Nonetheless, they dutifully sat through our training sessions, listened attentively, and contributed not a whit to class discussions.

The regiment was responsible for guarding a gasoline pipeline which ran from a fuel depot located 12 miles south of our camp. Standing orders were to shoot-to-kill any Korean man found to be tampering with the pipeline – not, however, women and children. Under the best of circumstances, it was all but impossible for the average GI to tell Korean men and women apart, especially when they were dressed in similar fashion and suffering so greatly from the depredations of war.

Their homes and factories had been destroyed, food crops decimated, and all life's essentials pretty well diminished. Most folks had to steal and all were dependent upon the Allies to take care of them. Korea was a very poor country by western standards. Her people had to be tough and resilient in order to survive centuries of invasions by foreign powers and more recently forty years of brutal occupation by Imperial Japan.

The refugee population-built shelters from any matériel which was available – card board boxes, beer cans, bottles, crates, scraps of tin, and sandbags, etc. These were the only shelters most of them had access to even in the coldest weather. Keeping warm was a struggle for them. Holding the hordes of rats at bay was also a challenge. Prevention of communicable diseases was nigh on impossible.

Understandably, most would do anything for a meal or an article of fresh clothing. When it came to scrounging, scavenging, call it what you will – the Koreans were phenomenally proficient at obtaining the supplies needed to endure as a community in the face of total war. Certain Korean smugglers, it was said, could pilfer a train load of supplies right under the noses of the armed GIs tasked with providing security.

According to reliable reports, Korean entrepreneurs accomplished such feats by tunneling from outside the rail yard perimeter to positions directly under the tracks above which sat the objects of their desire. By carefully removing floor boards from the targeted box car(s), one of the confederates would be hoisted up into the car above, from whence he would then feed its contents to others below, who in turn would hand off their booty to tunnel runners who in turn delivered the goods to waiting transports without detection.

Our Korean neighbors had a good thing going while it lasted. It was a fluke which led to the unravelling of their enterprise, when by chance we discovered a related group of locals was busy siphoning gasoline from several points along the 12-mile pipeline mentioned earlier. Several locals had tunneled under the pipeline at various points by using the large number of rice paddies throughout the neighborhood to their advantage. By cutting holes in the underside of the pipeline at irregular intervals, the guards were unable to either observe or detect the stealthy operations.

Over time a sufficient volume of gasoline accumulated on the surface of one of the paddies, which from a distance looked like "*pure*" paddy water. One night, however, an older fellow lit his pipe in the middle of the "*gas*" paddy and the whole thing went up with a terrific roar. At the time of the explosion, there were several people in the paddy filling drums. There was no telling how many casualties were involved, but I can say when the sun came up all that remained was a burned-out hole in the ground. From that day forward, every paddy along the pipeline route was inspected and physical security was the order of the day.

My job as S-3 kept me busy all the time. The hardest task was to keep everything and everyone at peak operational readiness. Among the biggest headaches we faced on a day-to-day basis were supply chain related. Vehicle parts, in particular, were hard to come by through regular channels. We also persistently encountered problems in obtaining spare parts for our weapons.

There was no shortage of all manner of US manufactured goods, e.g., original parts, spares, cigarettes, and foodstuffs, etc., available on the black market. One could readily procure almost anything at the drop of a hat by way of the burgeoning underground economy – where cigarettes by the carton were the coin of the realm. In many instances, it often simply made sense to circumvent the Army's supply system, rather than to go through the agony of necessary paperwork, approvals, and other rigmarole. Trading on the black market became so prevalent and such a problem that by early 1955, an entire regiment, the 19th Infantry, was designated to scour the peninsula for contraband and round up all US equipment, vehicles, and supplies which were displayed by black market operators. Our aim was to retrieve as many goods as possible and get it back into the US Army and US Air Force supply systems.

The armistice which ended hostilities in the Korean War was signed on July 27, 1953. When the armistice took effect, it seemed as though the Chinese People's Volunteer Army (PVA) and the Korean People's Army (KPA) occupied all the high ground along the 38th Parallel. My recollection is that with very few exceptions our defensive positions – named the *"Kansas Line"* were virtually all situated below the enemy's positions. There was one notable exception to this rule. In July 1953, US Army units, elements of the 25th Infantry Division, held the high ground at a place called Munsan-ni (elevation: 315'/96m). It was a lone strategic outcropping on the south side of the Imjin River overlooking the primary invasion route between the two Koreas. From its top, one could look to the south and see the capital city of Seoul, which was a mere 22 miles away.

I was keen to do a good job as S-3, so I worked hard at it. I did my best to always meet and even exceed the Commanding Officer's expectations with respect to the operational readiness of the battalion. Our battalion's officers were young and mostly inexperienced, but they were all eager to do well. It made for a most satisfactory feeling in very a dismal place. The 2nd Battalion had only a few cases of frostbite, during the winter of 1954. It was a miracle of sorts, because there was consensus that Korean winters were the coldest of those any of us had ever experienced. I have neither forgotten how cold it was nor the vow I made so long ago -- never to be that cold again.

After six weeks on the job, every indication was that I had hit my stride as the battalion S-3. Arriving for work one morning, it abruptly came to my attention that I was being transferred to Regimental Headquarters to be the Regimental S-1, i.e., Regimental Adjutant. My transfer came as a surprise not only to me, but also to the Commanding Officer, 2nd Battalion. It was stated that because I had acquitted myself so well as battalion S-3, my talents were sorely need on the regimental staff.

7th Infantry Division, 31st Infantry Regiment
Regimental Adjutant (S-1)

January – September 1955

At the time the entire regimental staff consisted of Colonel Walter E. Sewall, Regimental Commanding Officer; Lieutenant Colonel John Pratt, Regimental

Executive Officer; a Captain who served as S-3, Regimental Operations Officer; a Captain who served as S-2, Regimental Intelligence Officer; a Captain who served as S-4, Regimental Logistics and Supply Officer; and a Captain (me) who served as S-1, Regimental Adjutant; a Warrant Officer who was in charge of the Regimental Motor Pool; and a Warrant Officer who was in charge of Regimental Personnel.

Photo of the entire Regimental Staff of the 31st Infantry Regiment
Pictured left to right: Floyd R. Mulvany, Jr. (S-1), Hostetler (S-3), Unidentified (S-2), and
Unidentified (S-4) w/camera
January - 1955

Several companies were commanded by Second Lieutenants with Sergeants serving as Platoon Leaders. The shortage of officers was a very real problem, but it seemed as though there were none available in the entire US Army who could be assigned to us. Battalion staffs were also short of qualified officers.

Upon my departure from the 2nd Battalion, the Major then serving as Battalion Executive Officer assumed the role of S-3 as an additional set of duties. It was a tough situation all around. Everyone up and down the chain-of-command was working their butts off on the double-quick to make things work as necessary and expected.

Concurrent with my assignment as the Regimental Adjutant (S-1), a new Regimental Commanding Officer was named to replace Colonel Walter E. Sewall.

Our new Commanding Officer was Colonel George E. Fletcher, USMA Class of 1930. Colonel Fletcher was born in England in 1904, he and his family immigrated to the US in 1910, and he grew up an American. Fletcher was a very fine man with a Commander's sensibilities and a common touch when it came to understanding his men's feelings. When the realization hit him that his staff only consisted of three young Captains, we could see that this fact somewhat took him aback and was something which had not been confided to him in advance. Nevertheless, Colonel Fletcher took the news in stride and simply complemented his staff on their youthful appearance.

Upon Colonel Fletcher's arrival, we knew nothing about him either personally or professionally. We quickly learned, however, that our CO was on familiar speaking terms with most of the General Officers then serving in Korea. This included Major General Edmund B. Sebree, Commanding General, 7ᵗʰ Infantry Division, USMA, Class of 1919. At some point, we learned that during World War II, Colonel Fletcher had served as the Special Services Officer attached to the Allied High Command in the European Theater of Operations. We could only imagine the things he had done for those Generals a far as creature comforts may have been concerned. We also understood why he remained so popular with them. Colonel Fletcher was an Officer and a Gentleman *and one of the boys*, though he personally never said as much.

Colonel Fletcher was not terribly enchanted with the state of our regimental area, so he decided to do something about it. When the 7ᵗʰ Infantry Division left Japan for Korea in late 1950, the funds for the Officers Clubs (~$250,000) had been left in the bank. By late 1954, the interest on the principal had increased the amount of the fund by quite a bit. Colonel Fletcher asked for, and received, the 31ˢᵗ Infantry Regiment's share of the funds. He put out the word that there would be an Officers, NCOs, and Enlisted Men's Club in each battalion area and a regimental Officers' Club in the regimental headquarters area. Each battalion received its share of the money to build its own clubs.

I was given the job of building the regimental club. Lacking the time and the know-how to design and construct it, I found a young Corporal who had been an architect in civilian life. I told him he was excused of all other duties because he had only one mission in life – to build an Officers Club. I urged him to spare no expense and get it built as quickly as possible. He really took to the job – all I had to do was check in with him from time-to-time so that I could report progress to the Colonel. While we were at it, Colonel Fletcher also had a movie theater and a Pagoda-like guard shack built at the entrance to the regimental area.

Last but not least, we also procured a real nice flush toilet and a genuine shower stall which we installed in the Colonel's private quarters. Normally, it was customary for us Officers to take our showers at the Quartermaster's shower point. Water was obtained by an engine-operated pump which sucked river water through a series of filters and then discharged into a large holding tank. After passing through the filtration system and treated, the water was nominally clean and potable.

Several large squad tents, equipped with about a dozen shower heads and "duckboard" walks, were erected next to the storage tanks. Bathers entered at one end of the tent, removed all clothing, and tossed dirty clothes into big boxes. Each man got his five minutes' worth of red-hot water, free soap, and a clean towel. In a separate heated tent adjacent the exit, there were piles of clean socks, drawers, and tee shirts, etc., which the newly washed masses picked through and put on. We participated in this drill every seven to ten days – whether we needed to bathe or not.

Since the Quartermaster had a portable laundry unit in the vicinity, we never had to worry about washing our own clothes. On more than one occasion, it occurred to me that it wasn't a bad way to keep warm either – at least for a while. Not a bad system, or so it seemed at the time. At some later date, we managed to secure several clean 55-gallon drums, punched holes in the bottoms, set them up on wooden frames, and had Korean workers pour water into them so we could shower more frequently. Of course, this option only proved feasible when the weather was warm. We finally had to build sheds with Sibley stoves installed in order to have access to hot water during the winter months.

There wasn't much flat ground to be found in Korea. Our regimental headquarters area was situated on relatively flat ground. The battalion areas were mostly situated on undulating surfaces. In fact, most of the men's tents were anchored to hillsides above ravines. Owing to its mountainous terrain, there are ravines, rivers, and streams everywhere. During the monsoon season, typically from early June through late July, it is commonplace for streams to become raging rivers. There were occasions on which

I saw it rain so hard one could scarcely see the hand in front of the face. During one torrential downpour, I saw the Han River completely inundate the main bridge which linked the north and south banks. The main span of this particular bridge stood about 60 feet above the normal flow, so perhaps the reader can appreciate the magnitude of mother nature's might.

Under such circumstances, it was not uncommon to see giant flotsam, whole trees, houses and cars simply washed away. Perhaps the most memorable flash flood event was the one which saw several of the 3rd Battalion's vehicles swept away because they had been parked overnight in the floodplain. We were fortunate we didn't lose any men, but property losses were substantial.

Although there was not much in the way of entertainment, which was the main reason Colonel Fletcher ordered the clubs built, there was an overabundance of liquor. There was every kind of booze known to man, to say nothing of those which were not particularly well-known. Liquor stocks were sent over to us from Japan. Stockpiles were stored in a very large tent. A fifth of Canadian Club sold for .75 cents.

'Doughnut Dolly' Follies

There was a contingent of Red Cross females billeted at the 7th Infantry Division Headquarters, which was located several miles from the 31st Infantry Regiment's area. The 31st and 32nd Regiments were separated by about one mile; and the 17th Regiment was on Flank Guard about six miles distant. All Artillery, Armor, Engineer, and Signal units were positioned around the periphery of Division Headquarters.

From the day I became Regimental Adjutant, the head Red Cross female kept asking for permission to visit our area with all her girls. I kept telling her we neither needed nor wanted females in our area because our men were not used to being around women – or words to that effect. She was highly indignant over the fact that I had effectively barred her "girls" from visiting the 31st Regiment's area.

Owing to the fact that the Red Cross crew was billeted in close proximity to Division Headquarters, she must have complained to *"someone"*, because shortly thereafter Major General Sebree, Commanding Officer, 7th Infantry Division placed a personal call to Colonel Fletcher. When the call came in, I overheard the Colonel say, *"What did she tell him*"? Judging from the tone of his inquiry, the General must have repeated what he was told verbatim, because Colonel Fletcher replied, *"Well, screw her!"* I thought to myself, "*nice try*" Colonel, but it was my guess that that wasn't the sort of response the General would be expecting.

The following day, a half dozen Red Cross females paid us a visit and spent the afternoon handing out doughnuts and playing Bingo with the men. As anticipated, some of the men handled the situation well. A small number of others got drunk and became unruly and a few ended up in the guard house.

Predictably, it was the first and only time the Red Cross ladies paid a visit to the 31st Regiment's area on my watch.

31st Infantry Regiment
Officers Club

Grand Opening

As mentioned, Colonel Fletcher knew just about every General Officer (one, two, three star) in Korea. When our Officers Club was finally finished, Colonel Fletcher decided to host a grand opening of sorts. He detailed me to make the rounds in Seoul to personally present invitations on his behalf to the entire General Officers Corps. Only one General declined the Colonel's invitation.

Generals travelled from all points around the country by aircraft, sedans, ¾ ton trucks, and Jeeps. We had arranged quarters for those who planned to stay overnight. Other guests included the divisional and regimental staffs, doctors and nurses from the nearby Norwegian Hospital, and several British nurses who worked with the Norwegian medical contingent.

We hired Korean entertainers, a jazz ensemble from the 7th Infantry Division, and of course the Colonel's soiree featured an open bar. As a result, the 31st Infantry Division and its leader became famous throughout Korea and the envy of other units of the Eighth United States Army. It set a precedent which endured for the entirety of Colonel Fletcher's tour. For the men of the 31st IR, it had the effect of boosting our morale and made those 18 hours days seem more than worthwhile.

Rest & Recuperation (R&R)
Tokyo, Japan

January 1, 1955

After serving in Korea for 12 months, I was entitled to take a break for *"rest and recuperation"* (R&R) in Japan. As a combat veteran of the China-Burma-India (CBI)

Theater of Operations during World War II, I was somewhat ambivalent about the prospect of spending any leisure time with those *"little people."* After all, the bastards killed my good friend Warren B. Winkler and damn near killed me and the rest of our crew when we were shot down over the Burma-Siam Railroad near Rangoon on April 5, 1944. My fear was that I might not be able to mingle with the masses without doing someone bodily harm.

Our regimental Executive Officer, Lt. Colonel John Pratt, told me it was time to take a break and ordered me to take seven days R&R in Tokyo. On my way out the door, Colonel Fletcher entrusted me with $400.00 to purchase a strand of genuine pearls for his wife. Also, he directed me to investigate where we might find a local (Japanese) vendor to manufacture cigarette lighters, key chains, and such with our regimental crest affixed to the products.

These were to be given to all *"Polar Bears"* when they rotated back to the States. It was beginning to look as though there wouldn't be much time for R&R. Especially given all the shopping, I was likely to be doing at the behest of my superiors. After a good night's rest, I dug out my olive drab (OD) uniform which had been tucked away in my footlocker for over a year, dusted off my Paratrooper boots, and headed for the Kimpo Airfield near Seoul. I was soon surrounded by a group of officers from units stationed all over Korea. Planes were making daily R&R runs to Japan at the time. We departed Kimpo Airfield mid-morning and arrived at Haneda Air Base in Tokyo about noon. From there, we took a bus to Camp Drake R&R Center.

Almost ten years had passed since Japan had surrendered on September 2, 1945. US troops still occupied the country and the scars of all our bombings were still very much in evidence. I did not observe one building that had a fresh coat of paint on it. The people in the streets were shabbily dressed. All the cars, trucks, and streetcars appeared as though they were on their last legs.

I did not feel the least bit sorry for the Japanese people. As far as I was concerned, they had started the war and had proven themselves cruel masters and unmerciful conquerors. I remembered all the rotten things they had done for so many years to so many others. Still, though victorious in the war, none of us would walk the streets alone day or night. We always travelled in groups of two, three, or more. Surprisingly, the stores were filled with those items the Japanese were famous for producing: cameras, pearls, silks, and lacquered boxes, etc.

For several days, I noticed Japan seemed to smell an awful lot like Korea. Every place visited seemed to have the same sort of night soil odor about it. It finally dawned on me that *"that"* odor was emanating from my own clothing. My uniform had acquired its distinctive bouquet from being packed in a footlocker for over a year. I couldn't stand the scent so it was off to one of the famous bath houses known as the Tokyo Ansan.

I had my uniform cleaned and pressed, while my body was thoroughly cleansed in Japanese style. Unless one has not experienced the joys of a traditional Japanese bath house, it is difficult to convey how well it soothes both body and mind. Attendants wash you, dip your body of scalding hot water, wash you again, soak you in a hot tub, and top the whole experience with an unforgettable body rub. By the time it was over, I was loose as a goose and too tired to move -- but what an experience.

As for the Colonel's pearls, I had heard of the Mikimoto Pearl Company, so I went directly to their shop. It was reputed to be the finest store of its kind in the entire country. The store manager cheerfully greeted me in English. I told him what we were looking for and how much we were prepared to spend. He did not direct my attention to the counter displays, but instead invited me into the vault to examine their finest offerings. With the benefit of his good counsel, I selected a beautiful matched strand of pearls for Mrs. Fletcher. The price was exactly $400.00. Exactly.

As for the regimental crest souvenirs, I had no idea either where to go or exactly what sort of shop to seek out. At first, I poked about in a couple of import/export nick knack shops which typically were willing to ship items to Korea on consignment. Eventually, I did find a shop whose owner was an American-born Japanese fellow, Augi Naroomi, whose parents had taken him to visit relatives in Japan in 1939.

While in Japan on holiday, he was drafted into the Imperial Japanese Army and served for six years. I neither asked him where he served nor what he had done, but I was curious as to where he had grown up and where he attended school. When he explained he had grown up in the Silver Lake District of Los Angeles, I almost fell over. He went on to say he had graduated from King Junior High School. His old neighborhood was a stone's throw away from the place in which I had grown up, before entering Hollywood High School in 1936.

Augi and I hit it off on the spot. He fulfilled our orders in spades and all at competitive prices. Having stuck our bargain, he pledged to send an array of prototypes directly to our regimental area for review and approval. We were then free to order whatever we desired at fixed prices for as long as we had a need for additional supplies. For the next couple of days, this gentleman acted as my personal guide and generous host – he showed me a side of Tokyo few foreigners could hope to visit and we were entertained at some fine dining establishments and private clubs.

Return to Korea
Land of the Morning Calm

January 8, 1955

After my week-long furlough, I returned reinvigorated to my hectic routine at regimental headquarters in Korea. For some Second Lieutenants arriving in Korea, either straight from West Point or right out of ROTC, their first tour of duty as officers just happened to be as Company Commanders.

Frequently, new arrivals were stunned when I assigned them the duty upon reporting to the 31st. While no one liked the idea of subjecting inexperienced officers to a baptism by fire, it simply was unavoidable at times. We were always short of officers and Second Lieutenants, who were neither assigned staff duty nor platoons, when there were command vacancies to fill in the field.

During my time serving as Regimental Adjutant, I was responsible for maintaining the service records of all officers and enlisted men in the Regimental Personnel Office (records covering more than 3,300 authorized personnel); all courts-marshal records, except those pertaining to General Courts which were conducted at the regimental level; all orders and monthly payrolls which were prepared by the Personnel Office; all special service functions which came under the Adjutant's jurisdiction, including the operations of all Officers', NCO, and Enlisted Men's Clubs, and accountability for their funds.

I was kept busy seven days a week, 18 hours a day, for over one year. I was young, healthy, and eager to accept responsibility, and fearless when it came to questions of accountability. I was grateful for having been afforded the opportunity to serve as Regimental Adjutant as a Captain, inasmuch as it meant acquitting myself well in a Major's billet at an early stage in my career. We were a good team, we got along well together, and we got the job done.

Guest of Honor
Regimental Officers Mess
Devonshire and Dorset Regiment

March 1955

One of the most memorable of my experiences while serving in Korea, came about as a result of a chance encounter with several officers of the British Army's Dorset Regiment. The Regiment's motto was *"Primum in India"*, which meant *"First in India."* The *"Dorset"* Regiment was a line Infantry regiment in the British Army, organized in 1881. In 1958, the regiment amalgamated with the Devonshire Regiment to form the Devonshire and Dorset Regiment.

When it was learned that I had served in India during World War II, I was invited to attend a traditional British Officers Mess which was to be held in my honor. It was hosted by the Commanding Officer, Dorset Regiment, and attended by his entire staff. The regimental Mess Sergeant, had as it turned out, also served in India, so he was delighted to put on a good show. It was a memorable occasion; one I'll never forget.

**Members of the famed UK Dorset Regiment and
Captain Floyd R. Mulvany, Jr.
[Seated, far right, wearing *"Green Beret"*]
March 1955**

Rotation back to the United States
September 1955

Colonel Fletcher was an excellent Commander. Lieutenant Colonel Pratt was the right man for Executive Officer. We had our share of challenging moments, bad experiences, and a few truly joyless days. These, however, were in the minority. All-in-all, I survived 16 months service in Korea in good spirits and with many unforgettable memories.

For my service in Korea, I was awarded the Army Meritorious Service Medal. I received an excellent ER from LTC. Pratt and COL. Fletcher. And on the way out the door, I swore that I would never again be as cold as I was during my last winter in Korea with the 31st Infantry Regiment.

CHAPTER 14

FORT BENNING, GA
(OCTOBER 1955 – MAY 1957)

**Infantry School, Logistics Instructor: Orientation,
Education, and Training, October – December 1955 |
Practicum Training/Classroom Presentations, January –
March 1956 | Garrison Supply Officer, April 1956 – May 1957**

"Praise the Lord and Pass the Ammunition" (1942)

Frank Henry Loesser
(1910 – 1969)

I was delighted with my new assignment as an Instructor at Fort Benning. It was a choice assignment and a bit of good fortune, too. I was glad to be out of Korea and back in the United States. At the time, it was customary to offer such assignments only to those officers who had demonstrated outstanding abilities and high potential for promotion. Since my graduation from Air Corps Instructor School in 1944, I had served as a Platoon Leader, Company Commander, and Regimental Adjutant so the intrinsic nature of the Instructor's job itself I felt was unlikely to present many new challenges.

Logistics Instructor

Orientation, Education, and Training

October – December 1955

There were many different departments at the Infantry School wherein one might be assigned as an Instructor. Never in my wildest imagination did I ever expect to end up in the Logistics Department. Never having held a Logistical MOS, I asked whether it might be possible to be assigned elsewhere – *anywhere* but in the "*Log*" Department.

A representative of the Personnel Branch reiterated I was assigned to fill a Log Department slot, period. I was already discouraged by the response from Personnel, when I reported to the Commanding Officer, Logistics Department. He was a Full Colonel and a leg type character. He saw my Senior Parachutist Wings and the first words he uttered were, *"I don't like Paratroopers."*

I didn't have an answer for that one, so I said nothing in reply. Instead, I inquired as to whether there was a jump slot in the Logistics Department. I knew there was one, and it was my understanding that it was vacant. However, the Colonel stated he did not know the answer to my immediate question, but that he would look into the matter and revert to me.

I later learned that, in point of fact, the Colonel had long before gone through jump school, earned his Paratrooper's Wings. He had placed himself in the Logistics Department jump slot. He might have hated Paratroopers, but he sure didn't object to collecting jump pay as a Colonel.

The Colonel went on to explain that my tour would begin with my enrollment in a four-week Instructor's School. Its purpose would be to ascertain whether I was capable of *"cutting the mustard."* If I passed the course, I would be assigned as an Instructor, then I would learn *how* to be a Logistics Instructor, before I ever got in front of a class – a process which would take two to three months.

Instructor School was intense. Individuals were required to create original lectures on topics of one's own choosing. Presentations started out at three minutes in duration, gradually increasing to one hour in length. Each presentation was critiqued, in its turn, by the class as a whole in terms of contents, treatment of key points, voice, mannerisms, responses to questions, appearance and command presence, etc.

Class Instructors filled out evaluation forms as well. All presentations were tape recorded, so that speakers could hear themselves deliver their own commentary and observe the reactions of their audience at the same time. It was hard work writing speeches and rehearsing them since these activities had to be done largely after hours. My practice was to lock myself in a bedroom for three or four hours every night. Four weeks later, I graduated with a "*Superior*" rating.

At that point, I was ready for the next phase, learning all there was to know about various subjects covered under the rubric of "*Army Classes of Supply.*" Principal areas of study included the following: Class I – Food, rations, and water; Class II – Clothing; Class III – Petroleum, oil, lubricants; Class IV – Fortification and barrier matériel; Class V – Ammunition; Class VI – Personal Items; Class VII – Major End Items; Class VIII – Medical supplies, minimal amounts; Class IX – Repair parts; and Class X – Miscellaneous supplies. Areas receiving particular emphasis at the Logistics School included: Garrison Supply; Combat Supply; Food Service Management, Item Requisition; Records Maintenance; and "*Report of Survey*", i.e., accounting for any losses of property.

The Army had more regulations pertaining to Supply ("*Logistics*") than any other matter – even combat. It was said that before planning any operation, one should check with the Logistician to see whether it could be supported. Beans, bandages, and bullets were the Logistician's responsibility in combat.

There was a Logistics Career Field. It had a designated military occupational specialty (MOS) which was 4010. In the Army, there were NCOs and Officers who spent their entire careers in this field (separate and apart from the Quartermaster's Corps). It took me a couple of months of study to acquire a basic grasp of these regulations.

Although many officers considered Logistics (Supply) to be among the least important of all the duties they had to deal with as a Commander, those who were really smart understood the vital importance of the logistics and supply function. It was difficult, however, for most line officers to sit in a classroom for eight hours a day being lectured on the 'nuts and bolts' of mess hall management or some other like subject.

Personal accountability for either monetary or matériel losses could be a real hazard, especially for junior officers. Mismanagement of either property or funds could easily result in a large loss of money out of one's own pocket to say nothing of a damaging efficiency report (ER). After all, at the time, base pay for Captains and Lieutenants was hardly something to crow about. And a lousy ER could take as long as seven years to overcome for promotion purposes.

Actually, individual Unit Commanders did not have the time to become completely familiar with all Logistics related regulations. As a practical matter, there were simply too many of regulations and too little time available to achieve mastery of them. For this reason, our classroom instruction dwelt mainly on what the regulations entailed, which ones were most important, and what it took to ensure the beans, bullets, and bandages got to those who needed them most on time every time.

Logistics Instructor
Practicum Training/Classroom Presentations

January – March 1956

After I had gotten my arms around the regulations, I began making classroom presentations but only to fellow classmates and department heads. Critiques were brutal, questions were out of this world, and everyone seemed intent upon throwing me off balance in order to test my command of the subject matter.

My take-away from all this cross-examination: I could be confident in my command of the subject matter, I was unflappable under fire, and I was well prepared to share my knowledge with others in a classroom setting. My teaching philosophy was to be firm, friendly, and fair in order to maintain control of the class, employ humor when appropriate, encourage student participation, and always admit it if somebody posed a question that stumped me.

In addition to learning effective teaching techniques, we were also expected to develop examination questions. Our goal was to figure out clever ways to ask the same questions over and over, without altering the actual answer to a given question. This was no mean task, since there was a final exam associated with each class.

We taught at all levels of instruction, from Officer Candidate School to NCO classes and up through the Infantry Officer Advance Course. Instruction was varied according to the level of the particular class. There were a fair number of bright and highly motivated individuals in all classes, irrespective of rank. As might be expected, there were also a few smart asses who could be obnoxious on occasion, but always made a point of addressing us as *"Sir."*

It was a great learning experience to have had occasion to deal with all types of individuals from so many different units, each having his own interpretation of how to follow various rules and regulations. It was invariably necessary to warn students from the first day of class to set aside any preconceived notions about how things ought to be done. Students were encouraged instead to focus carefully on what was being taught in our classrooms. Their examinations would be based upon what we were teaching and often had little bearing on how people were accustomed to accomplishing tasks in their respective units.

Logistics Instructor
Garrison Supply

April 1956 – May 1957

I had been assigned to teach Garrison Supply. This course covered everyday supply matters, from the ordinary to the mundane, which routinely cropped up in every unit in the garrison day-in and day-out. It could be a deadly subject, which if not taught with skill and enthusiasm, it was difficult to keep students engaged for the duration of the class. We, in Garrison Supply, had to constantly refresh out repertoire of jokes and witticisms in order to leaven the subject matter.

Since I had a pretty good sense of humor and an ample supply of jokes, I could usually keep up a lively pace in the classroom. At the end of the term, students were given an opportunity to critique the Instructor in writing with no signature required, which was enough of an incentive to keep us on our toes.

Temporary Duty Assignments: Combat Operations Department, Prisoner-of-War (POW) Camp/Escape and Evasion Training/ Staff Officer Etiquette

Instructors were assigned duties unrelated to the classroom. Occasionally, for example, we would spend a weekend in the field assisting the Combat Operations Department in conducting the escape and evasion exercises and Prisoner-of-War (POW) Camp training. Escape and Evasion Training consisted of dumping out either an entire OCS or ROTC Officer Class at one end of the woods and telling them they were required to evade "*enemy*" patrols for a distance of two miles in order to escape to a safe haven. If they were detected, which was often the case because the evasion route was restricted and the "*enemy*" troops had the advantage of knowing the lay of the land like the back of their hands, they were entered into "*captured*" status.

When apprehended, the subjects became prisoners-of-war and were taken to a mock-up of a Korean War style POW compound complete with guards, solitary confinement, harassment, and other forms of psychological intimidation. POW training was as realistic as we could possibly make it. In no small measure, this approach to training was instituted as a result of the fact that so many US soldiers either had been captured or surrendered during the Korean War. Many of those POWs died in captivity and other remained incarcerated for years.

Escape and Evasion Training proved to be an effective means of enhancing a soldier's mental toughness. Properly conducted it could bring out the best and worst of a man, which in the end was all to the good. There were some who were profoundly shaken by the experience but, for the most part, it provided trainees with insights into what sort of treatment might be in store for them as POWs and thereby steeled their resolve to avoid capture altogether down the road.

When I was not detailed to conduct classes in Garrison Supply, I sometimes instructed the entire Officers staff of the Infantry School with respect to all the uniforms prescribed by regulations for Officers to wear. On one occasion, in particular, this included the first showing of the Army Green Uniform, introduced in 1956 to replace the old "*Pinks and Greens.*" When the Army Green Uniform was introduced, its trousers had a gold stripe down each trouser leg, which was later replaced by the black stripe.

I was able to obtain each kind of authorized uniform from a clothing store in Columbus, Georgia, which had been supplying uniforms to officers at Fort Benning for years. It was quite a show modeling each uniform, explaining on which occasions each was to be worn, etc. Moreover, I was highly commended by the Commanding General and School Staff for a job well done.

The Infantry was a proud, close knit society, and most of us served together in various places over the years. It was not uncommon to meet someone you had not seen in years, but when you met simply pick up the conversation just where you left off years before in some other time or place. This was one of the pleasures of serving as a member of a professional military organization.

Back in the classroom, I reached a point in my instruction where I was able to deliver a full eight-hour class relying minimally on notes, i.e., using only paragraph headings. I really enjoyed all aspects of teaching, especially the opportunities such an activity gave me to interact with my fellow soldiers. Until the end of my career, I was regularly running into people with whom there was a common bond of friendship and a rare *esprit de corps*.

Return to California
May 1957

Early in 1957, my mother had a serious illness and a lifesaving operation. It appeared, however, that her recovery would be long and difficult and too much for my father to bear alone. I deemed it necessary for us to be closer to the folks. Some friends in the Pentagon took up my case and arranged for a compassionate transfer to California. I was sorry to have to leave my instructional post, but I was fortunate to have been assigned to the Recruit Training Regiment at Fort Ord, California. It was with great reluctance that I left the Infantry School in May 1957.

I was never to return, but what wonderful memories and friendships were made in that place.

CHAPTER 15

FORT ORD, CA
(JULY 1957 – JUNE 1959)

**Post Logistics Office (G-4),
Supply Officer, July – December 1957 |
7th ID Briefing Officer, January 1958 – June 1959**

*"To despise our species,
Is the price one must too often pay
For our Knowledge of it."*

Charles Caleb Colton
(1780–1832)

Fort Ord was the home of the 7th Infantry Division. Upon reporting for duty, I was ushered into the Post Officer Assignment Branch. It was there I learned my supposed assignment to a training regiment was cancelled. I was being assigned instead to the G-4 Logistics Office, where it was thought my talents in logistics training could be put to good use. There was a shortage of Supply types, so it seemed to make sense to classify me as a Logistician assigned to the General Staff.

Logistics Office (G-4)
Post Supply Officer

July – December 1957

This 11th hour change of assignments was a career set back from a personal perspective. As an officer-of-the-line, I wanted troop duty, (i.e., troop related duty while *serving* on the General Staff, which was counted as "*troop*" duty in those days) in order to continue my professional development and advance my career. As the news sank in, I recognized there was nothing which could to be done to remedy the situation right away. Reluctantly, I removed my beloved 'crossed rifles' and put on the five-pointed star insignia denoting General Staff.

I found my new assignment to be very enlightening, but all too often from a negative point-of-view. What struck me early on, in particular, was the clash of cultures which separated Officers in the Logistics career field from the Officers-of-the-Line. From the perspective of the Logistics community, troops seemed to be viewed as mere numbers and treated as statistics – neither as individuals nor as the backbone of the organization.

As a rule, their concept of an Army career struck me as a hard-core staff-oriented one. Far too many of those with whom I interacted seemed much less concerned with taking care of soldiers than marking time and looking forward to retirement. It was hard to imagine any of them being assigned to troop duty, even in the event of war. In my view, such attitudes had no place in an organization whose mission it was to support the fighting man.

Initially, I was assigned to be the Post Supply Officer. A Captain (me) and a Master Sergeant comprised the entire staff of the Post Supply Office. In this capacity, I was personally responsible for checking, approving, and signing off on each individual requisition submitted from every unit on the post. I had a whole bookcase full of reference manuals devoted to pertinent regulations.

It was expected that I should be conversant with all aspects of their contents to ensure items requisitioned were properly authorized, available in sufficient quantities, and delivered on time to our customers. Since Fort Ord was a very large installation with Regular Army units as well as roughly 12,000 recruit trainees, the Supply Office received an average of 200 to 300 requisitions per day for processing and sign-off. My responsibilities kept me fully occupied, though not terribly satisfied.

I was living in the BOQ, so there wasn't much to do except work anyway. Mercifully, my workload actually helped to pass the time. After about six months, the G-4 Office increased the numbers of officers and enlisted personnel assigned. Around the same time, the G-4 Office appointed a Captain from the Quartermaster Corps to be *the* Post Supply Officer, which in effect rendered my role supernumerary. Since his date of rank was far ahead of mine, it was my lot to report to him. As a practical matter, this meant that a Quartermaster type would be giving me my annual ER.

This was the lowest point of my entire career up to that point. Naturally, I discretely inquired about the prospects of securing a transfer but to no avail. It happened to be the case that the G-4 was an older, very senior, Lieutenant Colonel who had been clinging to his commission for years. His Executive Officer was a Major, to whom I had taken an immediate dislike from the moment of our acquaintance. Unfortunately, his feelings towards me were reciprocated in spades.

In December 1957, an old friend also arrived on post. We had served together in Panamá and at Fort Benning. He was my Commanding Officer, when I served with the Company C, 33rd Infantry Regiment, when I served as a Platoon Leader following my graduation from OCS and commissioning in the Regular Army. It was great to have him around. As is customary in the military, I soon made other friends and gradually my attitude with respect to my assignment also improved.

7th Infantry Division
Briefing Officer

January 1958 – June 1959

In early January, 1958, the Commanding Officer, G-4 Logistics, a Lieutenant Colonel, decided to appoint me the official spokesman for the unit. As G-4 Briefing Officer, I had to be well-versed in Army procurement policies and procedures, rules governing expenditures, and the logistics practices that applied to Army Reserve and

National Guard units. In my new role, I spent a good deal of time on the road briefing on post units and various Reserve components.

This was a time in the Regular Army when all officers who did not have a college degree were required to obtain one. Since I had only three years of college equivalence credits, I had to enroll in the local college in nearby Monterey. I attended classes four nights a week and studied on weekends. My academic studies were in addition to my regular duties on post.

When it came time for my annual performance review, I received a very poor ER from the G-4 Post Supply Officer, the senior Captain. The Major, serving as G-4 Executive Officer, for whom I could muster very little respect, had declared me "flippant" with him and reported his views to my boss. If it hadn't been for the fact that the recently assigned G-4 Lieutenant Colonel was an historian, I probably would have recorded a much lower score on my ER. The Lieutenant Colonel had asked me several questions about historical events and people to which I knew the correct answers. He was satisfied I knew what I was doing. He concluded as well that my raters were misinformed.

In the spring of 1959, I was told to prepare for another overseas assignment. I wrote to the Infantry Officer's Branch at the Pentagon and requested assignment in Europe. I had over 18 years of service and had not been anywhere close to Europe. I was delighted to receive orders assigning me to the 18th Infantry Regiment in Germany as a Company Commander. Before departing for Europe, I was ordered first to travel to Fort Hamilton in New York to prepare for travel to Germany. It was hot and humid in Upstate New York and while I am seldom troubled by warm weather, I discovered Fort Hamilton was an old installation without air conditioners or even fans. Thank goodness I only had to spend a few days in that place.

CHAPTER 16

FEDERAL REPUBLIC OF GERMANY (AUGUST 1959 – APRIL 1962)

1st Battle Group, 8th Infantry Division, 18th Infantry Regiment,
Commanding Officer, Company A, August 1959 – December 1960 |
7th US Army Support Command, Headquarters Commandant,
January 1961 – April 1962

"Friendship is the only thing in the World,
Concerning the usefulness of which,
All Mankind are agreed."

John Van Valkenburg
(1844 – 1900)

I arrived in Frankfurt the week of August 23rd. I can recall this because I had celebrated my 37th birthday on the previous day. It felt good to be heading back to a line unit. I was assigned as Company Commander, Company A, 1st Battle Group, 18th Infantry Regiment.

1st Battle Group, 8th Infantry Division, 18th Infantry Regiment, Commanding Officer, Company A,

August 1959 – December 1960

The 18th Infantry Regiment was a really fine old Regular Army unit. It was constituted in May 1861 as the 2nd Battalion, 16th Infantry Regiment. During the previous century, the unit had compiled a distinguished record in armed conflicts: American Civil War, Indian Wars, Spanish-American War, Philippine-American War, World War I, and World War II.

In 1957, the US Army rolled out a 'new' Pentomic [1] structure for Infantry and Airborne divisions in response to the perceived threat posed by the introduction of tactical nuclear weapons on the battlefield. By December 1960, the Army began studying proposals to reorganize again – a move which was hastened by the newly elected President John F. Kennedy's *"Doctrine of Flexible Response."*

This latter development led to the Reorganization Objective Army Division (ROAD) initiative by 1963. [2] It was created by the US Army in an effort to overcome the perceived shortcomings of the Pentomic divisions that existed in the late 1950s. In effect, the ROAD concept was a subset of several previous reorganizations put into motion in the aftermath of the Korean War.

It was a concept which envisioned, among other considerations, the rotation of an entire US Army division from its home station in the United States to an overseas station as a complete unit. All parts of the division would go overseas together, serve three years, and then return to its original home station.

In effect, the division that was to be replaced overseas would trade places with the incoming unit and in due course the process would be repeated at prescribed intervals. At its core, the rationale underpinning the ROAD concept was to keep all the people

---

[1] The "Pentomic" structure for infantry and Airborne divisions was adopted by the US Army in 1957. See: https://en.wikipedia.org/wiki/Pentomic.

[2] The ROAD division was created in an effort to overcome the perceived shortcomings of the Pentomic divisions that existed in the late 1950s. See: https://www.armyupress.army.mil/Portals/7/combat-studies-institute/csi-books/sixty.pdf.

in a division together, thereby promoting unit cohesion and raising readiness. It was a capital idea, or so it seemed to US Army leadership at the time.

Soldiers everywhere generally prefer to consider one station as their home base, a place where they can put down roots where they will more or less 'permanently' serve throughout their careers. When the 1st Infantry Division was pulled out of Fort Riley, Kansas, its home station, and sent to the Coleman Barracks at Mannheim, Germany, for a three-year tour, members of the division knew they would be returning to Fort Riley at the end of their tour.

The Army's Pentomic system of organization lasted long enough for all the units of the *"Big Red One"* to become parts of the 8th Infantry Division. While the *"Big Red One"* was known the world over, practically nobody had ever heard of the 8th Infantry Division. What a blow it must have been to the old soldiers of the 1st Infantry Division. Many of them had served in the same regiment, battalion, and even the same company for years. It was bad enough going from a three-regiment (e.g., the 18th, 16th, and 26th) organization with three battalions of four companies each to some new-fangled *"Battle Group"* setup.

The Battle Group organization called for four rifle companies, a support company armed with 4.2" mortars commanded by an Artillery Officer, and a Battle Group headquarters company. Later, for good measure, a fifth rifle company was added to the mix. Battle Groups were commanded by an Infantry Colonel, with a Lieutenant Colonel as Deputy Commander (Operations), and a second Lieutenant Colonel as Executive Officer (Administration). The colors of the 1st Infantry Division, the "Big Red One", were returned to Fort Riley where the Division was reorganized into new Battle Groups.

The Army's experiment with the Pentomic system of organization illustrated the risks associated with change for its own sake, *read owing to political rather than practical considerations,* while failing to take into account unintended consequences as, for example, its effect on morale. When Major General William C. Westmoreland relinquished command of the 101st Airborne Division in 1960, he recommended the Pentomic structure be abolished.

By August 1957, the 8th Infantry Division had been in place for over two years. It was straight-leg Infantry, meaning its troops didn't jump out of airplanes or ride in armored vehicles of its own – it got from one position to the next on foot. I was really looking forward to having my own Company to command. My attitude was it was the best job an Infantry Officer could ever hold, a challenging assignment, but one worth its weight in gold. At that point in time, at age 37, I had almost 19 years of active-duty service, I was at the top of my game, and still capable of running the butts off kids half my age.

Army Training Test (ATT)

At the time of my arrival, the entire Battle Group was in the field undergoing its annual Army Training Test (ATT) at the Baumholder Training Area (BTA). This field test marked the culmination of a whole year's training during which every facet of Battle Group Operations and administration was graded. It was the most important event of any combat unit's existence.

Since I was soon to assume command of Company A, I was issued field gear and ordered into the field to observe the Battle Group in action. The ATT was being staged at the BTA, near Lager Aulenbach, a large (~30,000 acres) maneuver area located about 77 miles west northwest of Mannheim. It was about a ninety-minute drive via the A6 Autobahn through what can only be described as a magnificent rainstorm.

Upon my arrival at Baumholder, I was introduced to some of the finest *"Infantry mud"* ever encountered up to that point in my career – thick, gooey, and 18 inches deep – an Infantryman's nightmare. The Infantry has several platitudes, for example, *"You can only get so wet."* Another states, *"You can only get so cold."* I experienced both truisms on that first night in the field with the 18th Infantry Regiment. I felt right at home slogging around in the mud with all those foot soldiers. It was a great feeling, but *oh* what a night.

This particular ATT was not a good one for the 18th. It had failed its annual performance review. Failing an ATT was absolutely the worst thing that could happen to any combat unit during peacetime. Surely, heads would roll starting at the top with that of the Battle Group's Commander. In an interesting turn of events, the expected outcome was trumped by the unexpected one -- which was to say nothing quite so dramatic took place. Company A had failed its ATT miserably. This outcome was attributable, in no small measure, to the fact that the young Second Lieutenant in *temporary* command simply lacked the experience to effectively do the job. He was relieved.

The Battle Group Commanding Officer (CO) was not relieved, however. He was instead praised by the Division Commander during the post-mortem review. It followed in the immediate aftermath of the ATT. As an observer, I suspected this action was part of the old Army game known as, *"You take care of me, I'll take care of you."* This sort of exception to the rules was not unheard of at higher levels of command. Seldom, however, in my experience did this sort of thing ever come into play with respect to actions of commanders at a company level.

I assumed command of Company A in early September, 1957. Company A's performance during the ATT was a disappointment to its NCOs and enlisted personnel, but they did not blame themselves. They had obeyed orders and done their best to do their duty.

The ATT training regimen changed very little year-to-year. Each year's training program was essentially a repetition of previous years. It commenced with squad training, followed by platoon training, company training, and Battle Group training. It was a fact of life that this training had to be repeated yearly because the Army was dependent upon draftees to keep the ranks filled.

Draftees were inducted for a single two-year term, before being discharged and returned to civilian life. As draftees were discharged, their places were taken by newly drafted men who had to be trained from the ground up in the sequence described above. It was the only way a unit could have people in all positions who were able to function as a unit and a team.

It was a tiresome set of tasks which befell the NCO cadre, some of whom had served in Company A for years either as Squad Leaders or Platoon Sergeants. Soldiers like these knew their jobs and were damn good at them. It was an honor and privilege to command such troops.

I was one of those officers who knew first-hand it was the NCOs who, on a day-to-day basis, really ran the Army. Sergeants and Corporals could make or break a Commanding Officer. They *knew* it too and so did those officers who were worth their salt. For my part, I wasted no time in ensuring that the NCOs of Company A knew I had served almost six years in the ranks and 3 ½ years as a Sergeant.

Sharing this personal information did not earn me outright respect, but it did get their attention, and I still had to prove my worth to them. Commanding Officers came and went, but the NCOs were generally in the mix for the long haul. Officers had to demonstrate their leadership skills. Talk was cheap.

I found it easy to take on the heavy burden of responsibilities associated with the training of 200+ men. It was a difficult and challenging assignment. One could delegate authority, but one could not delegate responsibility.

At all times, I made it known that I respected each of them for their knowledge and skills, knew they were good at their jobs, expected individuals to be good at them, but that final responsibility for anything that did or did not happen was mine alone. I was always open to new ideas and opinions, but the authority and responsibility rested with me alone to make any and all final decisions.

When the Cold War was at its height, West Germany [3] was literally on the frontlines in Western Europe. Every Army combat unit was expected to always be ready to fight, always know how to fight, and always be prepared to carry out any mission which might be assigned. It was a tall order.

Combat readiness demanded 12 to 16 hours of preparation each day. It required being 100% combat effective at all times, ready to move out smartly at any hour with all our men and equipment. All equipment, except that which was carried by each individual, was packed and kept in boxes which could be loaded onto a vehicle within thirty (30) minutes of being placed on alert. Our own company vehicles were always locked, loaded and ready to for launch at a moment's notice.

Each unit stationed (pre-positioned) in Germany was assigned to a predesignated *"alert area"* to which they were required to deploy when placed on alert. Responding

---

[3] The Federal Republic of Germany is the proper English language name for the German republic, founded May 23, 1949. During the Cold War (1947-1991), Germany was divided into two competing political entities – "East" and "West" Germany. Following the *de facto* collapse of East Germany, November 9, 1989, the two entities were subsequently reunified under the aegis of the Federal Republic on October 3, 1990. See: https://en.wikipedia.org/wiki/West_Germany.

to alerts was part of our daily routine. At any hour of the day, we could be alerted to move out. In order for combat units to respond in good order, it was necessary to keep 90% of our manpower available at all times. This meant no more than 10% of a unit's manpower could be on pass or leave at any one time.

Commanding Officers could not be absent from their quarters without leaving a telephone number at which one could be reached. Any absence over two hours would require issuance of a written pass. Each officer and key NCO maintained a list of people to call when an alert was sounded. In this way, an entire company could respond in less than thirty (30) minutes. It was not unheard of for some soldiers to report to an alert area individually in civilian clothes, but always with their equipment. Each man always kept a duffel bag that contained, among other items, a complete uniform.

As one would expect, *"leg"* Infantrymen knew how to march. Once each week, we all took a ten-mile march. Once each month, we took a twenty-mile march. Once each quarter, we took a fifty-mile hike. On all hikes, we carried our individual equipment and weapons.

Our training was intense. We trained for every tactical operation known to the Infantry: attack; retrograde movements day and night; helicopter assaults; armored personnel carrier assaults; chemical, biological, and radiation (CBR) warfare; atomic blasts; river crossings; and Armor and Infantry assaults. We were in the field at least two weeks out of four and sometimes for 20 to 30 days at a time.

Baumholder Training Area (BTA)

During the 16 months I commanded Company A, we were at the Baumholder Training Area (BTA) on 62 separate occasions. As a Rifle Company Commander, I was also frequently detailed to *"umpire"* other companies in other Battle Groups throughout Germany. As if our training regimen wasn't demanding enough, we had to be prepared at all times to undergo a Command Maintenance Inspection (*"CMI"*). CMIs were not usually announced in advance, could occur at any time, and thus there was no fool proof way to prepare for such scrutiny.

1st Battle Group, 18th Infantry Regiment, Company A
Captain Floyd R. Mulvany, Jr. [c], Commanding
Returning from a 50-mile march
(1959)

CMIs entailed a thorough examination of every facet of company operations and administration. Inspections were conducted by a team of experts in records, weapons, motor maintenance, mess halls, and training – everything a Commanding Officer either personally did or had responsibility for was subject to inspection. Each piece of individual clothing and equipment had to be scrupulously maintained at all times.

A hole in a jacket was unacceptable. Stripes and patches had to be sewn on according to regulations. It was chicken shit and everyone knew it, but it was all part of the game. We also knew there was no way to avoid it. Unit commanders were relieved if any major deficiencies were identified.

By way of example, I recall an instance in which we had just returned from four or five days in the field. As we were off-loading our equipment in front of the barracks, I looked up and saw the Commanding General, 8th Infantry Division, accompanied by a delegation of about twenty *"experts"* bearing down on our position. Glory be, we had been selected for a CMI right then and there.

The Commanding Officer of our own Battle Group and his immediate staff were present as well. I am certain the leadership of the CMI team began their inspection thinking they had caught us flat-footed, but quickly realized this was not the case.

As a result of our daily work ethic, to say nothing of the fact that we had some of the best NCOs in the Army, we not only passed the damn inspection but received a "*Superior*" rating. Moreover, the Commanding General remarked that Company A had the best maintained weapons in the entire 8th Infantry Regiment.

My time as Commanding Officer, Company A, was extremely rewarding from a professional standpoint. It was also challenging in many respects, but especially so in terms of the strain it often placed on one's family life. There was never enough personal time available for being with our families, going on a pass, going shopping, or indulging in tourism and the like.

Each officer and every enlisted man (i.e., "*sponsor*") was held accountable for the actions of his dependents. With so little time to contribute to maintaining a household and parental supervision, regrettably some of the wives and children did get into trouble and ultimately the sponsor was held accountable.

During my tour in Germany, one of the saddest duties which befell me was when I was compelled to reduce an NCO one grade because his children were guilty of improper behavior and subsequently arrested by the Military Police (MPs). Sadly, this fellow was not only reduced in rank, but his family was sent back to the States while he had to complete his tour alone.

There was a well-known slogan in the Army, which asserted "*The shit stops at the Company level.*" It meant ideas, no matter how impractical or foolish, which originated with anyone above the grade of Captain, ought to be passed onto the Company level for execution. Invariably, the ones who came up with these hot "ideas" had either never served as a Captain or had not done so for a very long while.

'Voluntary' Giving

Such ideas might include mandating the purchase of government bonds, contributing to the United Way Fund, etc. Naturally, all charitable contributions were supposed to be "*voluntary*" contributions. The term "*voluntary*", of course, was a euphemism for compulsory. God help those units that did not go on record as having scored 100% in voluntary contributions. Apparently, it was not enough to be fully trained and combat ready. No, every member of the unit had to be a *"voluntary"* contributor to every campaign that came along to boot.

I recall one fundraising campaign, in particular, which was sponsored by the Seventh US Army Headquarters in Europe. Its occurrence came about near the end of the holiday season, at the point when we were all about *"contributed"* to death. As it turned out, contributions by members of Company A fell short of the unspoken 100% standard for *"voluntary"* contributions and I opted not to demand that it be met.

As a consequence, I received a nasty letter of reprimand from someone at Battle Group Headquarters. I showed the letter to the First Sergeant, noting the degree to which I was fed up with the whole charitable-giving charade. To make a long story short, not long afterwards another Sergeant came to me with a personal check made out in an amount which would put the Company slightly over the 100% contribution threshold.

I did not want him to do this, but at his insistence his additional contribution was accepted on behalf of the Company as a whole. In consideration of his generosity, he was given a three-day pass, which was the only way I could possibly thank him. He was an old Regular Army type and it showed.

On Parade

Once a month, the Battle Group held a parade. Our men all enjoyed showing off for family, friends, and visitors. We also had parties sponsored on Post by the Company and the 1st Battle Group as often as possible. We were Infantry and damn proud of that fact. No one worked harder and there were no soldiers better than us to be found anywhere.

At the annual Army Training Test (ATT) in September 1960, our Battle Group was rated the best in the 8th Infantry Division and within the European Theater. Company A received a 98.7 rating, the highest in the Battle Group. Boy, we were proud. All the time and effort had paid off. On a personal note, something that really made me proud and I'll never forget is the fact that all five Rifle Company Commanders had been former enlisted men. We had all come up through the ranks.

1ˢᵗ Battle Group, 18ᵗʰ Infantry Regiment, Company A
Captain F. R. Mulvany, Jr. [r],
Commanding Officer
On Parade
(1960)

"Probably the best job I ever had in my entire service career."

Promotion List

In October 1960, it came to my attention that I was about 300 numbers from being promoted to Major. I had been a Captain for almost eight years, so I had all but given up any hope of ever seeing another promotion. It was soon to be my time, but it would mean I would have to give up my company command. From a personal point-of-view, giving up my company would be the sad part of an otherwise happy story.

In December 1960, I was offered the Battle Group, Operations Officer (S-3) job. I wondered whether I ought to accept the job. After much reflection, I decided to decline the assignment knowing that I would be transferred out of the 18ᵗʰ Infantry Division and assigned elsewhere.

Captain Floyd R. Mulvany, Jr. (l)
Commanding Officer, Company A
18th Infantry Regiment

"On Maneuvers"
September 1960

SEVENTH UNITED STATES ARMY HEADQUARTERS
7th US Army Support Command
Headquarters Commandant

January 1961 – April 1962

At about the same time I joined the 8th Infantry Division, the then current Battle Group Commander had been transferred to the 7th Army Support Command as Chief of Staff. The 7th Army Support Command was commanded by a Major General and consisted of all the support units in the 7th US Army in Europe. It was a sizable organization.

The Chief of Staff was aware I had been promoted and knew I was not looking for another field assignment. He invited me to become his Headquarters Commandant, the overseer of support command staff activities and the company, which was comprised of all the enlisted men working within Headquarters. It was really a *"route step"* outfit from the word *"go"*, i.e., one whose style of 'marching' *per se* maintained prescribed intervals but did not require one or another to keep in step or maintain their silence, etc.

In other words, this was an outfit comprised of individuals no longer committed to the notion of *"one for all and all for one"*, but instead wedded to the ethos of every man for himself. It was comprised of no less than 20 Full Colonels, 40-50 other field grade officers (Lieutenant Colonels and Majors), and roughly 200 enlisted men, most of whom were all *specialists* of one sort or another, but very few were either well trained or combat tested soldiers.

Having spent 14 years in service at the Company level, the 'ins-and-outs' of this staff job came as quite a revelation to me. I never knew there was so much brokering and back-stabbing going on behind the scenes in the Army. My general impression was that officers hardly cared at all about the enlisted men. As a class, they were only concerned about getting themselves promoted. Undoubtedly, all the Full Colonels thought they were sure to be General Officers someday. As for me, I was undoubtedly looked upon as a simple paper pusher and a flunky.

On the other hand, my boss, the Chief of Staff, knew there was a lot lacking in efficiency, particularly in moving men and equipment out on alerts. Each section in the command, G-3, G-1, G-2, G-4 and so on and so forth, had 1 ½ ton trailers loaded with equipment which was supposed to have been inventoried and checked every 30 days. Of course, all the Colonels claimed they couldn't possibly spare their enlisted men to do this tedious work, much less for training, etc., other than on-the-job training for their paperwork within the sections.

As a consequence, the trailers and their contents were thoroughly screwed up. Moving this Headquarters into the alert area was like trying to teach a bunch of baboons to do close order drill. Alerts were all pure screw ups. The situation was so bad that finally the Commanding General ordered his Chief of Staff to clean up the mess. The Chief of Staff gave me the job and said, *"Do what it takes and report directly to me, and nobody else."*

I started by getting the men relieved from staff duties for two to three days a week. We unloaded all the trailers, inspected the equipment, and made all needed repairs. I then turned my attention to the alert area and had signs made which designated who would go where on each alert. I did it the Infantry way, every man was made aware of when and where he was supposed to be and how to get to his assigned position.

The Commanding General and Chief of Staff were pleased with the results, but the Colonels were not. I had aroused their animosity, in part because I had failed to give them a heads up before doing what I had been ordered to do before the fact. Some of the Birds were real doozies.

Fellows like them would complain if they detected even a smattering of mud on their sacred reserved parking spaces, come rain or come shine. Still others declared there was too much wasted paper, but when I gathered all the waste paper and made scrap tablets for them to jot notes thereupon, they refused to make use of them. It was simply beneath their dignity.

Geez, was I ever out of my element? Out of step and adrift. If this was any reflection of what other high-level commands were like, I was bound someday to lament having been ever promoted to the rank of Major. I was a gung-ho type in an outfit where there was neither another 'gung' nor a 'ho' in sight. I was dealing with a bunch of fuds whose asses I'd have gladly kicked up between their ears at least once a day – if only I were King of the Hill.

In late 1961, the 18th was sent to Berlin via the highway that went through East Germany – as a show of force. Russian forces had closed the highway to all Western traffic. The 18th was chosen to drive through the blockade to Berlin, the prospect of WW III be damned. Happily, their trip was uneventful and without incident. Soon the Soviets relented and the highway was reopened to all traffic.

By this time, I found myself at a low point in my career. On the job, I was growing weary of all the intrigue and infighting which was not my cup of tea. There were times, I seriously considered requesting a tour cut so I could return to the States early. Fortunately, I was still living in the Ben Franklin Village, so I was occasionally able to fraternize with my former colleagues from the 18th Infantry Regiment. Thank goodness.

A Call for Volunteers

Hoping for a miracle, there it was -- a new door opened up as another was closing fast.

In February 1962, the Pentagon sent out a TELEX (TWX) message to all CONUS and Overseas Commands outlining a need for officer volunteers to serve in the Republic of South Việt Nam. It described the requirements that volunteers had to meet. Weighing in at more than 23 inches in length, the TWX meticulously stated who, what, when, where, why and how of one's prospective duty in Việt Nam. Only combat arms officers (e.g., Infantry, Armor, and Artillery) need apply.

The duty was to advise and assist the South Việtnamese Army (ARVN) in building up its strength and combat effectiveness by being assigned as advisors at the corps, division, regimental, and battalion levels. The requirements of each officer accepted for this duty were stringent. They included being the rank of Major or above, having completed ten years of commissioned service, having had combat experience, having experience at training and operations at the regimental level or higher, and having at least two years of remaining active duty.

These criteria, plus quite a few other things, limited the number of those who could even volunteer, let alone accepted. As I recall, I was one of only two officers accepted from the 7th Army at the time. It was an honor to have been highly recommended by my boss. He often stated that his high grades as a Battle Group Commander were due to his officers, one of whom was me.

The opportunity to serve in Việt Nam was a blessing because, at the time, I really didn't know how much longer I could remain as Headquarters Commandant before I did or said something that might end my Army career. In April 1962, orders came through to report to Fort Bragg, NC, for my "Counter-Insurgency Training" before shipping out to Việt Nam.

It was not difficult to leave my job in Germany. The opportunity to serve in Viet Nam was, I thought at the time, probably the last best chance available to extend my career as a member of the officer class in the US Army. Within a matter of days, I departed for Ft. Bragg with and thirty days of schooling in the art of jungle warfare.

CHAPTER 17

REPUBLIC OF VIỆT NAM
(JUNE 1962 – DECEMBER 1963)

**Military Assistance Advisory Group (MAAG),
I Corps – ARVN Senior Advisor, Civil Guard (CG) and
Self Defense Corps (SDC) Units, Huế City, June – July 1962 |
ARVN I Corps Headquarters, Đà Nẵng City,
Senior Advisor, G-3
(Airborne, Operations, and Training)
August 1962 – December 1963**

"Tôi thích cơm rất nhiều."
("I like rice very much.")

The training program at Fort Bragg had been thrown together rather hastily. It was conducted by the Special Forces personnel in residence. It devolved to US Army Special Forces personnel to take the lead in counter-insurgency (CI) training since, at the time, they were the only outfit within the US military establishment which was actually trained in such operations.

Back to the Future
Counter-Insurgency Training

Fort Bragg, NC

My class was the first to go through the course. For many of us, the training left a lot to be desired. Except for the Việtnamese language training, we were all acutely aware the course curriculum was no more than a review of things we already knew. As 'select' volunteers it meant, by definition, that we had already met some fairly stringent criteria in order to be accepted into the program. And so, as it happened, we were called upon to endure instruction in map reading, a night cross-country compass course, first aid, jungle sanitation, radio communications, and training related to the several types of weapons being used throughout Việt Nam.

Weapons instruction included training on the 1903 model, bolt action, Springfield rifle which had been replaced by the M1 in 1940; the Thompson submachine gun; single- and multiple-shot shotguns; the M1 carbine; the Colt 1911 model .45 caliber pistol; the M1 Garand rifle; light .30 caliber and heavy .50 caliber machineguns; the 75mm recoilless rifle; and the 3.5-inch rocket launcher.

At times, it seemed as though we were revisiting and about to re-live World War II. We also received instruction in the assembly of improvised demolition devices and booby traps. Horrendous explosive devices could be made from the most ordinary combinations of objects, such as bamboo poles filled with gravel, broken glass, and nails.

We had genuine native speakers of Việtnamese as Instructors. Our language training consisted, however, mainly of listening to instructional tapes over and over so the sound of the language would become normal to our ears. By the time the program was over, we had probably acquired a level of language proficiency equal to that of a two- or three-year-old child. While not great, we figured that this exposure to the language would probably be sufficient to enable us to get by in country until our proficiency improved with the passage of time.

I made several friends through the program. We tended to spend most if not all our time as a tightly knit group. At every turn, we all tried to help one another succeed from day one. One of my very good friends, known within our little community as "*Tuff*", had one hell of a time getting the hang of the Việtnamese language. He learned only one phase really well, *"Hai mươi mốt"*, which means "21."

During one of our classroom sessions, our Instructor asked Tuff *"How many children do you have?"* He responded, simply, *"Hai mươi mốt"*. Naturally, the Instructor was astonished to learn that Tuff was the father of 21 children.

Well, this statement made Tuff an instant hero in the eyes of our teacher. For the typical Việtnamese family had only eight children. Funny thing was that Tuff didn't have a clue with respect to the meaning of the Instructor's question, but he damn sure coughed up a good answer.

California Here We Come

Upon completion of our training, we were ordered to report to Travis Air Force Base, located north of San Francisco. Travis was to be our port of embarkation to the Republic of Việt Nam. It was left up to each individual to decide how best to get to the West Coast, so long as we reported in time to make our flight.

Tuff had his car with him at Fort Bragg, so I decided to accompany him on the coast-to-coast drive to the Bay area. We took the southern route to California across North Carolina, Georgia, Mississippi, Louisiana, Texas, New Mexico, and Arizona. It was the first week of June, so we were travelling in shorts and t-shirts most of the way. Naturally, as fate would have it, we were caught in a snowstorm as we approached the outskirts of Flagstaff, Arizona. We couldn't believe it – snowfall in the desert southwest in June.

When we arrived in the Los Angeles area, Tuff and I temporarily broke ranks, so that I could spend a few days with my parents before deploying overseas. It had been more than three years since I had last seen my parents, so I was looking forward to our reunion. When my time was up, my parents decided to drive me up to Travis, by way of a short stopover in San Francisco. We had had an enjoyable visit in Los Angeles and it was a nice send-off as well.

I was traveling light to Việt Nam because I fully expected to be running about in the jungle, in which case I'd have no use for anything but fatigues and a couple pairs of Khaki uniforms. Field equipment would be issued to me in country, so it was not necessary to take anything else along. We had a single stopover for refueling at Honolulu, then continued on our way to Tan Son Nhat International Airport near Sài Gòn.

Republic of Việt Nam
1955 - 1975

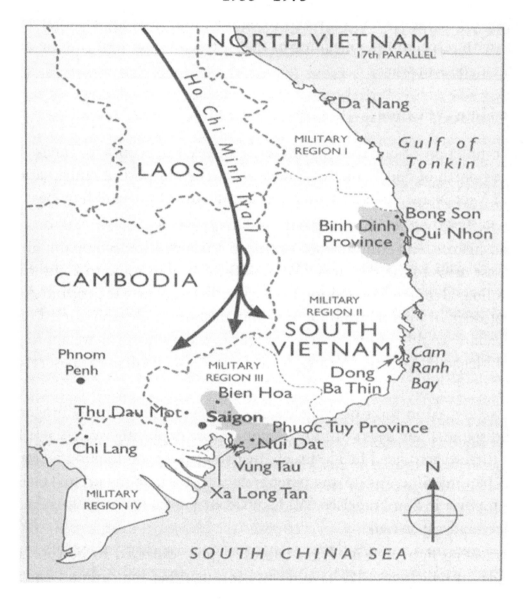

Arrival in the Republic of Việt Nam

We arrived in Sài Gòn at 2:00 AM on June 10th. At that hour, there was no one on hand to meet us except a small convoy of 2 ½ - ton trucks which were dispatched to ferry us to our temporary billets. We Majors and Lieutenant Colonels loaded our own baggage onto the trucks, which the enlisted GIs got a kick out of seeing, as we newcomers climbed aboard to be driven across town.

Our billets consisted of a large squad tent with no flooring and some GI canvas cots indiscriminately strewn about. In the moment, it seemed unbelievable to us to discover there was neither a BOQ nor a hotel available where we could put up for the night. After all, we were all field-grade officers with years of active duty under our belts. We had had an established Military Assistance Advisory Group (MAAG) headquartered in Sài Gòn for years, but nobody had thought to construct suitable transient housing?

My first encounter with an indigenous person occurred the next morning. I greeted him in my very best Fort Bragg Việtnamese, but he didn't seem to comprehend anything I said to him. Others also tried to speak with him, as well, but to no avail. In short order, a Việtnamese fellow who spoke pretty good English appeared on the scene.

We asked this gentleman why we had gotten no response to our inquiries. He told us we had spoken in the Hà Nội dialect and, therefore, our Việtnamese was incomprehensible to the first person with whom we had tried to communicate. We had been taught the northern Hà Nội dialect in anticipation of carrying out operations in the south of the country. At least for the moment, it seemed as though our language studies were all for naught.

Onboarding in Country

The following day, we were all processed by the MAAG personnel. Our records were checked, we received a half-assed physical examination, and to my complete dismay, I was told there was no record of my having received the required immunizations before I left the States. I protested, declaring it an odd bit of news, because I had been given sixteen shots prior to departing Fort Bragg.

No arguments were accepted, so it was back to square one for me. I was compelled to go through the whole process one more time – all sixteen vaccinations. With a total of 32 shots, I was practically immune to any diseases known to be prevalent in Southeast Asia.

During our processing, we received lectures concerning how to behave in order to mitigate the prospect that I might come down with anything. I recall, in particular, one medical Sergeant making the profound statement that every time we wiped ourselves after defecating there was always going to be a trace of feces under our fingernails. In addition, he cautioned us against drinking any water other than what was provided to us by the US types. On both points, it occurred to me that I had actually learned as much as a Private twenty years before his lecture on personal hygiene.

Personnel Assignments

Tuff and several others were assigned to form and train the Army of Việt Nam's (ARVN) 25th Infantry Division, based in III Corps. We had not been in country more than thirty (30) days, when I learned that Tuff had been out on a reconnaissance mission with five ARVN officers and enlisted men. One of the enlisted men tripped and detonated an anti-tank mine booby trap. Tuff's left leg was blown almost entirely off and he was medevacked to the States. Even at that, Tuff was lucky, since he survived his injuries. Four of the ARVN soldiers were killed outright and one ARVN officer had his testicles blown off. The officer died before he reached the hospital.

For my part, I was expecting to be assigned either to a Regular ARVN regiment or battalion as its US Army Advisor. Instead, I was sent north to the City of Huế to work with Civil Guard (CG) and Self-Defense Corps (SDC) units. The CG were analogous to our own National Guard units. There was at least one CG battalion in every province of South Việt Nam. The SDCs defended an area with a circumference of about three kilometers from the center of a given village.

I wasn't too pleased about being assigned to advise CG and SDCs, but their need for training was even greater than that of the ARVN because these auxiliary units had been neglected for so long. The VC were becoming stronger and bolder, so the need for well-trained local troops was tremendous. Local resistance to the VC was badly needed because the ARVN could not possibly cope with the situation countrywide.

CG battalions were under the direct control of each province chief and consisted of squads, platoons, and companies. Soldiers in these units were generally equipped with M1 Garand rifles, machine guns, and bazookas. SDCs were equipped with whatever was available: M1903 Springfield bolt-action rifles, French MAS-36 Infantry rifles, Stevens Model 77E short barreled pump action shotguns, and occasionally a Thompson SNG .45 caliber submachine gun. Generally speaking, all the equipment was in disrepair. SDC units were not well-versed in the ways of even rudimentary weapons maintenance.

In many cases, weapons could not be fired at all, because they were missing parts and spare parts were difficult to come by more often than not. In a nutshell, SDC units were in the tank and that hole was mighty deep. We had our work cut out for ourselves. Moreover, it seemed as though the prevailing attitude within the South Viêtnamese leadership was that as long as the CG companies could function and operate well – no one really cared whether the SDCs survived as a fighting force.

This was to be my introduction to *"counter-insurgency"* (CI) warfare in the real world. At the time, US military personnel were serving in South Việt Nam solely in an advisory capacity. We were expressly not intended to be serving as combatants. Our job was to equip and train South Viêtnamese forces to counter the insurgency.

For many years to come, CI was the hottest ticket in US military circles. Active-duty personnel from all service branches had to complete CI training and have such training entered into their service records. Completion of CI training was *the* ticket if one expected to attend the *"right"* schools and get promoted.

Geopolitical Context

At the time, American policy makers were convinced there was an 'insurgency' underway which pitted the Republic of (South) Việt Nam against the Democratic Republic of (North) Việt Nam. In those days, the conventional wisdom in Washington was that there was neither a revolution nor a civil war underway, but an 'insurgence' by the North Viêtnamese (a Communist state) into South Việt Nam (a Democratic republic) to overthrow the established government below the 17th parallel and take over the country.

The Influence of South Viêtnamese Domestic Politics and the Roots of Sectarian Strife

President Ngô Đình Diệm was an absolute and autocratic ruler, a despot, someone who masqueraded as a champion of democracy. All the people in his government, however, all high-ranking military, and all province chiefs, or so it seemed, were in his pocket. He had put them in power and rewarded them in the expectation that they would never oppose him.

Graft, bribery, lying, thieving, and cheating were all acknowledged as being part and parcel of how his government functioned. These characteristics were also prevalent throughout the lower echelons of the government and military establishments. As long as Ngô Đình Diệm was in power, there were to be no changes to the inviolable *status quo*. Furthermore, it was plain to see the peasantry were apathetic for a good reason – they were either ignorant or had long since lost any hope of a better life.

From 1955 – 1963, Madame Nhu (Trần Lệ Xuân) was the *de facto* First Lady of the Republic of South Việt Nam, though in reality she was actually the wife of Ngô Đình Nhu, who was the brother and chief-advisor to President Ngô Đình Diệm. Mme. Nhu was a very influential advisor to the President and insisted that the female population of the country be organized, trained, and armed. It seemed that everyone over the age of 18, male or female, carried a weapon everywhere all the time. Surprisingly, scarcely any of those gun toting folks seemed to have any idea how the weapons functioned. Mercifully, we Advisors had no responsibility for the training of Mme. Nhu's constituents.

This, too, was a real mess since these females mostly carried M1 carbines, a better weapon than anything the SDC was able to field. The Nhu family was strictly aligned with the Roman Catholic Church and antithetical to the Buddhist majority and its political factions. President Ngô Đình Diệm's eldest brother, Pierre Martin Ngô Đình Thục (1897 – 1984) was the Roman Catholic Archbishop of Huế, Việt Nam.

The Archbishop was also a prominent protégé of Francis Cardinal Spellman of New York City. Cardinal Spellman was perhaps the most powerful Catholic in America and an outspoken proponent of America's prosecution of the Việt Nam War. Nepotism was alive and well in the Republic of South Việt Nam.

Huế City

Huế was a beautiful city. For centuries, it had been the capital of all of Việt Nam. It was the seat of training for all the Mandarins who governed the country. Each Man who successfully completed the required education was given the title of "Mandarin" and had a large, carved stone turtle placed amongst the other stone turtles.

The Citadel, the Việtnamese emperor's palace city, was an outstanding architectural shrine with the tombs of many emperors laid to rest within its walls. The Perfume River ran through the center of Huế and it was the main artery for waterborne traffic. The University of Huế was the most prominent educational institution in all of Việt Nam.

The female students at the University were drawn from the highest ranks of Việtnamese society. They were off-limits and entirely unapproachable even by the Việtnamese males. All US Army Advisors in Việt Nam were cautioned never to stare at such women and, above all else, never to approach them without their family's express approval.

Vestiges of French Colonial Rule

The French plantation owners and political officials were still quite influential throughout Việtnamese society in 1962. Their 'official' meeting place in Huế was *"Le Circle Sportif"*, a large elegant club house located by the Phu Xuan Bridge over the Perfume River. Despite the war, golf and tennis were still being played on the grounds. There was also a large swimming pool, weekly dances, and afternoon gatherings by French and Việtnamese officials. Occasionally, even some American diplomats and officers were among the invited guests.

Where was the war, I wondered? Well, truth be told, just a few miles outside of Huế and any other large Việtnamese town. It was in those out of the way places that people were fighting, being killed, and wounded every day. The Army of South Vietnam

(ARVN) took charge in the countryside during daylight hours. The Việt Cộng (VC), however, were in charge after darkness fell. And in the countryside, the ARVN troops holed up in all the old French forts and bunkers that peppered the landscape.

This was a strategy the ARVN had learned from the French, who were defeated decisively by the Việt Minh at Điện Biên Phủ (May 7, 1954) and ultimately driven out of Indochina. In the aftermath of the humiliating French defeat, the prosperous French plantation owners and operators swiftly moved to cut their own deals with the Việt Minh to ensure their commercial interests were unmolested.

Later, the VC, successors to the Việt Minh, collected protection money from French business interests to finance their war against the central government in Sài Gòn and their new enemy – the Americans.

Our Allies:
Ideologically Divided and
Reluctant Warriors

My compatriots and I had not been in the country more than sixty (60) days before many of us had figured out that the war was not being effectively prosecuted. If we were going to win the war (remember, this was 1962), our concept of operations would need to be adjusted in order to align our operational plans with the realities we found on the ground. One of two things were true: either the United States officers and troops would have to lead the ARVN or all training would have to be *"counter-insurgency"* and *"guerilla-warfare"* oriented training.

We could foresee early on in the war there was no way the ARVN was ever going to defeat the VC, much less North Vietnamese Army (NVA) regulars, by relying on conventional warfare strategies and tactics. In retrospect, since the politicians in Congress, the civilian leadership, and military brass at the Pentagon were in charge of all Vietnam operations, neither of these ideas ever seemed to have merited serious consideration.

Instead, the Army of the Republic of Việt Nam (ARVN) was going to be reorganized, trained, and equipped to fight a conventional war against an *unconventional* enemy. I'm sure nothing could have pleased Uncle Ho and his followers more than that sort of decision. It was clear to the leadership in Hà nội, I was sure, that they knew it was only a matter of time before the ARVN would be defeated. Had not the People's Army of Vietnam (PAVN) defeated the French for the same reason?

In any event, there really wasn't much the poor and dispossessed could do to change fate, since all phases of their pitiable existence were controlled by those who would be temporal gods among men. After all, the Việtnamese peasantry had been dominated, at times subjugated, by the Chinese for over 2,000 years, and more recently over the past century by the French Colonialists, to say nothing of their Japanese occupiers during World War II.

By this time, ordinary Việtnamese peasants had become accustomed to being subjugated and oppressed. It looked to me as though all they really wanted was to be left unmolested, free to live out their lives in peace and harmony. Most, it seemed, could care less about who was running their country.

The Republic of Việt Nam
I Corps, Huế City

June – July 1962

When I arrived in Việt Nam, there were fewer than 1,000 US Advisors in country. The troop buildup began with our initial wave of Advisors and increased steadily to a peak troop strength of 543,482 as of April 30, 1969. During the early years of the war, most of my time was spent seeing to it that CGs and SDCs were being properly equipped and trained.

Training centers were set up throughout South Việt Nam in order to teach ARVN soldiers personnel as much as we could about military tactics and operations. We also had our ARVN officer counterparts to deal with as well. We were there, of course, to advise our indigenous allies and though we carried firearms, we were ordered *never* to discharge them unless fired upon first.

This was not a good situation. It was a good bet that those who promulgated the rules of engagement were nowhere proximate to an operational area where shooting was commonplace day in and out. My immediate boss was a very eccentric Lieutenant Colonel who ate Việtnamese food, drank Việtnamese water, and, as a consequence, was ill much of the time. Fortunately, American food and drink was available in our billets. We also had individual Jeeps and drivers. Such amenities were available to us 24 hours a day.

Speaking of amenities, I had never seen so many vehicles in one place and with so many drivers on call. How, I wondered, could the ARVN possibly spare so many men to serve as drivers? Hell, I knew where the Jeeps came from – Uncle Sam, of course. What a colossal waste of men and matériel. In any event, it was customary to permit my driver to ferry me about the town and countryside close to Huế.

When it came to driving long distances, I drove the Jeep alone because the drivers were afraid to go out into the more distant countryside. During my off-duty hours, I spent several hours a week teaching English to the SDC Headquarters officers. Most ARVN officers seemed eager to improve their English language skills.

Tactical Military Zones [1],
Transportation Lines, and
Logistical Challenges

The Republic of Việt Nam was divided into five military zones, plus the "Special Capital Zone." The French Colonial government in its infinite wisdom, which grew out of their 80 years of colonial rule, built only one railroad and one [real] highway. Both the thoroughfares ran north and south between Sài Gòn to Hà Nội and covered a distance of roughly 1,726 kilometers (~ 1,072 miles).

These two corridors were the main supply lines and traffic arteries for the entire country. It was easy for the VC to interrupt these routes at will, anywhere it struck their fancy, and at any hour of the day. It didn't take long to figure out that air transport would be the primary means of resupply and transportation.

---

[1] The country was subdivided into four Corps Tactical Zones, I, II, III, and IV, sometimes referred to as Military Regions (e.g., MR-1, MR-2, MR-3, and MR-4), plus the Special Capital Zone (i.e., the Sài Gòn metropolitan area).

The US Air Force had been established in Sài Gòn at Tân Son Nhat Airfield since 1956. It was the USAF's primary base of operations in Việt Nam until the fall of Sài Gòn on April 30, 1975. Secondary airbases were located at Đà Nẵng, Huế, and Quảng Trị.

Also, the Việtnamese airline (we knew it as *"Air Nhuc Bam"*) flew daily throughout the country. *"Nhuc Bam"* is a terrible smelling and worse tasting fish oil sauce popular with locals, who spread it on virtually anything edible before it was ingested. It surrendered a rather pungent aroma of rotting fish, the hotter the weather the more pervasive its stench.

In the early years of the war, the US Army was operating the H-21 *"Shawnee"* (aka, the *"Flying Banana"*) helicopter. In early 1963, the H-21 was being replaced by a squadron of US Marine Corps H-34 choppers based at Đà Nẵng. The H-34 was not permitted to operate below 1,500 feet owing to the fact that it was unarmed. Despite its limitations, the USMC H-34s played a vital role in resupplying outposts and shuttling

US Army troops and ARVN personnel all over. We also relied on the US Army's de Havilland DHC-4 *"Caribou"* aircraft to transport troops and handle resupply missions.

Army of the Republic of Việt Nam (ARVN)
I Corps Headquarters, Đà Nẵng
Senior Advisor - Airborne, Operations and Training (G-3)

August 1962 – December 1963

In late July, I managed to get transferred from Huế to ARVN, I Corps Headquarters, at Đà Nẵng. The city of Đà Nẵng was a large metropolis located on the coast of the South China Sea south of Huế. Since Đà Nẵng was a Corps Headquarters, there were many ARVN, CG, and SDC training camps in the area.

I was assigned as the ARVN I Corps G-3 (Airborne, Operations and Training) Advisor. In this capacity, I was not directly assigned Corps Operations. Nevertheless, I made it a point whenever possible to go into the field on combat operations with ARVN and CG units.

My new residence was located at #9 Pasteur Street. It was a large private home rented by the US government to house two Lieutenant Colonels and two Majors.

We had a man servant and a female laundress to assist with the maintenance of the household. The house next door was occupied by four Air Force field grade officers. Our neighborhood consisted mainly of high-ranking ARVN officers and local civilian officials. The ARVN I Corps Headquarters complex was located about three miles from the house. Transportation to and from the HQ was no problem for anyone, since we all had our own individual Jeep and driver both of which were available on demand around the clock.

As the ARVN I Corps G-3 Advisor, I was occasionally invited by the odd provincial Chief to social events. On one particular occasion, as I recall, I was invited to a join the province Chief and a number of local worthies for a traditional meal at his home. The first course consisted of roasted blackbirds, complete with head, feathers and feet, covered with some kind of sweet sauce. Each guest was served his own bird 'belly up' as it were on a plate. I was so taken aback by the sight of this delicacy; I feigned an upset stomach and confined my dining experience to the cooked rice side dish. Admittedly, this was my practice at all such public dinners and when out on operations with ARVN and CG units in the field. Throughout my first tour, I never added an ounce of fat over a period of 18 months. For better or worse, I never did develop much of a taste for Việtnamese cuisine.

Sanitation and personal hygiene were virtually unknown throughout the ARVN, CGs, and SDCs, to say nothing of the society-at-large. I saw food in Việtnamese restaurants completely covered with flies. When the diner was ready to taste his dish, he simply brushed the flies away with a wave of the hand and scarfed up a hearty portion. With that the flies once more descended on the plate and the process resumed in harmonious fashion.

An Early US Army Helicopter Assault Operation
Tam Kỳ in Thui Thien Province

August 11, 1962

On August 11, 1962, I took part in what might have been the first major helicopter assault operation planned by the US Army. A battalion of CG/SDC types were airlifted in Sikorsky H-34s piloted by ARVN personnel into an area west of Tam Kỳ in Thui

Thien Province. As luck would have it (read poor 'intelligence'), the battalion was set down smack dab in the middle of a Việt Cộng (VC) regimental headquarters area.

As soon as all the troops were on the ground, all hell broke loose as the weather turned bad. Our choppers couldn't return in the two hours' time allotted for the operation so the battalion really took a beating. We were socked in in a very bad spot.

The troops were on the ground for six hours before the weather cleared enough to do an extraction. As one might have expected, casualties were high with many dead and seriously wounded. If the VC hadn't stopped firing, probably because they had not been prepared for a lengthy engagement, we would have been lucky to have gotten anyone out alive.

The operation was a fiasco from the start. As a result, it was a good while before we got our troops back into the field. It was plain our troops were sorely in need of more in-depth operational training before another operation could be effectively executed.

Early Field Operations – Part 1
Searching for a Missing ARVN
Battalion

There was a single ARVN ranger battalion assigned to each tactical area of operations within the Republic of Việt Nam. These were their best troops, so they were constantly in the field on operations. Each battalion was advised by two American officers. I became good friends with a young First Lieutenant who advised the I Corps battalion. He was assisted by another First Lieutenant. Both spoke Việtnamese, lived, slept, ate, and fought with their battalion. In addition, both officers were terribly conscientious and did their jobs very well. Since they were in the field most of the time, I did whatever I could to make their daily existence tolerable.

At one point, after I had not heard from them for several days, I persuaded the pilot of a US Air Force spotter plane to help me locate them and their units. I had made up a bundle of supplies to air drop to them. It included several packs of cigarettes, candy bars, and a book entitled, *"How to Live Alone and Like It"*, by Marjorie Hillis. My US Air Force aviator buddy found my junior confreres and successfully made his drop. Later the two of them confided that they really appreciated my offbeat sense of humor.

They left no doubt it had the desired effect of uplifting their morale. It certainly wasn't easy to locate ground troops in the jungles of I Corps. The triple canopies could rise above the jungle floor to soar 200' to 250' in places. At ground level the vegetation was so thick visibility was often restricted to less than ten feet in any direction.

Early Field Operations – Part 2
Lost and Found Beneath the
Triple Canopy Jungle

On another occasion, I was in a helicopter searching for the main elements of our battalion. For more than an hour, we hovered over their reported position without spying a trace of their presence. In desperation, I leaned out the side of the helicopter and craned my neck to obtain a better view.

While my troops remained out of sight, it soon became apparent that our presence in the area had drawn unwelcome attention from *Victor Charlie*. Suddenly, muzzle flashes and machine gun rounds were zipping by from all directions. We were about to haul ass when, as if by magic, an *"arrow"* appeared on the ground beneath us.

It was just like an animated movie. First, the initial portion of the shaft appeared and then another, and soon the image was complete. The arrow itself was clearly pointing in the direction we were to follow, since it strongly resembled an approximation of a prearranged signal.

We were not certain who was making the arrow, but we decided to take a chance that it was the Ranger unit we had been seeking to contact. Off we flew in a nick of time and out of range of those nasty .51 caliber heavy machine guns hidden in the hills below. In the clear, we descended and saw flashes of color in and amongst the trees.

Glory be, it was our 'lost' battalion. When we landed, I asked the young Lieutenant how the arrow had appeared like magic. His response was as direct as it was simple. He told me that some of his men had discovered a large cache of rice nearby, so they decided to pour the rice over the ground in the shape of a directional arrow. What a perfect example, I thought, of a *"field expedient"* means of communication.

We had only a few minutes to confer on the ground and go over our maps before we began receiving artillery fire within 50 meters of our position. Where in the hell was it coming from? We knew of no friendly troops or enemy artillery positions in the vicinity, but *'there it was.'* We scattered quickly and within moments we were again airborne and headed back to base.

Early Field Operations – Part 3
Still Looking for the Perfect

Jungle Drop Zone

The senior US Army Advisor to the ARVN I Corps, as mentioned, was a full Colonel who constantly had me looking for suitable drop zones for possible airborne operations. I was a Major at the time, so it was an assignment ideally suited to my skills and experience. Most of the time, the Colonel had me looking for a DZ in an area where it always seemed as though the jungle was its most dense.

**Unidentified ARVN Sub-lieutenant (l) and
Major Floyd R. Mulvany, Jr., Đà Nẵng City
Republic of Việt Nam, I Corps
(1962/63)**

He had the idea that if we could find a way into such a morass it would prevent the VC from knowing where the actual drop would be made. While on assignment for the Colonel, I spent quite a lot of flying time in choppers, liaison aircraft, and *Caribou* transports all over I Corps.

Early Field Operations – Part 4
West of Đà Nẵng: The A Shau Valley,
Khe Sanh, and Beyond

I was present in the A Shau Valley and operating in and around Khe Sanh long before the names of either place were well-known by the American public. Khe Sanh is the district capital of Hướng Hóa District, Quảng Trị Province. It is located about 39 miles (63 km) west of Đông Hà.

During the Vietnam War, the Khe Sanh Combat Base was located to the north of the city. The famous *siege* known to history as the Battle of Khe Sanh later commenced there on January 21, 1968.

ARVN Outpost
I Corps, A Shau Valley
Suspected Việt Cộng Cadre

(1962 – 1963)

During the latter part of 1962, I was busy inspecting Special Forces Camps, ARVN battalion areas, Civil Guard (CG) installations, and Self Defense Corps (SDC) units throughout the A Shau Valley. My former Executive Officer of Company A, 18th Infantry Regiment (Germany), was a Captain serving as a Battalion Advisor in the A Shau Valley at the time. In those days, it was my custom to accompany ARVN and CG battalions on routine combat operations.

Major Floyd R. Mulvany, Jr. (l) and
Warrant Officer 3 Herbert L. ("Jack") Evans (r)
Republic of Việt Nam, I Corps
(1962)

Most such operations were worthless exercises because many of the Việtnamese commanders refused to accept battle. I can recall one engagement, in particular, when after several hours of hard fighting, we had managed to bottle up an entire company of VC – they had no way to escape our grip. We had a company of ARVN in reserve awaiting insertion by helicopters at the open end of the valley to block the enemy's escape.

When we Advisors sent word to the Company Commander to insert the reserve company, he refused to comply arguing it was too late in the day to extend combat operations. His response was absurd, since we had sent the 'word' in plenty of time to make certain there would be enough daylight left over to successfully close out the fight. We made no fewer than three attempts to get him to move out smartly, but to no avail.

Major Floyd R. Mulvany, Jr. (m)
In the field with fellow US Army Advisors in the Au Shau Valley
Republic of Việt Nam, I Corps
(1963)

The ARVN commander refused battle. The VC, of course, melted away right before our eyes in the late afternoon. Adding insult to injury, no action was taken against the offending Company Commander after the fact.

There were plenty of times, at I Corps Headquarters, I could not get my Việtnamese counterparts to go into the field with me. I asked, requested, cajoled, ridiculed, and hollered at them without managing to get them on board. Ultimately, it was only at the insistence of the senior US Army Advisor that they finally assented and agreed to participate in field operations, but *not* combat operations. Instead, we headed out invariably to the nearest ARVN battalion base camp.

Australian Army Training Team
Vietnam (AATTV)
Mates from Down Under

The Australian Army Training Team Vietnam (AATTV) was active in the A Shau Valley in the early 1960s. In 1962, the AATTV operated there with two teams of 40 each Australian Army Advisors. Having fought, of course, in several jungles throughout the British Commonwealth throughout the 20th century they wanted to join the fight in Việt Nam. These were a top flight group of Advisors and, as such, their primary mission was to train the SDCs and CGs at two camps in I Corps. Remember, this was 1962.

Early Field Operations – Part 5
Making a Silk Purse from the
Proverbial Sow's Ear

When I wasn't out in the field, either on combat operations, reconnoitering prospective drop zones (DZs), or inspecting SDC and CG training areas, I had several administrative functions to perform. For example, I might be testing new equipment, writing evaluation reports, writing training memorandums, and trying to get marksmanship medals for the SDCs as an incentive to improve their generally miserable marksmanship abilities.

God as my witness, I saw some of those folks hold a rifle at arm's length to one side of their body, then close their eyes, when they fired. It's nigh on impossible to hit a target when you don't aim and keep your eyes wide open. It took eight months of persistent 'negotiations' with the Việtnamese I Corps Commander and staff, the SDC National Commander, and the province chiefs to inaugurate the simple marksmanship medal program.

It was a great day, indeed, when medals were presented to the first class of SDC men who had completed their training. There were neither any 'expert' nor 'sharpshooter' badges handed out, but the awards ceremony was a tangible sign of progress. There were only marksmanship medals, because none of the SDCs had enough training to become experts or sharpshooters.

Nevertheless, it was notably a step in the right direction. At least all the US Army types were of that mind. Sadly, I later learned that our Việtnamese counterparts apparently did not share our enthusiasm, inasmuch as it was on the very day of my departure from ARVN I Corps Headquarters that the program ended.

Inspiration from Above
Missive from MAAG Headquarters
Sài Gòn City

As for administrative work, I recall having received a telegram from MAAG Headquarters in Sài Gòn requesting that I survey all cognizant US military personnel in country for their ideas concerning how best to conduct jungle warfare. When I read the message, all I could do was shake my head in wonderment and disbelief. After all, the US Army had fought four years of jungle warfare in World War II and all around the world. Had everyone at MAAG simply forgotten the lessons of our history?

I certainly didn't conduct any such survey. Instead, I merely suggested the author of the telegram obtain and study the US Army Field Manual, FM-31-21 1961. For the record, it was entitled, *"Guerrilla Warfare and Special Forces"* (Jungle Operations).

Early Field Operations – Part 6
Still Seeking that Elusive
'Needle in the Haystack'

As part of my normal routine, I was kept busy looking for suitable drop zones (DZs) in the jungle, but they were few and far between. However, the US Army's Senior Advisor to ARVN I Corps persisted in goading me into such pursuits. He never did roger up to the fact that jumping wasn't the problem. It was landing on the rocks and in the trees that would be the real problem.

It's hard enough to avoid injuries under the best of circumstances, to say nothing of trying to keep some semblance of formation, prevent injuries, and get out with all men and equipment intact. Still, all this was difficult for a leg to comprehend. Fortunately, the message must have resonated with my boss because in the end we never did make any jumps with airborne troops on my watch in I Corps.

I jumped a number of times with the Viêtnamese Special Forces stationed at Đà Nẵng. They were a cocky bunch when it came to jumping, but the same was seldom the case when it came to fighting. They made a practice of jumping only with a "main" parachute, i.e., without a "reserve."

It was American practice to always jump with both a "main" and a "reserve" 'chute. Furthermore, in contrast to American custom, the Viêtnamese usually did not have a pre-designated DZ – their custom was to jump more or less in the general vicinity of a particular area. It seemed to be the prevailing theory that jumping into any area, rather than a safe, soft one, made for good combat training.

As far as I can recall, no ARVN Special Forces outfit ever made an actual combat jump prior to June/July 1963. I was always leery of jumping with a Viêtnamese-packed parachute, even though there were US Special Forces "Riggers" (parachute packing) Advisors to supervise their work. Fortunately, I never had a chute malfunction, although I did experience several jumps during which I almost *"bought the farm."* Yes, friends, I really earned my jump pay.

Early Field Operations – Part 7
ARVN – Scout Dog Platoon
Risky Business

As part of overall combat operations, there was a Scout Dog Platoon in I Corps, where an American Sergeant served as an Advisor. It consisted of 10 – 12 beautiful, well-trained police dogs from the USA. Viêtnamese handlers were trained and given control over individual scout dogs. Each animal was valued at about $1,000.00.

Scout dogs were trained to detect (smell) an enemy at quite a distance, which greatly mitigated the prospect of an ambush under most circumstances. When handlers were considered to be adequately trained, they and their dogs were sent out on combat operations. After several such operations, reports began coming in of dogs being killed by hostile fire or turning up missing.

After a time, we US Army type Advisors became suspicious about the number of such casualties. We requested the US Sergeant Advisor to accompany his Viêtnamese charges on an operation. He was to report back to us if any of the dogs were reported KIA or MIA.

The Sergeant protested because he had never been in the field with the troops, so we simply ordered him to get his ass out in the field on the next operation. When he reported back to us, he stated that there was some incoming small arms fire, but he was sure it wasn't enough or in the right places to kill a scout dog as was reported by the Việtnamese handlers. An investigation revealed that those Việtnamese bastards had been killing and eating those beautiful, highly trained, dogs.

This brought all scout dog deployments to a screeching halt. To make matters worse, the US Sergeant demanded he be awarded his Combat Infantry Badge (CBI) for his role in breaking up the dog meat scam. It was bad enough he was not Infantry; he hadn't been in combat. He was, however, attached to the Quartermaster's Corps.

A Changing of the Guard,
International Intrigue, and
A Deadly Reckoning

On November 2, 1963, President Ngô Đình Diệm and his brother, Presidential Advisor Ngo Dinh Nhu, were assassinated by troops under the command of General Dương Văn Minh and backed by the US Central Intelligence Agency (CIA). About three weeks later, on November 22, 1963, our own president John F. Kennedy was assassinated in Dallas, Texas.

Almost overnight, the entire officer structure of the ARVN, CG, SDC, and the array of province chiefs was changed. Suddenly, Diệm's men disappeared and most were never heard of again. The remaining officers left in I Corps, who had not been aligned with Diệm, were promoted and given new jobs. For several days, no one was in charge of the training centers and various ARVN, CG, and SDC units.

Within a matter of a few days, a whole new cast of Commanders and province chiefs appeared seemingly out of nowhere. An officer who had been formerly a Captain in the ARVN I Corps G-3 office was now presented as a Lieutenant Colonel and as the new I Corps G-3 Officer. Several Lieutenants and Captains with whom I had worked were gone and replaced.

There were so many new faces, but no new methods or incentives for pursuing combat operations. The Ranger Battalion and the CG Battalions, as usual, continued to be the combat units of choice and they were in action most of the time. The Strategic

Hamlet Program (SHP) was officially defunct. And Madame Nhu's "Women's Army" replete with its ubiquitous M-1 Carbines suddenly disappeared.

Recruitment and Training
Of Indigenous Manpower for
SDC and CG Components

Recruiting and training continued for the SDC and CG formations. I use the term *"recruiting"* advisedly, because actually the ranks were filled through forced conscription. Conscripts were rounded up from the jungle areas as well as the countryside and were brought to the training centers with malarial diseases, tubercular diseases, eye, ear, and skin infections, and venereal diseases, etc. They were really a sad group of recruits, indeed.

US assistance included providing the centers with best, most effective vitamins and medicines available. Recruits had to be cured and restored to good physical condition before they could be trained. Montagnards were excluded from the draft. The "Yards", as we called them, were despised by the Việtnamese.

The Việtnamese, north and south, were utterly detested by the Yards. These diminutive souls were treated as savages by the Việtnamese. It was very rare to come across anyone of Montagnard descent in any branch of the Việtnamese armed forces.

Onward and Upward

I had extended my one-year tour for an additional six months because I was anxious to complete the work that had begun on my watch. I had been in country for 17 months, when a team from the Officers Branch in the Pentagon came into the country with our records in order to discuss future assignments. At that time, I was told I ranked in the upper 10 percent of the entire US Army Officer Corps and that I had been selected for promotion to Lieutenant Colonel.

News of my impending promotion came as a pleasant surprise. Since I had been an Officer for 17 years, I asked about going to the Command and General Staff College (C&GS) at Fort Leavenworth, Kansas. After all, I had attended the Advance Officers

Course as a Captain in 1953; I had served in several staff assignments at the Army and Corps level; and I had commanded a rifle company for 16 months prior to coming to Việt Nam.

He asked me whether I preferred the short course (six months), which was designed to cater to Reserve and National Guard Officers, or the long course (12 months), which was primarily geared to the needs of members of the Regular Army Officers Corps. I chose the short course because coming off 18 months in Việt Nam, I wasn't thrilled about the prospect of sitting in a classroom for a year.

Happily, my orders for C&GS and promotion to Lieutenant Colonel arrived at the same time. It was encouraging to know I had made both lists. Since I had been deployed overseas for the better part of four years, I was looking forward to duty stateside.

First Farewell to Việt Nam

I enjoyed the time I spent in Việt Nam, though the duty was not without its hardships. I had made a number of friendships which would last the better part of my lifetime. In addition to working hard to shore up the South Việtnamese government, we also did a lot to improve the lot of ordinary citizens. Many Americans had contributed to the building of orphanages and the care of Việtnamese children.

What a terrible world those children had been born into and bequeathed. As an aside, I was always amused by the wonderment displayed by Việtnamese children when they saw us US-types with so much body hair and weird physical features. I fondly recall their fascination as they stroked my arms just to experience the feel of so much hair. Việtnamese people did not seem to have much hair anywhere except upon their heads. If a male had a few chin hairs and a scraggily moustache, he was a rare bird indeed. Việtnamese peasants were relatively small creatures, most coming only up to my chin.

And the *"Yards"* were smaller still, only chest high.

CHAPTER 18

FORT LEAVENWORTH, KS
(JANUARY – JUNE 1964)

Command and General Staff College (C&GS)

"We have met the enemy and he is us ... " [1]

The Command and General Staff College (C&GS) teaches tactics at the division, corps, and Army staff levels. Its curriculum consists of a graduate level program, which includes instruction on leadership philosophy, military history, and the military planning and decision-making processes. Upon graduation, an officer is considered qualified to either to hold command or serve in a staff capacity at any one of the aforementioned levels.

Historically, on an annualized basis, no more than 10% of the US Army's Officer Corps has been selected to attend C&GS. If one expected to graduate from the C&GS course, an unwritten rule held that students were to forget everything they *thought*

---

[1] Quote from the Pogo daily comic strip from 'Earth Day', 1971, by Walt Kelly. Kelly's quote was a 20th century parody of a quote by American naval officer Oliver Hazard Perry after defeating and capturing ships of the British Royal Navy in the Battle of Lake Erie on September 10, 1813. On the occasion of his victory at sea, Captain Perry famously declared, among other things, *"We have met the enemy and they are ours."* See: https://en.wikipedia.org/wiki/Pogo_(comic_strip)#%22We_have_met_the_enemy_and_he_is_us.%22 and https://en.wikipedia.org/wiki/Battle_of_Lake_Erie#Aftermath.

they either knew or had ever learned about the profession of arms. Supplicants, all, we 'students' were to keep our powder dry, listen intently, and learn whatever it was our Instructors intended to impart.

As an experienced leader, this was not an easy thing to do, especially if one was serving as an officer in one of the combat arms, e.g., Infantry, Armor, or Artillery. How on earth, I wondered, could students be expected to check their hard-earned experience and accumulated wisdom at the door for the sake of conforming to nonsensical unwritten rules? After all, the everyday training experiences of the three combat arms were the very stuff which enabled an officer to perform successfully in combat.

If one lacked the capacity to profit from experience, then he lacked the 'right stuff' to hold command. Up to this point, all of one's previous schooling had been explicitly based on the *actual* conduct of combat operations in the field. On the other hand, students hailing from one of the supporting arms, e.g., Quartermaster, Ordnance, or Transportation Corps, etc., by definition had neither tactical combat training nor experience to forget – at least generally speaking. And as if intended to reassure the assembled body, I distinctly recall that on the first day of classes it was announced in no uncertain terms that *"everyone graduates from C&GS."*

This reassuring declaration did not mean, by any means, that no one failed tests. It did mean, however, that everyone could expect to graduate irrespective of their actual academic performance. From my point-of view, this notion was antithetical to my values as a professional soldier and citizen.

Well, it seemed to me as though we were off to an unpromising start to an otherwise necessary and important career step. Officers from all arms of the US Army were enrolled in the program. In addition, there were many officers from other branches of the United States' military and various allied armed forces.

Each C&GS class consisted, as a general rule, of about 400 students divided into 40 10-man sections. As mentioned previously, the Command and General Staff College (C&GS) offered prospective candidates two options for attendance. There was the short course (six months), which was designed to cater to Reserve and National Guard Officers; or the long course (12 months), which was primarily geared to the needs of members of the Regular Army Officers Corps.

388

Pedagogical Instruction

The six-month short course was said to be modeled on the 12-month course variant, but its instructional content was intended to be pared back to accommodate the more limited time available. Accordingly, all subjects were supposed to be taught in lesser detail though that's not the way things played out. By way of example, the course in *"Nuclear Warfare"* consisted of a single Instructor reading from a typewritten manuscript for roughly eight hours and largely without interruption.

Whenever someone attempted to ask a question, the Instructor invariably replied that he could not stop to answer any questions, because he was required to READ the entire script to us. As a consequence of this sort of instruction, more than half the section failed the final examination. It took the school staff three weeks to re-examine the test papers and post new scores, which with only a few exceptions were passing grades.

Another example of this misguided form of instruction related to a class entitled, *"Armored Division in the Attack, Desert Operations."* All during its instruction, the Instructor hammered into us that the attack ought to be made taking advantage of all cover and concealment available, such as ravines (Wadi) or high sand dunes. When we sat for the examination, naturally we all answered with the "cover and concealment" approach as it had been taught.

However, for purposes of our section's exam, the school's *"correct"* solution was that the attack should be made in the open, across the desert and avoiding as much as possible, any and all terrain features. This time around, there was no re-appraisal of answers. As a result, over half the section received a failing grade.

When it came to discussing the tactical methods to use in Việt Nam, the Instructor's offered up the same tactics used by the French between the years 1946 – 1954. It was the French, of course, who were so roundly defeated by the Việt Minh at the Battle of Điện Biên Phủ (March 13 - May 7, 1954). I became so perturbed listening to our section lecturer one day, I stood up and sounded off.

I asserted that we were losing our asses in Việt Nam, precisely because what was being taught at the C&GS School bore no relationship to the realities on the ground. Our section Instructor had not served in Việt Nam, so he welcomed my comments and criticisms. As it turned out, there were eight other members of my section who had also served in Việt Nam. As I recall, a consensus emerged that there was an urgent need for the US military leadership, from the Joint Chiefs on down, to radically rethink our concept of operations in Việt Nam. Remember, this dialogue took place fully 18 – 24 months before the massive troop buildup which got underway in earnest in 1965.

The Chief of the Tactical Department at the Command and General Staff College was, Lieutenant Colonel Frank Barnhart, my former 188th Airborne Battalion Commander. He and I had always enjoyed a good professional relationship, so I decided to schedule a visit with him to share my thoughts concerning my misgivings about what was being taught in his classrooms. When we met, I explained my sense of frustration with respect to the quality of instruction on offer at C&GS especially when it came to the discussion of how best to prosecute the war in Việt Nam.

As a 'friend', he assured me that I was not alone in my misgivings about the trajectory of the war. He pointed out that even if he could order changes to the curriculum in an instant, it would still take more than a year to work new ideas into classroom lectures and teaching materials. As a practical matter, his argument was that established doctrine changes slowly, proposed changes would have to be promulgated, revised, approved, and reviewed again and again – and the pace of change would inevitably lag changes in the field.

My God, I asked myself, could the US Army really be so incredibly hide bound? We had gotten ourselves into a war on the Asian continent, quickly found ourselves barking up the wrong tree, and seemed unable to see the bloody forest for the trees. Wasn't anyone interested in actually coming up with a winning strategy and improving tactics?

According to official US government statistics, between 1964 and 1975, more than 2.5 million US military personnel served in Việt Nam. Troop strength peaked at 543,482 on April 30, 1969. In the process of having had our heads handed to us on a platter, we suffered 58,220 killed-in-action (KIA); experienced 303,704 wounded-in-action (WIA) -- more than half of whom required hospitalization; allied deaths (KIA) were estimated to have been about 282,000; and others reckon as many as 2.3 million perished as a result of the war.

As telling as these statistics are, they do not reveal the full extent of our losses inasmuch as they neither reflect the fact that our 'unofficial' involvement in Việt Nam began as early as 1946 nor the fact that the Department of Defense 'officially' began compiling our battle-related casualties as early as 1955.

There was at least one really excellent course on offer at C&GS which was entitled, on *"Military Writing"*. I later concluded, it was one of the few courses offered at C&GS in which everyone could actually learn something new and useful. Mercifully, it was also one of the few courses that did not entail inane instruction in strategy and tactics in relation to the war in Việt Nam.

Walking down the hall one day, I ran into an old acquaintance Lewis L. (*"Lew"*) Millett, Sr. [2]. Lew was carrying a sheaf of papers in one hand. I was immediately struck by the fact that the only ribbon he wore was the Good Conduct Medal, which was awarded to any enlisted man for having a "clean" three years of service. I asked him why he wasn't wearing any other devices, including the Medal of Honor (MOH), and he replied that he had been assigned as an Instructor on the Military Writing Committee. He went on to say that he chose not to wear the MOH or any other ribbons because they carried no weight at C&GS. Those 'papers' he was carrying included his request for either a transfer out of the school or reassignment to the Tactics Committee.

This was a typical case of the US Army trying to force fit a *"round peg"* into a *"square hole"*. It was especially noteworthy because it involved a young, highly decorated combat veteran who happened to be a recipient of the Medal of Honor. Lew later served in Việt Nam following the Tet Offensive in 1968. While in Việt Nam, he worked closely with the US Central Intelligence Agency (CIA) as part of its Phoenix Program. Colonel Millett retired voluntarily from active duty in 1973, apparently frustrated over the fact the US had by that time *"quit"* the Việt Nam war.

---

[2] Lew Millett was awarded the Medal of Honor for his service during the Korean War. On February 7, 1951, while serving as Commanding Officer, Company E, 2nd Battalion, 27th Infantry Regiment, 25th Infantry Division, Millett led his company in a bayonet charge in relief of a beleaguered platoon which had been pinned down by a superior enemy force atop Hill 180 near the city of Anyang, South Korea. He was subsequently awarded the Distinguished Service Cross for his leadership during another bayonet assault later in the same month.

While I enjoyed the writing course, I did find it annoying that we were required to read an unreasonable number of field manuals, pamphlets, and other documents. Most were never used in class and most others were never even referenced. My essential beef came down to the fact that the reading assignments encompassing two to three hundred pages of material per day were entirely too much to be fully absorbed and retained.

Our instructors seemed to have concluded that reading assignments could be substituted for lectures, since this was after all the short (six month) course. As part of the class syllabus, students were required to write a thesis on a military topic of their own choosing. It was to be composed in perfect English and produced free from grammatical, spelling, and typographical errors.

All statements of fact or opinion from any source other than ourselves had to be footnoted. Finished manuscripts were required to include charts, maps, and photographs, etc., since papers would be formally presented before a panel of Instructors during the final week of the course. The topic of my paper dealt with the question of how Self Defense Corps (SDCs) units ought to be armed in order to maximize their overall effectiveness. It was a topic I actually knew a good deal about coming off my tour in Việt Nam.

I received a 'Superior' rating for my research and for my presentation before the panel. In all honesty, the superior rating conferred on my work marked the high-water mark of my participation during the entire six months at C&GS. As the end of C&GS came into sight, we were given a test to determine those assignments we would most likely be suited to perform. When the results of my evaluation were presented, it was revealed that I would be a *poor* Company Commander but an *excellent* field Army Chief of Staff.

Well, now, what a revelation by whatever means such results were obtained. My service record reflected the fact that in all the companies I had commanded, I had consistently received 'Superior' ratings on all Efficiency Reports (ERs). In contrast to a company command which is made up of about 200 troops, a field Army consists of approximately 80,000 personnel.

Naturally, I appreciated the richness of the irony in the C&GS evaluation of my prospects for higher command responsibility. At the risk of citing the obvious, I felt the time spent while at C&GS had been largely a waste of time. Graduating at the top of our class was none other than a Lieutenant Colonel attached to the Medical Service Corps. In retrospect, his accomplishment did not come as a surprise, since lacking any tactical training and combat experience there was nothing to forget while enrolled at the College. His was a 'natural' born success story.

Harry S Truman, the 33rd president of the United States of America, was the keynote speaker at our graduation ceremony. Personally, I was not a huge fan of the man. He was the president who eschewed the opportunity to use the atomic bomb to stop the Chinese from overrunning United Nations forces in the early stages of the Korean Conflict (June 25, 1950 – July 27, 1953). Our US armed forces alone suffered 33,652 killed-in-action (KIA) and 36,914 fatalities in total.

He was also the president who relieved (fired) General Douglas A. MacArthur, April 11, 1951. At the time of his dismissal, I felt strongly that MacArthur was relieved of command because he had the audacity to argue the war could be won. He advocated using all the resources at our disposal to defeat communist aggression, but found his views at odds with many politicians, including Mr. Truman.

After six months of frustration mixed with success, I received my diploma which declared me a graduate of The Command and General Staff College. Shortly thereafter, I wasted little time in disposing of every field manual, pamphlet, and scrap of paper accumulated during the previous six months. I threw away my diploma, too (though later I requested a replacement copy).

To this day, however, I wonder about the fellow, the Medical Service Corps Officer, who graduated first in our class. Did his experience at C&GS do him any good? Was he ever able to apply the 'lessons learned' at the US Army's highest-level tactical school?

CHAPTER 19

SIXTH UNITED STATES ARMY HEADQUARTERS
THE PRESIDIO OF SAN FRANCISCO
(JULY 1964 – DECEMBER 1965)

**State of California's National Guard Bureau,
Regular Army Staff Officer/Liaison, July – August 1964 |
US Army Reserve Center (Pasadena), Commanding Officer,
September – December 1964 | US Army Reserve Components
(Commerce City), Commanding Officer, January – March 1965 |
Nuclear Materials Courier, Asia-Pacific Region, April – December 1965**

A Penitent's Lament:
"Even our misfortunes are a part of our belongings."

Night Flight (1931)
Antoine de Saint-Exupéry
(1900 – 1944)

Upon receiving orders to report to Sixth United States Army Headquarters in San Francisco, I immediately requested reassignment to Việt Nam. It was in Việt Nam, not in the backwaters of the Bay Area, where my experience and skills could be put to best use in the service of the nation. Much to my chagrin, someone up the chain-of-command had other ideas and decided that my talents could best be employed instead in the service of the State of California's National Guard Bureau at The Presidio. I tried in vain to escape this assignment, because it was clearly not a good place for me to do time. It was my previous experience serving as Headquarters Commandant, 18th Infantry Regiment, 7th US Army Support Command, which convinced me before the fact that this assignment was a bad idea waiting to happen. Notwithstanding my objections, I was ordered to report for duty in early July.

State of California's National Guard Bureau
Regular US Army Staff Officer - Liaison
San Francisco, CA

July – August, 1964

My new boss was a Lieutenant Colonel in the National Guard. He was serving a four-year active-duty hitch, so that he could get his 20 years of active service. Achieving this milestone would make him eligible for full retirement benefits immediately upon his retirement. Not only was this fellow a civilian soldier, but I soon figured out he knew nothing about the Regular Army and could care less about the good of the institution.

Having recently been promoted to Lieutenant Colonel, in the Regular Army, it struck me this assignment was shaping up as a lousy reward for my years of service-to-date. The Presidio was crawling with full Colonels and Lieutenant Colonels, most of whom were queued up for retirement and few had little if any professional ambition left in them. While observing the day-to-day rhythm which characterized the place, I was reminded on more than one occasion of the title of the Gershwin brothers' show tune from the late 1930s entitled, *"Nice Work If You Can Get It"*. It *was* and *they* did.

Life at The Presidio could be good under the right circumstances, especially if one was married while riding out the waning days of 'active' duty service. For such folks, the typical housing available to senior officers was wonderful, huge, and almost permanent in nature. On the other hand, if you were an officer assigned to The Presidio (but living without immediate family) living quarters were pretty dismal. My place was situated in a World War II barracks. It consisted of a single room with exposed 2x4s, furnished with an Army cot, and a makeshift closet area featuring a single pole resting upon two supports. My quarters at The Presidio were strikingly reminiscent of those I enjoyed as a Second Lieutenant.

The Sixth US Army Headquarters was a complete and utter boondoggle. Our primary mission was to provide administrative support to Army Reserve and National Guard units in nine western states. It was under the command of a Lieutenant General (three stars) He was supported by a cadre of Major Generals (two stars), Brigadier Generals (one star), and a cast of many others of lesser ranks on his staff. It truly was an *"Old Soldiers Home"*, an administrative headquarters only. While the political infighting and back-stabbing were not new to my experience, I confess it was never easy for me to suffer gladly the legions of fools which populated the field of play in and around The Presidio.

I visited as many of the National Guard Units as possible throughout the nine state Western Region. As often as possible, I also travelled with Reserve Headquarters types and participated in their inspections of the college ROTC units and the Reserve units under its command. I was always on the lookout for an opportunity to get out of the office and on the road to spend time with our people.

US Army Reserve Center
Commanding Officer
Pasadena, CA

September – December, 1964

In August 1964, my father died unexpectedly. Since I was an only child, my dad's untimely demise left my mother alone in her grief. As a result, I requested a compassionate transfer to the Los Angeles area in order to be close enough to our family home in case my mother needed emotional support.

I was given command of the US Army Reserve Center in Pasadena. It was located at 655 Westminster Drive, just off Colorado Boulevard, and beneath *"Suicide Bridge."* At the center, I was in charge of thirteen Reserve units, one of which was an Infantry Brigade Headquarters commanded by a Full Colonel. As a Regular Army Officer, I was appalled to observe that the officers and men were *"buddy-buddy"* with each other at regular training meetings. Individuals addressed one another in familiar terms, without reference to rank and military decorum, etc.

I was aware, of course, these people were neighbors, colleagues, and friends, but still it was difficult to accept their undisciplined manner of behavior while serving on active-duty time. In an improbable turn of the worm, there was even a case in which a Private First Class happened to be the boss of several of the officers. Military decorum was hard to come by with that lot and the situation really vexed me to no end.

A Regular Army Captain and I were assigned to instruct, observe, maintain records, and continually evaluate these units. It was their job to learn their duties and perform them professionally. Once each year, each unit was inspected by the Inspector General (IG) from the Sixth Army. My job was to see that they were prepared for the annual inspection. Moreover, it devolved to me to ensure that individuals passed the inspection with at least a 'Satisfactory' rating.

Both the young Captain and I went on record with the Colonel reminding him of some of the more serious performance deficiencies which had carried over from the previous year. We warned him of the need to correct such deficiencies before the next inspection. He acknowledged our criticisms. He stated he had a corrective plan in place. When the inspection was completed, the IG report noted that many of the previous deficiencies were still found. They had not been corrected. This was a grievous matter.

The one fatal sin any US Army Unit Commander can commit is to fail to correct previous IG specific deficiencies before the current following year's IG inspection rolls around. It was my duty to report the results of the IG inspection to Army Headquarters, then recommend the Colonel be relieved of command. To my knowledge, such a request on the part of a US Army Reserve Center commander was unprecedented. While pleased my recommendation was accepted without objection, it was more pleasing to witness the immediate effect of this action on discipline and morale.

Sixth US Army - Reserve Components
Northeast Los Angeles Sub-Sector
Commanding Officer
Commerce City, CA

January – March, 1965

Within weeks of completing my work in Pasadena, I was transferred to the Northeast Los Angeles sub-sector of the Southern California Sector, Sixth US Army - Reserve Components. I was assigned as commander of the sub-sector component, which was located at Patton Barracks, in Commerce City, CA. My command consisted of 69 separate Reserve Units, which was under the overall command of a very senior Lieutenant Colonel, 15 years in grade, and working for a Full Colonel who was busy planning for a comfortable retirement in the area.

Our Colonel, I soon learned, had already purchased a retirement home and had only about one year to go before hanging up his spurs. For his part, the Lieutenant Colonel was an obnoxious bastard who spent every afternoon, on government time, attending a local college to obtain a teaching certificate which he intended to use to later secure a sinecure in higher education. Honestly, up to that time, I don't think it had ever occurred to me that anyone would use government time and taxpayer dollars to underwrite their private, personal, economic gains.

Looking back on this period, I can see there was a streak of naivety which influenced my expectations about how 'normal' people could be expected to behave. This assignment probably marked the nadir of my career as a professional soldier. Disappointed by the dysfunction at work within my immediate organization, I resolved to bring about several necessary changes on my watch. I recognized, however, that my work was going to be cut out for me since neither the Full Colonel nor the Lieutenant Colonel were concerned about much beyond their own personal agendas.

Standard operating procedure called for the Reserve Units to undertake formal drills for not less than two hours each Friday evening. As it happened, I soon discovered the majority of individuals who showed up for 'drills' were spending most of their time waiting in line to purchase items from the Post Exchange (PX) shops in the Armory. As a consequence, very little time was actually devoted to learning about the art of military science and regrettably few officers required the enlisted men to engage in drills.

This was a situation which I found intolerable, so all units were immediately placed on notice that henceforth they would be held strictly to their service obligations. Failure to regularly drill would be recorded, drill credits denied, and no payments would be made to any offending parties. As one can imagine, this action on my part caused a furor. Delegations of officers and NCOs from various units called on me to register their displeasure with my edict. From my point-of-view, it was one thing to object to the injustice, but quite another to bitch and moan over the fact people were simply being required to do their duty – nothing more or less.

I responded to the backlash by reminding all comers that I was Sub-Section Commander. It was explained in firm, friendly, and fair terms that it was my job to see to it they acquired the necessary skills attendant their respective military occupational specialties (MOSs) and were able to demonstrate and maintain proficiency through regular drills. They were reminded too that I was the only individual who signed their paychecks. My bottom line was that anyone unable abide by US Army regulations, and abide in my authority as their Commanding Officer, would be welcome to submit their resignation from the US Army Reserves – no harm no foul.

As had been the case at the US Army Reserve Center in Pasadena, this Regular Army approach to doing business did not generally sit well with our local cadre of Army Reservists. It was the first time in a very long time that anyone in authority had challenged the *status quo* and threatened to hold everyone accountable up and down the chain-of-command. Initially, my admonitions were greeted with skepticism until it was discovered that the PX had been placed off-limits to all Reservists during drill periods without written permission from their Commanding Officer. Shopping at the PX was a privilege, not an entitlement. And I would not permit the privilege to be abused.

My actions in connection with this matter were met with widespread derision, most notably on the part of the two senior officers to whom I nominally reported. Among other considerations, they were pissed off because I had taken the time and made the effort to increase drill period efficiency and to *actually* train our personnel. It will be recalled that my tenure at Sixth US Army Headquarters, National Guard Bureau and

Reserve Components, coincided with the accelerating buildup of US armed forces in Việt Nam (1964-65).

The draft was in full swing and people serving in either the National Guard or Reserves were not being drafted to serve in the war in Southeast Asia. I suspected many of our personnel were closet draft dodgers, so I did my level best to ensure every one of my people got the most out of their training experience. Every one of them knew if they quit the Guard or Reserves, they would be drafted soon thereafter and, in all probability, sent to Việt Nam. Having already experienced my first tour, I didn't have one ounce of sympathy for any of them. Incidentally, morale gradually improved and not a single one of our troops left the shelter of their comfortable units.

All of the National Guard and Reserve units were required to spend two weeks at a training center each summer. Summer exercises were to put the finishing touches on what was to have been *in theory* an entire year of training. Other than being in charge of advisory training teams at the summer camps, my job was a real bummer. I devoted seven days and five nights per week fully invested in my work. I was conscientious to be sure, but I was also well aware of the storm rising up and spreading throughout Indochina. God help us all, I thought, if some of these Reserve units were to be called up for active duty in Việt Nam.

Frankly speaking, the time I spent while serving with the Sixth United States Army Headquarters' Command, where my services were so badly needed, did little to enhance my career prospects. So much for having graduated from The Command and General Staff College, then having been denied the opportunity to return soon thereafter to Việt Nam where my skills and experience might have made a real difference.

SIXTH UNITED STATES ARMY HEADQUARTERS
The Presidio of San Francisco
Nuclear Materials Courier
Asia-Pacific Region

April – December 1965

Somewhere along the way, I accepted a "*hush-hush*" assignment to serve as a Nuclear Courier Officer. It entailed delivery of nuclear weapons components and matériel all over the South Pacific, Korea, and Japan. I did not mind this duty, because the travel was good and enjoyable. My orders always stated that I was to be given any transportation required, to any place, at any time, and without questions.

During this period, I travelled extensively to Guam, Saipan, Okinawa, Wake Island, Kwajalein Island, Korea and Japan. I travelled by C-124 Globemaster II heavy lift cargo aircraft. It had a maximum speed of 264 knots at 20,800 feet (6,340 meters), a cruise speed of more than 200 knots, and a nominal range in excess of 3,000 nautical miles with about 30,000 kg of payload (~35 short tons).

Douglas Aircraft Company
C-124C Globemaster II
"Old Shaky"
(1965)

I didn't really mind the lack of creature comforts associated with flying aboard the C-124, as long as she got me to the final destination on time and in one piece. Since no one was authorized to quiz me about either my business or my baggage, I didn't have many questions to answer along the way. On arrival, I was invariably met by a security team to hand off my load. Lacking much in the way of accountability, I usually plotted my path back to The Presidio with considerable care. I seldom failed to make the most of being more or less footloose and fancy free.

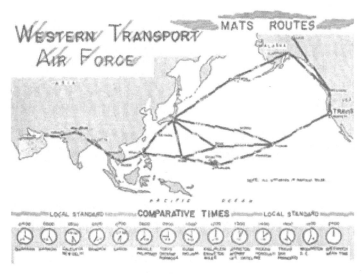

Military Air Transport Service
WESTAF Route Map
(1965)

SIXTH UNITED STATES ARMY HEADQUARTERS
The Presidio of San Francisco
End of Tour Report

December 1965

In my *"End of Tour Report"*, I categorically stated that no Regular Army Officer should ever be called upon to either command or serve in Reserve Units. You can imagine how well this idea went over with the *"Chairborne"* Commanders at the Sixth US Army Headquarters and 5th Corps Headquarters, US Army Reserve. Needless to say, my efficiency Report (ER) reflected the pain inflicted on their egos as a function of my candor.

A Bolt Out of the Blue

Nearing the end of my tour, I received a call out of the blue from a friend in the Pentagon. He calmly announced I was being assigned to a Special Operations unit in

Paris, France. At first, I thought he was pulling my leg because the offer seemed too good to be true.

Assignment to a Special Operations unit with jump pay and a billet in Paris, too? He said it was not possible to say more over the phone, but that he'd follow up with details via TELEX (TWX) within the ensuing 24 hours. Did I want the job? You bet.

Mark my words, this assignment came just in time to lift my spirits from the depths of despair and restore my fighting spirit. Following six months at The Command and General Staff School and more than 18 months with the National Guard and Reserves, I had had my fill of being sidelined and passed over by the system. After doing penance of a sort for nearly two years, I was ready to emerge from the backwaters and get back into the fight.

I was ready for another overseas assignment and chomping at the bit to renew my old habit of jumping out of airplanes.

CHAPTER 20

EUROPEAN THEATER
(JANUARY 1966 – APRIL 1969)

**Support Operations Center, Europe (SOCEUR) |
Support Operations Task Force, Europe (SOTFE),
Support Operations Officer, (Paris, FR),
January – December 1966 / (Panzer Kaserne, FRG),
January 1967 – April 1969**

"Dulce bellum inexpertis"
("War is sweet to those who never experienced it.")

Desiderius Erasmus Roterodamus
(1466 – 1536)

The Supreme Headquarters Allied Powers, Europe (SHAPE) was located on the outskirts of Paris, France. At the time I reported for duty, the Supreme Allied Commander, Europe (SACEUR) was US Army General Lyman L. Lemnitzer (1962 – 1969). Lemnitzer was succeeded by US Army General Andrew J. Goodpaster (1969 – 1974).

When the North Atlantic Treaty Organization (NATO) was formed, and the position of Supreme Allied Commander Europe (SACEUR), identified, it was determined that the nation contributing the largest number of troops to the NATO Alliance would hold that senior commander position. It has always been a US Flag or General Officer and SACEUR has been "dual hatted"; as the NATO operational commander and as the Commander of US European Command which was established as the US command over all US Forces in Europe on 1 August 1952. When the designated 4-star commander is fulfilling his NATO duties, that individual is referred to as SACEUR. When fulfilling his US-only command duties, that individual is referred to as Commander, US European Command (COMUSEUCOM).

The Support Operations Center, Europe (SOCEUR) was a joint staff unit responsible for controlling all US Army, US Air Force, and US Navy special operations units in the European Theater. The Support Operations Task Force, Europe (SOTFE) was also a joint staff entity responsible for the planning of all guerilla and counter-guerilla operations in the European Theater and for the training of US Special Forces and allied nation's forces participating in such combined operations. SOCEUR was based physically within SHAPE Headquarters.

All US Army personnel assigned to SOTFE held Special Forces military occupational specialties (MOSs). All US Navy, US Air Force, and US Marine Corps personnel were either Airborne or Support Operations qualified. We operated directly under the SACEUR wearing his Commander, US European Command hat, but our headquarters occupied facilities separate and apart from SHAPE Headquarters. We worked in a secure, top secret, facility with controlled access 24/7/365. Admission to the area was by special identification badges only. Almost every piece of written material produced was classified "*Top Secret*" (TS) or higher and each of us held a "*Special Strategic Intelligence*" (SSI) clearance as well.

Support Operations Officer
Support Operations Center, Europe (SOCEUR)|
Support Operations Task Force, Europe (SOTFE)
Paris, France

January – December 1966

Our place of work was in a building which formerly was the site of the Wehrmacht's communications center for the German Army of the West during World War II. It was a five-story reinforced poured concrete edifice with walls 10 feet thick, no windows, with only a single point of access and egress at grade. The entrance to the facility was under armed guard 24 hours a day.

We observed, only half in jest, that even a direct hit overhead with nuclear munitions might have been mistaken for distant thunder. It was located about two blocks from the Arc de Triomphe de l'Étoile, just off Avenue Kleber, and adjacent to the famed Majestic Hotel (formerly the actual Headquarters of the German Army of the West, 1940 -1944). One block removed, off Avenue Foch, was the site of the former Gestapo Headquarters. By the 1950s, it had reverted back to being a rather nice apartment complex not far from the Avenue des Champs-Élysées.

Team Members
Support Operations Task Force Europe (SOTFE)
Paris, France (1966)

"The author waving to the camera from the deepest recesses of the WC."

Since SOTFE was a top-secret unit, we always wore civilian clothes while working in Paris. It wasn't difficult, however, for the locals to readily pick us Americans out of a crowd. For a variety of reasons, we looked nothing like the rather ordinary, drab looking Parisian males. In fact, it was often remarked it was a shame that a beautiful city like Paris had to be inhabited by Parisians.

Very few Americans, military or civilian personnel, lived in the City of Lights proper and (for that matter) among the indigenous Parisians. Instead, most of us lived in an apartment complex in Saint-Cloud, a commune in the western suburbs of Paris. It is located about six miles from the center of Paris. In general, we made a practice of carpooling though public transportation was a reliable alternative as well.

Learning to drive in France was quite an experience. Becoming accustomed to their rules-of-the-road was a challenge too. Approaching, for example, a roundabout like the Arc de Triomphe, all traffic coming from the right *always* had the right-of-way irrespective of the circumstances – no *"ifs, ands, or buts"* about this immutable law. Since traffic flowed in a counter-clockwise direction, it was often difficult to break into the rapidly moving traffic pattern, owing in no small measure to the fact that seven major thoroughfares converged on the circle from every direction at once. From above, the traffic pattern below resembled a radiating star hence the formal name given to the site *"L'Arc de Triomphe de l'Étoile."*

One evening, in fact, I orbited the famed thoroughfare no fewer than 14 times before being able to exit onto the correct roadway. Lacking a certain courage, quick reflexes, and boldness of action could mean the difference between an on-time arrival and missing an important 'rendezvous.' Driving in Paris, certainly was not for the faint of heart and frequently took on the character of a battle royal. At the end of the day, it was all about being the last man standing, bloodied perhaps, but unbowed.

The SOTFE unit was commanded by a US Army Colonel, who's Deputy was a US Air Force Colonel. The US Navy contingent was led by a Commander (i.e., equivalent in rank to a Lieutenant Colonel) and the US Marine Corps contingent by two Majors. No officers below the rank of Major served at SOTFE. As a practical matter, this meant there was a great deal of experience at play within the joint command and all facets of Support Operations were well covered.

Our organization worked directly with the 10th Special Forces Group stationed at Bad Tolz in Bavaria. We could call upon US Navy SEAL units based at Little Creek, Virginia and the US Air Force's Special Air Commands Squadron, stationed at Rhine-

Main, Germany (Wiesbaden). SOTFE personnel participated in joint operations with teams from all North Atlantic Treaty Organization (NATO) member countries.

We planned, coordinated, and trained as one force. Naturally, all activities were carried out in concert with pertinent foreign affairs and defense ministries, etc. So-called *"Unconventional Warfare"* (UW) was very controversial in those days, so it was necessary to obtain in advance diplomatic and defense ministerial approvals before conducting UW operations in any NATO country.

Our operations were carried out relying solely on the highest caliber troops, e.g., the Special Air Service Regiment (UK); the Greek Raiders (Greece); the Spanish Airborne Command (Spain); and the Jaeger Corps (Denmark). In Germany, one of our priorities was to train the German Regular Army Airborne and German Army Reserves in rear area defense methods and guerilla warfare tactics and counter-measures.

We did not work with any French forces at the time, because the government of President Charles de Gaulle had recently announced his country's withdrawal from NATO. France had its nuclear weapons, a credible deterrent, and de Gaulle had decided it was preferable for the French to go it alone in Europe. De Gaulle was convinced his country was capable of defending itself against any foe from any quarter.

His declarations to this effect stuck many as odd. France's last victory in a war (without outside assistance) was under Napoleon Bonaparte at Ligny (Belgium) on June 15, 1815. Three days later, Bonaparte suffered his calamitous defeat at the hands of Arthur Wellesley, 1st Duke of Wellington at Waterloo.

Since we were all Airborne qualified and on jump status, we jumped frequently at US air bases in France and Germany, including many jumps made with the 10th Group at Bad Tolz in Barvaria. For most of us, the assignment at SOTFE was as good as it got and as close as we were ever likely to get to a 'dream job.' Hell, we were training day-in and day-out with some of the finest troops to be found anywhere, while drawing jump pay, and travelling all over Europe to boot.

The 10th Special Forces Group's area of operations (*"AOR"*) was comprised of the entire European Theater. The SACEUR would decide where UW training was most required each year. The leadership of SOTFE would conceive, plan, develop, and conduct training exercises with as much realism as possible. Because UW operations could be expected to be conducted deep in enemy held territory, up to 1,500 miles behind the lines, there was a paramount need for secrecy. It's the reason why the US Ambassador to each NATO country had to be briefed and approvals obtained in advance before any form of training commenced. Only those with a need-to-know were to be apprised of our activities.

As a general rule, Special Forces teams are usually infiltrated into an operational area during hours of darkness. All actions must be planned backwards from the actual time designated for the troops to hit their objective. Infiltration can be accomplished by various means, e.g., parachuting, swimming, rubber dinghy, submarine, or by simply walking in by foot or driving in by car.

In most cases, parachuting was the insertion method of choice and could be accomplished either by an individual or a complete "A" team. The US Air Force Commando Squadron's MC-130E aircraft were the platform of choice because they were so well suited to air drops and outfitted with sophisticated radar and electronic counter-measures.

Lockheed Aircraft Company
MC-130E *"Combat Talon"*
(1968)

We also made good use of the famous World War II era C-47s because they were ubiquitous and could readily be 'sanitized' to remove any trace of its flag of origin.

Douglas Aircraft Company C-47
US Air Force Commando Squadron
(1966)

Crews manning the MC-130Es were so well-trained they were able to routinely fly from bases in Germany to any drop zone within range and insert the teams within ten seconds of the designated drop time. Any time in excess of ten seconds was considered unsatisfactory. All things considered, theirs's was quite an achievement given the number of variables in play on any given day, e.g., distance, winds, and possible mechanical problems, etc.

Our Special Forces troops were well known and respected throughout Bavaria. Our troops' relations with the local population and, oddly enough, with the border guards who were responsible for preventing penetrations by foreign elements along the German frontier were excellent. These same people, however, did not seem to have any love lost for regular German Army personnel. In any event, anytime we wanted to use their barns or fields for our Special Forces types, they were most cooperative.

On many occasions, they assisted us by hiding our troops in haystacks, wood piles, barns, and telling the German troops to leave their property whenever such troops came looking for us. The German Airborne units were responsible for rear area security from enemy airborne and guerilla attack. The units really had no idea how to conduct anti-guerilla warfare. The German Army Reserve units were even less capable. Their idea of defending a vital power plant, hydro-electric dam, or industrial facility was to station troops around its perimeter. Little or nothing was ever done to prevent enemy troops from parachuting in and establishing mortar or artillery positions to destroy their objective.

Most high-ranking German Army officers of the period harbored the false idea that *"Teutonic minds"* were the best of the best and knew how to do everything correctly each and every time out of the blocks. We had a difficult time convincing them that static defense was only good in the context of static warfare. Guerilla warfare was anything but static. The guerilla way presupposed 'hit and run' tactics, unrestricted warfare, and without fixed lines or boundaries.

The Germany Army was not alone in its skepticism about the merits of guerilla warfare and other forms of unconventional combat. It was conventional wisdom after the end of the Second World War, especially among the armies of the West, to assume the continuing primacy of the established doctrines of war. It was taken as an article of faith that large standing armies of well-trained warriors could readily defeat small, motley, groups of lesser trained and experienced people.

Selling the establishment on the virtues of unconventional warfare was proving to be a tall order. In those days, it seemed as though the leadership of the US Army, in particular, was somehow oblivious to the fact the American military was losing its ass in Việt Nam because it lacked sufficient UW capabilities. In the early 1960s, it was difficult to be a qualified Special Forces officer in part because specializing in unconventional warfare was not a career field at the time.

An officer could serve in a Special Forces billet one tour, then be assigned to a non-UW unit in his next. In addition, time spent in Special Forces did not count for much when it came to promotion. We were viewed with suspicion by the *"Old Army"* types, as outsiders, and non-conformists. Very few Special Forces types made General Officer in that era.

Special Forces troops and their units are considered to be the crème de la crème of the mainstream armed forces today. It was a long hard struggle to gain the appreciation of the rest of the military establishment. Along the way, we felt the opportunity to work with elite forces from around the world was reward enough for us. When one works with the very best, it gives one a deep sense of pride and accomplishment which strengthens unit morale and *espirit de corps*.

Among the benefits of being attached to SOTFE was the opportunity to jump out of perfectly good aircraft while being paid a bit extra each month for the privilege of doing so. As frequently as possible, we also made it a practice to jump with the troops we were training. I routinely jumped in France, Germany, and Spain and had a number of 'interesting' experiences along the way.

For example, in France, we once had occasion to jump on a concrete parking strip. One of my friends landed so hard the tops of his feet were black and blue for weeks afterwards. He really hit the deck hard. For my part, I also hit hard but also got dragged by the wind face down along the length of the strip. Out of a sense of self preservation, I held my arms and legs up and let my reserve chute absorb the punishment threatening my body. When I finally came to a stop, there wasn't much left of my chute but happily I walked away no worse for the wear.

On a jump in Germany, the ground winds were so strong that I flew parallel to the ground (in my chute, of course) for about 100 yards. I was travelling so fast that all I could do was cling to my risers and holler a string of expletives. I had the sinking feeling something in my body was about to break. When the ground rose up to meet me it was my back that took the brunt of her embrace.

I completed two backward somersaults and came up running more or less in the same direction the wind was blowing. It was some kind of miracle, but once more I walked off unhurt when two of my buddies ended up in the hospital overnight with broken legs. Somebody, it would seem, failed to check the ground winds before the jump.

In Spain, I set out to test the drop zone in advance of a Special Forces team jump. It was daytime and I was the only one making this particular jump. I threw out a streamer to check the wind direction as we passed over the drop zone in a C-47. It appeared to be blowing across the drop zone from left to right. I told the pilot to come about for another pass flying to the *left* side of the DZ.

Douglas Aircraft Company C-47
"Skytrain" **Military Transport**
(1946)

Properly corrected to the left this flight path would enable me to make my jump with some assurance of actually landing in the zone. The pilot came around as requested, but he corrected to the right (not the left.) of the DZ and maintained that heading. My assumption was that as we approached the point over which I was to exit the aircraft, the pilot would naturally correct to the left.

He did not and I jumped in spite of the confusion. The wind was strong and blustery. In the blink of an eye, I passed over the edge of the DZ, over a stream, passed by a copse of trees, and headed at breakneck speed straight for a two story *"U"* shaped, tile roofed farm house. At this point, I was certain my two legs were about to be broken.

No matter how hard I tugged on my risers, the chute simply would not respond due to the wind velocity. In an instant, I reflexively lifted both my legs, skirted the top of the roof, and improbably landed in the middle of a 360 square foot courtyard without touching anything but Mother Earth.

My chute collapsed over me and almost instantly, or so it seemed, I was surrounded by several people, two dogs, and scads of youngsters. Everyone was hollering with one voice of surprise, when I rose up and calmly inquired, *"Halló mis amigos. Disculpe la interrupción, pero parece que me he perdido. Por favor, ayúdame a ir a casa.".* ("Hello my friends. Sorry for the interruption, but it seems I've lost myself. Please, help me go home.")

There was laughter all around, probably due at least in part to my poor Spanish language skills. Anyhow, all's well that ends well, inasmuch as someone showed up with a donkey, another folded up my chute and secured it to the other ass, and escorted my misbegotten and uninvited butt back to the DZ on foot.

Support Operations Officer
Support Operations Center, Europe (SOCEUR) |
Support Operations Task Force, Europe (SOTFE)
Panzer Kaserne, Böblingen (FRG)

January 1967 – April 1969

When the government of France announced its intention to withdraw from NATO's integrated military command in June 1966, the decision by the French president Charles de Gaulle, for a time, greatly complicated relations between the U.S. and Europe. Although France remained politically aligned with NATO, de Gaulle's action cast doubt about the organization's future as a counter to Soviet military power and influence in Western Europe.

As a direct consequence of this unilateral action on the part of the French government, NATO's Supreme Headquarters Allied Powers Europe (SHAPE) and SACEUR were relocated to Casteau, a village near Mons, Belgium from Roquencourt on the outskirts of Paris in 1967. The "US-Only" US European Command was transferred from Camp des Loges, just west of Paris to its new headquarters at Patch Barracks, near Stuttgart, Germany. SOTFE moved to Böblingen, the former headquarters of Erwin Rommel's armor command during World War II.

Rommel's own Officers Club was still in use when we took over the place. In anticipation of our arrival, the Germans constructed a special secure area for us in the Kaserne, which was guarded 24 hours a day. In comparison to our office accommodations in Paris, it was a joy to be in a secure location which featured windows and honest-to-God daylight.

What a difference a country can make. I was responsible for all UW exercises with the German Army Reserve units. Germany was divided into six Reserve areas. Their Reserve forces were known as "*Wehrbereich Commandos*, I bis VI" ("Military area Commandos, I to VI"). Each area was commanded by a Lieutenant General of the Bundeswehr. I became acquainted with each of the commanders. We enjoyed a close working relationship throughout my tour at SOTFE within the NATO command structure.

As it happened, during this period, I also became fast friends with the local German Airborne Battalion Commander, Oberstleutnant (Lieutenant Colonel) Werner Gruber. Gruber hailed from the old German "*Bundeswehr*" (Regular Army) and was captured by American forces at Cherbourg early in 1944. He told me he was fortunate to have been made an American prisoner-of-war because he was sent to an American POW camp. His Executive Officer was not so fortunate. He was catptured by the Russians in in 1945, survived his internment in the Soviet Gulag, and only returned to his Homeland as a free man in 1954.

During preparations for an UW exercise in Spain, I was detailed to brief NAVEUR Headquarters in London. The Commander in Chief, Naval Forces Europe (COMCINCNAVEUR) was Vice Admiral John S. McCain, Jr, a crusty old salt with a reputation for being a hard nosed individual. I briefed the Admiral and his staff on the planned exercise since we wanted to *borrow*, more or less, a US submarine to infiltrate a Navy SEAL Team and some Special Forces troops onto the coast of Spain.

It had appeared the Admiral's staff was dead set against diverting a submarine from its on "station" patrol just to participate in a delivery venture in support of a wayward UW team. Admiral McCain then asked me why and how the proposed exercise might be of relevance to US national security. I stated that this was to be the first time since General Francisco Franco came to power in 1939 that the US would be able to land our forces onto the Spanish mainland. My explanation seemed to satisfy him, because he turned to his staff and said *"Get them the god damn sub, any questions?"*

There were no questions. And we got the sub. While I was occupied in England, our boss was briefing the US Ambassador in Madrid. It was a challenge to sell the Spanish government on the merits of permitting anyone to 'violate' their national sovereignty, especially for the sake of an unconventional warfare exercise. It must be remembered that Franco, Spain's ruler for life, had by this time been in power for more than three decades.

Under Franco's fascist regime, Spain was a totalitarian police state and a closed society where there were few personal freedoms and certainly no freedom of the press. The Franco regime held an iron grip on all aspects of civil life through its "*Guardia Civil*", its secret police force which pervaded every corner of society. They were present even in the smallest and most remote towns and villages.

No one did anything without first checking with the local representatives of the Civil Guard. The country was governed and controlled by senior military leaders appointed by Franco and fiercely loyal to him. In order to win approval for our planned exercise, each provincial Governor (Regular Spanish Army General Officers) had to be individually briefed on the particulars of our infiltration plan before the fact. Operational security was the first casualty to befall our planned exercise.

Having secured the necessary approvals from Spanish authorities, our plan was to fly an *"A"* team from Bad Tolz (Germany) to Grenada (Spain) where they were to be dropped after nightfall on day one of the exercise. The Special Forces team would first land at Saragossa, the capital of northeastern Spain's Aragon region, to off load themselves and their equipment for inspection before proceeding to Granada. The SEAL team was to rendezvous at sea with Spanish naval forces and the local Civil Guard before infiltrating by sea into their appointed exercise area.

We were compelled to agree to these restrictions since so much time and effort had already been expended on the exercise. As a result of the many restrictions placed upon us by the Spanish government, this exercise marked the first and (probably) only time an entire Special Forces *"A"* team was arrested and put in jail because the leadership of the *very* local Civil Guard had not been told about our presence. As fate would have it, a local resident had seen the *"A"* team enter a cave to hide. Like any other good citizen, the local fellow reported what he saw as suspicious behavior by strangers to the authorities.

All exercises were well planned and executed, but it was the exception rather than the rule that exercises came off without any hitches. On one occasion, as I recall, we invited the Turks to participate in a UW exercise that was planned to take place in northwest Turkey. In advance of the exercise, the Turkish armed forces sent many of their top officers and men to participate in a 20-hour UW training course in Germany.

In anticipation of the exercise itself, the government actually removed all the inhabitants of the designated exercise area before it commenced. This particular exercise turned out to be a tremendous success. It laid the foundation for close collaboration between our respective armed forces for many years to come.

We brought several contingents of Turkish Airborne troops to Bad Tolz in later years for airborne instruction and a couple of parachute jumps. After completing the training, participants were awarded US Army parachute wings. The memory of one Turkish jumper still stands out in my memory.

He was caught in a thermal draft rising and falling vertically for more than 20 minutes before alighting in the drop zone. By the time he finally touched down, the entire post was on hand to welcome him back to earth and offer to buy him a beer. This young man had earned his US Parachute Wings.

I had the pleasure of being the guest of the Danish Army's Jaeger Corps. The personnel of this unit, both enlisted and officers, were the best men in the Danish armed forces. During the Olympic Games in 1968, held in Mexico City, about 80% of the Danish team was drawn from the ranks of the Jaeger Corps.

The mission of the Corps was, in the event of nuclear war, to stay behind while other troops were evacuated and to find, fix, and destroy the enemy's atomic installations, emplacements, and weapons. They were organized into strike teams of five individuals. Rank was of secondary importance until each member of every team had served in all five positions within the team. Until that milestone was achieved, the team commander was the most experienced member, irrespective of rank.

The philosophy of the Jaeger Corps was that leadership only came with experience through which one earned the right to be a leader. The Corps was commanded by a Major. Members of the Corps also wore dark green berets quite similar to our own Special Forces personnel. The beret I have in my possession to this day, the one I wore throughout my second tour in Việt Nam, was the very one given to me by the Corps Commander.

While visiting his command, I was privileged to be given a top secret briefing on the Jaeger organization, its equipment, and operational capabilities. As a matter of professional courtesy, he also gave me an extensive guided tour of their operational areas. I vividly recall standing at lands' end on the northern most point of the Alborg Peninsula and gazing out to sea through the darkness, at the place where the Battle of Jutland had taken place during World War I. In the end, I was as impressed by the view as I was with the caliber of the men who served in the Danish Jaeger Corps.

In the late spring of 1968, I was wrapping up my tour with SOTFE while planning my next career move. In March, I made seven parachute jumps in two days, including a couple of night jumps, so that I could secure my Master Parachute Wings. They were presented to me right after my 65th qualifying jump in the DZ at Bad Tolz. My wings were presented to me by Colonel Bob Jones, Commanding Officer, 10th Special Forces Group. Joining the ranks of Master Parachutists was among the proudest moments of my career as a professional soldier.

In April 1969, I received orders for my second Việt Nam tour. I was being assigned directly from SOTFE to the Studies and Observations Group (SOG) Headquarters as Deputy Director, OPS-35. What had proved to be probably the best three-year tour of duty of my Army career was coming to an end.

While the tour with SOTFE was memorable for lots of reasons, its most rewarding feature had been the opportunity it afforded me to serve with so many fine men from all branches of the US armed forces. US Special Forces troops were our very best.

CHAPTER 21

REPUBLIC OF VIỆT NAM
(JUNE 1969 – JUNE 1970)

Military Assistance Command Vietnam (MACV),
Headquarters, (Sài Gòn),
Studies and Observations Group (SOG),
Deputy Director – (OPS-35), June – November 1969 |
ARVN National Training Center (NTC),
Senior Advisor – MACV Team 61, Chi Làng,
December – June 1970

"Xin loi …"
("Sorry … about that.")

I returned to Sài Gòn on June 10, 1969 to begin my second tour in Việt Nam. It did not take long to notice how much things had changed during my 5 ½ year absence and not for the better. All the men, money, and matériel that had been poured into the country had not made the slightest difference in the conduct of the war.

Studies and Observations Group (SOG) [1]
MACV Headquarters [2], Sài Gòn City

June – November 1969

We were still fighting a contained conflict which we were not expected to win. Most of us Regular Army types knew we would not and could not win the war. I was thankful to God that I would be working with the best of the best – US Special Forces soldiers as part of Military Assistance Command's (MACV) Studies and Observations Group (SOG).

Although the mission of the *"Studies and Observations Group" (SOG)*, was openly described as tasked with the evaluation of combat missions in Việt Nam, very few people were fooled by this cover. It was, in fact, an open secret that "*SOG*" actually stood for a "*Special Operations Group*", an outfit with a highly classified operational mission. At the time, its mission was so highly classified that even these many years later some of its activities remain classified.

Military Assistance Command, Vietnam (MACV) – Studies and Observations Group (SOG) command was activated on January 24, 1964. Through MACV, SOG was directly accountable to the US Joint Chiefs of Staff's Special Assistant for Counter-Insurgency and Special Activities (SACSA). It was a joint services unit drawing on all four branches of the US military establishment.

SOG's mission was to carry out all cross-border operations in which regular combat units were not permitted under US law. It was comprised of units drawn from the ranks of the US Navy SEALs, US Marine Corps' Force Recon, US Air Force Special

---

[1] The Studies and Observations Group (MACV-SOG) was a highly classified, multi-service United States special operations unit which conducted covert unconventional warfare operations prior to and during the Vietnam War.
See: https://en.wikipedia.org/wiki/Military_Assistance_Command,_Vietnam_%E2%80%93_Studies_and _Observations_Group.

[2] U.S. *Military Assistance Command, Vietnam (MACV)* was a joint-service *command* of the United States Department of Defense. *MACV* was created on 8 February 1962, in response to the increase in United States *military assistance* to South *Vietnam*.
See: https://en.wikipedia.org/wiki/Military_Assistance_Command,_Vietnam.

Operations Command (inclusive of air assets and Combat Control Teams), and the US Army's Special Forces troops and its Long-Range Reconnaissance Patrol (LRRP) assets.

Military Assistance Command Vietnam (MACV) HQ
Studies and Observations Group (SOG)
COL. Steven E. Cavanaugh, Jr., Commanding Officer [r]
LTC. Floyd R. Mulvany, Jr., Deputy (OPS-35) [l]
June 20, 1969

These units were augmented by highly trained indigenous Montagnards, Chinese Nùngs, and Cambodian detachments and a cadre of highly qualified ARVN helicopter pilots.

In addition, in some instances, special naval craft *("Nasty Boats")* were available to carry out clandestine insertions and extractions. SOG Headquarters was located in Sài Gòn. It was co-located in a building shared with the civilian run US Agency for International Development (USAID). Both entities were, of course, engaged in running various forms of counter-insurgency programs.

Organization

Although all mission planning and coordination was done at headquarters, under the direction of Colonel Steve Cavanaugh (1968-70), Chief SOG, all missions were launched from Forward Operational Bases (FOBs). All FOBs reported to Command and Control (CC) sites, which had operational control of a given mission. There were three such sites: Command and Control North (CCN) at Đà Nẵng, Command and Control Central (CCC) at Kontum, and Command and Control South (CCS) at Ban Mê Thuột. CNN missions were conducted in Laos and North Việt Nam. CCCs took place in those areas where the borders of South Việt Nam, Laos and Cambodia intersected. CCS was responsible for the central Cambodia border area to the southern border, where Cambodia meets the Gulf of Thailand.

Field Operations

The primary operational unit in all the CCs was known as a Reconnaissance Team (RT). RTs usually consisted of three US Special Forces types and nine indigenous types. These teams were backed up by "Hatchet Forces" [3] which were comprised of five US Special Forces troops and up to 50 indigenous soldiers.

Hatchet Forces were well-trained specialists in staging ambushes and exploiting the finds of the RTs. Other units existed, too, such as *Roadrunner*, small pseudo-force indigenous units operating under the auspices of the US Army Special Forces, which would be employed as required. In effect, RT teams provided the intelligence on enemy activities for these and other units to act upon.

SOG operations were the most covert and direct actions against the enemy in Việt Nam and other areas where operations were conducted. SOG itself was broken down into separate operational commands, including ground operations (RT teams), air operations, naval operations, psychological operations, and rescue operations. My assignment was to serve as Deputy Director of Ground Operations (OPS-35).

---

[3] A Hatchet Force or Hatchet Team was a special operations team of American and South Vietnamese members of MACV-SOG during the Vietnam War, who operated in small covert operations along the Ho Chi Minh trail from 1966.[2] The units specialized in search and destroy missions and in locating missing American servicemen in Laos, Cambodia and North Vietnam.

See: https://en.wikipedia.org/wiki/Hatchet_Force.

SOG OPS-35 (Ground Studies Group)

Within SOG, OPS-35, it was our job to dispatch reconnaissance teams (RTs) from all three CCs into their respective operational areas of responsibility (AORs). My previous training exercises while serving with SOTFE became the '*real*' thing with SOG. We worked seven days a week, from 7:00 AM to 7:00 PM as normal duty hours. We worked even longer hours when circumstances required as much of us. I spent many days at all three CCs and their launching sites.

These sites were located in the midst of established bases or camps of conventional type forces. Usually, they were located at or near helicopter landing zones. For example, CCN launched teams from a site located in the middle of the 101st Airborne Division at Huế (Phú Bài).

Hardly anyone paid any attention to these launches since helicopters and other types of aircraft were constantly coming and going. Such circumstances enhanced our cover vis-à-vis prying eyes and enhanced our clandestine capabilities. The other two CCs possessed similar launch sites. All SOG teams were billeted in separated areas, which were proximate to other units, but segregated from regular allied ground forces.

'Insertion' Activities

Although not expressly authorized to do so, on at least one occasion I accompanied one of our teams on an insertion which originated from CCN. I flew in the Medevac chopper which always accompanied an insert or an extraction. This craft flew over an area until the RT team had been safely inserted or extracted.

With my strategic intelligence clearance and my knowledge of UW operations and their locations, I would have made a highly valuable prisoner-of-war. Since the operation proved to be uneventful, this episode served as a very valuable learning experience from a personal point-of-view. Moreover, my participation gained me the respect and admiration of those formally engaged in the insertion operation.

Often, our operations were supported by an Air Force Commando (Special Operations) Squadron which flew the specially equipped EC-130H aircraft. These craft were outfitted with specialized Electronic Warfare (EW) equipment and EW Officers on each mission. EW was a suite of electronic countermeasures which were employed to mislead and confuse enemy radar installations as to the actual location, direction, and speed of an aircraft.

At its most effective, active EW countermeasures were a tremendous aid to our forces in support of mission objectives. Some of these aircraft were also equipped with Terrain Following Radar (TFR). With TFR in use, the plane was capable of safely flying itself over virtually any terrain at very low altitudes, avoiding all obstacles, by automatically banking and increasing altitude as required.

My first experience with this type of equipment was on a night flight over Laos. Although the pilot and co-pilot were flying *'hands-off'*, their eyes were glued to the small radar screen, their hands hovered no more than an inch away from the stick, in case the need arose to override the TFR system. While they were comfortable with TFR, theirs' was not exactly *"blind trust"* but something more akin to *"trust but verify."*

Inspection Tours

On the night in question, we flew all the way across Laos to Thailand. As it happened, another SOG Officer and I had been sent to observe some training facilities operated under the aegis of the Central Intelligence Agency (CIA).[4] SOG Command had a Special Forces Unit (46th Company) in western Thailand which was busy conducting the hands-on training of Thai Special Forces. In addition to its training mission, the 46th was also actively engaged in combat operations on regular basis side-by-side with Thai forces along the Thai border. All US Army Special Forces troops either killed in action (KIA) or missing in action (MIA) along the frontier were reported as having been lost in South Việt Nam.

CIA personnel always had it made or so it seemed to us SOG types. For example, CIA personnel always seemed to have beautiful, spacious living quarters and the

---

[4] The Central Intelligence Agency conducted active operations in Vietnam from the 1950s to the late 1960s, before and during the Vietnam War.

See: https://en.wikipedia.org/wiki/CIA_activities_in_Vietnam.

best training equipment money could buy. Although I had worked closely with CIA personnel during my first tour, 1962 – 1963, I never did quite figure out how the organization managed to live so well in the midst of war.

At the outset of US involvement in the wider war in Indochina, e.g., Thailand, Laos, and Việt Nam, all Special Forces troops and operations were under the direct control of the CIA. The CIA's *primacy* over covert operations in Indochina began in the late 1940s and persisted until the early 1960s. In policy making circles in Washington, DC at the time, it was widely assumed the CIA possessed the requisite know how and more importantly the access to the funding needed to parry the advance of communism in Southeast Asia.

USAF Intelligence Computer Center (ICC)

While in Thailand, we made a stop in Bangkok to check out the US Air Force operated Intelligence Computer Center (ICC). My first exposure to the area came about during World War II, when Thailand was known as Siam. On more than one occasion during the previous war, I had not only flown over the country, but I had also been shot at by the Japanese during those overflights.

The ICC maintained an array of powerful, high capacity, high-speed mainframe computers used to collect and disseminate intelligence in support of combat operations throughout Southeast Asia. It was a very large installation initially conceived to support and sustain what was then known as the "*McNamara Line.*" [5] The so-called "line" was itself an allusion to Defense Secretary Robert S. McNamara's project to construct a multi-billion dollar 2,000-foot-wide barrier across the Demilitarized Zone (DMZ).

McNamara's concept envisioned the installation of an elaborate array of electronic sensors to provide early detection of North Việtnamese troop movements into South Việt Nam, either through the DMZ itself or over the Ho Chi Minh Trail through

---

[5] The so-called "McNamara Line", was the physical manifestation of an operational strategy employed by the United States during the Vietnam War (1966–1968), designed to prevent infiltration of South Vietnam by NVA forces from North Vietnam and Laos. See: https://en.wikipedia.org/wiki/McNamara_Line.

Laos. Electronic devices used were designed to resemble the flora and fauna which were common to the area. Some were shaped like banana leaves, plants, and ferns, etc., so they would blend in with the surrounding foliage.

These devices were linked into a network which fed data back into the USAF Intelligence Computer Center in Bangkok. The Air Force was very proud of its intelligence gathering apparatus. When I asked a young Captain to pull up the latest intelligence on a certain area where one of our RT teams had been operating, he did so and reported that five "somethings" had passed through the area only 48 hours earlier.

I asked, *"Five what?"* *"Were they cows, buffaloes, elephants, wild boar, or what?"* *"Which way did "they" go?"* The poor Captain could not answer my questions. So much for "McNamara's Line" and its much vaunted *"white elephant"* which produced little actionable intelligence and cost billions of dollars.

In reality, it *was* our SOG reconnaissance teams which were the primary source of reliable, up-to-the-minute intelligence throughout the war. It should be noted that RT teams, however, were limited to a 12-mile insertion limit imposed due to political concerns. This range limitation was extended to 18 miles later in the war.

CIA Operations

On our way back from Thailand, we stopped in Savannakhet, Laos, located on the extreme eastern Thai border to check in with the local CIA station chief, whose wife served as his assistant. He had a beautiful eight room home which doubled as his headquarters. Security was provided by his own private mercenary force.

I was sure everyone in the town knew who he was and what he was up to in that place, which was to organize Laotian mercenaries to fight rear-guard actions with the local Communist forces. He had a good organization supported by well-trained troops under his direct command. Our stop was well worth the trouble inasmuch as our inspection yielded valuable insights into the war out on the frontier.

We watched, learned, and reported our findings upon our return to SOG Headquarters.

Reconnaissance Teams (RTs) [6] in Action

Our RT teams frequently experienced perilous contacts in the field, since they routinely operated deep in enemy held territory. We were often able to monitor their missions over the communications network at SOG Headquarters back in Sài Gòn. It could be eerie to listen to a team calling for an extraction while under fire and being chased by NVA forces after insertion, all of which was happening in places where US ground forces were not supposed to be operating.

Probably the worst part of all our operations was having to leave some of our dead behind because of hot pursuits and emergency extractions. Every effort was made to avoid leaving our wounded behind. Some super human efforts were accomplished in rescuing wounded team members, some of which produced Medal of Honor recipients and other awards for valor under fire.

Regrettably, it was not always possible recover our dead. At times, entire teams perished. Worse, still, was the necessity on occasion to lie to next-of-kin about how and where their loved ones either perished or were wounded. On a personal note, I always found it very difficult to speak about these young men after they were killed.

Command and Control
Field Leadership
(CCN/CCC/CCS)

I was well-acquainted with all the CC Commanders because I made it a point to visit with all of them on a regular basis in the field. The Commanding Officer of the CC Central (CCC/Kontum) was a first-class individual. He was a soldier's soldier,

---

[6] Military Assistance Command, Vietnam, Studies and Observations Group (MACV-SOG) conducted strategic reconnaissance missions in the Republic of Vietnam, the Democratic Republic of Vietnam, Laos, and Cambodia. Its reconnaissance teams (RTs) carried out the capture of enemy prisoners: rescued downed pilots: conducted rescue operations to retrieve prisoners of war throughout Southeast Asia; and conducted clandestine agent team activities and psychological operations. See: https://en.wikipedia.org/wiki/Military_Assistance_Command,_Vietnam_%E2%80%93_Studies_and_Observations_Group.

someone who would do anything for his men and to a man they all responded to his leadership in kind. The Commanding Officer of the CC South (CCS/Ban Mê Thuột) was an old school Special Forces type who instinctively knew what needed to be done and how to make things happen. In contrast to his peers, the Commanding Officer CC North (CCN/Đà Nẵng) was a West Point graduate with a *"Ring Knocker"* mentality and very little Special Forces experience.

His manner of dealing with others suggested he felt West Pointers were the US Army's elite, superior in all matters, relative to all others engaged in the profession of arms. All things considered, this fellow was blessed to have had as his Executive Officer someone with plenty of experience and three previous tours in Việt Nam to his credit. Without the XO's steady hand in play every day, the CO would not have accomplished much in the way of results.

When we heard reports about possible sightings of US POWs being led around in the Delta, the CCN Hatchet Force was placed on stand-by status to assist regional Special Forces, i.e., a 'Mike Force', which was inserted to proceed to the area of the sightings to attempt a rescue operation. We spent more than a week in the bush searching for our quarry, but never saw any trace of the presumed contingent of POWs. As MACV/SOG Deputy Director - OPS-35, I was ordered to accompany the RT team to bring back first-hand reports to SOG Headquarters.

Upon my arrival back at SOG HQ, I reported the negative results of the mission. Evidently, the enemy's early warning systems had provided the captors with ample time to escape and avoid contact with our search team. Within two weeks, paperwork was received at SOG HQ recommending the Silver Star award (America's third highest award for bravery under fire) for the Commanding Officer of CCN for *his* actions in connection with the search mission. It was an astonishing act of hubris on the part of the CCN CO to have his name placed in nomination for the Silver Star medal. Clearly, he had not actually participated in the operation. Rightfully, the nomination for the award of the Silver Star medal was not approved. The CO was relieved of command. He was soon transferred out of the unit. Later I heard that he had put in for retirement, rather than face a courts-marshal proceeding.

LTC. Floyd R. Mulvany, Jr., OPS-35
MACV | SOG | HQ
September 11, 1969
"Your hero in Vietnam"

Moving Up, Moving On

During my time at SOG Headquarters, I often requested that I be given the first CC command job which became available. With the recent opening at CCN and another opening soon to be open at CCS, I made an urgent request that I be considered for assignment to one or the other CC billets. I never made any bones about my desire to command a line unit as opposed to staff duty. For reasons never formally addressed, the Commanding Officer, SOG Headquarters, told me in no uncertain terms I would never be assigned to command a line unit on his watch.

About the time I was denied a CC command, two Colonels with whom I had worked while at SOCEUR reached out to me with an offer which I found difficult to turn down. These individuals were looking for a senior Lieutenant Colonel to serve as Senior Advisor to the ARVN's National Training Center (NTC) located in IV Corps.

LTC. Floyd R. Mulvany, Jr., OPS-35
MACV | SOG | HQ
October 28, 1969
"SOG Soldier."

When the opportunity for a command assignment arose, my former SOCEUR colleagues confided it had been necessary to relieve the former Senior Advisor at the NTC. While my sponsors declined to specify why such action had been necessary, they hastened to assure me the MACV Team 61 assignment would be a good fit. They asserted, however, that there was an urgent need to 'plug the leadership gap' at Chi Làng and expressed their confidence in my ability to get matters at Chi Làng squared away. I pledged to give their proposal careful consideration and revert to them within the ensuing 24 hours.

In the interim, I once again petitioned SOG leadership for a command assignment. Once more I was rebuffed, though the leadership reaffirmed their desire that I stay on as Deputy Commander, OPS-35. With that final decision, I decided step away from SOG and to accept the leadership position in the field at Chi Làng.

Senior Advisor, National Training Center (NTC),
IV Corps, MACV Team 61, Chi Làng

December 1969 – June 1970

The following morning, I accepted the assignment at Chi Làng. My transfer took effect immediately. I received the requisite briefings over the next few days. Unexpectedly, on my way in the door, I met the Lieutenant Colonel (my predecessor) who had recently been relieved as Senior Advisor at Chi Làng. His story was that he was convinced the NVA coveted Chi Làng because it was the last large ARVN installation in the Mekong Delta flying the colors of the Republic of South Việt Nam. He was certain the NTC was going to be attacked, so on his own authority, he and his ARVN counterpart had cleared a 500-meter (~550 yards) area around the NTC perimeter and placed barbed wire, trip flares, Claymore anti-personnel mines, and various types of booby traps.

He and his ARVN counterpart had also ordered the reinforcement of bunkers and built a six-foot high berm (dirt embankment) around the perimeter inside the wire. For these actions, he stated, he had been relieved of command because the brass back in Sài Gòn refused to accept the possibility that Chi Làng might be overrun. At the time, I thought it was a strange reason for an individual to be cashiered.

On its face, it was clear he was only acting out of an abundance of caution to protect his command and the people in his charge. Having heard the word, I elected not to pursue the questions begged by his story. My theory was that reality would soon enough settle the issue.

'Vietnamization' of the War

In January 1969, the Nixon Administration promulgated what became known as its *"Vietnamization"* [7] policy." It was intended to end U.S. involvement in the Vietnam War through a program to "expand, equip, and train South Vietnamese forces and assign to them an ever-increasing combat role, at the same time steadily reducing the number of US combat troops.

---

[7] "Vietnamization" was a policy of the Nixon administration to end U.S. involvement in the Vietnam War through a program to "expand, equip, and train South Vietnamese forces and assign to them an ever-increasing combat role, at the same time steadily reducing the number of U.S. combat troops." See: https://www.google.com/search?client=firefox-b-d&q=vietnamization+policy.

The National Training Center (NTC) at Chi Làng was under the direct command of a senior ARVN officer, Colonel (Đại tá) Đại. [8] Its resident contingent could train up to 5,000 troops at one time. It was customary for ARVN Regulars and Civil Guard (CG) battalions to cycle through the NTC for periodic retraining, reequipping, rest and recuperation from combat duty. In time honored fashion, they often came accompanied by their wives and children. While staying at the training center, they generally occupied the bunkers around the perimeter of the camp.

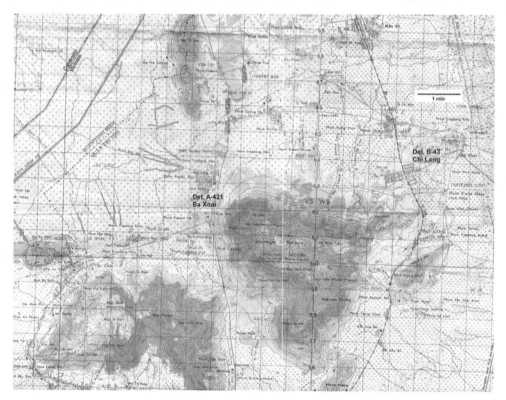

Grid Map highlighting local topography and
US Special Forces Detachments in the vicinity of
ARVN National Training Center (NTC),
IV Corps, MACV Team 61, Chi Làng
(1969)

---

[8] In the Vietnamese language the rank of Colonel (06), "Đại tá", is pronounced *"die ta"*. Colonel Đại's family name gave rise to a predictable (if grim) play on words among American troops at Chi Làng – as in *"it's a good day ta die."*

ARVN National Training Center (NTC)
IV Corps, MACV Team 61, Chi Làng
(1970)

(Photo courtesy of former S/SGT Mike Fieldman)

Role of ARVN National Training Centers (NTCs)
In Relation to the Policy of Vietnamization

1969 - 1970

Chi Làng was one of four National Training Centers in the Republic of Việt Nam, one NTC apportioned to each of the four Corps tactical districts (I-IV). It had warehouses, mess halls, billets for ARVN troops stationed at the center, and an airfield with a 1,000-foot runway. In addition, there were fuel and ammunition dumps, to enable helicopters to land, refuel, and rearm. No choppers were permanently based at Chi Làng. Choppers merely used the place when passing though while on operations in the Mekong Delta region.

At Chi Làng, all facilities were staged in the open, i.e., without the benefit of any protective cover whatsoever. We had a small US Army Signal Corps detachment *in situ* to handle all communications with aircraft in the area and with the Delta Region Headquarters Command, located about 30 minutes flying time away. We also had the luxury of having two US Air Force pilots and one observation fixed-wing aircraft on permanent assignment to the center.

The pilots were Forward Air Controllers (FACs) whose job it was to coordinate all aircraft operations in and around Chi Làng. About 880 yards from the NTC compound, there was a 5th Special Forces "B" Detachment (B-43) which controlled four or five "A" detachment camps in our area (e.g., A-421 at Ba Xoai). The presence of these units made us feel right at home.

Adjacent to the northwest edge of the NTC compound was the village of Chi Làng. Several hundred people lived in the village. Mainly many of our ARVN NCOs and their immediate families.

Team 61 Compound

The US Advisor Team, better known as MACV-Team 61, compound was located near the main NTC Headquarters structure. Our team consisted of 17 US Army

**Aerial View of ARVN National Training Center (NTC) Compound and
That Son Airfield at Chi Làng, IV Corps
Home of MACV Team 61
(1970)**

officers and enlisted men. We had our own bunkers, billets, and a thick berm (courtesy of my immediate predecessor) surrounding our perimeter.

We were responsible for our own defense and possessed the weapons, ammunition, and supplies on hand to do the job. Our bunkers were constructed of poured concrete with six-inch thick walls. Piled in front of its walls were several sand-filled 55-gallon gasoline drums. Piled in front of the sand-filled drums were alternating layers of sandbags interlaced with PSP matting (i.e., steel mats designed to be laid down over landing strips on makeshift air fields). Similar protective layers were also installed over the top of our billets, mess hall, and headquarters building.

Impromptu photo opportunity at the National Training Center (NTC) Headquarters Building, Chi Làng, IV Corps (1970)

LTC. Floyd R. Mulvany, Jr., Senior Adviser
(Fourth from left above)
(Photo courtesy of former S/SGT Mike Fieldman)

In the center of our compound stood a large 5,000-gallon capacity steel water tank. Drain gutters on the tin roofs of our buildings emptied into the water tank. Water collected and stored in this tank was our only source of potable water.

During the rainy season, May to October, the water level in the Mekong Delta could be expected to rise as much as six feet. For this reason, all structures intended for human habitation were built on high ground. From November through April, it was generally dry as hell in the Mekong Delta, but when the monsoons arrived the Mekong River basin became like an inland sea.

Bell Helicopter Company
AH-1 *"Cobra"* Gun Ship at Chi Làng
(1969)

Water Tower in the background

Offensive Threats and Defensive Capabilities

The NTC was defended by an artillery battery of four 155mm Howitzers and two ARVN rifle companies. One platoon drawn from these companies was permanently stationed on an outcrop atop Nui Cam Mountain. At 710 meters, an elevation of about 2,300 feet, *Nui Cam* is the highest point in the Bay Nui Seven Mountains area of An Giang province (aka, the "*Seven Sisters*").

An array of Regular NVA units held the high ground in all directions, which afforded them a direct line of sight into the heart of the NTC compound. From their vantage point, they were able to shower us with mortars, rockets, recoilless rifles, and heavy machine gun fire at will and with impunity. In Infantry operations, it is axiomatic to seek to *"take the high ground."* In our case, the only high ground we held was the platoon perch just above the camp which was vulnerable itself to being fired on from NVA positions at higher elevations. In short, this elementary rule governing Infantry combat was never brought into play at Chi Làng.

Our defenses (e.g., gun emplacements, mortar positions, etc.) were in plain view of the enemy at Chi Làng. The air strip was well within mortar and machine gun range. We were situated right on the Cambodian border, separated by a canal, and Cambodia was off-limits to US forces at the time. In fact, there was an NVA training center located on the opposite side of the canal and within ear shot of us.

For all intents and purposes, the NVA training area was hidden in plain sight and readily observable to the naked eye when riding in our observation plane. We could see the enemy training his troops, but there was not a damn thing we could do about it. Simply put, the NVA were able to cross over the canal at will into Việt Nam in order to transport troops and equipment up the mountains largely unimpeded.

At the ARVN NTC, our mission was training, not combat operations. Troops were there for a rest, so the NVA could move in and about the neighborhood without being harassed. Ours was not an easy assignment, especially in view of the fact we were taking fire daily largely without meaningful recourse.

Initially, we were peppered with 82mm mortar rounds and occasionally we took RPG-2 and RPG-7 (B40/B50) rocket fire. The first time I heard a B50 projectile explode, it landed less than 100 feet from our headquarters building. When the explosion occurred, I was sitting down and it caused me to literally leap about eight feet in the air. In spite of the fact that I had previously experienced artillery fire in combat, the concussion from that particular blast struck me as the loudest I had ever heard and frankly scared the living hell out of me.

As time passed on station, the firing which rained down on the NTC compound became heavier and more frequent. I was beginning to have a genuine appreciation for why my predecessor and his ARVN counterpart had had the 500-meter field of fire cleared, installed obstacles, and built the series of berms about the camp perimeter. The NVA really did seem to want to destroy the NTC and permanently close it down.

LTC. Floyd R. Mulvany, Jr., Senior Advisor
IV Corps | ARVN National Training Center at Chi Làng
Commanding Officer MACV Team 61
December 3, 1969

"Inside the wire"

Personalities, Politics, and Turf

Colonel (Đại tá) Đại, Army of the Republic of Việt Nam, Commanding Officer, NTC - Chi Làng, my ARVN counterpart, had been fighting Communists for 15 or 20 years by the time we met. He had been badly wounded in his left arm by a mortar shell and was placed on limited duty as the NTC Commander. Đại knew his business and we got along really well professionally.

He and I were both harassed by our respective higher headquarters on a daily basis. Neither his superiors nor my own, all of whom were ensconced safely in Sài Gòn, believed the NTC to be in any real danger of being overrun. Up to that time, of course, none of those higher up in the chain-of-command had been to the NTC to see for themselves what we were up against.

The Senior Advisor to IV Corps was a US Army Major General, whose headquarters was located at Cần Thơ, a thirty-minute flight from Chi Làng. Soon after my arrival at the camp, the Senior Advisor flew in to inform me he was in charge of activities in the Delta. I dutifully reminded him that, of course, I understood his role but that I had been told I was expected to take my orders from others in Sài Gòn.

COL. Đại (l) and LTC. Floyd R. Mulvany, Jr. (r)
ARVN National Training Center (NTC)
IV Corps, MACV Team 61, Chi Làng
December 17, 1969

In my capacity as a senior Lieutenant Colonel, I explained to the Major General, ARVN Senior Advisor - IV Corps, I felt as though I was caught between a "*rock and a hard place*", which was to say that I felt the Senior Advisor ordering me to do certain things his way while the Sài Gòn "commandos" were invariably promulgating contradictory instructions to be executed "*their*" way. I made it clear to the Senior Advisor that Colonel Đại and I had enough challenges to deal with at Chi Làng without being drawn into turf battles behind the lines in the capital.

Finally, I reiterated the belief held by Colonel Đại and me that the camp was in imminent danger of an all-out assault by the NVA. I assured him we were preparing to answer the threat, but that doing so had had a degrading effect on certain aspects of our ongoing training activities. In response, the Major General ordered two enlisted men to begin manning a night scope each evening from atop the NTC water tower (Elevation: ~20 feet).

After our initial encounter, we never heard much again from the Major General, ARVN Senior Advisor, IV Corps, who hailed from Cần Thơ. He had paid us a visit and tested our mettle. He apparently was pleased with what he saw and heard.

In the ensuing days and weeks, the NVA began ramping up its shelling of the NTC compound. As a result, we informed the MACV Training Command and the Sài Gòn "commandos." Soon thereafter, the new Commanding General of the MACV Training Command, IV Corps, paid us a follow up visit.

Arriving by helicopter, we took him on a tour of the compound in a Jeep. We had only just begun our tour, when we started to take incoming mortar fire. In artful fashion, our NVA adversaries began skillfully 'walking in' rounds directed at the Commanding General's modest entourage. It was not necessary for us to paint the Commanding General a picture of our dilemma.

We took flight and quickly found shelter within my command bunker, where I thoroughly briefed the General on our situation. My briefing reaffirmed the message which had been repeatedly sent to higher command in Sài Gòn for the past several weeks. Our 'situation' was straightforward: the NVA were perched atop Nui Cam Mountain, we were in their direct line of sight, and we were coming under fire with increasing regularity, intensity, and lethal effect.

I went on to point out that if more than 3-5 men assembled in one spot, some kind of fire would be directed on them. I also pointed out that the NVA gunners were directing their fire towards the fuel and ammo dumps as well as incoming and outgoing aircraft. He asked what sort of assistance we had received from higher headquarters.

I reported we had not received any material support to date, save for the two enlisted personnel who had been detailed from Cần Thơ to man the night scope, which was mounted on top of the water tower, after dark. He understood our situation and ordered us to redouble our efforts to fortify our fox holes and strengthen our defenses. With that, he too was gone.

Before long the radio channels and telephone lines between Sài Gòn and Chi Lăng were burning up with several persons demanding to know, *What the hell did you tell the new CG?* In reply, I told them exactly what had been discussed with the CG. My interlocutors were really pissed, as if somehow, I had shared insights with the CG which had been denied to others at MACV Headquarters.

**COL. Herbert L. Roye, US Army [c], COL. Đại (r) and
LTC. Floyd R. Mulvany, Jr. (l)**

**Inspection tour of ARVN National Training Center (NTC)
IV Corps, MACV Team 61, Chi Làng
January 12, 1970**

I later learned the new CG had returned to headquarters in a foul mood, summoned several Full Colonels (including my two erstwhile mentors) while standing them at attention, in order to deliver a scathing ass chewing. Naturally, Colonel Đại and I were next up in the barrel when our respective immediate superiors called to dress us down for an apparent breach of etiquette.

A young Major came down alone to tour the NTC compound and deliver a message to me on behalf of my bosses in Sài Gòn. The moment he alighted from his chopper, he informed me that (*in his opinion*) one of our machine guns was not properly positioned. Owing to the tenor and substance of his remarks, I looked him straight in his eyes and told him his opinions were of no interest to me unless or until he was placed in command of the NTC compound.

Until that time, he should keep his mouth shut, because if he ever set foot on my camp without an invitation I'd knock his block off and leave his sorry ass on the ground to rot in the sun. Well, my intemperate remarks were duly noted. Although unintended, they quickly sparked a new round of squabbling with my superiors at MACV headquarters.

It was not long before another round of verbal harassment gave rise to nit picking and bad blood. Reports were wrong, fortifications were deficient, and training was sub-par. There were also lots of questions coming in which seemingly were designed to call into question my competence and leadership abilities.

"Why are there three million rounds of .30 caliber rifle ammunition sitting around in your warehouse?" "How come you have so much .30 ammo laying around, when everyone at the camp is armed with .223 caliber M16 rifles?" "Looks like it's about time somebody ought to look into matters at the NTC at Chi Làng!"

Winning a Battle, Losing the War

Sure enough, it turned out we actually did have three million excess .30 caliber rounds in storage. Colonel Đại had requested permission on multiple occasions to return them to the supply system, but on every occasion, he was ordered to keep them on hand because nobody else in IV Corps had any use for them. In any event, moreover, it would cost too much to have the stockpile hauled off.

Colonel Đại was told he could expect a few visitors in the coming days who would be anxious to "look into the matter." As an aside, I suggested to Colonel Đại it might be in our interests to commandeer our own bulldozer that evening, dig a long and relatively deep trench outside the southern perimeter of the camp, bury the ammo, cover the trench, and spread the excess fill material along the existing berm. We were fairly confident that none of our exalted visitors would be too eager to extend their 'inspection' activities beyond the defensive perimeter.

Sure enough, a contingent of about 20 inspectors, *"armchair commandos"*, arrived the next morning. In charge of the delegation was a half-assed Coastal Artillery Lieutenant Colonel. He waltzed up to me and announced he had Permanent Change of Station (PCS) orders for everyone on the team – except for me.

I immediately inquired what had happened to my orders. Why was I left out of the mix? He didn't have an answer. He did say, however, that he and his confreres had been ordered to conduct a 100% inspection of the NTC. I asked the visiting Lieutenant Colonel if the Center Commander, Colonel Đại, had been made aware of his inspection visit. He opined it was unlikely that Colonel Đại, in fact, had been notified. At that remark, I asked whether he thought it might not be a good idea to alert Colonel Đại before the inspection got underway.

The chief of the inspection team agreed, so I contacted Colonel Đại by phone and later introduced him to the head of delegation. At about this point in the game, it dawned upon me who was behind this boondoggle. It had to be my former Airborne Colonel and *erstwhile* mentor, who had been instrumental in my assignment to Chi Làng. He had gotten his teat in the ringer and his butt chewed out by the new Commanding General at MACV Training Command following his visit to the NTC a few days earlier.

As soon as Colonel Đại was able to join us, the physical inspection of the warehouse got underway. As the delegation wandered about the building, it became apparent to them that the spaces were stocked with lots of supplies but no surplus .30 caliber ammunition was anywhere to be found. One could sense the air of growing distress among the inspectors as they failed to get the goods on us.

With no smoking gun, there could be no justification for implementing the PCS orders. Shortly thereafter the 'inspection' petered out. After completing their rather cursory inspection and a brief meeting with Colonel Đại, the delegation beat a hasty retreat back to Sài Gòn in time for their steak dinners and cocktails.

Back to the Action

Meanwhile, the NVA occupying the heights on Núi Cam and Núi Bắc Khơi, a few klicks down the road from Chi Làng, really began to increase the pressure on the NTC compound. In response, Special Forces Strike Teams from the 5th Group at Nha Trang were sent in to assault Núi Bắc Khơi. Not long afterwards, our ARVN platoon on the outcropping at Núi Cam came under intense fire which commenced at dawn and lasted six to eight hours.

The platoon was hit hard and suffered more than 20 casualties, several KIAs and about a dozen WIAs. The Platoon Leader was killed outright and the remaining men were afraid to descend the mountain under such heavy fire, even though we urged them to evacuate themselves and their wounded. Colonel Đại asked me to spare an officer to go up and lead his platoon to safety.

Colonel Đại had no one to send because he was expecting an all-out attack along the center of his defensive line. I asked for a volunteer and my Executive Officer, a very able young Infantry Major named Tom Ragusa, offered to lead the rescue mission. I told him to take a radio and one of Colonel Đại's radio operators with him and to maintain radio contact with me. *"Keep on the air,"* I told him.

Ordinary People, Extraordinary Courage

It took Major Ragusa a good while to climb the mountain and reach the beleaguered platoon. The platoon was still receiving fire when he reached his objective. Ragusa immediately reported there were at least 11 WIAs to transport off the mountain. He also noted he had no means of extricating the wounded, since it would take four able bodied men to carry each casualty.

As Ragusa was speaking to me, there was a very loud explosion. When I asked Tom what had happened, he told me a mortar round has killed his radio man. Luckily, despite their proximity to one another, Ragusa was not injured.

With that I ordered him to sit tight until the smoke cleared.

Slick to the Rescue

While all this was going on, a Huey helicopter (Bell UH-1 Iroquois) with a crew of four landed next to our compound. They had been flying over the NTC area, noticed all the fighting on Núi Cam, and seen the mortar explosions. What were the odds of this crew showing up when they did, I wondered?

The pilot asked to know the situation, so I explained we had 11 WIAs and an American Advisor up there unable to come down. The pilot and co-pilot said they would try to pick up our troops and bring them in from the mountain. I asked if they clearly understood the risks, they said they did, and off they flew.

We watched the Huey ascend the mountain and land amidst the mortar explosions and other incoming. From our vantage point, it appeared as though the shells were bursting right on top of their ship. No one was on the radio, so we had no idea how things were playing out above us.

Bell Helicopter Company
UH1 Iroquois *"Huey"*
(1970)

After what seemed an eternity, we watched the chopper lift off the mountain and race down its face deadheading for our position. Within a matter of minutes, the Huey landed with all 11 WIAs and one very happy Major Tom Ragusa. It was some kind of miracle, because the helicopter had several holes in it yet there were no additional injuries to either the WIAs or the crew.

All in a Day's Work

What fine, brave, and daring young aviators. The pilot said it was all in a day's work, he and his crew expected nothing in return, so I insisted he provide me with their names and unit affiliation. Later I wrote them up for the Distinguished Service Cross (the nation's second-highest combat award) and sent it off to their Commanding Officer. I never saw or heard of those young men again. I have no way of knowing whether they were awarded recognition for their valor. Still, I hope they did receive appropriate recognition for their heroic actions in due course.

With no wounded soldiers to worry about, Ragusa returned to the mountain. He was successful in bringing out the rest of the lost ARVN platoon. I put Major Ragusa in for the Bronze Star medal with "V" device for extraordinary bravery under fire.

I would have put Major Ragusa in for the Combat Infantry Badge ("*CIB*"), but no one serving in the MACV Training Command was eligible to receive the CIB -- no matter how much combat they participated in the course of executing their duties. [9]

Dwindling Manpower, Increasing Threats

Soon after this episode, Ragusa was transferred out to another unit. No one asked either me or him whether he wanted a transfer. He simply received orders out of the blue. My First Sergeant rotated out to return stateside soon thereafter. He was not replaced.

As circumstances played out, the shelling of the NTC increased to the point where it no longer made sense to keep the airfield open. It was closed down. As a consequence,

Forward Air Controllers (FACs) and their aircraft were transferred out. From that day forward, all air operations at Chi Làng ceased. Aircraft were warned that Chi Làng was closed, except for extreme emergencies, because the strip was routinely under direct attack by heavy machine guns, mortars, and rocket fire.

Endeavoring to Persevere

We did not stop our training efforts, in spite of the ongoing reductions in force at the center. On the contrary, the actual number of trainees increased to 5,500 during this period because MACV was planning to turn over all combat operations to ARVN. At this point in the war, the bloom was off the rose and the US was looking for a way out of the conflict.

What remained of the MACV Training Command team at Chi Làng had to be resupplied with food and supplies by helicopter from Cần Thơ. ARVN resupply was accomplished by convoys overland. All of us had more than enough ammunition in our bunkers and more available within the NTC compound.

---

[9] In order to qualify for the award of the Combat Infantryman's Badge (CIB) a soldier must meet the following three requirements: (*i*) Be an infantryman satisfactorily performing infantry duties; (*ii*) Assigned to an infantry unit during such time as the unit is engaged in active ground combat; and (*iii*) Actively participate in such ground combat.

Since we were pretty isolated at Chi Làng, I spent many hours at night in my observation post (OP), a 5,000-gallon capacity open-top steel water tank which was situated on a platform at an elevation of roughly 20 feet. Looking out from the OP, I had an unobstructed view of the entire camp, as far as the berms about the perimeter, and over to the near side of Núi Cam.

Harassment and Interdiction

The US Air Force had dropped hundreds of *"shoe mines"* on the slopes of Núi Cam. Such seeding of anti-personnel mines was an effort to keep the NVA from going and coming as they pleased. Our 155mm Howitzers poured round after round on top of that mountain.

ARC Light Strikes [10]

We observed numerous periodic ARC Light B-52 strikes in and around Núi Cam. On at least one occasion, in particular, the B-52s put on a strike during daylight hours. Such strikes were among some of the most horrendous bombardments I had ever witnessed.

During ARC Light strikes, the earth shook beneath our feet and buildings rattled as if a tremendous earthquake had struck the province. I often wondered how anyone could survive such events, but as often as not the NVA certainly seemed to be up to the task.

---

[10] Operation Arc Light (1965-1973). The United States deployed B-52F Stratofortresses from bases in the US to Guam to provide battlefield air interdiction (BAI), including strikes at enemy bases, supply routes and behind the lines troop concentrations, as well as occasionally providing close air support (CAS) directly to ground combat operations in Vietnam.

See: https://en.wikipedia.org/wiki/Operation_Arc_Light.

Operation Arc Light Strike
(1970)

(Photo courtesy of the USAF Museum)

Action and Reaction

Seemingly and without fail, within about 20 minutes of a cessation of a bombardment at Núi Cam, the NVA would make a point of dropping a single mortar round -- just one – into the center of the NTC compound. Sir Charles certainly knew how to make a pointed statement. Remarkable, but true.

Waiting for the 'Big Bang'

I received an alert one day to be on the lookout for a lone aircraft which was scheduled to drop a 12,000-pound bomb (5,443 kg) on Núi Cam. The aircraft in question would be instantly recognizable by the very large parachute trailing it which would be used to guide the bomb to the target. We all waited with great anticipation as the H-hour approached.

Sure enough, the plane arrived over the target area. The parachute deployed and the bomb hit its target. Instead of the much-anticipated mega-explosion, we witnessed only a plume of smoke and dust rising from the earth.

Since this incident took place before the withdrawal of my FACs, I ordered one of the pilots to reconnoiter the impact zone and report to me with his observations.

**Cessna OH-1 *"Bird Dog"* Spotter Plane,
'Swamp Fox 25', at Chi Làng Airstrip
(1970)**

Well, the bomb turned out to be a dud. During his flyover, the pilot reported having observed three individuals at the site who appeared to be engaged in the dismantlement of the misbegotten device. So much for the 'Big Bang'.

Night Fights

We used to refer to bright moonlit nights as "our night", because there was enough light to see for a long distance without (necessarily) the benefit of "Starlight" Scopes (e.g., AN/PVS-1 & 2) and other types of night vision aids. Such bright nights were especially welcomed by the troops who manned the watch tower and might or might not have had the benefit of specialized scopes. If it was really dark, the night was said to belong to *"Charlie"*.

"Charlie" was sometimes known also as either *"Sir Charles"* (i.e., NVA Regulars) or *"Victor Charlie"* (i.e., Việt Cộng Cadre). In any event, the enemy used the cover of night to transport troops and equipment back and forth across frontiers in the Seven Mountains (Bảy ngọn núi) region of IV Corps.

On many nights, we were presented with a grand display of fire power from both the AC-47 "Spooky" (aka *"Puff, the Magic Dragon"*) gunship which featured 7.62 mm mini-gun modules and the AC-130 *"Spectre"* which featured an array of M61 Vulcan 20mm guns and a twin 40mm Bofers cannon. These gunships came in a variety of configurations, but every one of them delivered an astonishing amount of lethal firepower to the tune of 6,000 rounds per minute per gun, with every 5th round a tracer.

Lockheed Aircraft Corporation
AC-130 Gunship (aka, *"Spooky"*)
US Air Force Commando Squadron in Laotian Airspace
(1967)

Typically, the first indication the enemy had that our gunships were overhead was the sound of Vulcan mini-guns firing three second bursts on their positions. The spooky in *"Spooky"* referred to the aircraft's camouflage paint scheme, which featured a flat black undercarriage which made those ships blend into the night sky. So, to enemy soldiers, these aircraft were 'ghost-like'.

"Charlie" could run, but he could not hide from the light of either AC-47 or the AC-130 gunships in Việt Nam. Whenever we saw these beasts, we knew that *"Charlie"*

was up to no good in the neighborhood. He was headed for a close encounter with a world of hurt. Bearing witness to either the "Spooky" or the "Spectre" light show and fireworks made us feel a whole lot safer and more secure than might otherwise have been the case.

On a separate but related note, whenever I saw small explosions on Núi Cam, I knew *"Charlie"* was hiking through the field of *"shoe mines"* laid down by the gunships and other US Air Force planes. "Shoe mines" were very small explosive devices designed to maim, rather than to kill the victim outright. They were just potent enough to blow off a foot if stepped on and sounded an awful lot like fireworks when triggered.

We Were Not Alone

Other than seeing all the firing and explosions from my observation post, I could look out over the berm in the direction of the nearest ARVN mess hall where the ground appeared to be in perpetual motion. The cause of the commotion was the confluence of tens of thousands of rats munching their way through the mounds of garbage discharged from the mess hall daily.

The rats only came out at night, but seldom frequented our (US) compound. We had the local population of feral cats on our side, while the ARVN troops enjoyed the company of no fewer than 43 native species of such vermin -- some of which actually made it on to the menu from time-to-time.

Our cats lived in the spaces between our buildings and the sand bags/PSP coverings which served to strengthen and bomb proof our structures. Local felines had pointed ears, no tails, bred like rabbits, and fed on rats. It seemed as though every couple of weeks a mama cat would stroll by with a half dozen kittens in tow.

They would shimmy down a tree from the roof and scatter throughout the compound in search of a hearty meal in and around the ARVN mess. Since we did not occupy our bunkers for the most part, I'm sure they scouted them out and made good use of our auxiliary quarters. We treated our felines with great respect and that *certain* deference which was accorded only to the kind of royalty which could assure peace and tranquility in our living quarters. Plenty of hungry cats meant fewer rats.

Replacement Personnel

It took some time to adjust to Major Ragusa's abrupt departure and the loss of our unit's First Sergeant, because the transfer of such capable individuals without securing capable replacements had an adverse effect upon our ability to get things done in a place like Chi Làng. It will be recalled that neither my former Executive Officer nor the First Sergeant were slated to be replaced.

Unexpectedly, however, I received word through the chain-of-command that a replacement to fill the post of Executive Officer was assigned to the NTC staff and would be arriving within days. When he showed up, Ragusa's 'replacement' turned out to be a dissipated, overweight, and Cretan-like character. An Artillery Major, this fellow had zero combat experience and little apparent appetite for line duty.

As it turned out, it was his first tour in Việt Nam to boot. What in the hell, I wondered, had this fellow been doing for the past 5-6 years? Your guess is as good as mine.

Routine Perimeter Patrols

During my command time at Chi Làng, it was standard operating procedure (SOP) to have an officer from our team patrol the range area whenever either any night training was scheduled or firing took place. The officer in question would be fully armed, locked and loaded. He would be accompanied by at least one enlisted man while making his rounds.

Whenever I went on patrol, I had a .45 caliber sidearm, carried an M16 rifle, and wore a special high-capacity ammunition harness. My harness held 20 M16 magazines, each of which contained 20 x 5.56mm rounds (i.e., 400 rounds total), two canteens of water, and a first aid kit. My ensemble was topped off with an elegant stiletto style knife.

The day my new Executive Officer arrived happened to coincide with my regular turn for range patrol. Having welcomed him to the team, I ordered him to accompany me as we made the rounds. It was a perfect opportunity to get acquainted with him and to take the measure of my new number two. We had him properly outfitted with the requisite weapons and equipment, then threw in a flak jacket and a steel pot for good measure.

Too Close for Comfort

It was *"Charlie's"* night, moonless, and pitch black. I was walking along with the Major in tow, about ten yards behind in file, when a sudden burst of machine gun tracers filled the gap between us about belly high. As I retreated smartly to avoid being hit, the Major dropped to the ground and I lost my fix on his position in the chaos of the moment. At that point, I had no idea whether he had been hit, but I heard no cries which would indicate he had been wounded.

Under cover I waited for some sign he was alive when, finally, I detected movement in my direction. I was readying my aim, when I heard his muffled grunting and groaning. It was a good bet no Việt Cộng or NVA regular would be making that kind of racket, so I held my fire.

It was, indeed, my new XO who emerged from the underbrush, muddy, wet, and breathing hard. He had received his baptism of fire and a proper introduction to the everyday underbelly of life at Chi Làng. Where the fire originated from remained a mystery, but it mattered not one whit since neither the Major nor me were hit.

Snap, Crackle, Pop

One day while working in our Headquarters building, one of my men reported there was a *Caribou* (i.e., a de Havilland Canada DHC-4 *Caribou*) cargo/transport aircraft making an approach for landing. Its appearance was surprising to us because there appeared to be no onboard emergency and it was well-known throughout IV Corps that our field had be closed for some time. When it landed, the pilot taxied off the strip and parked astride the fuel dump.

The aircraft bore the distinctive insignia of the Royal Australian Air Force (RAAF). She and her crew were attached to No. 35 Squadron, call sign *"Wallaby"*, nicknamed the *"Wallaby Airlines"*, which was based at Vũng Tàu. Her crew disembarked and strode over to our location and introduced themselves.

Royal Australian Air Force
No. 35 Squadron *"Caribou"* **on approach**
during the Vietnam War
(1971)

I asked whether they were aware that the field was closed due to the close proximity of enemy fire power in the heights overlooking our position. The pilot responded that the closing of the field was news to him. Curiosity, it seemed, had gotten the best of them and they simply popped in to find out what was happening at Chi Làng.

Two USAF Fairchild C-123 *"Provider"* **Aircraft**
On the tarmac at Chi Làng Airstrip
(1970)

(Photo courtesy of former S/SGT Mike Fieldman)

Well, it certainly didn't take long for our friends to figure out what was *"happening"*, because within moments *"Charlie"* had sent several rockets into our position, directed at the *Caribou*. The incoming ordnance was a combination of 122mm rockets, several RPGs (B40s/B50s), and many more 82mm mortar rounds.

Our fuel and ammo dumps had been exposed for a good while and the enemy had been (undoubtedly) awaiting the right opportunity to take them out. What better time to do so than when a relatively high value target presented itself close by and out of the blue? The whole lot of us took refuge in the nearest bunker and watched the dumps go up in flames punctuated by the sound of snap, crackle, and pop as the ammo cooked off.

Flames shot up in the air a good 800 to 1,000 feet. Heat from the conflagration was so intense the *Caribou* was literally sucked into the flames. Initially the aircraft seemed to move slowly, but as the flames intensified, she was simply overtaken by events. Finally, the aircraft burst into flames, exploded, and was consumed. All of us stared at the spectacle in disbelief. What a sight.

Our new found Aussie friends were flabbergasted. How were they to explain their presence at Chi Làng and the loss of their aircraft? In the end, our friends were picked up the following day, returned to their squadron at Vũng Tàu, and we never got word about the fates of our allies.

Hell's Kitchen Redux [11] – Part 1

On the day before Easter in 1970, Saturday, March 28th, we were lounging around outside of our billets after a hard day of work. No sooner than we were seated, a mortar round landed about 500 meters from our position and just outside the camp perimeter. It was a commonplace occurrence, so none of us paid its arrival any particular heed. About five minutes later, however, a second round fell about 100 meters closer and in a direct line from the first shell. Then a third round landed still nearer to our position.

I realized right away the enemy were registering their fire by using the 50-foot-tall radio antenna which stood in the middle of the compound as an aiming stake. By

---

[11] This action was part of the much wider North Vietnamese Army (NVA) offensive operations launched throughout the IV Corps during the Easter Sunday period March 26-30, 1970.

the time the fourth round feel on the berm, it was apparent the enemy was ready to commence an attack. As quickly as the firing had begun, it suddenly ceased – at least for the moment.

I manned the observation post throughout the black of night. It was another one of *"Charlie's"* nights. Around 10:00 PM, I heard an explosion near our 155mm Howitzer positions. First one explosion, then another, and another joined in short order by the rattle of small arms fire. Bright orange flames were cropping up from all quarters. My team was disciplined, well trained, and we made an orderly retrograde movement to the relative safety of our respective bunkers.

At dawn, I took up a position in my Command Post. We were under attack by a strong and determined enemy force and the fight was getting nasty. I contacted Colonel Đại, my ARVN counterpart, to obtain a situation report (SITREP) and solicit his assessment of the threat we were dealing with across the compound.

He confirmed the attack was in force and the enemy was inside the wire, wreaking all kinds of havoc, all over the compound. Enemy infantry was firing RPGs at our positions and busy little Sappers were tossing satchel charges into bunkers. He added, too, with an unmistakable measure of pride that his two ARVN rifle companies, positioned outside the berm, were engaging with the attackers in hot and heavy fighting but more than holding their own.

Having concluded my business with Colonel Đại, I immediately got on the radio to call in air support. I was told there was a well-coordinated offensive under way throughout the Mekong Delta (IV Corps/MR-4). All ARVN installations and American 5th Special Forces Group camps were being attacked simultaneously. Neither inclined to be discouraged nor denied, I kept working the radio in an effort to rustle up some air support for the NTC compound.

It soon became apparent the 5th Special Forces Group (SFG) camp located about 880 yards up the road from us was really being hammered. Helicopter gunships from the 5th SFG's own Aviation Company were fully engaged fending off their assailants and unable to come to our aid. For the time being, it looked as though we were likely to be fighting on our own at Chi Làng. The fighting was intensifying by the minute.

Hunkered down in our bunkers, the men of MACV Team 61 were pinned down and unable to effectively return fire. We were, however, hell bent on keeping the NVA out of our compound, with or without the benefit of close air support. While I continued to work the radio in search of aid, I also kept busy trying to gather as much intelligence in real time in order to keep my fingers on the pulse of battle.

At least for the moment, the outcome of the fighting throughout IV Corps was in doubt and we were in serious jeopardy. It was by no means clear things would be getting better anytime soon. The battle in the vicinity of Chi Làng went on unabated for roughly eight hours.

As dawn approached, the fighting began to noticeably taper off and the enemy melted away. It was only then we were able to critically take stock of our situation. It was evident we took quite a few casualties, but the ARVN units held, and the enemy had left 69 dead on the field.

The number of enemy dead left behind was significant. Indeed, it was rare for *"Charlie"* to leave any evidence of his losses in the open. It suggested their losses were many times greater than those indicated by our body count.

Upon closer examination, it was later revealed that our compound was hit by two battalions of NVA regulars (about 1,000 men) and a company of Sappers. Sappers were brave, well-trained, highly disciplined, motivated individuals, and hard fighters. It was customary for these specialized troops to go into battle wearing only a loin cloth or shorts, while carrying satchel charges designed to destroy bunkers and kill their enemies at close quarters.

Members of the attacking Sapper company had managed to work their way through 500 yards of ground covered with barbed wire, sprinkled with trip flairs, Claymores, and other obstacles virtually undetected. Incredibly, they made it through our inner defensive perimeter to attack our bunkers and to seek out and attempt to destroy our defensive positions.

One of the two infantry battalions had followed the Sappers though our outer perimeter, so that they could take up positions atop the berm and fire RPGs (B-40s) directly into some of our bunkers. Our two ARVN rifle companies had engaged the other NVA battalion outside the perimeter and fought them to a standstill and in spite of having been slightly outnumbered. When the smoke had cleared, it was plain the enemy had taken a punishing beating.

Before policing up the grounds, some ARVN commanders made a point of leaving some of the bodies where they had fallen so that local villagers could see the NVA were mere mortals too. As I went about the business of inspecting the entire perimeter on Easter morning, I witnessed sights which haunt me to this day. Dismembered bodies were strewn about the landscape willy-nilly.

Disparate body parts were all over the place. Men had been blown out of their bunkers. Their bodies blown apart, yet I cannot recall having seen even a single ounce of blood flowing forth from any of those corpses.

Colonel Đại dutifully prepared his after-action report (AAR). It was passed up through ARVN channels back to higher headquarters in Sài Gòn. His superiors, in turn, passed his report on to my superiors at MACV Training Command in Sàigòn.

Much to my dismay, there were no inquiries directed to me from anyone within the MACV organization about the action within the NTC compound or at Chi Làng. No one at MACV asked *any* questions. Neither about the action itself nor about US casualties.

Hell's Kitchen Redux – Part 2

On the evening of Easter Sunday, March 29th, barely 24 hours after the battle, we received a smattering of incoming mortar rounds. It was just one of those things, absent any obvious indications of a renewal of a ground attack. Still, I had a funny feeling that something simply wasn't quite right.

Accordingly, I ordered the men back into the bunkers for the night. It was not a popular order, but that was of no particular concern of mine. I slept in the Command Post and at around 2:00 AM, all hell broke loose.

It was a new day, but the same old routine. We were being hit with everything the enemy could throw at us. Since the cessation of the previous day's fighting, the enemy had used the interregnum to regroup, resupply, and make sighting adjustments.

With respect to sighting adjustments, it couldn't have taken much effort or skill to zero in on a stationary target as prominent as our center – especially given the enemy had a direct line of sight to the target from its position in the heights above our camp. Over the next 22 minutes, the enemy poured 632 rounds into the heart of the NTC compound.

Every structure sustained multiple direct hits. We were grateful for the structural integrity build in to our bunkers. My Command Post reeked of cordite smoke from the shells exploding on the roof.

A single 82mm mortar round broke through the ceiling and exploded in my room, but resulted in little damage and no casualties. All the vehicles parked in the compound were hit: blown tires, broken windshields, and plenty of shrapnel holes. As near as I could tell, the only structure within the compound which was not struck was our huge steel 5,000-gallon capacity water tank.

Incredibly, or so it seemed at the time, there was not a mark on either the tank itself or its fairly substantial supporting structure. In contrast, our communications infrastructure (e.g., PTSN, relays, and radio antennae, etc.) was thoroughly demolished despite its proximity to the water tank *cum* 'aiming stake'. Three of our team members were wounded by shrapnel which penetrated some apertures, but none of the injuries were found to be either serious or life threatening.

In round two, we had been hit hard and come away bloodied perhaps but unbowed. The camp was a shamble, but it was impossible not to give the devil his due. *"Sir Charles's"* attempt to overrun and hold the camp might have fallen short, but surely, he did an artful job of degrading our camp in the process.

As the sun rose on Monday, March 30th, we emerged cautiously from our shelters to survey the damages, tend to our wounded and dead, and clean up the mess. Our ARVN allies suffered a few more casualties as a result of the previous night's assault. As a result of the fighting over the preceding 48 hours, I learned (later in the day) that our camp had suffered 392 casualties killed and wounded.

Given our overall troop strength of 5,500 combat effectives at the outset of fighting on the night of March 28th, our losses totaled slightly more than seven percent of the total of men under arms. Since our communications infrastructure was destroyed, it was not possible to readily contact other units. Standard operating procedure (SOP) mandated we make situation reports (SITREPs) at hourly intervals each day to IV Corps at Cần Thơ.

After the Storm

Our last SITREP had gone out at 2:00 AM, yet we were still waiting for somebody to investigate our circumstances. It was late in the afternoon before a Brigadier General arrived by helicopter from Cần Thơ to check us out. By the time 'help' arrived, I was the only one in camp stirring about in the Command Post.

When the General presented himself, I was still wearing my steel helmet, flak vest, fast fading and ready to drop from fatigue. It didn't take him long to roger up to the situation. All he had to do was look at me and he could see we were running on fumes.

He told me he'd muster a contingent of engineers as quickly as possible to help clean up and rebuild the compound. Our training mission was placed on hold while we and our ARVN forces regrouped. Soon the word got around about the pounding we had taken at Chi Làng.

Even before the events of Easter weekend had transpired, there had been a lot of chatter about how "hot" the place was because of its proximity to the "Seven Mountains" area astride the border with Cambodia. Word was we were regularly being shelled by the NVA, which was true, especially by their contingent on top of Núi Cam. People were generally not eager to visit the NTC at Chi Làng, especially if it might require being there for any length of time.

The MACV Team 61's reputation for hazardous duty was well-known. It was perfectly well-justified too. When a detachment of combat engineers was sent out to rebuild the camp, there was some an audible gnashing of teeth and visible wringing of hands as the team came to terms with the fact this reconstruction project was likely to take more time than they had hoped.

Helipad at Chi Làng
(1970)

Camp Reconstruction

Fear can be a powerful motivator. At the NTC, our compound was repaired in record time. It was clear from the get-go that our detachment of combat engineers was in no mood to dither in completing their appointed tasks.

Restoring the training and education institution was another challenge altogether. All trainees continued to live in tents adjacent the bunkers because all the more permanent billets had been destroyed and not yet restored. In the redesign of the camp, dispersal was the order of the day so as to reduce the number of easy targets on offer to *"Charlie"*.

As fate would have it, the night before the engineers arrived, enemy marksmen placed a single 122mm rocket right beside the undamaged water tank and blew scores of holes in it. Their strike was a dandy feat of marksmanship, especially considering the rocket had to clear the tops of our buildings to get to the tank. This said, however, the NVA were pros after all in their own right.

By the time they administered the *coup de grâce*, they had had plenty of practice firing down range and nailing their targets. A civilian engineer had been designated to accompany the combat engineer detachment to Chi Làng while it was on loan from Cần Thơ. A nice enough fellow, but someone with a classic and very visible case of the 'shakes.'

Poor guy had to leave his nice bed, his club, his booze, and probably his babe (too), to spend time on assignment in a certifiably inhospitable place out in the boondocks. One of his pals swore he had chain smoked an entire pack of cigarettes on the thirty-minute flight from Cần Thơ.

The instant he stepped off the chopper, he started bitching about being called upon to participate in our reconstruction enterprise. After about 30 seconds, I informed him to get his ass back on the chopper. He was told to get back to Cần Thơ and never dare to come back to Chi Làng on my watch.

ARVN Armored Cavalry to the Rescue

About one week later, we got word that there was an ARVN operation planned to attack Núi Cam, so that we could resume our training activities at Chi Làng. The

ARVN's designated attack formation arrived, but it turned out to be an Armored Calvary unit. They planned to use tracked vehicles to assault an enemy stronghold at an elevation of 716 meters (~2,350 feet) which featured nearly vertical slopes on all sides.

I spoke briefly with the Commanding Officer of the assault team, an ARVN Lieutenant Colonel, and confided my concerns about his plan of attack but he was not about to be confused with the facts. His mind was made up. He was loath to be confused by facts. He was determined to "take the hill" on his own terms. He was *absolutely* convinced he could do the job his way.

Well, predictably, this officer and his troops had their heads handed to themselves in short order. They pulled out later that evening and were never heard from again. Shortly after my séance with the Commander of the ill-fated mission to take the heights at Núi Cam, the Deputy Commander of MACV, a Major General, visited Chi Làng.

The Deputy Commander of MACV, a Major General, was second in command at MACV at the time. He initiated a conversation with me inquiring of my opinions concerning our immediate needs, etc. Among other things, I told him we needed to uproot the NVA from Núi Cam, so that we could get about our training mission in relative safety.

Having shared my views, it occurred to me that I had better hope this particular General was not the same fellow who encouraged the ARVN to send out an armored formation to nonsensically attempt to *"take the hill."*

Within moments, out of left field, the General launched into a rant berating me over the fact that one of our ARVN trainees had been observed firing his weapon into the ground on the firing range. I was, of course, aware that some of our trainees had a hard time learning how to properly fire a weapon.

But I was also acquainted with the incident to which the General referred and told him so. He then remarked that *"unfortunately"* the three-star ARVN General Officer in charge of training had witnessed the incident. I explained to the General that I was still investigating the case.

I briefly stated that I would have to get back to him with a proper fact-based explanation concerning the circumstances of the incident, what had transpired, why it had occurred, and how we would mitigate the possibility of future failures. My explanation obviously failed to satisfy the General, so he had me stand at attention while he persisted in chewing me out.

All thoughts about the near collapse of the NTC at the hands of the NVA, the valiant defense of its turf by ARVN trainees, was all but overlooked and forgotten.

I was still standing at attention when the General departed my office.

On a Lighter Note

As my inspection of the compound progressed, following the battle, I noticed something which struck me as a bit odd. At every turn, I was coming across an astonishing surfeit of rat bones. Feral felines, it seemed, reigned supreme behind our lines. While I was proud of the defense mounted by our ARVN allies in the face of the NVA assault, I came away equally impressed and, indeed, awed by the vigilance displayed on the part of our feline cadres.

International Press Corps

A few days after the battle, a couple of French newspaper correspondents showed up thinking there might still be some fighting in and around Chi Làng. It was a quiet day, so they politely asked if I might kindly direct them to "where the action" might be found. At that time, the 5th Special Forces Group – Mobile Strike Force based at Nha Trang (SF HQ VN) was (*once again*) trying to take Núi Khét.

Núi Khét was located three or four klicks down the road, so I sent them there. A couple of hours later, they came back in a Jeep to be evacuated – each individual had been shot in their respective French derrieres. Their wounds were not serious, so I feigned innocence and inquired as to whether they had "found" the action.

Enough said.

End of the Line

Heading into the summer months, I was then approaching my estimated date of return from overseas duty (DEROS) June 10th. President Nixon gave an order on or about April 15, 1970 to invade Cambodia in order to eliminate the Kingdom as an enemy sanctuary. The decision to launch the Cambodian incursion on May 1, 1970 had the effect of forcing the NVA to abandon their positions in the Seven Mountains region in general and atop Nui Cam Mountain in particular.

Such NVA troops were off to fight in Cambodia for the foreseeable future. The shelling from Nui Cam Mountain had stopped, but not the harassment from the powers up the chain-of-command. Ten days before my DEROS, my boss called to tell me that I was not to depart the NTC at Chi Làng prior to June 7th.

I affirmed my intent to stand firm until my tour was up, yet he reiterated his admonition that I was not to depart my station a moment too soon. Abruptly, he hung up the phone. To add insult to injury, no one in Sài Gòn even bothered to tell me what transportation might be available to get me from Chi Làng to MACV Headquarters.

I placed a call to my friends at 5th Special Forces Group at Nha Trang and requested a helicopter set down about one klick from the NTC at dawn on June 6th. "No sweat", we'll be there to pick you up at 6:00 AM and get you on your way.

On the night of June 5th, I packed my bag and cleared my desk without a word with anyone. At 5:00 AM on June 6th, I picked up a Jeep from the motor pool, told the Sergeant where and when he could pick it up and walked out the door. I said no "*good byes*" to anyone, with the sole exception of Colonel Đại, whom I deeply respected. He was the only Việtnamese officer I ever worked with who would have no part in graft or corruption. His integrity was beyond reproach, he cared for his troops, and led them well.

I had no regrets about leaving Chi Làng, Việt Nam, or leaving the politics of MACV HQ behind. I had already requested assignment to Fort Bragg, NC. From Fort Bragg, I could retire unburdened following completion of my final tour of duty.

A Chill in the Air

When I arrived at MACV Headquarters – Training Command on Monday, June 8th, the reception which greeted me was a chilly one. Everyone seemed surprised to see me. Moreover, it was plain that no one was delighted by my presence.

There were neither warm greetings nor congratulations for a job well-done. I was, however, curtly informed that I was not to depart Việt Nam without first completing Efficiency Reports (ERs) for each of the officers still serving with Team 61 at Chi Làng. In the meantime, I was told to report to the office of my immediate boss, Colonel Herbert L. Roye.

He and I had served together with the 11th Airborne Division in the early 1950s. He was the individual who was chewed out by the Major General from Cần Thơ. Shortly after my arrival at Chi Làng, it will be recalled that the Major General had visited Team 61 and received a briefing from me. Colonel Roye was also the man who had been busting my chops ever since that sad occasion.

When I entered his office, he ordered me to stand at attention in front of him. A certain Lieutenant Colonel, whom he had invited to join us, behind closed doors was also present. One of the US Army's time-honored *unwritten* regulations within the Officer Corps, when it came to ass chewing's, was that such disciplinary actions were to be administered in private and one-on-one. By involving a third party, Colonel Roye had willfully broken faith with tradition in order to satisfy his need to publicly humiliate one of his subordinates, for some real or perceived slight, which had taken place in the past.

Well, no matter, he had his way with me. It was in the manner of his own choosing. He spoke his piece, I spoke mine, and when the chewing out was done, the whole matter was officially put to rest.

I had had the pleasure of serving with a terrific group of individuals who made up Team 61 at Chi Làng in support of Colonel Đại's team. Naturally, I gave all of my subordinate officers and NCOs excellent ERs, especially noting their duties had been carried out under combat conditions.

My final act was to recommend that Colonel Đại be awarded the Bronze Star Medal for his leadership of the National Training Center (NTC). Colonel Đại, in turn, nominated me for the Vietnam Armed Forces Honor Medal, First Class (later awarded). By the end of my second stint in Việt Nam, I was ready to head back to the world – *really* ready.

LTC. F. R. Mulvany, Jr.
Binh Thuy Air Base at Cần Thơ
June 7, 1970

CHAPTER 22

FORT BRAGG, NC
(JULY 1970 – AUGUST 1972)

Airborne Test Board (ATB)/Special Operations
Executive Officer

"Only two things fall from the sky: bird shit and fools"

Vintage Army Airborne Saying

I arrived at Fort Bragg in early July 1970. Having been a long-time member of the Special Forces community, I had many old friends and acquaintances working at the base. At the time, in fact, one of my former compatriots was serving as the Director of the Special Warfare Center ("*SWC*"). Shortly after my return to Fort Bragg, I was offered an opportunity to serve as his Deputy Director. Having previously accepted an assignment to the Airborne Test Board ("*ATB*")/Special Operations, it was infeasible to accept the appointment to the Special Warfare Center team.

Airborne Test Board/Special Operations - Mission

The Airborne Special Operations and Test Board (1940-1990) was responsible for the development and testing of new parachutes, and test dropping all manner of US

469

Army equipment by parachute from the Lockheed C-5A *"Galaxy"* military transport aircraft. Special rigging had been developed to drop any piece of equipment in the military inventory, e.g., tanks, armored personnel carriers, artillery, helicopters, small fixed wing aircraft, earth moving equipment, pontoon bridges, and (occasionally) a variety of top secret highly sophisticated developmental aircraft, etc. Air dropping a medium tank, for example, required that six 100' diameter chutes be rigged (attached) to the payload.

Lockheed C5-A *"Galaxy"*Transport
"The Original Big Ass Bird"
(1968)

In addition, personnel and cargo chutes were modified and tested for smaller payloads such as soldiers, palletized supplies, communications gear, and other types of components.

**Executive Officer
Roles, Responsibilities, and
Reporting Relationships**

I served as Executive Officer, second-in command, to the Board's Commanding Officer. My job was not only challenging from a physical, intellectual, and technical perspective, but it also enabled me to continue making regular parachute jumps and Colonel jump pay as well. It also afforded me the luxury of personally deciding when, where, and how often I would make those jumps.

My boss, Colonel Francis J. Kelly, was an old 11ᵗʰ Airborne Division type. [1] When my boss and I initially became acquainted, we were both working at Fort Campbell, Kentucky. At the time, he had been in charge of the Division Jump School, while I had served as a First Lieutenant, Platoon Leader (HWP), H Company, Second Battalion, and 188ᵗʰ Airborne Infantry Regiment. As long-time respected colleagues and friends, he and I got along famously while working together at the ATB.

C5-A Testing Program

Our boss was the C5-A testing program Project Officer, a Full Colonel. In its day, the C5-A was one of the most complex and expensive weapons related programs ever undertaken by the Pentagon. In point of fact, it holds the dubious distinction of having been the first acquisition program to rack up cost overruns in excess of one billion dollars.

---

[1] Colonel Francis J. Kelly, Commanding Officer, US Army Airborne Test Board (ATB)/Special Operations, was a legendary figure within the Special Forces ("Green Beret") community. He was born February 18, 1919 and died December 26, 1997, age 78. A combat veteran of the European Theater commencing with the D-Day landings on Omaha Beach in World War II, he later served in the Korea War and in Vietnam. As commander of the Fifth Special Forces Group (Airborne) in Vietnam from June 1966 to June 1967, Colonel Kelly led an elite corps of a few thousand men who teamed up with South Vietnamese soldiers and ethnic-minority civilian irregulars like Montagnard tribesmen to wage counterinsurgency warfare against the Vietcong and North Vietnamese in some of the most remote areas of South Vietnam.

Kelly and Mulvany were among the first wear the coveted Green Beret (ca 1953/54) and initially served together with the 11ᵗʰ Airborne Infantry Division, 188ᵗʰ Airborne Infantry Regiment (AIR), at Fort Campbell, KY between May 1951 and June 1953. While working through their respective 'twilight cruises' at the ATB, COL. Kelly and LTC. Mulvany became the first two individuals, by order of seniority, to make parachute jumps from the C5-A Galaxy.

Colonel Kelly was also the author of "US Army Special Forces – 1961 – 1971."

Library of Congress Catalog Card Number: 72:600263

First Printed 1973—CMH Pub 90-23

As the late Senator Everett M. Dirksen (R-IL) reputably noted [2], when discussing the pattern of defense program related cost overruns in the late 1960s, "… *a billion here, a billion there, pretty soon, you're talking real money.*" Senator Dirksen was correct in his assessment, but in the end the American taxpayer got quite a bang for their bucks when it came to the C5-A.

At the time of its maiden flight, June 30, 1968, the C5-A was reputed to be the largest aircraft in the world. She has a wingspan of 233 feet, a length of was 247 feet, and weighs in at a svelte 380,000 pounds (tare). Her maximum payload capacity was rated (initially) at 180,000 pounds, but this standard was later revised downwards after some aircraft began showing signs of structural failures in the wing design. Her cargo deck runs the full length of the aircraft, while the upper deck provides accommodations for flight operations and seating for up to 75 passengers, including the embarked loadmaster and crew, all who face to the rear of the aircraft during flight. The cargo compartment is 121 feet (37 m) long, 13.5 feet (4.1 m) high, and 19 feet (5.8 m) wide, or just over 31,000 cubic feet (880 m³). Full-open(able) bay doors at both nose and tail enable drive-through loading and unloading of cargo.

The ATB spent two full years loading, rigging, and dropping whatever piece of equipment which came through the pipeline. As large as the C5-A was, there was only enough room for 72 paratroopers per flight. Seating was provided on the upper deck, but jumpers had to leave the equipment on the main cargo deck stacked beside whatever else was being transported. Before jumping, the troopers came down to the main deck to put on their gear.

Deploying from the C5-A was the easiest way to make a parachute jump because, relatively speaking, jumpers were transported in comfort to their drop zones and unencumbered by their chutes and other gear during flight. The C5-A would slow down to an incredibly slow 120 knots for the jumps. The huge exit doors on each side opened wide enough to deflect the wind. Jumping from the C5-A was like leaping into a vacuum. Colonel Kelly was the first person to jump from the C5-A and I was only the second such individual. Doing so was a tremendous thrill for both of us.

---

[2] The saying, "A billion here, a billion there, pretty soon, you're talking real money" has been attributed to Dirksen, but there is no direct record of Dirksen saying the remark.

See: https://en.wikipedia.org/wiki/Everett_Dirksen.

A Brief Trip Down Memory Lane

About 18 months into my tour at Fort Bragg, we were visited by a team from the Inspector General's (IG) office. Among its members was a Lieutenant Colonel who had recently returned from Việt Nam. Our conversation revealed that he had spent the past year and a half serving as MACV Team 61, Senior Advisor to the NTC at Chi Làng. He had been my replacement.

What a small world, indeed. He told me that during his entire tour at Chi Làng, not a single shot was fired in anger into the camp. He had not been bothered in the least by *"Charlie."* It was difficult to believe, but apparently true.

When I asked if anyone had ever visited the heights of Núi Cam, he responded in the affirmative and said they had discovered a huge cave complex large enough to accommodate several hundred people. The cave's entrance was small. It would allow two or three people to enter or exit at any one time.

His reporting explained why all our efforts to get rid of the NVA squatters had failed. The cave complex shielded NVA troops from our air strikes and shelling. Now, I understood how it came to pass that *"Sir Charles"* was able to deliver those single 82mm calling cards to the center of our camp like clockwork following our attacks. Amazing.

Visiting Dignitaries

As Executive Officer, I was attuned to everything which was going on at any one time, what was being planned, and who was doing what to whom. My role evolved over time. Eventually, in addition to my other duties, I became the Board's permanent Briefing Officer. During this stretch, I became acquainted with many very interesting people.

One such person was Brigadier General Samuel W. Koster, formerly Major General and Commander of the 23rd Infantry Division, known as the Americal Division. Koster was demoted in the aftermath of the Mỹ Lai Massacre, March 16, 1968.

In this capacity, I also met three Secretaries of the Army and lots of other visiting dignitaries.

A 24/7/365 Jump Slot

I jumped from whatever sort of aircraft might happen to be available. Whenever jumps were being planned, I invariably received a heads up to inquire as to whether I would like to go along for the ride. If I was able to jump, someone would be sent to pick me up, deliver me to the waiting aircraft where a chute would be waiting for me, and invariably someone would be sent to pick me up following a jump. I never had it so good.

I especially enjoyed jumping from helicopters. There was seldom any wind, except that which emanated from the rotor blades, so it was a straight down fall away. A new chute, the MC1-1, was introduced in 1971. It was equipped with toggles on which one could pull to change direction rather than having to strain with the risers to go wherever you wanted to go.

What a change this was, especially where you had a lot of equipment with you. Then came the modified T-10 parachute. It featured a 12-inch nylon skirt which was attached around the entire edge of the canopy. This modification was made to ensure that a parachute would open without any shroud lines becoming entangled in the canopy.

As required, the chute was tested using 200-pound dummies which were dropped a total of 500 times. A chute had to deploy flawlessly for at least 90% of the 500 drops before testing could proceed further. When this standard was met, it was time for human tests to begin.

This was accomplished. So, it was time for humans to test the modified T-10 chute. We dropped from a helicopter from 1,500 feet. Four of the chutes performed exactly as they were designed to perform. Regrettably, however, my chute did not open. Instead, it had a perfect streamer. Not good.

Nothing I did made the chute open. I fell for 800 – 900 feet at about 125 mph, all the while shaking and pulling the lines in an attempt to get the chute to open. At about 400 feet, I pulled the reserve chute. It worked.

I landed behind a large mound of sand, out of the line of sight for the officers observing the tests. They only saw my streamer and a few were certain that I had *"bought the farm."* It came as quite a surprise to them when they found me alive when they arrived in an ambulance to scrape me off the ground. Needless to say, the chute was returned for further modification before another human jumped with it.

Changing Times

In late 1971 and early 1972, the US Army implemented what it lovingly referred to as the *"All Volunteer"* Army. Universal conscription was one of the casualties of the American experience in Việt Nam. From that moment on anyone in the Army would be there, in theory, because he or she wanted to be a part of the organization and thus was considered a "volunteer."

Incentives for people to *"join up"* and to remain in the service were done away with for good. Eventually, civilian contractors replaced GIs in the mess halls and kitchen police (KP) duty became a thing of the past. The heretofore sacred *"Eleven General Orders"* which every soldier who hailed from the *"Old Army"* could recite verbatim were summarily reduced to three orders which any moron could repeat.

Gone were the morning roll calls. Unmarried Privates and Privates First Class were suddenly permitted to have quarters off-post. Commanders no longer knew with certainty where their men might be at any given moment. NCOs were no longer deigned to be the lords of the barracks. They could no longer scold or touch their subordinates.

Discipline went to hell in a hand basket. Everything I had grown up with and knew and respected and practiced were gone for the sake of quantity over quality. For many NCOs and officers, junior and senior alike, such changes were simply more than they could take.

My own enthusiasm for the whole notion of the *"All Volunteer Army"* was nil. And I wanted no part of the changes overtaking the US Army and other service branches. In the aftermath of Việt Nam, the US Army suffered greatly from its involvement in an unpopular war.

A Change of Seasons

And so, it was with great sadness, I put in my retirement papers and looked forward to a future separate and apart from my most beloved of institutions. My Army career ended on August 1, 1972. True to form, I simply packed my bags and left just as I had done at the end of my second tour in Việt Nam. I did not request a retirement parade to which I was entitled after 31 years, six months, and nine days of active duty.

During those years, I rose through the ranks from Private to Lieutenant Colonel. I was a *"Mustang"* from the ranks with a Regular Army commission. My body left the Army that day, but my soul did not. To this day, I miss being on active duty and wearing my uniform. No matter how long I live, this piece of my spiritual fabric will never be altered.

I might wear civilian garb, but I remain a proud soldier at heart.

"ARMY PRO"
He always knows when it's time to go...

Photo – Provenance Unknown
Courtesy of Lieutenant Colonel F. R. Mulvany, US Army (Retired)
(Undated)

AFTERWORD

Shortly after his retirement from the US Army in August 1972, Russ joined the administrative staff at California State University, Northridge, where he served as assistant to the Vice President until 1976. He went on to earn a Certificate of Fine Arts at Los Angeles City College; and a two-year Certificate in Archeology at Moorpark College in Ventura. Later he commanded the Civil Air Patrol Squadron at Truckee, California for 4 years. He then went on to serve as a docent at the Palm Springs Air Museum from 2002 - 2017.

Russ and I first met on the occasion of my initial visit to the Palm Springs Air Museum (PSAM) in the fall of 2014. In the ensuing months, we quickly became good acquaintances and later fast personal friends. As our friendship grew, we eventually took to meeting regularly at the museum's *"Freedom Fighter Café"* adjacent to *Miss Angela's* berth and occasionally at offsite locations near his home for lunches and dinners.

During a business trip to Southern California in April 2018, Russ invited me to join him for lunch at his country club in Indian Wells. Following our lunch, he suggested I join him for a cup of coffee at the house. While relaxing in his study and chewing the fat about his Army Air Corps experiences, out of the blue he declared, *"Hey, Chris, I've got something which might be of interest to you."*

Well, as I recall, I responded with a puzzled look and mustered a quizzical *"really, what might that be?"* Russ responded by suggesting I open the closet door which was situated behind my chair. *"There's a three-ring binder up on the top shelf which contains a copy of a memoir which was written several years ago."*

As I casually reviewed the text, it quickly became apparent that fate had thrust upon me an unusual gift. Russ explained he had written the memoir principally for the benefit of his immediate family, but indicated a willingness to share his story with me. Russ agreed to loan his only known copy of the text with the proviso that it be returned to him within the following week.

Upon my return to the East Coast, I had the document scanned and returned his original document to him within seventy-two hours. It was returned along with a USB thumb drive containing a digital version of the text in order to make it easy for his heirs to make additional copies. After careful study, I concluded Russ' memoir was worthy of a place in the public domain.

Soon, thereafter, Russ and I agreed to collaborate on the further development and restructuring of his story, which entailed many months of historical research to fill in some gaps in the historical record and ultimately rewrite with care portions of the book. Our immediate goal was to produce a tightly written manuscript which would become a valued family keepsake. In the longer term, it was hoped we might eventually be able to have "ARMY PRO" published.

In retirement, Russ maintained a busy schedule and active lifestyle. He was an inveterate reader, social critic, and 'old school' personal correspondent extraordinaire. As a rule, he continued to visit his friends at the Palm Springs Air Museum one Thursday per month and his schedule invariably included weekly outings with friends for lunches and other forms of entertainment until the last few months of his life.

Christopher J. O'Shea V

Editor and Co-Author

Dover, DE 19901

September 1, 2019

PALM SPRINGS AIR MUSEUM

B-17G *"Miss Angela"*
Her 'Thursday' Crew
2016

**From left to right: Eitan Hedram, Greg Robarge, Russ Mulvany, Ray Lucky,
Bob Mitchell, Dave Kaplan, John Temple, Gary Lueders**

(Photo courtesy of Gary S. Lueders, February 25, 2016)

Russ at home in his study
April 17, 2018

Lunch at the Freedom Fighter Café
Russ and Michele Van Niekerk
June 21, 2018

(Photo courtesy of *"The Management"*)

POSTSCRIPT

"Army Pro: A Memoir of a Soldier's Life" came to life more than fifteen years after the author's retirement from active duty in 1972. Its contents, initially drawn largely from memory, were written out in longhand over a period of about 5 years between 1989 and 1993. As noted in the Introduction, these reminiscences were later transcribed into a typewritten format, single-spaced, which totaled 253 pages when completed in early 1994. According to the author, it was shortly thereafter that a 'handful' of Xerox copies, perhaps as many as 3-6, were reproduced and circulated among family members, friends, and colleagues.

As suggested by events described in the Afterword, during the ensuing years a single copy of the typewritten manuscript, bound in a three-ring binder, was stored on a closet shelf in the author's home study undisturbed until April 2018. At the time, the author offered to let me read his memoir because he thought it might be of interest to me. My own review of the manuscript gave rise to a rolling dialogue with the author about the merits of undertaking to edit his manuscript with the aim of ultimately rendering it a more thorough, accurate, and complete work. On July 7, 2018, a concerted effort was initiated to transcribe the typewritten manuscript into a digital format. An initial updated baseline digital transcription, approved by the author, was completed on September 10, 2018.

With the author's endorsement of the updated digital transcription, the tedious and time-consuming work of editing was begun. Between September 15th and December 30, 2018, the line editing process resulted in 5 progressive iterations of the manuscript during which creative content, writing style, and language use on the sentence and paragraph level were evaluated in terms of their effectiveness in communicating the author's story. Once the task of line editing was completed, we transitioned into classical editorial mode wherein our focus was on combing the manuscript for errors, checking and rechecking facts, while all the while conducting additional historical research on an *ad hoc* basis in order to strengthen the manuscript.

Between January 5th and February 10th, two further iterations of the manuscript were produced, the latest of which (aka, a "Keepsake" version) was submitted to the author for his approval on February 15, 2019. Approval of the "Keepsake" version was forthcoming within 7-14 days. During the week of May 26th through June 1st, numerous hours were spent in conversation with the author concerning progress on the final manuscript and conducting additional archival research. At each step throughout the editorial process, from start to finish, all proposed changes to the document were reviewed and approved by the author prior to their adoption and incorporation into subsequent versions of the manuscript through May 30th. LTC Floyd R. ("Russ") Mulvany died in his sleep of natural causes on June 18, 2019.

From my first reading of the author's original draft manuscript, I knew he had a good story to tell, had told it remarkably well, and done so with a remarkable degree of honesty and plain-spokenness. We both recognized early on the limitations of the original draft manuscript, most of which were rooted in the fact that there were so few official records available to document many aspects of the author's thirty-one years, six months, and nine days in uniform. It will be recalled, that on July 12, 1973, a catastrophic fire engulfed a section of the National Personnel Records Center, the Military Personnel Records Center (MPRC) at Overland, MO, a suburb of St. Louis.

As the primary custodian of military personnel records, the destruction of the MPRC, dealt a tremendous blow to the government and the public-at-large. According to the National Archives and Records Administration, the fire destroyed approximately 16-18 million official military personnel records though the actual number will probably never be known. According to the online encyclopedia Wikipedia, *"a massive effort to restore destroyed service records began in 1974. In most cases where a military record has been presumed destroyed, NPRC [has been] able to reconstruct basic service information, such as military date of entry, date of discharge, character of service, and final rank."* Suffice it to say, *"massive"* though the effort might have been to reconstruct lost military personnel records, those efforts have fallen far short of satisfactory based on our own particular experience.

Fortunately, the author's vivid recollections of his military service offered up plenty of clues which enabled our reconstruction of his service record, combat experiences, and also many other aspects of his life and times.

Christopher J. O'Shea V
Editor and Co-Author
Boryspil, Kyivs'ka Oblast
Ukraine 08301

May 2, 2021

ACKNOWLEDGMENTS

This work was made possible by the collective efforts of many individuals, several of whom were themselves veterans of the US Armed Forces.

First and foremost, I wish to thank the late LTC Floyd Russell Mulvany, Jr., US Army (Retired) for having afforded me the opportunity to collaborate with him in bringing his story to life. Special thanks are due as well to Lieutenant General Frank J. Kisner, Jr., USAF (Retired), Lieutenant Colonel Robert T. Mounts, USAF (Retired), and Command Sergeant Major Dennis J. Woods, US Army (Retired), each of whom was especially generous in the commitment of time and attention to the critical review of various iterations of the draft manuscript.

Other individual contributors included:

Michael S. Baechle. Mike is a lawyer by trade and former litigator living near Chicago, IL. A widely read student of military history and aviation, his editorial suggestions and literary criticisms were the source of innumerable improvements to multiple iterations of the manuscript. Mike's navigational expertise, in particular, proved invaluable in ferreting out the best online digital mapping tools. A veteran of the US Air Force: June 1963 - May 1967, Mike was based (primarily) at Hunter AFB GA. He was attached to the Military Airlift Command (MAC) and flew missions throughout the world. An "Aircraft Loadmaster" (MOS 1A2X1), he was responsible for properly loading, securing and escorting cargo and passengers. In this capacity, his specialty was *providing information concerning navigation and [occasionally] suggesting other sources of useful information.* Honorable discharge. Rank at separation: Senior Airman (E-4).

Dennis W. Duerr. Dennis is a civil engineer living in Dover, DE. Dennis made valuable contributions to Chapters 17 and 21. His keen attention to detail and critical commentaries, especially with respect to the work of the Studies and Observations Group's (SOG) activities in III Corps during 1969/'70, had a positive influence on the overall quality of the early manuscript. A graduate of Dover High School, class of 1968, Dennis soon thereafter enlisted in the US Army to *Ride the Iron Beast* as did an uncle in WWII. So, with tales of armor campaigns in his mind, he was inducted into the service on January 5, 1969. Following basic training at Fort Bragg, NC he received advanced training as an Armor Crewman/Sheridan Crewman, at Fort Knox, KY. In the summer of 1969, he arrived in Việt Nam and was assigned to the 11th Armored Cavalry Regiment, 3rd Squadron, L-Troop, where he served as a Sheridan tank commander and Lead Scout in operations throughout III Corps, including those related to the Cambodia Campaign (1969/'70). Combat wounded/medivacked ('70) from Cambodia to Japan. Honorable discharge June 15, 1971. Rank at separation: Corporal (SP-4).

Michael N. Fieldman. Mike Fieldman is an architect practicing his art in Jerusalem, Israel. It is difficult to overstate the nature and scope of Mike's material contributions in enhancing the quality of the present manuscript – front to back. Alone among collaborators, he is the only one to have served under the command of the late author while attached to the staff of the US Army's Senior Advisor - MACV Team 61 at Chi Làng (IV Corps), 1969/'70. Mike received his invitation to join the ranks of the US military establishment in late 1965. Having dropped out of high school earlier in the year, he elected to join the US Army in order to retain a modicum of control over his career path. He enlisted and began his service on February 24, 1966. Following basic training, he was detailed to the Defense Language Institute/Department of State's Foreign Service Institute in Arlington, VA. His course of study was Mandarin Chinese: 44 weeks. Việt Nam service: Headquarters – Military Assistance Command Vietnam (HQ MACV, March/August) | MACV Team 61 - Chi Làng, IV Corps, September '69 – April '70). Honorable discharge: April 6, 1970. Rank at separation: Staff Sergeant (E-6).

Gary S. Lueders. Gary is a former commercial airline pilot. He retired as a Captain with American Airlines in June 2000. He is a long-time member of the docent community at the Palm Springs Air Museum (PSAM), whose individual members regularly volunteer to share their aviation expertise with the visiting public. He lives in Rancho Mirage, CA. Active duty: US Air Force, 909th **ARS at March AFB, CA**: July 12, 1964 – August 4, 1969. A KC-135A pilot, he flew 123 Combat Air Refueling Missions during 3 deployments to Southeast Asia in support of the Việt Nam War: November 1966 – January 1967; March 1967 – September 1967; October 1968 – December 1968. Honorable discharge from USAFR February 20, 1985. Rank at Separation: Captain (03).

Ryan Lorimer. Ryan is a master automotive technician in his 'other' life, who works by day for a major package delivery service outlet in Rancho La Quinta, CA. Among other considerations, he is a wizard when it comes to the restoration of old photographs, maps, and other images. His handiwork is on display throughout the text of the author's memoir. Our manuscript would be the poorer for the lack of his extraordinary computer and software related skills.

Michael S. Mulvany. Mike is a former commercial airline pilot. He retired as a Captain with Northwest Airlines June 27, 2004. During the war, he served as a naval aviator aboard the USS Ranger (CV-61) off the coast of North Việt Nam, August '68 - May '69. Later he served as a flight instructor at the Naval Air Station (NAS) Corpus Christie, TX. Received an honorable discharge from the US Navy July 31, 1972. Mike's rank at separation from Active Duty was Lieutenant (03). His rank at separation from the US Navy Reserves was Lieutenant Commander (04). He resides in Kona, HI.

Robert G. Quirk. Robert G. Quirk lives in Winnipeg, Manitoba, Canada. He compiled and edited a 2-volume compendium entitled, *"354 Squadron RAF, 1943 – 1945, A Record of Their Operations"*, first published in draft format in 2003. Volume I consisted of RAF SF 540s ('After Action Reports') which documented every mission flown by the RAF "M" 354 Squadron. Volume II consisted of scores of squadron related photographs. An entry from Volume I, dated 6 April 1944, was authored by F/O Robert ("Bob") Banks. Banks' AAR provided the key to unlocking the mystery over who was at the controls of the RAF *Liberator* Mark V whose crew discovered the survivors of Captain R. G. Bailey's aircraft which ditched in the Bay of Bengal on 5 April 1944. Royal Air Force (RAF) Squadron No. 354, part of the No. 225 RAF Group,

Southeast Asia Command (SEA), was a general reconnaissance squadron of the RAF during World War II. It was first formed at Karachi (India) on May 10, 1943 as part of Coastal Command. On August 17, 1943, it was posted to RAF Station Cuttack (Odisha), where it took delivery of *Liberator* Mk. V bombers built by Consolidated Aircraft. Squadron No. 354 was disbanded on May 18, 1945.

Karl L. Swartz. Karl lives in the San Francisco Bay area. A Product Manager for a leading technology company by day, he is also the creator of the Great Circle Mapper (http://www.gcmap.com/) online tool kit. It was Karl's tool kit which enabled us to bring to life the narrative of Mulvany's aerial combat experiences with the USAAF Tenth Air Force in the China/Burma/India Theater of Operations, January – May 1944. See: Chapter Five - Pandaveswar Air Base (India)."

Paul H. Vivian. Paul is a retired civilian employee of the US Department of Defense. He is an historian, intelligence analyst, Russian language linguist, former member of the Army National Guard and a retired Colonel (06). A graduate of Ransom-Everglades School, Union College (NY), Indiana University at Bloomington, IN, and the US Army War College, Carlisle, PA. He lives in New England.

Institutional contributors included:

1. **US Air Force Historical Research Agency (AFHRA)**
   600 Chennault Circle
   Maxwell AFB, AL 36112-6424
   Tel: (334) 953-5697

2. **National Personnel Records Center**
   1 Archives Drive
   St. Louis, MO 63138
   Tel: 314-801-0800
   https://www.archives.gov/personnel-records-center

3. **National Archives and Records Administration**
   8601 Adelphi Road
   College Park, MD 20740
   https://www.archives.gov/college-park

4. **Military Assistance Command Vietnam | MACV Teams – Blog**
    https://macvteams.org/team-61/

5. **Australian War Memorial**
    Postal address: GPO Box 345, Canberra ACT 2601, Australia
    Street address: Treloar Crescent, Campbell ACT 2612, Australia
    Internet: https://wartime@awm.gov.au

CODA

"AN PAEAN TO MILITARY SPOUSES"

The times change. Methods change. Institutions of longstanding such as the United States military, however, steadfastly strive to maintain the integrity of their core principles and ingrained attitudes.

Today's military is, on the surface, vastly different from what I experienced as a dependent from 1946-1962, especially in terms of its demography. For example, in that time I never laid eyes upon a female Soldier, Sailor, Marine, or Airman in uniform. In those days, except for those who served as nurses, there simply were no women members of the military cadre. As a member of the military family, a woman's place was in the home.

Over time, of course, the demographics of the U. S. military have changed and continue to change -- albeit at a glacial pace. As social mores have evolved, alterations to longstanding customs, norms, and behaviors have ushered in a number of important changes in military culture. In many cases, such changes have had the effect of improving the quality of life for service personnel, their families, and thereby arguably resulted in an enhanced state of military readiness. At the same time, the underlying character of the military 'mindset' has not necessarily been altered. Indeed, its mission-driven bedrock traditions, philosophy, reason for existence, structures, behaviors, standards, and practices, remain fundamentally the same to this day.

A career in the armed forces comes at a price, one that is all too often is disproportionally borne by military spouses and their dependents. In my own case, for example, I attended one kindergarten, six elementary schools, two junior high schools, and two high schools (K-12) before college. Those who have experienced a conventional civilian upbringing might find such circumstances almost beyond belief. For the families of active-duty military personnel, it's the norm and simply one more fact of life to which one must become accustomed to without complaint in order to prosper and grow. From the perspective of the military "Brat", the butcher's bill was repeatedly paid in missed opportunities to put down roots, make lasting friendships, and secure a sense of belonging beyond the confines of wherever installation our father was stationed at a particular point in time.

The community of a military spouse and their dependents is defined, by order of precedence, in terms of the (*i*) military institution; (*ii*) immediate family; and (*iii*) whoever is around when and where you happen to be in the moment. We moved every two to three years. "We" were the nuclear family, literally my mother, me and my two younger brothers. My father, per protocol at the time, invariably proceeded to his next duty station with all deliberate speed. For this reason, father rarely participated in the relocation process: packing, cleaning, clearing quarters, loading up, and (usually) driving to the next post.

Upon arrival at our destination, as a rule, we were assigned 'temporary' quarters for a period of 45-60 days. Eventually, we were assigned to 'permanent' quarters for the remainder of the current tour. Sooner or later, father would join us though he rarely participated in the setting up our new household. Mom invariably led the charge on this front with assistance of me and my siblings. In her spare time, mom also assumed responsibility for getting our household integrated into the neighborhood, the wider community, got her three boys registered for school, extra-curricular activities, and established our family routine. While all this was going on in the background, my father went about the business of soldiering. For his part, my father could be gone for days, weeks, and months at any given point in time. Every few years, the cycle of uprooting the family would repeat itself with numbing regularity.

The lifestyle associated with the profession of arms bore little resemblance to the civilian norms epitomized by television series like *"The Adventures of Ozzie and Harriet"* (1952-1966), *"Father Knows Best"* (1954-1955), *"Leave It to Beaver"* (1957-1963), and

"My Three Sons" (1960-1972). By way of contrast our family life was itinerant, arbitrary, and understandably governed by the needs of the military and the national defense. In retrospect, it is revealing to consider what young people in particular can become accustomed to, even learn to like, about the military lifestyle in spite of its notable drawbacks. It is also remarkable to consider that even in the face of perpetual hardship, my mother never threw in the towel and never wavered in her responsibility to her family.

What was my mother to do? To even the most casual observer, the foundation of the military family is the spouse. Military spouses know something about the wages of war, the insecurity, stress, anxiety, loneliness and mental fatigue that is part and parcel of the role such persons play on the home front in support of warfighters. As a kid, I didn't give much thought to my mother's reality, probably took her for granted, and like most kids might not have shown my appreciation of her sacrifices often enough. As for my father, he rarely showed any interest in the quality of our home life. When he did so, it was generally to express dissatisfaction with some aspect of our domestic routine in terms of either perceived efficiencies or deficiencies.

While our father was a good provider, he was never truly emotionally engaged with his wife and children. Growing up, my siblings and I were entirely reliant on our mother for emotional support, care, and nurturing. She was always there for us, ever loving, and devoted to our emotional and spiritual well-being. At the time, I did not fully comprehend how mom was able to cope with the vagaries of a life on the lam so to speak. Even now, I struggle to understand how she managed to maintain her equanimity. Given the magnitude of her family, household, and spousal duties, I have often found myself wondering what kind of life she had had that she could really call her own. She never complained, simply dug in each day, and soldiered on.

Eventually, something had to give and it did. As the years passed by, the stress and strain could no longer be sustained. She succumbed ultimately to the pressures and obligations associated with the military lifestyle. I'll never know the depth of her resolve or the source of her pure love and devotion that she showed unfailingly to me and my siblings. In my eyes, my mom was a saint.

This is my unique story but it is very similar to most other military family experiences. I cannot describe my ongoing admiration and respect for all military spouses then and now, female and male. Under the most stressful and spirit-sapping conditions what you do/did for your families and friends can never be forgotten or praised enough. Would that I had the ability to express in words your strength of character, devotion and love. Thank you. From my heart.

Michael Shane Mulvany
Kona, HI

November 16, 2020

Portrait of an "ARMY PRO"
Lieutenant Colonel Floyd R. Mulvany, Jr., US Army
Fort Bragg, NC
July 1972

(Painting by the late Barbara Evans Mulvany)